CORE TAX ANNUALS

Capital Gains Tax 2013/14

CW00321986

CORE TAX ANNUALS
Capital Gains Tax 2013/14

Rebecca Cave FCA CTA MBA

and

Iris Wünschmann-Lyall MA (Cantab) TEP

Series General Editor: Mark McLaughlin CTA (Fellow) ATT TEP

Bloomsbury Professional

Bloomsbury Professional Ltd, Maxwelton House, 41–43 Boltro Road, Haywards Heath, West Sussex, RH16 1BJ

© Bloomsbury Professional Ltd 2013

Bloomsbury Professional, an imprint of Bloomsbury Publishing Plc

ISBN: 978 1 78043 155 0

Typeset by Phoenix Photosetting, Chatham, Kent
Printed and bound by CPI Group (UK) Ltd, Croydon, CR0 4YY

Preface

Capital Gains Tax Annual 2013/14 is one of the Core Tax Annuals series published by Bloomsbury Professional. It aims to provide a clear and a quick guide to the taxation of capital gains for busy tax practitioners and taxpayers alike.

We have taken a practical approach to the subject, concentrating on the most commonly found transactions and reliefs. The commentary is cross-referenced to the tax legislation, as well as to the HMRC Manuals where appropriate. Decisions from recent tax cases have been referred to where they are particularly relevant to the text. In Chapter 11, reference is made to the ICAEW Tax Faculty guidance note (TAXGUIDE 01/12) on entrepreneurs' relief, which summarises the responses given by HMRC to questions posed by the professional bodies concerning entrepreneurs' relief.

This edition includes three new examples, on conditional contracts, selling assets situated abroad, and transfer of interest in a main residence to a spouse. The other 130 examples have been updated to the current tax year. New focus points have been added to highlight the practical application of the law, which may not be obvious on first reading.

Chapter 5 has been rewritten to highlight the effect of the new statutory residence test on taxpayers who move into and out of the UK tax regime. The new taxes that apply from April 2013 to high-value residential properties held by companies, trusts and partnerships (namely, ATED and CGTED) are discussed in Chapter 4.

The commentary on tax planning and tax avoidance in Chapter 10 has been rewritten and rearranged to reflect the new emphasis on tax avoidance and the general anti-abuse rule (GAAR). Chapter 16 now contains commentary on the CGT reliefs which are available under three venture capital schemes: EIS, SEIS and VCTs.

The *Finance Act 2013* introduced two new tax reliefs for capital gains: disincorporation relief (see Chapter 9) and relief for shares acquired under an employee shareholder contract (see Chapter 17).

Chapter 17 also includes a brief summary of two proposed CGT reliefs which are the subject of consultation at the time of writing.

This edition has been fully revised and updated by Rebecca Cave and Iris Wünschmann-Lyall, and is up to date to the *Finance Act 2013*, which received Royal Assent on 17 July 2013.

Preface

We hope you enjoy using this book and would welcome any suggestions for improvements or changes.

Rebecca Cave
Rebecca@taxwriter.co.uk
August 2013

Contents

Contents

Contents

Table of statutes

[All references are to paragraph number]

Table of statutes

Table of statutes

Table of statutes

Table of statutes

Table of statutory instruments and other guidance

[All references are to paragraph number]

Table of cases

[All references are to paragraph number]

List of abbreviations

AIM	alternative investment market
APR	agricultural property relief
ARTG	HMRC Appeals, Reviews and Tribunals Guidance Manual
ATED	annual tax on enveloped dwellings
BES	business expansion scheme
BIM	HMRC Business Income Manual
BMT	bereaved minor trust
BPR	business property relief
CAA 2001	Capital Allowances Act 2001
CG	HMRC Capital Gains Manual
CGT	capital gains tax
CGTED	CGT charge on ATED-related gains
CH	HMRC Compliance Handbook
CPI	consumer prices index
CTA	Corporation Tax Act
CVS	corporate venturing scheme
DOTAS	disclosure of tax avoidance schemes
DPT	disabled person trust
EEA	European Economic Area
EIS	Enterprise Investment Scheme
EMI	enterprise management incentive
ER	entrepreneurs' relief
ESC	Extra-Statutory Concession
FA	Finance Act
FHL	furnished holiday lettings
GAAR	general anti-abuse rule
HMRC	HM Revenue and Customs
ICTA 1988	Income and Corporation Taxes Act 1988
IHT	inheritance tax
IHTA 1984	Inheritance Tax Act 1984
IHTM	HMRC Inheritance Tax Manual
IPDI	immediate post-death interest
ISA	individual savings account
ITA 2007	Income Tax Act 2007
ITEPA 2003	Income Tax (Earnings and Pensions) Act 2003
ITTOIA 2005	Income Tax (Trading and Other Income) Act 2005

LLP	limited liability partnership
NBCG	HMRC Non-statutory Business Clearance Guidance Manual
NIC	National Insurance contributions
PIM	HMRC Property Income Manual
PIP	personal independence payment
PR	personal representative
QCB	qualifying corporate bonds
RBC	remittance basis charge
RPI	retail prices index
SA	self-assessment
SACM	HMRC Self Assessment Claims Manual
SAV	shares and assets valuation division
SDLT	stamp duty land tax
SE	small enterprise
SE	Societas Europaea
SEIS	Seed Enterprise Investment Scheme
SI	Statutory Instrument
SIPP	self-invested personal pension
SME	small or medium-sized enterprise
SP	Statement of Practice
SSE	substantial shareholdings exemption
TAAR	targeted anti-avoidance rule
TCGA 1992	Taxation of Chargeable Gains Act 1992
TIOPA 2010	Taxation (International and Other Provisions) Act 2010
TMA 1970	Taxes Management Act 1970
TSI	transitional serial interest
VCM	HMRC Venture Capital Schemes Manual
VCT	venture capital trust

Chapter 1

Introduction to capital gains tax

SIGNPOSTS

- **CGT changes** – Summary of recent changes to CGT and where they are covered in this book (see **1.2–1.3**).

- **Who and what is chargeable to CGT** – Including the territorial limits of this tax (see **1.4–1.7**).

- **Exempt assets and gains** – A summary of the gains or particular assets that are exempt from CGT (see **1.8–1.11**).

- **Calculating CGT** – Once the gain is computed what other deductions or reliefs apply (see **1.12–1.25**).

- **Tax return entries** – Including valuations, helpsheets, toolkits and deadlines (see **1.26–1.39**).

- **HMRC powers and penalties** – A summary of the HMRC investigation powers, penalties that may apply and the tax appeals system (see **1.40–1.55**).

BASIS OF CHARGE

1.1   Capital gains tax (CGT) is charged on capital gains, defined as chargeable gains accruing to a person on the disposal of an asset (*Taxation of Chargeable Gains Act 1992* (*TCGA 1992*), *s 1*). Spouses and civil partners are chargeable separately, but where the members of such a couple are living together transfers of assets between them are deemed to take place for a consideration that gives rise to no gain and no loss (see **3.62**). There is no CGT on death, and the deceased's assets are deemed to be inherited at their market value.

A 'person' may be an individual, a trustee or personal representative (PR), or a company. Companies are generally excluded from CGT, and are chargeable instead to corporation tax on their chargeable gains (*Interpretation Act 1978, Sch 1*; *CTA 2009, s 2*). However, an exception has been made for CGT due on disposals of certain high-value residential properties from 6 April 2013 (see **4.39**).

In very broad terms, the chargeable gain arising on the disposal of an asset is the excess of the disposal value over the acquisition value. **Chapters 1–6** focus on rules as they apply to individuals and particular assets. There are special rules for personal representatives of a deceased person (see **Chapter 7**) and trustees of a settled property (see **Chapter 8**). The chargeable gains accruing to a company for an accounting period are included in the company's total profits for the accounting period and are chargeable to corporation tax unless another tax or relief applies (see **Chapter 9**). **Chapters 10–17** focus on the reliefs that can reduce, defer or eliminate CGT.

HISTORY OF CGT

1.2   CGT was introduced in 1965, at the same time as corporation tax. Previously, short-term gains on the disposal of capital assets were chargeable but were taxed as income.

From its introduction CGT taxed inflationary gains as well as real ones. Indexation allowance attempted to remove the effect of inflation from March 1982, but older assets were still taxed on pre-1982 inflation. From March 1988, taxpayers had the option of excluding pre-March 1982 gains from their capital gains calculations by rebasing the asset at its 31 March 1982 value. However, this rebasing was not universal, so taxpayers could still compare calculations using the asset's March 1982 value and the original cost, taking the lower gain or loss to be taxed. This was known as the kink test. All assets held by individuals and trustees were compulsorily rebased at 31 March 1982, with effect from 6 April 2008, so the kink test became irrelevant.

Indexation allowance was frozen for disposals made by individuals, PRs and trustees from 6 April 1998, so no further indexation could accrue from that date. Indexation allowance was finally abolished for these taxpayers from 6 April 2008, but it remains in place for companies.

Taper relief was introduced on 6 April 1998, partly to compensate for the freezing of the indexation allowance. However, when the indexation allowance was withdrawn completely on 6 April 2008, so was taper relief (see **1.15**).

Special share identification rules were enacted from 6 April 1998, as it was necessary to identify a holding period for separate acquisitions of shares. These identification rules were simplified considerably from 6 April 2008 for individuals, trustees and PRs, but not for companies (see **Chapter 9**).

The rate of CGT has swung from a flat rate set below the top income tax rates, to the taxpayer's marginal income tax rate, back again to a single flat rate, and now to three rates as summarised below. Low flat rates tend to encourage the re-categorisation of income as capital, and that problem has been partially addressed by raising the rate of CGT for those in the higher income tax bands for gains realised from 23 June 2010.

Period	Rate of CGT
5 April 1965–6 April 1982	30%, no relief for inflation but with retirement relief for business assets.
6 April 1982–5 April 1987	30%, with relief for inflation.
6 April 1987–5 April 1998	Marginal income tax rate up to 40%, with relief for inflation.
6 April 1998–5 April 2008	Marginal income tax rate up to 40%, taper relief gives enhanced relief for business assets.
6 April 2008–22 June 2010	18%, no relief for inflation, entrepreneurs' relief gives limited relief for gains from certain business assets.
23 June 2010–5 April 2014	18% for gains falling in basic rate band, 10% for all gains qualifying for entrepreneurs' relief. 28% for gains falling in higher or additional rate bands. 28% for all gains made by trustees and PRs. No relief for inflation.

Trustees and PRs have paid CGT at different rates from those applicable to individuals for many years (see **Chapter 8**).

The *Taxation of Chargeable Gains Act 1992*, as amended by subsequent *Finance Acts*, now contains the main provisions concerning taxation of chargeable gains.

Changes in 2013/14

1.3   *Finance Act 2013* introduces a number of changes to capital gains tax which may become more significant as time moves on. These are:

- The statutory residence test and removal of the concept of 'ordinarily resident', both from 6 April 2013 (see **Chapter 5**).

- The annual tax on enveloped dwellings (ATED) and the associated CGT charge on gains realised on the disposal of dwellings subject to that tax (see **Chapter 4**).

- Disincorporation relief for small companies, applicable for a five-year period from 1 April 2013 (see **Chapter 9**).

- A new type of tax-favoured employee share awarded in conjunction with employee shareholder status, due to apply from 1 September 2013 (see **Chapter 17**).

CHARGEABLE PERSONS

1.4   A person is chargeable to CGT in respect of chargeable gains accruing to him in a year of assessment, ie a 'tax year' ending on 5 April, if the residence condition is met (*TCGA 1992, ss 1, 2(1)*). The residence condition is defined in *TCGA 1992, s 2(1A)* for periods from 6 April 2013 onwards. Before that date, the taxpayer could be subject to CGT if he was ordinarily resident in the UK.

'Accruing' means realised or deemed to be realised, rather than accumulated over a period.

Anti-avoidance rules provide for a person to be chargeable to CGT on gains accruing to others in certain circumstances. For example, the gains of a non-resident trust or company may be attributed to a UK-resident individual (see **5.52**). Residence and the remittance basis are discussed in detail in **Chapter 5**.

Where a donor has not paid the CGT due on a gift, the tax may be recovered from the donee (*TCGA 1992, s 282*). Where the donor has died, his personal representatives stand in his shoes, and become liable to pay the CGT owed by the deceased on disposal made during the deceased's life. This was the case in *Zoe Hamar v HMRC* [2011] UKFTT 687 (TC), where the deceased had made gifts to his daughter Zoe, but unfortunately died without paying the CGT due. The estate did not pay the CGT, so HMRC raised an assessment on Zoe Hamar in August 2009 purporting to be an assessment for 2002/03, the year in which the gifts were made, and charged interest on the late paid tax due from 31 January 2004. The First-tier Tribunal found that the assessment should have been raised for 2009/10, as it is not possible to treat an assessment for one year as an assessment for another (see *Baylis v Gregory* [1987] STC 297). Mrs Hamar could not be charged interest for the late payment of the CGT due by her father and his estate, but could only be charged interest on her own default of the tax.

Territorial limits

1.5   The UK comprises Great Britain and Northern Ireland. It includes the UK's territorial seas, but excludes the Isle of Man and the Channel Islands. A person who is a 'temporary non-resident' may also be chargeable to CGT. A non-resident person carrying on a business in the UK through a branch or agency (or through a permanent establishment, in the case of a company) is chargeable to CGT (or corporation tax) on gains arising from assets in the UK that are used for the purposes of the business (*TCGA 1992, ss 10, 10A, 276*). A non-resident person who does not fall into that category cannot generally be chargeable to CGT on gains made on UK situated property. However, from 6 April 2013, CGT is extended to gains made on the disposal of high-value residential properties in the UK, where the owner is a non-resident or a UK-resident, non-natural person such as a company (see **4.39**).

CGT is not limited to gains on disposal of UK assets. However, an individual who is not domiciled in any part of the UK may not be chargeable on gains arising on non-UK assets if that individual has claimed, or has the automatic right to, the remittance basis and those overseas gains are not remitted to the UK. See **Chapter 5** regarding residence, remittance and the location of assets.

Beneficial ownership

1.6   The beneficial owner of the asset disposed of is normally the chargeable person in relation to the disposal. There is no disposal where an asset is transferred between a beneficial owner and a nominee for him (*TCGA 1992, s 60*).

CHARGEABLE GAINS VERSUS INCOME

1.7   Every gain accruing on the disposal of an asset is a chargeable gain, but it should only be chargeable to CGT if it is not taxed by income tax. *TCGA 1992, s 37* expressly excludes from the chargeable gains calculation amounts charged to income tax or corporation tax as income. However, this rule does not prevent the same sum from being subject to two different taxes as HMRC may raise alternative assessments on that sum under income tax and CGT (*IRC v Wilkinson* [1992] STC 454, 65 TC 28 and *Bye v Coren* [1986] STC 393, 60 TC 116).

There are a number of types of transaction that may result in the profits being taxed as income rather than as capital due to the impact of anti-avoidance legislation. For example an artificial transaction in land may give rise to an income tax or corporation tax charge on the profit under *ITA 2007, s 775* (*CTA 2010, ss 818–822* for corporation tax).

It is difficult, but not impossible, to convert income (taxed at 20%, 40% or 45%) into capital (taxed at 10%, 18% or 28%). For example, a high earner may decide to invest in bonds that provide a return in the form of capital redemptions subject to CGT, rather than investments that return dividends or interest that are subject to income tax. Schemes that seek to convert employment income into an asset that would be subject to CGT on disposal may have to be reported to HMRC under the DOTAS regulations or the GAAR (see **10.2, 10.8**).

Capital losses are computed, as a general rule, in the same way as gains. If a gain accruing on an asset would be exempt from CGT, a loss accruing on the same disposal cannot generally be an allowable loss. However, there are exceptions for losses arising on EIS or SEIS shares (see **Chapter 16**).

In theory, capital gains and losses can arise from the relative movement in exchange rates in respect of sums held in foreign currency bank accounts, crystallised by the withdrawal of funds from the account. Generally, such gains would be covered by the taxpayer's annual exemption; but, from April 2008, non-domiciliaries are denied the use of the annual exemption if they also claim the remittance basis (see **1.17**). This need to calculate and report numerous small gains and losses has been removed by *TCGA 1992, s 252* from 6 April 2012, but it remains for earlier tax years.

EXEMPT ASSETS OR GAINS

1.8   The main exemptions applied to particular assets or gains by virtue of *TCGA 1992* are set out in Table 1.1, in the order in which they appear in the legislation. Exemptions provided elsewhere in the tax legislation are set out in Table 1.2. There are also a number of special rules relating to particular assets (see **Chapter 4**) and a variety of reliefs which either provide a reduction in the CGT liability or defer it until a later date (see **Chapters 11–17**).

Exemptions provided by TCGA 1992

1.9

Table 1.1	
Exempt assets or gains	**TCGA 1992**
Sterling is not an asset for CGT purposes (but currency other than sterling is an asset).	*s 21(1)(b)*
Wasting assets: No chargeable gain accrues on a disposal of tangible movable property that is a wasting asset as defined, subject to certain exceptions (see **Chapter 4**).	*s 45*
Winnings from betting, lotteries or games with prizes are not chargeable gains.	*s 51*
Compensation or damages for any wrong or injury suffered by an individual in his person or in his profession or vocation are not chargeable gains.	*s 51*
Death: The assets of which a deceased person was competent to dispose are deemed not to be disposed of by him on his death (see **Chapter 7**).	*s 62*

Exempt assets or gains	*TCGA 1992*
Interests in settled property: No chargeable gain accrues on the disposal of an interest in a settlement by the original beneficiary or by any other person except one who bought the interest. The trustees must be resident in the UK. There are also other exceptions (see **Chapter 8**).	*s 76*
Government stock and qualifying corporate bonds (QCBs): A gain accruing on a disposal of government-issued securities known as gilts, or any QCB whoever issued it, or of any option or contract to acquire or dispose of such assets is not a chargeable gain. The official list of gilts which are exempt from CGT is given at www.hmrc.gov.uk/cgt/gilts-list.htm.	*s 115*
Savings certificates and certain government securities are not chargeable assets, so that no chargeable gain accrues on a disposal.	*s 121*
Business expansion scheme (BES) shares: A gain accruing to an individual on disposal of shares issued after 18 March 1986 for which tax relief was given under the BES and has not been withdrawn is not a chargeable gain. Special rules apply to losses on disposal of such shares.	*s 150*
Enterprise investment scheme (EIS) shares: Gains accruing on the disposal after the end of the 'relevant period' of shares for which income tax relief under the EIS regime has been given (and not withdrawn) are not chargeable gains. Partial CGT exemption is available where income tax relief was restricted. Special rules apply to losses on disposal of such shares (see **Chapter 16**).	*ss 150A–150C*
Seed enterprise investment scheme (SEIS) shares: Gains accruing on the disposal after the end of the 'relevant period' of shares for which income tax relief under the EIS regime has been given (and not withdrawn) are not chargeable gains. Partial CGT exemption is available where income tax relief was restricted. Special rules apply to losses on disposal of such shares (see **Chapter 16**).	*ss 150E–150F*
SEIS reinvestment of gains: Gains realised from disposals in 2012/13 or 2013/14, that are reinvested in SEIS shares in the same tax year, for which income tax relief is received and not withdrawn, are exempt or partially exempt from CGT (see **Chapter 16**).	*s 150G* *Sch 5BB*

Exempt assets or gains	TCGA 1992
Individual Savings Accounts and Personal Equity Plan investments: No tax is chargeable on either the investor or the account manager in respect of gains arising on ISAs, Junior ISAs or PEPs, provided certain conditions are met.	*s 151*
Venture capital trusts: A gain accruing to an individual on a 'qualifying disposal' of ordinary shares in a venture capital trust is, subject to certain conditions, not a chargeable gain. Special rules apply to losses on disposal of such shares (see **Chapter 16**).	*s 151A*
Substantial shareholdings exemption (SSE): A gain on a disposal of a 'substantial shareholding' (broadly, an interest of at least 10%) that has been held for at least 12 months is not a chargeable gain, provided various conditions are met (see **Chapter 9**).	*s 192A, Sch 7AC*
Life insurance and deferred annuities: A gain accruing on a disposal of (or of an interest in) rights conferred by a policy of insurance or contract for a deferred annuity is not a chargeable gain unless the policy etc (or the interest in it) has been acquired for actual (not deemed) consideration.	*ss 204, 210*
Main residence: All or part of a gain on the disposal of a dwelling house which has been the individual's only or main residence at some time in the period of ownership will be exempt from CGT (see **Chapter 12**).	*s 222*
Employee shares: Shares acquired through the adoption of 'employee shareholder' status are exempt from CGT on disposal (see **Chapter 17**).	*ss 236B–236G*
Pension funds, purchased annuities, and superannuation funds:	*ss 237, 271*
Gains on the disposal of investments held for the purposes of a registered pension scheme are not chargeable to CGT. No chargeable gain accrues on the disposal of a right to payment out of a qualifying superannuation fund. This covers the majority of occupational pension schemes. Also the disposal of rights to payments under purchased annuities or covenants not secured on property is exempt.	

Exempt assets or gains	*TCGA 1992*
Woodlands: Any part of the consideration for a disposal of woodland in the UK that is attributable to trees (including saleable underwood) growing on the land is excluded from the CGT computation together with the related costs. Where the occupier of woodlands manages them on a commercial basis with a view to the realisation of profits, consideration for the disposal of trees standing or felled or cut on the woodlands is excluded from the computation. Any capital sum received under an insurance policy relating to the destruction of (or damage to) trees or saleable underwood by fire or other hazard is also excluded.	*s 250*
Debts: Where a person (A) incurs a debt to another person (B), no chargeable gain accrues to the original creditor (B) on a disposal of the debt or an interest in the debt, except in the case of a debt on a security.	*s 251*
Foreign currency bank accounts: Gains and losses arising from withdrawals from foreign currency bank accounts are removed completely from the scope of CGT for individuals, trustees and PRs with effect from 6 April 2012.	*s 252*
Works of art etc: A gain is not a chargeable gain if it accrues on the disposal of assets such as works of art, historical building etc to which a conditional exemption from inheritance tax could or does apply, or the exemption for gifts to the nation applies.	*s 258*
Chattels: A gain accruing on a disposal of tangible movable property is not a chargeable gain if the amount or value of the consideration for the disposal is not more than £6,000 (see **Chapter 4**).	*s 262*
Motor cars: Vehicles which are commonly used as private motor cars are not chargeable assets, which means no chargeable gain or loss can accrue on their disposal. This exemption covers vintage cars, but not vehicles of a type not commonly used as a private vehicle and unsuitable to be so used.	*s 263*
Renewables obligation certificates: Where an individual disposes of a renewables obligation certificate in relation to an electricity generation system installed at their home and other conditions apply, there is no chargeable gain.	*s 263AZA*

Exempt assets or gains	*TCGA 1992*
Decorations for valour or gallant conduct: A gain accruing on the disposal of a decoration awarded for valour or gallant conduct is not a chargeable gain unless the taxpayer acquired it for a consideration in money or money's worth.	*s 268*
Foreign currency for personal expenditure: A gain accruing on the disposal by an individual of currency acquired for his own or his family's or his dependants' personal expenditure outside the UK is not a chargeable gain.	*s 269*
SAYE savings schemes: Interest on certified SAYE savings arrangements within *ITTOIA 2005, s 702* is disregarded for all purposes of CGT.	*s 271(4)*

Other exemptions

1.10

Table 1.2

Exempt assets or gains	Source
Cashbacks: Lump sums received by a customer as an inducement for entering into a transaction for the purchase of goods, investments or services, and received as a direct consequence of entering into the transaction (eg a mortgage), are not considered to derive from a chargeable asset for CGT purposes, so that no chargeable gain arises. This practice does not extend to other incentive payments, or to 'trail commission' paid to investors which may be subject to income tax from 6 April 2013.	SP 4/97, para 35 HMRC Capital Gains Manual at CG13025–CG13029 R&C Brief 04/13
Child Trust Funds: Assets held by a named child as account investments are regarded as held by him in a separate capacity from that in which he holds similar assets outside the CTF. The child will be treated as selling the account investments and reacquiring them in his personal capacity at their market value on attaining the age of 18. Losses accruing on account investments are disregarded for CGT purposes.	*Child Trust Funds Act 2004, s 13; SI 2004/1450*

Exempt assets or gains	Source
Compensation paid by foreign governments: By concession, and subject to conditions, certain capital sums paid as compensation by a foreign government for the confiscation or expropriation of property outside the UK are not treated as giving rise to a chargeable gain.	ESC D50
Lloyd's underwriters' special reserve funds: Profits and losses arising from disposal of assets forming part of a special reserve fund are excluded from CGT.	*FA 1993, Sch 20, para 9*
Compensation for bad pensions advice: compensation for misleading pensions advice given between 29 April 1988 and 30 June 1994 is not a chargeable gain.	*FA 1996, s 148*
Compensation to Equitable Life policy holders: compensation paid under the Equitable Life payments scheme are disregarded for the purposes of capital gains tax.	*SI 2011/1502* R&C Brief 26/11

Exempt persons

1.11 The main exemptions likely to be met in practice are set out in Table 1.3. Others include full or partial exemptions for the Crown, local authorities, health service bodies, friendly societies, certain museums, housing associations, self-build societies, pension schemes, trades unions, scientific research associations, certain central banks, visiting forces and diplomats.

Table 1.3

Exempt person(s)	Source
Nominees and bare trustees: Where assets are held by a person (A) as nominee or bare trustee for another person (B), the property is treated as vested in B and acts of the nominee or bare trustee are treated as acts of B, so that there is no occasion of charge where the bare trustee, for example, passes assets to B.	*TCGA 1992, s 60*
Charities: A gain is not a chargeable gain if it accrues to a charity and is applicable and applied for charitable purposes (subject to restrictions found in *ITA 2007, Part 10*).	*TCGA 1992, s 256*
Community amateur sports clubs: A gain accruing to a registered club is not a chargeable gain if the whole of it is applied for qualifying purposes and the club makes a claim.	*CTA 2010, s 665*

THE CAPITAL GAINS TAX CALCULATION

1.12   Individuals, trustees and PRs pay CGT at the rate or rates applying in the relevant tax year (see **1.23**).

See **Chapter 3** for a discussion of the detailed computation of chargeable gains. **Chapter 11** deals with entrepreneurs' relief and the complications that arise when qualifying gains are made both before and after 23 June 2010.

The amount chargeable

1.13   Once the gains have been computed as set out in **Chapter 3**, several adjustments may be required before the taxpayer can ascertain the taxable amount and then apply the appropriate rates of CGT.

CGT is charged on the total amount of chargeable gains accruing in the tax year, after deducting:

- any allowable losses accruing to the taxpayer in that tax year; and

- any allowable losses accruing to him in a previous tax year (not earlier than 1965/66) that have not already been allowed as a deduction from chargeable gains.

Generally, allowable losses cannot be carried back to an earlier tax year.

Focus

The no carry-back rule is broken in the following circumstances:

- where the loss is sustained by an individual in the tax year in which he died (see **Chapter 7**); or

- where a loss is made on the disposal of a right to unascertainable consideration, it may be carried back to set against the earlier taxation of that consideration (see **3.29**).

The taxpayer can set allowable losses against gains in the most beneficial way in the current tax year, which may involve setting the loss against gains chargeable at a higher rate before those chargeable at lower rates of CGT (*TCGA 1992, s 4B*). Relief cannot be given twice for the same loss under *TCGA 1992* and is not available for a capital loss that has been, or may be, relieved under the income tax legislation (*TCGA 1992, s 2(2), (3)*).

Losses and gains arising from a single business disposal subject to entrepreneurs' relief must be aggregated, before entrepreneurs' relief is applied to the net gain (see **Chapter 11**).

Gains accruing to others

1.14 This general rule for the off-set of losses is modified where gains have accrued to others but are attributed to the taxpayer, as settlor or beneficiary of a trust, under any of the following provisions (read, where appropriate, with the rules in *TCGA 1992, s 10A* relating to temporary non-residents):

(a) *TCGA 1992, s 86* – attribution of gains to settlor with an interest in a non-resident or dual-resident settlement;

(b) *TCGA 1992, s 87* – attribution of gains to a beneficiary; and

(c) *TCGA 1992, s 89(2)* – migrant settlements etc.

The effect of these special rules is that the taxpayer's own capital losses cannot be set against such relevant deemed gains (*TCGA 1992, s 2(4)–(7)*).

Taper relief

1.15 Taper relief was automatically given against gains arising on disposals made by individuals and trustees between 6 April 1998 and 5 April 2008. Losses were deducted before the net gain was tapered by a percentage dependent on the type of asset and the period the asset had been held. The taxpayer had the choice of which gain to set against any available loss (*TCGA 1992, s 2A*). For further discussion of taper relief, please refer to the 2011/12 or earlier edition of this book.

Entrepreneurs' relief

1.16 Entrepreneurs' relief (ER) may be claimed where certain qualifying shares or business assets are disposed of after 5 April 2008. Where the qualifying gain is realised on or after 23 June 2010, CGT is applied to that gain at 10%, where the gain lies within the taxpayer's lifetime limit for the relief. However, the gains subject to ER must be first set against the taxpayer's basic rate band. This reduces the basic rate band available to set against any non-ER gains in the same tax year; see Example 1.1 below. The chronological order in which the ER gains and non-ER gains are realised during the tax year is irrelevant, as the ER gain will always take priority over the available basic rate band (see CG21210).

For qualifying gains realised before 23 June 2010, the relief reduces the effective rate of CGT to 10%, by reducing the qualifying gain by 4/9ths. Entrepreneurs' relief is examined in detail in **Chapter 11**.

Annual exemption

1.17 Most individuals are entitled to an annual exemption, the effect of which is to provide that a slice of the 'taxable amount' (see **1.19**) for a tax year is not chargeable to CGT. Any unused part of the annual exemption is lost – it cannot be carried forward to the following tax year. Spouses and civil partners are entitled to their own annual exemption, which is not transferable. Non-UK domiciled individuals are not entitled to an annual exemption where they claim or are entitled to use the remittance basis, subject to certain exceptions, see **Chapter 5**.

The amount of the annual exemption is as set out in Table 1.4 (*TCGA 1992, s 3*).

Table 1.4		
Tax year	*Individuals, certain trustees (see 1.22) and personal representatives: £*	*Other trustees £*
2013/14	10,900	5,450
2012/13	10,600	5,300
2011/12	10,600	5,300
2010/11	10,100	5,050
2009/10	10,100	5,050
2008/09	9,600	4,800
2007/08	9,200	4,600

Indexation of the annual exemption

1.18 From 2013/14, the indexation of the annual exemption is tied to the consumer prices index (CPI) rather than the RPI, but this will still be subject to parliamentary override. For 2014/15 and 2015/16, the annual exemption will be increased by only 1%.

The 'taxable amount'

1.19 The taxable amount is usually the amount of chargeable gains accruing to the taxpayer for a tax year after deduction of losses and reliefs. In some cases, gains accruing to others but chargeable on the taxpayer under anti-avoidance rules will be added at this stage in arriving at the taxable amount (see **1.14**) (*TCGA 1992, s 3(5)*).

Losses and the annual exemption

1.20 Allowable losses must be set against chargeable gains arising in the same tax year, even if this means reducing the taxable amount below the annual exemption. In other words, the set-off of current-year losses cannot be restricted in order to utilise the annual exemption and preserve some of those losses for future use.

Allowable capital losses carried forward from an earlier year (or carried back from the year of the taxpayer's death) need not be deducted where the 'adjusted net gains' (see below) of the current tax year are covered by the annual exemption *(TCGA 1992, ss 2(2), 3(5A))*.

If the taxpayer's adjusted net gains exceed the annual exemption, then the amount set off in respect of losses carried forward (or back) is restricted to the excess. For this purpose the 'adjusted net gains' are, in most cases:

- the chargeable gains accruing to him for the year, before deduction of losses and reliefs, less

- allowable losses arising in the current year *(TCGA 1992, s 3(5B), (5C))*.

However, where gains have accrued to others but are attributed to the taxpayer as beneficiary of a settlement under the rules mentioned in (b) or (c) of **1.14**, then the smaller of the following amounts is added in arriving at the adjusted net gains:

- the amount of gains so attributed to him; and

- the amount of the annual exemption *(TCGA 1992, s 3(5C))*.

Personal representatives

1.21   The CGT treatment of personal representatives is considered in **Chapter 7**. Personal representatives of a deceased individual are entitled to the same annual exempt amount as an individual for:

- the tax year in which the individual died; and

- the next two following tax years *(TCGA 1992, s 3(7))*.

Trustees

1.22   The CGT treatment of trustees is considered in **Chapter 8**. Two sets of rules, set out in *TCGA 1992, Sch 1*, fix the annual exemption. Broadly, trustees generally are entitled to an annual exemption equal to one-half of the exemption available to an individual, but trustees of settled property held for people with disabilities and others in receipt of attendance allowance or disability living allowance are entitled to the full annual exemption *(TCGA 1992, s 3(8), Sch 1, para 1)*.

Rates of tax

Individuals

1.23   For disposals made, and deemed to be made, on or after 23 June 2010 and in subsequent tax years, there are three possible tax rates of CGT that apply to the gains realised, which depend on the taxpayer's level of income and gains:

Taxpayer or gains:	*Rate of CGT*
Individuals with income and gains within their basic rate band:	18%
Individuals with income and gains exceeding their basic rate band:	28%
All trustees and personal representatives:	28%
Gains subject to entrepreneurs' relief:	10%

The higher rate of CGT at 28% applies where the taxpayer's total taxable income and taxable amount of gains (see **1.19**) exceeds their basic rate threshold for the tax year. The taxpayer's total taxable income is his or her income subject to income tax for the full tax year, less personal allowances and all allowable deductions. The taxpayer's basic rate band will be the amount set for the tax year (£32,010 for 2013/14, £34,370 for 2012/13), expanded by the gross amounts contributed to registered pension schemes and donated under the Gift Aid scheme (see CG21220).

The rate of CGT was set at a single rate of 18% for gains made from 6 April 2008 to 22 June 2010. During this period, this flat rate of CGT applied irrespective of the level of other income taxed in the same tax year (*TCGA 1992, s 4*).

Focus

For the Gift Aid donation to expand the basic rate band for the tax year, it needs to be made or treated as made in that tax year.

A Gift Aid donation can be carried back to be relieved in the previous tax year if it is made before the tax return for that tax year is submitted. A claim to carry back a Gift Aid donation cannot be made in an amended tax return (see *Cameron v HMRC* [2010] UKFTT 104 (TC)).

The taxpayer can choose which gain should be reduced by their annual exemption and/or capital losses, including capital losses that arise in the tax year and losses which are brought forward from an earlier tax year.

Example 1.1

Sid's taxable income for 2013/14 is £60,000 after his personal allowance and all tax-allowable expenses have been deducted. He sold shares in his personal company in May 2013, realising a gain of £17,000, which qualified for entrepreneurs' relief. In November 2013, he sold an investment property for a gain of £50,000. Sid made a contribution to his registered pension scheme of £40,000 net (£50,000 gross) in December 2013. Sid has no capital losses to use in 2013/14. The CGT on those gains is calculated as follows:

2013/14	May 2013 gain £	November 2013 gain £	CGT payable £
Higher rate threshold	32,010		
Expanded by pension contribution	50,000		
Total basic rate band	82,010		
Taxable income	(60,000)		
Available basic rate band	22,010		
Gross gains	17,000	50,000	
Less annual exemption		10,900	
Net taxable gains	17,000	39,100	
Basic rate band deemed used	17,000	7,010	
Gain taxable at 10%	17,000		1,700
Gain taxed at 18% (using basic rate band)		7,010	1,261.80
Gain taxed at 28%		32,090	8,985.20
Total CGT payable			11,947

Sid has chosen to set his annual exemption of £10,900 against his later gain, as that gives him tax relief at 28%. Although the first gain is subject to entrepreneurs' relief and is thus taxable in full at 10%, it is deemed to take priority before other gains over the available basic rate band.

Sid's total CGT liability for 2013/14 of £11,947 is payable by 31 January 2015.

Trustees and personal representatives

1.24   For gains realised on disposals made on or after 23 June 2010, all trustees pay CGT at 28%.

Where the disposal was made between 6 April 2008 and 22 June 2010, the trustees pay CGT at 18%.

Companies

1.25   Companies do not generally pay CGT but, in the case of properties subject to the annual tax on enveloped dwellings (ATED), a CGT charge can apply for disposals made after 5 April 2013 (see **Chapter 4**). As discussed in **Chapter 9**, companies are chargeable to corporation tax on their chargeable gains (*TCGA 1992, s 1(2)*; *CTA 2009, s 2*).

SELF-ASSESSMENT

1.26   The self-assessment system has applied to individuals, trustees and personal representatives, broadly, since 1996/97. An individual's tax return must include a self-assessment of income tax and CGT liabilities. The taxpayer is required to pay the tax on or before the due date, based on that self-assessment.

Self-assessment and related matters, including compliance with the regime for disclosure of tax avoidance schemes, are examined in detail in Chapter 2 of *Income Tax 2013/14* (Bloomsbury Professional). This chapter focuses on the fundamental aspects of self-assessment relating to capital gains.

HMRC provide general guidance on CGT at www.hmrc.gov.uk/cgt/index.htm. There is also specific guidance on keeping records for capital gains tax purposes at www.hmrc.gov.uk/cgt/intro/record-keeping.htm. Technical guidance on CGT and chargeable gains for companies can be found in the HMRC Capital Gains Manual at www.hmrc.gov.uk/manuals/cgmanual/index.htm.

HMRC also provide toolkits, which are interactive checklists covering the most difficult or problematic areas of tax returns (see www.hmrc.gov.uk/agents/prereturn-support-agents.htm). There are four toolkits that deal with capital gains issues:

- capital gains tax for land and buildings;
- capital gains tax for shares;
- capital gains tax for trusts and estates; and
- chargeable gains for companies.

The use of the toolkits is completely optional when preparing a tax return. However, HMRC state that, if the relevant toolkits are used when preparing a tax return, this will demonstrate that the preparer has taken 'reasonable care'. Tax advisers may equally prove they have taken reasonable care by using alternative checklists or review procedures. Reasonable care could be a significant factor if errors are subsequently discovered on that return and penalties are imposed (see **1.48**).

Focus

The HMRC toolkits are updated for each new tax year:

● ensure the HMRC toolkit you are using is the one written for the tax year under consideration; and

● CGT toolkits for the tax years 2010/11 onwards are available on the HMRC website.

Tax returns

1.27   Taxpayers may file their tax return online via the HMRC website, in which case a paper return form is not required. All the self-assessment tax return forms for the years 2011/12 back to 2009/10 can be downloaded from the HMRC website at www.hmrc.gov.uk/sa/forms/content.htm. You need to follow the links on that page to access the 2012/13 forms.

The capital gains summary pages are required if an individual taxpayer answers 'yes' to question 7 in the section entitled 'What makes up your Tax Return' on page TR2 of the 2012/13 form SA100. Page TRG5 of the Tax Return Guide sets out in greater detail the circumstances in which the capital gains summary pages (SA108) should be completed. Trustees and personal representatives need to complete the SA900 Trust and Estate tax return, with supplementary pages SA905 to report capital gains and losses. Settlors and beneficiaries of trusts may need to report income or gains from a settlement, in which case form 50(FS): Trust Gains and Capital Payments is required.

HMRC provide notes to the capital gains pages (SA108 Notes for individuals, SA905 Notes for trustees), including examples. HMRC also provide detailed helpsheets on various topics. Those relevant to capital gains are set out in Table 1.5, and listed on page CGN 22 of SA108 Notes. You can order a hard copy of the helpsheets from the HMRC orderline on 0845 9000 404 or download them from the HMRC website, (search for the specific helpsheet by number, or try using a wildcard such as HS***).

Table 1.5

HS261	Foreign tax credit relief: capital gains
HS275	Entrepreneurs' relief
HS276	Incorporation relief
HS278	Temporary non-residents and Capital Gains Tax
HS281	Husband and wife, civil partners, divorce, dissolution and separation
HS282	Death, personal representatives and legatees
HS283	Private residence relief
HS284	Shares and Capital Gains Tax
HS285	Share reorganisations, company take-overs and Capital Gains Tax
HS286	Negligible value claims and Income Tax losses on the disposal of shares you have subscribed for in qualifying trading companies
HS287	Employee share and security schemes and Capital Gains Tax
HS288	Partnerships and Capital Gains Tax
HS290	Business asset roll-over relief
HS292	Land and leases, the valuation of land and Capital Gains Tax
HS293	Chattels and Capital Gains Tax
HS294	Trusts and Capital Gains Tax
HS295	Relief for gifts and similar transactions
HS296	Debts and Capital Gains Tax
HS297	Enterprise Investment Scheme and Capital Gains Tax
HS298	Venture Capital Trusts and Capital Gains Tax
HS299	Non Resident Trusts and Capital Gains Tax
HS301	Beneficiaries receiving capital payments from non-resident trusts and the calculation of the increase in tax charges
HS390	Trusts & estates of deceased persons: foreign tax credit relief for capital gains
HS393	Seed Enterprise Investment Scheme – Income tax and capital gains tax relief

Notice to deliver a return

1.28 An HMRC officer may give notice to the taxpayer requiring him to make and deliver a return to enable the officer to establish the amount of any income tax or CGT liability. The notice may request such accounts, statements and documents, relating to information contained in the return, as may reasonably be required (*TMA 1970, ss 8, 12*).

Information required to be sent with the return

1.29   The notice may require different information, accounts and statements for different periods or different sources of income. While there is no statutory authority for HMRC to require a taxpayer to provide a list of investments or other assets held at a particular date, HMRC guidance indicates that they may possibly ask for such a list if they are aware that one exists (CG20224). The return includes a declaration by the person making it to the effect that the return is, to the best of his knowledge, correct and complete.

The capital gains summary pages must be submitted together with detailed computations of each capital disposal made. HMRC do not prescribe a format for the CGT computation, but it does include a worksheet for simple disposals in the notes to the capital gains pages (page CGN21 of SA108 Notes).

For online submission, the tax return must also include CGT computations for each disposal. This can be included in the 'any other information' space (box 36) on page CG2, if the computation does not exceed the data limit for this box. Otherwise, the CGT computations should be submitted as a PDF file attached to the tax return.

Reporting limits

1.30   A return of capital gains is required only if certain reporting limits, set out below in relation to individuals, personal representatives and trustees respectively, are exceeded. However, the capital gains pages should be completed if there are allowable losses or the taxpayer wishes to make a claim or election for the year (see **1.39**).

Individuals

1.31   HMRC do not require the taxpayer to complete the capital gains summary pages where any of the following apply:

(a)   the taxpayer's chargeable gains accruing in a tax year do not exceed the amount of the annual exemption (see **1.17**);

(b)   the aggregate amount or value of the consideration for all 'chargeable disposals' (see below) that he made in the year does not exceed four times that annual exemption (ie £42,400 for 2012/13, £43,600 for 2013/14), and the chargeable gain arising was less than the annual exemption; or

(c)   the gain relates to a private residence and is wholly relieved by main residence relief (see **Chapter 12**).

For this purpose, the amount of chargeable gains accruing in the year is taken to be the amount before any deduction for allowable losses. An individual cannot take advantage of the exemptions in (a) and (b) above if they claim the remittance basis for the tax year, or where they may have a claim under *TCGA 1992, s 16ZA* for foreign chargeable gains to be taxed in a tax year after a year in which they accrue (see **Chapter 5**).

'Chargeable disposals' for the purpose of these reporting limits exclude both disposals on which any gain accruing is not a chargeable gain and 'no gain, no loss' disposals between spouses or civil partners (*TCGA 1992, s 3A(1), (2), (3)*).

Personal representatives

1.32   The above reporting limits are applied to personal representatives for the tax year in which the individual concerned died and for the next two tax years (*TCGA 1992, s 3A(4)*).

Trustees

1.33   The reporting rule in **1.31** also applies to trustees of a settlement, but the reporting limits are calculated by reference to the reduced annual exemption available to the trustees, where appropriate (see **1.17** and **Chapter 8**) (*TCGA 1992, s 3A(5)*; *Sch 1, para 2(6A)*).

Estimates

1.34   A taxpayer who has used estimated figures to calculate gains or losses should:

- tick the relevant boxes on page CG1 or CG2 of the capital gains pages; and

- identify and give reasons for the estimates, either in the detailed computations or in box 36, the 'any other information' box on page CG2 as appropriate.

Estimates may be needed where property which was held at 31 March 1982 is disposed of. The Valuation Office has provided a report which can be used as a source of historical values for land and buildings as at 31 March 1982 (see www.voa.gov.uk/DVS/propertyMarketReport/1982/index.html).

Valuations

1.35   The use of any valuation in a CGT computation should be indicated in the detailed computations. HMRC Statement of Practice 1/06 recommends that the following details should be given in the 'other information' space on the tax return:

- the firm or named individual who carried out the valuation, whether they were independent or suitably qualified; and

- the basis on which the valuation was carried out (eg as at 31 March 1982).

In addition, the notes to the CGT pages ask for the following information in respect of valuations for land or buildings:

- description of the property;

- whether it is held freehold or leasehold;

- any tenancies that affect the ownership at the date of valuation; and

- a plan of the property where that may aid identification.

HMRC may check the valuation and, in the absence of any agreement, the disputed valuation may be referred to the Tax Tribunal.

Before finalising the tax return, the taxpayer may ask HMRC to carry out a 'post-transaction valuation check', by using the form CG34 (see www.hmrc.gov.uk/forms/cg34.pdf). In most cases, the completed CG34 should be submitted, together with a valuation and all supporting documents, to HMRC at:

Local Compliance
Individuals & Public Bodies S0927
PO Box 3900
Glasgow
G70 6AA

If the taxpayer is a company, or their tax office is Public Department 1 or the High Net Worth Unit, the form CG34 should be submitted to the tax office that deals with the taxpayer's tax return. Trustees should submit the CG34 form to:

HMRC Trusts & Estates
Compliance S0923
PO Box 204
Bootle
L69 9AQ

Focus

- The form CG34 must be submitted to HMRC at least two months before the filing date for the tax return.

- If HMRC become aware that the tax return has been submitted, they will not proceed with the valuation check.

- Once the tax return has been submitted, the only way to resolve the valuation issue is to open an enquiry into the return.

The advantage of using the CG34 procedure is that, if HMRC agree a valuation, they will not challenge the use of that valuation in the tax return. This does not mean that the final gain or loss is agreed, as factors other than the valuation may be relevant. If HMRC cannot agree the valuation as suggested on CG34, they will use specialist valuers to suggest alternatives.

The taxpayer should indicate, in the detailed computation of the gains or losses submitted with the tax return, which transactions are, or have been, the subject of a CG34 valuation check.

It is possible to request a ruling on the application of recently passed tax legislation to a non-business transaction under Clearances and Approvals 1 (CAP1). 'Recently passed' tax legislation means that passed in the last four years. However, HMRC will also give a view where the subject of the query is derived from older legislation and the matter is not covered in the HMRC published guidance.

Before using the CAP1 service, the taxpayer or their adviser is expected to read the HMRC online guidance concerning the type of transaction in the query, or to have contacted the relevant HMRC helpline. HMRC will only provide a response under CAP1 where there are genuine points of uncertainty concerning the taxation of the transaction, and the enquiry window for the period in which the transaction falls has not closed.

The CAP1 service should not be used in place of the CG34 procedure. Further details are available at www.hmrc.gov.uk/cap/cap1.htm.

Provisional figures

1.36   HMRC advise taxpayers not to delay filing a tax return just because some of the required information is not available. Provisional figures should be provided and identified in the main pages of the return (by putting a cross in box 20 on page TR6 and a note in the 'any other information' box to indicate which figures are provisional). HMRC also want to be told why final figures could not be given and when those final figures will be provided.

The tax return guide (SA150) warns that a taxpayer may be liable to a penalty if they do not have good reasons for supplying provisional figures, or provide unreasonable figures. Pressure of work, or the complexity of the individual's tax affairs, are not good reasons to provide provisional figures. A taxpayer who uses provisional figures must ensure that the final figures are submitted as soon as they are available.

Filing date

1.37   The return must be delivered to HMRC by the filing date, which for electronically submitted returns will normally be 31 January following the end of the relevant tax year, ie 31 January 2014 for the year ended 5 April 2013. Taxpayers filing a paper return must do so by 31 October following the end of the tax year. Missing either deadline will generate a late filing penalty, which is not reduced to the level of tax outstanding. Tax returns for certain individuals, such as MPs and members of the security forces, cannot be submitted electronically, so may be submitted in paper form up until the final deadline of 31 January. Where a notice to deliver a return is given after 31 July following the end of the tax year, the filing deadline is three months after the date of that notice.

Where a paper tax return is submitted by 31 October, or an electronic tax return is submitted by 30 December, HMRC will adjust the PAYE notice of coding for the following tax year to include underpaid tax of up to £3,000, if this is requested.

Payment of tax

1.38   CGT for a tax year is payable in one sum by 31 January following the end of the tax year for which the liability arose. Unlike the combined income tax and Class 4 national insurance liability, the CGT is not payable as part of the on-account payments due on 31 January in the tax year, and 31 July after the end of the tax year. See Chapter 2 of *Income Tax 2013/14* (Bloomsbury Professional) for details of how payments on account are calculated.

Where CGT is unpaid more than 30 days after the due date, a penalty of 5% of the tax unpaid is imposed, with a further 5% charged if the tax remains unpaid six months after the due date. Once the CGT due is over 12 months late, an additional penalty is imposed of 5% of the unpaid tax at that date.

Time limits

1.39   The time limits for direct taxes, including CGT, were revised and generally shortened for all tax assessments, claims or elections submitted after 31 March 2010 (*SI 2009/403*).

Tax practitioners should pay particular attention to the tax periods covered by assessments raised by HMRC officers on and after 1 April 2010, to ensure that the periods assessed are not time barred. Table 1.6 summarises the current claims and assessment periods, as introduced by *FA 2008, Sch 39*.

Table 1.6

Statutory provision	Description	Effective from 1 April 2010
TMA 1970, s 28C(5)(a)	Determination of tax where no return delivered	3 years from filing date
TMA 1970, s 33(1)	Error or mistake claim	4 years from end of tax year
TMA 1970, s 33A(2)	Error or mistake claim – partnership	4 years after end of tax year
TMA 1970, s 34	Ordinary time limit for individuals	4 years from end of tax year
TMA 1970, s 35	Disclosure of late receipts of income	4 years after year received
TMA 1970, s 36(1)	Assessment to make good loss of tax through carelessness	6 years
TMA 1970, s 36(1A)	Assessment to make good loss of tax through fraud	20 years
TMA 1970, s 40	Assessment on personal representatives	4 years from end of tax year of death
TMA 1970, s 43	Claims	4 years after end of tax year
TCGA 1992, s 203(2)	Capital losses	4 years
TCGA 1992, s 253(4A)	Loans to traders	4 years from end of tax year
TCGA 1992, s 279(5)	Foreign disposal, delayed remittance	4 years from end of tax year
FA 1998, Sch 18, para 36(5)	Determination of tax for companies	3 years from end of accounting period
FA 1998, Sch 18, para 46	General time limit for assessment for companies	4 years from end of accounting period
FA 1998, Sch 18, para 51(1)(c)	Relief for mistake by companies	4 years from end of accounting period
FA 1998, Sch 18, para 55	General time limit for claims by companies	4 years from end of accounting period

COMPLIANCE ASSURANCE AND PENALTIES

HMRC's powers

1.40 HMRC have a single set of powers in order to monitor the accuracy of all tax returns, documents and information submitted to them, and to check the taxpayer's tax position at any time (**1.42**). They also have special powers to manage deliberate tax defaulters and to publish their details (**1.47**).

The system of penalties has been aligned and modernised across all taxes, with a number of new penalties introduced to encourage timely filing and payment. The previous penalty system continues to apply to errors and mistakes in tax returns or documents submitted to HMRC before 1 April 2009, and so it will run in parallel with the current system for some years (**1.48**).

Interest rates on the late payment or overpayment of tax were harmonised across all taxes from September 2009. However, the circumstances in which interest will be paid or charged have not yet been aligned across all of HMRC's responsibilities.

The time periods in which HMRC are permitted to raise tax assessments have been largely aligned with the periods available to taxpayers to make certain claims and elections (**1.39**). The system of tax appeals was also completely reformed from April 2009 (**1.55**).

Training and guidance

1.41 The HMRC internal guidance concerning its compliance powers and penalties is contained in the Compliance Handbook (www.hmrc.gov.uk/manuals/chmanual/Index.htm). HMRC have also produced a series of over 20 compliance factsheets to explain taxpayers' rights and the duties of HMRC officers during a compliance check (www.hmrc.gov.uk/compliance/factsheets.htm). These factsheets also cover the penalties that can be imposed.

HMRC have designed a number of training packages for tax agents and HMRC to use on a variety of topics including resolving disputes and penalties (www.hmrc.gov.uk/agents/lt-training.htm).

Compliance checks

1.42 HMRC can use the information and inspection powers introduced by *FA 2008, Sch 36* to undertake compliance checks on individuals and businesses for most of the taxes and duties they administer. In this section, references to paragraphs are to paragraphs of *FA 2008, Sch 36*.

A compliance check includes carrying out an investigation or enquiry of any kind (*para 58*), but it will not necessarily develop into a full-blown tax investigation.

HMRC have the power to request information ahead of the submission of any tax return, and conduct checks of business records before the accounting period has finished. The business records check (BRC) programme is targeted on businesses who are likely to have kept inadequate businesses records. If, after a second BRC visit, the business records are still inadequate, HMRC will impose a penalty.

HMRC officers may use their powers to obtain information and documents from the taxpayer and third parties which are reasonably required for the purpose of checking the tax position of the taxpayer. The 'tax position' is defined in *para 64* as the person's past, present or future liability to pay any tax. This includes:

- UK taxes: income tax, CGT, corporation tax, VAT, NIC and relevant foreign taxes;

- penalties paid or payable in respect of any tax; and

- claims, elections, applications and notices that have been made or may be made or given in connection with any tax.

Visits by HMRC

1.43   As part of the compliance check HMRC may visit business premises to inspect the premises, business assets and statutory records. 'Business premises' means any premises or any part of them that HMRC have reason to believe are used in connection with the carrying on of a business, so this includes homes that are partly used for business purposes. However, HMRC officers do not have the power to enter or inspect any part of the premises that is used solely as a dwelling. The Compliance Handbook instructs HMRC officers only to arrange to visit a person's home if it is essential to checking the person's tax position, and they must obtain their line manager's agreement first (CH254510).

HMRC officers do not have the power to force entry to the premises or to search the premises (para CH25120). *Paras 15–17* give HMRC powers to copy documents, to remove them and to mark assets and record information. HMRC are liable to pay the owner reasonable compensation should they lose or damage the document. HMRC officers may also inspect any computer used by the business (*FA 2008, s 114*), but the officer must first seek the advice of an HMRC data-handling specialist (CH23360).

Information notices

1.44 The HMRC officer will normally ask informally, either orally or in writing, for the information he requires. However, if this does not produce the required result, he can issue a formal taxpayer's notice, or a third party notice or an identity unknown notice. A 'third party notice' is one issued under *para 2* by an HMRC officer to check the tax position of someone whose identity is known to the officer and which names that taxpayer, except where approval has been obtained from the First-tier Tribunal to the issuing of the third party notice without the requirement to name the taxpayer.

The notice will usually specify or describe the information or documents to be provided or produced and stipulate a time limit for production. If the notice is given with the approval of the tribunal this must be stated in the notice. Where a tax return has been submitted, *para 21* only permits an HMRC officer to issue a taxpayer notice if one of the following conditions applies:

(a) the enquiry window for the return is still open, or an enquiry into that return is still open;

(b) HMRC have reason to suspect that tax has been over- or underpaid or too much tax relief has been given for the period;

(c) information is needed to check the taxpayer's VAT position; or

(d) information is needed to check the taxpayer's PAYE position.

Situation (b) is similar to the old discovery assessment position where an HMRC officer could make an assessment to tax if he discovered some relevant information or facts that were not disclosed in the tax return. However, the hurdle for this condition is much lower. The HMRC officer only needs to have reason to suspect there are tax irregularities, not the actual evidence (see CH23560). Having said that, the HMRC officer should not make random requests for information; he needs to identify a specific risk that tax was underpaid.

Safeguards

1.45 The taxpayer can only appeal against the taxpayer notice if it asks for something that is not part of the taxpayer's statutory records. Statutory records are very loosely defined as any information or document required to be kept by the *Taxes Act* or *VAT Act* (*para 62*). In the case of *Beckwith v HMRC* [2012] UKFTT 181 (TC), it was decided that personal bank account statements formed part of the taxpayer's statutory records, as that bank account had been used to pay a number of business expenses.

HMRC may also ask for what it calls 'supplementary information' that does not comprise statutory records, such as appointment diaries, correspondence and employment contracts. However, if this information concerns a person's physical, mental, spiritual or personal welfare, the taxpayer or third party cannot be required to produce it (CH22180).

There are also restrictions on the power of HMRC officers to inspect documents in the following categories (*paras 18–28*):

- information older than six years;

- documents relating to the conduct of tax appeals;

- journalistic material;

- legally privileged information or documents;

- auditors' statutory audit papers; and

- tax advisers' papers giving advice.

Where the taxpayer has died, an information notice may not be given more than four years after the death (*para 22*).

Partnerships

1.46 For CGT purposes, the tax practitioner should particularly be aware of *FA 2008, Sch 36, para 37* relating to partnerships. The restriction in *para 21* on taxpayer notices where a return has already been filed (described at **1.44**) applies as if the partnership return had been made by each of the partners, with extension where an enquiry is open in relation to any partner. Notice to one partner may effectively be notice to all (see *para 37(6)*). An information notice given to one of the partners, to check the position of one or more of the other partners whose identity is not known, does not require approval of the First-tier Tribunal.

The current penalty regime

1.47 The current penalty regime is largely defined in *FA 2007, Sch 24*. HMRC may impose penalties in the following circumstances:

- failure to notify certain tax-related events, such as becoming chargeable to tax;

- failure to provide information, or concealing or destroying documents requested in an Information Notice;

- obstructing an inspection approved by the First-tier Tribunal;

- inaccuracies or errors in returns/information given to HMRC (see **1.48–1.54**);

- VAT and Excise wrongdoing;

- failure to pay on time;
- failure to submit a return on time.

The current penalty regime for errors or inaccuracies applies to documents or returns concerning VAT, NIC, PAYE, CIS, income tax, CGT or corporation tax submitted to HMRC on or after 1 April 2009 which relate to a return period that commenced on or after 1 April 2008. The old penalty rules continue to apply to tax returns or information submitted for earlier periods.

Taxpayer behaviour

1.48   The basis of all the current penalties is the taxpayer's behaviour, which is categorised as falling into one of four categories in relation to each particular error or inaccuracy. The penalty charged is a percentage of the 'potential lost revenue' (see **1.49**). The range of penalties which can be imposed for each category of taxpayer behaviour is summarised in the following table:

Table 1.7

Type of taxpayer behaviour	Maximum penalty	Minimum penalty – unprompted disclosure	Minimum penalty – prompted disclosure
Took reasonable care	0%	0%	0%
Careless action	30%	0%	15%
Deliberate but not concealed	70%	20%	35%
Deliberate with concealment	100%	30%	50%

If the taxpayer took reasonable care but nevertheless made a mistake, or has a reasonable excuse for the failure to comply, the penalty should be reduced to nil under the current regime.

If several errors or inaccuracies are discovered, each error must be categorised separately according to the taxpayer's behaviour. *Schedule 24, para 6* requires careless inaccuracies to be taken as corrected before deliberate inaccuracies. Deliberate inaccuracies that were not concealed are taken to be corrected before those that have been concealed. However, these rules do not apply to the penalties imposed on third parties.

If the error, failure to file, or failure to notify, relates to income or gains in an overseas territory, the penalty can be up to 200% of the potential lost revenue (see **5.62**).

Potential lost revenue

1.49   The 'potential lost revenue' is defined by *Sch 24, para 5* as the additional amount due or payable in respect of tax as a result of correcting the inaccuracy or understatement. This includes an inaccuracy that is attributable to the supply of false information or the withholding of information. To summarise, the potential lost revenue can be:

(a)   the additional tax due and payable;

(b)   any excessive repayment of tax made by HMRC;

(c)   5% of the tax delayed for each year of the delay; or

(d)   10% of any unused loss.

Point (b) can include the situation where HMRC make an assessment that the taxpayer knows is too low, but where the taxpayer does not, within a reasonable time, tell HMRC of their error. This inaction by the taxpayer could also trigger a penalty (see Factsheet CC/FS7b, 'Penalties for not telling us about an under-assessment').

Disclosure

1.50   Disclosure (whether of an inaccuracy, the supply of false information, or of withholding of information, or failure to disclose) is achieved by taking three measures:

•   telling HMRC;

•   giving HMRC reasonable help in correcting the error; and

•   allowing HMRC access to the records.

By *Sch 24, para 9(2)*, disclosure is 'unprompted' and therefore qualifies for a greater reduction in penalty if it is made at a time when the person who makes it has no reason to believe that HMRC have discovered, or are about to discover, the inaccuracy, the supply of false information, the withholding of information or the under-assessment. In all other situations, disclosure is 'prompted' and the minimum penalty which can be imposed is defined in Table 1.7 above.

Deliberate defaulters

1.51   Where a tax investigation has resulted in additional tax payable of over £25,000 and a penalty has been imposed in respect of a deliberate default (not careless behaviour), HMRC may publish details of the 'deliberate defaulting' taxpayer on their website (see www.hmrc.gov.uk/defaulters/defaulters-list. pdf). An additional list of deliberate tax defaulters is published every quarter, but the details should not remain online for more than 12 months.

Third party documents

1.52 *FA 2007, Sch 24, para 1A* can impose a penalty on the taxpayer where the error in the taxpayer's document is attributable to another person, where:

- a third party gives HMRC a relevant document which contains an inaccuracy; and

- that inaccuracy is attributable to false information that was attributable to the taxpayer;

- who supplied the third party with that false information or who deliberately withheld information from the third party;

- intending that the document sent to HMRC would be wrong.

For this purpose, the 'relevant inaccuracy' is one that leads to an understatement of the tax liability or a false or inflated loss claim or repayment claim. A penalty becomes due under this paragraph in respect of the inaccuracy, whether or not the person who supplies the document to HMRC is also liable to a penalty under the main provision in *Sch 24, para 1*.

Suspension of penalties

1.53 HMRC may agree to suspend the whole or part of a penalty for up to two years to encourage the taxpayer to improve his systems, so that a further similar mistake could not occur. Only penalties imposed as a result of careless inaccuracies can be suspended, but the HMRC officer must consider all penalties imposed for careless inaccuracies for suspension.

In order to suspend the penalty, the HMRC officer is required to impose at least one specific condition on the taxpayer which, if met, will avoid further penalties for careless inaccuracies. The taxpayer can suggest a specific condition to be imposed, such as using a suitably qualified tax adviser to submit future tax returns. HMRC will also set a generic condition aimed at ensuring the taxpayer complies in general with his tax obligations (see CH83151). Although CGT generally applies to isolated disposals, this does not mean that an improvement in record keeping would not prevent an error concerning a future capital disposal (see *David Testa v HMRC* [2013] UKFTT 151 (TC)).

Focus

A penalty relating to CGT may be suspended if:

- the taxpayer is likely to make another capital gain in the future; and

- his systems for reporting or recording can be improved.

Tax agents

1.54   The taxpayer cannot escape penalties completely by engaging an agent to help prepare his tax return. If the tax agent makes a mistake in the return, the taxpayer is still liable unless he can show HMRC that he took reasonable care to avoid the inaccuracy (*FA 2007, Sch 24, para 18*; see CH84540). In *Hanson v HMRC* [2012] UKFTT 95 (TC), the taxpayer relied entirely on his accountant to make the appropriate CGT relief claim in his 2008/09 tax return. The CGT claim was incorrect. The judge held the taxpayer had taken reasonable care in instructing his accountants; and, as the mistake was made by the agent, the penalty was quashed.

It is possible for the tax agent to suffer a penalty where that tax agent has deliberately supplied false information or has withheld information, and that action has resulted in an understatement of tax liability, a false or inflated loss, or a false or inflated repayment of tax.

Tax disputes

1.55   At any stage in a dispute with HMRC, the taxpayer or his agent can apply to use the alternative dispute resolution (ADR) service.

ADR provides taxpayers with an alternative way of resolving tax disputes by using a facilitator (appointed by HMRC but independent to the case) who mediates discussions between the taxpayer and the HMRC caseworker. This may be particularly useful where the facts of a case need to be firmly established, but where communications have broken down between the taxpayer and HMRC. Using ADR does not affect the taxpayer's right to appeal or review.

Large businesses that have a customer relationship manager or dedicated caseworker within HMRC should approach that person to discuss ADR. Small businesses and individuals should apply to use ADR by completing the application on the HMRC website at www.hmrc.gov.uk/adr/smei.htm. Disputes concerning the removal of fixed penalties on the grounds of reasonable excuse, or tax payments, are not suitable for ADR.

Tax appeals system

1.56   Where a taxpayer disagrees with an appealable decision relating to a direct tax made by an HMRC officer he can submit a written appeal to HMRC, stating the grounds of the appeal within 30 days. At the same time the taxpayer (or his adviser) should make an application to postpone any disputed tax. HMRC may accept a late appeal where there is a reasonable excuse for the delay. There are slightly different procedures for indirect taxes.

Once an appeal has been submitted the taxpayer can ask for the decision to be reviewed by the HMRC internal review panel, or HMRC may offer a review. This is known as an internal review, or statutory review. The taxpayer must accept the HMRC offer of the review within 30 days, or it will lapse. The taxpayer can reject the offer of an internal review and notify the case directly to the First-tier Tribunal.

The internal review should be undertaken by HMRC staff who have not been involved in the original case. The review team are required to produce a decision within 45 working days, or such longer time as agreed. If the review is not completed within this time, the original decision stands and the taxpayer can take the case forward to the First-tier Tribunal.

The taxpayer has 30 days to ask the First-tier Tribunal to consider the appeal if they disagree with the result of the review. If the taxpayer does not respond to the review decision within 30 days, they are deemed to have accepted the HMRC decision.

Tax disputes are referred to the First-tier Tribunal (tax chamber) and then on to the Upper Tribunal. Some cases may go directly to the Upper Tribunal. An appeal from the Upper Tribunal will go to the Court of Appeal in England, Northern Ireland or Wales, or the Court of Session in Scotland. For further discussion of the new tax appeals system, see Chapter 2 of *Income Tax 2013/14* (Bloomsbury Professional). Guidance on the tax appeals system is also provided in the HMRC Appeals, Reviews and Tribunals Guidance Manual (ARTG).

Chapter 2

Disposals

SIGNPOSTS

- **Definition of assets and disposals** – What is considered to be a deemed disposal, part disposal, small disposal or not a disposal at all (see **2.2–2.9**).

- **When the value of an asset disappears** – Is lost or becomes negligible (see **2.10–2.11**).

- **Compensation and other sums received** – Such as insurance payout, for surrender of rights or for exploitation of assets. The funds may be used to replace or restore the asset (see **2.12–2.17**).

- **Whether these transactions create a chargeable gain** – Mortgages and charges, hire-purchase, gifts, settlements, deemed disposals by non-residents and capital distributions (see **2.18–2.23**).

DEFINITION OF ASSETS AND DISPOSALS

2.1   Every gain accruing on the disposal of an asset is a chargeable gain, unless otherwise expressly provided – see the exemptions listed in **1.9–1.11** (*TCGA 1992, ss 1, 15*).

The date of the disposal determines the period in which the gain is to be taxed. The rules for determining the date of disposal vary according to the nature of the disposal, for example by gift, under contract, or by deemed disposal (see **2.20–2.22**).

Meaning of 'asset'

2.2   All forms of property, wherever they are situated, are assets for CGT purposes, although there are special rules for assets owned by persons who are not domiciled or not resident in the UK (see **5.5**). Assets include options, debts, intangible property, and currency other than sterling. Property that has been created by the person disposing of it, or has otherwise come to be owned without being acquired, is also an asset (*TCGA 1992, s 21(1)*).

Meaning of 'disposal'

2.3   *TCGA 1992* does not define 'disposal'. HMRC guidance indicates that the word takes its natural meaning and that a disposal is 'an occasion when you sell an asset or give it away' (HMRC Capital Gains Manual at CG10242). A disposal for CGT purposes can include all of the following:

- sale, gift or exchange of assets;

- part disposal (see **2.4**);

- deemed disposal (see **2.6**);

- the entire loss or destruction of an asset (see **2.10**);

- money or money's worth received in respect of an asset (see **2.14**);

- transfer into a settlement (see **2.21**);

- receipt or entitlement to receive capital distribution in respect of shares (see **2.23**);

- grant of an option (see **4.6**); and

- repayment of a debt (see **4.34**).

HMRC may contend that a series of transactions is so closely linked that, as a matter of legal construction, the transactions should be regarded as a single disposal (CG14795).

There are occasions when a disposal of an asset does not constitute a disposal for CGT purposes, such as:

- transfer of legal ownership between nominee and beneficial owner (see **1.6**);

- on death, where assets pass to the personal representatives (see **2.9**);

- where assets are sold under alternative finance arrangements (see **3.70**); and

- on reorganisation of share capital or on a take-over of a company, where new shares are received for old shares, or shares are exchanged for securities (see **4.4**).

Part disposals

2.4   Any 'part disposal' of an asset is a disposal for CGT purposes. A part disposal occurs where a person makes a disposal and any description of property derived from the asset remains undisposed of. There is also a part disposal of an asset where the disposal itself creates an interest in, or a right over, the asset (eg where a lease is granted by the person holding the freehold interest in land) as well as in the case where the interest or right existed before the disposal (*TCGA 1992, s 21(2)*).

Where there is a part disposal, any allowable costs of acquisition and improvement which cannot be wholly attributed to either the part retained or the part disposed of are apportioned by reference to the following formula (*TCGA 1992, s 28(2)*; see also **Chapter 3**):

$$\frac{A}{A + B}$$

where:

- A is the proceeds received (actual or deemed); and
- B is the market value of the part retained.

Example 2.1—Part disposal

Robert buys a piece of land in April 1998 for £182,000. He subsequently sells half of it to Lesley in May 2013 for £150,000. The remainder of the land, because of its better position, is estimated to be then worth £200,000. Robert's capital gain is computed as follows:

A = £150,000

B = £200,000

The cost attributable to the part disposed of is:

$$\frac{150,000}{150,000 + 200,000} \times £182,000 = £78,000$$

2013/14

	£
Proceeds of land sold to Lesley	150,000
Less: Cost allocated to the part disposed of	78,000
Less: Annual exemption	10,900
Robert's chargeable gain is	£61,100

The cost allocated to the remaining land, when that is disposed of, will be:

	£
Original cost of all the land	182,000
Less: Cost of part disposal	78,000
Cost of remaining land	£104,000

'Small disposal' proceeds

2.5 Where a capital sum is received for an asset which is not lost or destroyed, the receipt is not treated as a disposal if certain conditions are satisfied (eg where the proceeds are small compared with the value of an asset). The capital sum is instead deducted from the allowable expenditure on a subsequent disposal.

In practice, 'small' for these purposes means the higher of the following (CG15703, CG57836):

- 5% of the value of the asset; and

- £3,000.

There are special rules for part disposals of land (see Statement of Practice D1). Where certain conditions are satisfied, the taxpayer may claim that the part disposal of land does not constitute a disposal for capital gains tax purposes. The disposal proceeds are instead deducted from the cost of the land when calculating a gain on its subsequent disposal.

For the relief to apply, the proceeds from the part disposal of land must (*TCGA 1992, s 242*):

- not exceed 20% of the market value for the entire holding of the land at the time of the transfer; and

- be no more than £20,000;

and the total consideration for all transfers of land made by the taxpayer in the same year must not exceed £20,000. In addition, the transfer must not be between spouses or civil partners or between members of a group of companies.

A similar treatment can apply where the disposal of land is to an authority that has compulsory purchase powers and the proceeds received are small (*TCGA 1992, s 243*).

The definition of 'small' in this context is as set out above (the £3,000 or 5% rule).

For relief to apply under either *TCGA 1992, s 242* or *s 243*, a claim must be made within one year of 31 January following the tax year in which the transfer is made; or, for corporation tax purposes, within two years following the accounting period of transfer.

Example 2.2—Part disposal of land

Cuniliffe owns farmland which cost £134,000 in May 1988. In February 1999, a small plot of land is exchanged with an adjoining landowner for another piece of land. The value placed on the transaction is £18,000. Cuniliffe makes a claim for this transaction not to be treated as a disposal for capital gains tax purposes.

The value of the remaining estate excluding the new piece of land is estimated at £250,000 in February 1999. In May 2013, Cuniliffe sells the whole estate for £500,000.

	£	£
Small land swap in February 1999		
Allowable cost of original land		134,000
Less: Disposal proceeds		18,000
Adjusted allowable cost		116,000
Allowable cost of additional land		18,000
Disposal in May 2013		
Disposal proceeds		500,000
Allowable cost:		
Original land	116,000	
Additional land	18,000	134,000
Net gain		366,000
Annual exemption		10,900
Chargeable gain 2013/14		355,100

If Cuniliffe had not claimed that the small disposal should be ignored for capital gains tax purposes, the capital gain in 1999 would be:

Disposal in February 1999	£
Disposal proceeds	18,000
Allowable cost:	
$\dfrac{18,000}{18,000 + 250,000} \times £134,000 =$	9,000
Unindexed gain	9,000
Indexation allowance frozen to April 1998 (£9,000 × 0.531)	4,779
Chargeable gain 1998/99	4,229

The above rules for small part disposals of land do not apply if the allowable expenditure is less than the part disposal proceeds. However, the taxpayer may elect that the costs are deducted from the part disposal proceeds, with none of the expenditure being an allowable deduction on subsequent part disposals. In other words, the gain is treated as in the same way as a disposal of the whole asset. A claim must be made within one year of 31 January following the tax year of the part disposal, or for corporation tax purposes within two years following the accounting period of transfer (*TCGA 1992, s 244*).

Deemed disposals

2.6   The legislation treats assets as having been disposed of in certain circumstances, including the following:

(a)   *Capital sums derived from assets.* A deemed disposal for capital gains tax purposes can arise where a capital sum is derived from an asset, even where the person who pays the capital sum does not acquire the asset (subject to the small disposal exception). The time of disposal in this context is when the capital sum is received (see **2.16**).

(b)   *Negligible value.* Where the value of an asset has become negligible, the owner may claim to be treated as having sold and immediately reacquired it at market value, in order to realise an allowable loss (see **2.10**).

(c)   *Death.* The assets of a deceased individual's estate are deemed to be acquired by the personal representatives at market value on death but are not deemed to be disposed of by the deceased (see **2.9**).

(d)   *Trusts.* Trustees are deemed to dispose of and immediately reacquire assets at market value in certain circumstances, eg where a person becomes absolutely entitled to assets as against the trustees, or if the trustees cease to be resident in the UK (see **2.21**).

(e)   *Migration of trade or company.* When chargeable assets are transferred abroad (see **2.22**).

(f)   *Value shifting.* A disposal or a part disposal of land or shares may be deemed to have to take place if certain conditions are satisfied (*TCGA 1992, s 29*). In this case, there is a corresponding acquisition by the person or persons who receive the value. These anti-avoidance rules are broadly designed to prevent value passing from one holding or interest into another without there being any disposal for capital gains purposes; see **Chapter 10**.

Deemed disposals between spouses or civil partners are exempt even where the value shifting rules apply (*TCGA 1992, s 58*). Relief may also be available under other capital gains tax provisions if the relevant conditions are satisfied, for example relief for gifts of business assets within *TCGA 1992, s 165* (see **Chapter 13**).

No gain, no loss disposals

2.7   Certain disposals are treated as giving rise to neither a gain nor a loss, known as no gain, no loss disposals, as follows:

- disposals between husband and wife or civil partners (*TCGA 1992, s 58(1)*) (see **3.62**);

- disposals within the same 75% group of companies (*TCGA 1992, s 171) (1)*) (see **9.34**);

- disposals of business assets where a claim is made to roll over the gain against a replacement asset (*TCGA 1992, s 152(1)(a)*) (see **Chapter 14**);

- transfers on a company reconstruction (*TCGA 1992, s 139(1)*) (CG52800);

- on the termination of pre-22 March 2006 (and certain other) interests in possession in settled property by reason of the death of the person so entitled, if the property reverts to the settlor (*TCGA 1992, s 73(1)(a)*) (see **8.12**); and

- gifts to charities (*TCGA 1992, s 257(2)(a)*) (see **3.63**).

The deemed disposal consideration (and the transferee's acquisition cost) is an amount equal to the original cost plus indexation allowance (if applicable).

Disposals under contract

2.8   Where an asset is disposed of and acquired under a contract, the time of the disposal (and acquisition for the purchaser) is the time when that contract is made, ie the date when contracts are exchanged. It is not the date of the completion of the contract, or time of the conveyance or transfer of the asset (if different). However, if the contract is never completed, the disposal never takes place, as confirmed in the House of Lords decision of *Jerome v Kelly* [2004] UKHL 25.

In the case of a conditional contract, the time of disposal and acquisition is the time when the condition is satisfied. This applies in particular to a contract that is conditional on the exercise of an option (*TCGA 1992, s 28(2)*).

There is no statutory definition of what a 'conditional' contract is, and the meaning of the term varies according to context. However, for capital gains tax purposes, a contract is only conditional if:

- the condition has to be satisfied before the contract becomes binding; and

- it is not something that one of the parties has agreed to bring about, such as to fence a plot of land.

A condition which must be satisfied before the contract becomes legally binding is termed a 'condition precedent'. Such a condition must be distinguished from a 'condition subsequent', which is broadly a condition that is not fundamental to the immediate performance of the contract. In such cases, the contract continues to be legally binding (see CG14270 and *Lyon v Pettigrew* (1985) 58 TC 452).

> **Example 2.3—Conditional contract**
>
> In January 2007, a landowner who held land in the East of Glasgow agreed to sell his land to a developer, conditional upon the 2014 Commonwealth Games being held in Glasgow. Until it was officially announced in November 2007 that the Commonwealth Games were to be held in Glasgow in 2014, there was no effective contract. The whole contract for the sale and purchase of the land would be conditional upon Glasgow hosting the 2014 Games. The liabilities and duties between the parties under that contract would only arise when the condition was fulfilled by the announcement in November 2007.

See **2.18–2.23** for special circumstances where the date of disposal may be different.

Disposals on death

2.9   The assets which the deceased was competent to dispose of are deemed not to be disposed of, whether or not they are the subject of a will. The deceased's personal representatives are deemed to acquire the assets at their market value at the date of death.

A disposal by way of *donatio mortis causa* is a lifetime gift that will take effect only if the donor dies. When the donor dies he is not competent to dispose of the relevant assets, so the above rule cannot apply and there is a disposal at the time of death. However, it is provided separately that no chargeable gain accrues on a disposal by way of *donatio mortis causa* (*TCGA 1992, s 62*). See **Chapter 7** for CGT issues arising on the administration of the deceased's estate.

WHEN ASSET VALUE IS LOST

2.10   There is generally a disposal of an asset on the occasion of the entire loss, destruction, dissipation or extinction of the asset. This applies whether or not a capital sum is received by way of compensation or otherwise. If a gain arising on the disposal would have been a chargeable gain, any loss arising will be an allowable loss (*TCGA 1992, ss 16(2), 24(1)*).

The owner of an asset that has become of negligible value cannot claim relief for a capital loss under the normal rules, because he has not disposed of the asset. However, the taxpayer may claim to be treated as having sold and immediately reacquired the asset, either at the time of the claim or at some earlier time (see below).

Focus

The taxpayer who makes the claim must prove that the value of the asset has become negligible during the taxpayer's period of ownership.

In *Harper v Commissioners for Revenue & Customs* [2009] UKFTT 382 (TC), the taxpayer claimed that the shares became of negligible value at 5 April 2004 (the time of the claim), but the tribunal found that the shares were of negligible value when Harper acquired them.

To support the claim for negligible value, the taxpayer needs to provide evidence of the asset's value at the time of acquisition. If unquoted shares have become of negligible value, it may be possible to make a claim for share loss relief against income (see **17.14**).

A negligible value claim can also be made when the taxpayer acquired the asset by way of a no gain, no loss transfer (see **2.7**). The asset must have been of negligible value at the time of that transfer and there have been no other transfers of that asset since it became of negligible value, other than no gain, no loss transfers (*TCGA 1992, s 24(1A)–(1C)*).

The deemed consideration for both the deemed disposal and the deemed reacquisition is the value specified in the claim. The legislation does not define 'negligible', but HMRC regard it as meaning 'worth next to nothing' (*TCGA 1992, s 24(2)*; CG13124).

The claim may specify an earlier time for the deemed disposal if the taxpayer owned the asset at that time and it had become of negligible value at that time. The earlier time must not be more than two years before the beginning of the tax year in which the claim is made. In the case of a company chargeable to corporation tax, the earlier time must fall within the earliest accounting period ending not more than two years before the date of the claim.

For these purposes a building may be regarded as an asset separate from the land on which it stands. The taxpayer is treated as if he had sold and immediately reacquired the site at its market value (*TCGA 1992, s 24(3)*).

HMRC operate a post-transaction valuation service for capital gains, which is accessed by submitting form CG34 to HMRC (see **1.35**). This service can also be used to check if an asset has become of negligible value. The form CG34 should be submitted at the same time as the negligible value claim, or shortly after that claim has been made. Acceptance by HMRC that the value of the asset is negligible should not be taken as agreement that all of the conditions for the negligible value claim are met.

HMRC maintain a list of the dates they have agreed that quoted shares became of negligible value; see www.hmrc.gov.uk/cgt/negvalist.htm.

Asset lost or destroyed: replacement asset acquired

2.11   If the asset is lost or destroyed, a capital sum received in compensation for the loss or destruction, or under an insurance policy against the risk of such loss or destruction, gives rise to a disposal, as described in **2.12**. However, a form of roll-over relief is available where the taxpayer applies the capital sum in acquiring a replacement asset within one year of receiving that sum, or within a longer period allowed by HMRC. The taxpayer is treated as if:

(a)   the consideration for the disposal of the old asset was reduced to an amount giving rise to no gain and no loss on the disposal; and

(b)   the consideration for the acquisition of the new asset was reduced by the excess of the capital sum received and any residual or scrap value over the reduced consideration in (a).

Partial relief is available where only part of the capital sum is reinvested in this way. As long as the part of the compensation not applied is less than the gain deemed to accrue on the disposal of the old asset, the owner can claim to reduce the gain arising to the amount not spent on the new asset.

Where the assets concerned are buildings, and the old building is destroyed or irreparably damaged, then for these purposes the old building is treated as lost or destroyed and each building is regarded as an asset separate from the land on which it stands (or stood) (*TCGA 1992, s 23(4)–(7)*). For a detailed discussion of the capital gains treatment of compensation see Chapter 12 of *Capital Gains Tax: Roll-over, Hold-over and Deferral Reliefs 2013/14* (Bloomsbury Professional).

Example 2.4—Treatment of compensation

Arthur bought a Hockney painting for £50,000 in February 1991. It was destroyed by fire in October 2011, and Arthur receives £900,000 compensation in December 2012. Arthur buys a Hirst painting to replace the Hockney in June 2013 for £1,000,000. Arthur makes a claim that the disposal of the Hockney painting should be treated as no gain, no loss and the allowable expenditure on the Hirst painting should be reduced by the amount of excess capital received.

2012/13		£
Compensation received		900,000
Cost of destroyed asset		50,000
Excess gain to be rolled over (ie the gain otherwise accruing)		850,000
2013/14		
Consideration for acquisition of new painting		1,000,000
Excess gain rolled into this cost		850,000
Reduced allowable expenditure on new asset		150,000

If Arthur only spends £800,000 on the replacement Hirst painting, he can make a claim to reduce the capital gain arising to the amount of compensation not applied.

2012/13	£	£
Excess gain on disposal (as above)		850,000
Compensation monies received	900,000	
Compensation monies reinvested	800,000	
Amount not reinvested in a new asset (being less than the gain of £850,000)	100,000	
Chargeable gain (the compensation not reinvested)		100,000
Net chargeable gain 2012/13		100,000
The chargeable gain to be rolled over is reduced to: (£850,000 – £100,000)		750,000
The allowable expenditure on the new asset is:		
Actual expenditure on new Hirst painting		800,000
Gain rolled over into cost of new asset, being amount of chargeable gain not already assessed		750,000
Total allowable expenditure		50,000

COMPENSATION AND OTHER RECEIPTS

2.12   There is a disposal of assets by their owner where a capital sum (which means any money or 'money's worth', see **2.14**) is derived from assets, whether or not the person paying the capital sum acquires an asset (*TCGA 1992, s 22(1)*; CG12940–CG13020). This general rule is applied, in particular, to the following receipts:

(a)   compensation for damage or injury to assets, or for the loss, destruction or dissipation of assets or for any depreciation (or risk of depreciation) of an asset, including infringement of copyright and 'injurious affection' of land;

(b)   capital sums received under an insurance policy against risk of damage or injury to (or loss or depreciation of) assets;

(c)   capital sums received in return for forfeiture or surrender of rights (or for refraining from exercising rights) such as an amount paid on the release of a person from a contract or restrictive covenant; and

(d)   capital sums received as consideration for use or exploitation of assets, such as a lump sum paid to a farmer in return for the granting of easements.

Incentive payments and inducements offered by financial institutions, such as free shares on demutualisation of a building society, can potentially fall within (b) and will be chargeable to CGT (CG13028). However, a cash-back offered to encourage a person to take on a mortgage is not treated as a capital sum derived from an asset and is not chargeable to CGT (CG13027). Repayments of commission are generally subject to income tax from 6 April 2013 (R&C Brief 04/13).

Capital or revenue?

2.13   Any sum received that is chargeable as income is excluded from CGT. In *Lang v Rice* [1984] 57 TC 80, the taxpayer carried on business in two rented bars in Belfast. They were both destroyed by bombs and neither business was restarted. He claimed compensation from the Northern Ireland Office (NIO) under the *Criminal Injuries to Property (Compensation) Act (Northern Ireland) 1971*. Although the claim referred to 'loss of profit, ie goodwill, 1.5 years' purchase of net profit', in making the payment the NIO specified a sum as 'in respect of the temporary loss of profit for ... the length of time allowed for the ... business to resume normal trading'. The Inspector of Taxes raised an assessment to CGT on the basis that these were capital sums in respect of compensation for loss of goodwill. The Court of Appeal in Northern Ireland held that there was no reason not to accept at face value the revenue nature of the sums paid, as stated by the NIO.

This case and others relevant to the treatment of compensation receipts as income are discussed in HMRC's Business Income Manual at BIM40101–BIM40130 (*TCGA 1992, s 37(1)*).

Money's worth

2.14   HMRC regard money's worth to be (see CG12980):

- something which is convertible into money; or

- something which is capable of being valued in monetary terms (*Chaney v Watkis* [1985] 58 TC 707).

There does not actually have to be a conversion into money, but it must be possible. The writing off of a debt cannot be turned into money, so it is not money's worth.

Capital sum derived from rights

2.15   Compensation may be derived from statutory rights, contractual rights or rights to take action for compensation or damages, rather than directly from the asset itself.

The decision in *Zim Properties Ltd v Proctor* (1984) 58 TC 371, Ch D established the general principle that the right to take court action for compensation or damages is an asset for capital gains tax purposes, the disposal of which (eg by negotiated settlement) could result in a capital gain. In that case, a company brought an action against its solicitors alleging that the solicitors had drawn a contract for the sale of land negligently. A compromise agreement was subsequently reached, resulting in a payment to the company by the solicitor's insurers. The court held that the capital sum was derived from an asset, ie not the land but Zim's right to take action against the solicitors for compensation or damages. The receipt of that capital sum for disposing of the right was therefore taxable.

HMRC subsequently introduced an Extra-statutory Concession (ESC D33) to remove some of the unintended consequences of this decision. The effect of ESC D33 is broadly that, although the receipt of damages and compensation payments can strictly give rise to a CGT liability, by concession the damages will be treated as derived from the underlying asset if there is one. Hence the receipt will be taxable if the underlying asset is taxable, or exempt if the underlying asset is exempt. Alternatively, the damages will be treated as exempt if there is no underlying asset (CG13020).

Time of disposal

2.16   In the four cases (a)–(d) in **2.12**, the time of the disposal is the time when the capital sum is received. In other cases where the capital sum is paid under a contract, the agreement of the contract will set the date of disposal. Where there is no such contract, HMRC regard the date on which the sum is received as the time of disposal (CG12960).

The full disposal proceeds must be brought into account at the time of disposal. There must be no reduction for postponement of the right to receive any part of it, or to allow for the risk of any part of the sum being irrecoverable, or any discount because part of the consideration may be contingent (*TCGA 1992, s 48*). However, there is effectively an entitlement to a form of 'bad debt relief' if a claim is made on the basis that any part of the consideration brought into account has subsequently become permanently irrecoverable (CG14930–CG14933).

Capital sum applied in restoring the asset

2.17   The taxpayer can elect for the receipt of a capital sum not to be treated as a disposal where the whole or a part of a capital sum within (a)–(d) in **2.12** is used to restore the asset. Instead, the consideration that would have been taken into account on that deemed disposal is deducted from the allowable expenditure on a later disposal of the asset (*TCGA 1992, s 23(1)*), where:

(a)   the whole of the capital sum is applied in restoring the asset;

(b)   all but a part of the capital sum is applied in this way, and that part is not reasonably required for the purpose and is small compared to the capital sum received; or

(c)   the amount of the capital sum is small in relation to the value of the asset.

The allowable expenditure is fixed by reference to the acquisition and disposal costs defined in *TCGA 1992, s 38* (see **3.36**). These rules are modified in relation to wasting assets.

Where there is no such allowable expenditure, or the consideration for the deemed disposal is greater than the allowable expenditure, (b) and (c) above do not apply. This means that the deduction from allowable expenditure on a later disposal applies only if the whole of the capital sum is applied in restoring the asset.

Where there is allowable expenditure, the taxpayer may elect for the amount of the consideration for the disposal to be reduced by the amount of the allowable expenditure. This would result in none of that expenditure being deducted in computing the gain accruing on a future disposal (*TCGA 1992, s 23(2)*).

In a case where the taxpayer makes no such election, and applies part of the capital sum (received as compensation or insurance proceeds) to restore the asset, he may make a claim for that part of the capital sum not to be treated as consideration for the disposal, as provided by *TCGA 1992, s 22*. Instead, the capital sum is deducted from any allowable expenditure deducted in computing a gain on a future disposal of the asset (*TCGA 1992, s 23(3)*).

SPECIAL SITUATIONS

Mortgages, charges and bank accounts

2.18   The following transfers are not treated as involving any acquisition or disposal of an asset:

- the conveyance or transfer of an asset (or of an interest or right in or over the asset) by way of security;

- the transfer of a subsisting interest or right by way of security in or over an asset (including a retransfer on redemption of the security); or

- the transfer of a dormant bank or building society account to an authorised reclaim fund and/or to one or more charities (*TCGA 1992, s 26A*).

A lender enforcing the security and selling the mortgaged property is treated as acting as nominee for the borrower (*TCGA 1992, s 26(1), (2)*).

Hire-purchase transactions

2.19   Under a hire-purchase transaction, a person obtains the use of an asset for a period, and at the end of that period the property in the asset will (or may) pass to him. The hire-purchase transaction is treated as the entire disposal of the asset to that person at the beginning of the hire period. An adjustment will be required if the hire period ends without ownership passing to him (*TCGA 1992, s 27*).

Gifts

2.20   A gift is treated as having been made when the donor has done everything within his power to transfer the property to the donee (*Re Rose, Rose and Others v Inland Revenue Commissioners* [1952] 1 Ch 499, [1952] 1 All ER 1217). However, general law principles will determine whether that transfer is effective. For example, contracts in respect of land must be evidenced in writing, so the disposal date will be the date of exchange of those contracts. In the case of shares, the disposal date will be when the share transfer form is sent to the company. In the case of a gift of a chattel, the gift is effective when the chattel is delivered.

Settlements

2.21   A transfer into a trust or settlement is a disposal of the property that becomes settled property, even if that transferor is a trustee of the settlement or has some interest as a beneficiary (*TCGA 1992, s 70*). The trust deed itself may transfer the legal title of the property to the trustees, so the date of the deed will be the disposal date (CG35730). In other cases, the disposal date of the gift into the settlement will follow the rules set out in **2.20**.

See **Chapter 8** regarding this and other rules relating to settled property, including:

- person becoming absolutely entitled to settled property (*TCGA 1992, s 71*);

- termination of life interest on death of the person entitled (*TCGA 1992, s 72*);

- death of life tenant: exclusion of chargeable gain (*TCGA 1992, s 73*);

- disposal of interests in settled property (*TCGA 1992, ss 76, 76A, 76B*); and

- trustees ceasing to be resident in UK (*TCGA 1992, s 80*).

Nominees or bare trustees may hold assets for beneficiaries who are absolutely entitled to those assets (or would be entitled but for being an infant or a disabled person). For capital gains tax purposes, disposals by nominees or bare trustees are treated as having been made by the beneficiary for whom they act (*TCGA 1992, s 60*).

Deemed disposal by non-resident

2.22   There is a deemed disposal and reacquisition of assets at their market value where 'chargeable assets' (see below) that have been used in a business carried on through a UK branch or agency (or a permanent establishment in the case of a company) are transferred abroad, unless the transfer occurs on the occasion of the cessation of the business (*TCGA 1992, s 25(1), (2)*).

Assets are 'chargeable assets' for this purpose if a chargeable gain on their disposal would be chargeable under *TCGA 1992, s 10(1)* or *s 10B* (non-residents with a UK branch, agency or permanent establishment). For further details, and the situation where the business ceases or is transferred overseas, see **Chapter 5**.

Capital distributions from companies

2.23   Where a liquidator is appointed to wind up a company on a formal basis, the distributions made to shareholders are treated as capital receipts. The disposal date for such a capital receipt is the date when the capital is received.

Many small companies are wound up informally without a liquidator being appointed, and the tax treatment of distributions made in such circumstances

2.23 *Disposals*

are governed by *CTA 2010, ss 1030A, 1030B.* These provisions apply to distributions made on or after 1 March 2012, whether or not permission for capital treatment was previously obtained under ESC C16. Where the total of all the distributions from the company in anticipation of the winding up does not exceed £25,000, those distributions are treated as capital for tax purposes. Otherwise, all the distributions made in anticipation of the winding up are subject to income tax. Note that any share capital returned to shareholders is always treated as capital and is not treated as a distribution under *CTA 2010, s 1000.*

Any capital gain arising on such a capital distribution may qualify for entrepreneurs' relief (see **11.32**).

For a detailed discussion of the tax and legal issues related to the winding up of small companies, see *Dissolving the Family Company* (Bloomsbury Professional).

Chapter 3

Computation of gains and losses

SIGNPOSTS

- **Computational rules** – Currency, rebasing, indexation, VAT and corporate exceptions (see **3.1–3.3**).

- **Determine the consideration** – Eliminate income, market value, series of transactions, aggregating and apportioning value (see **3.4–3.15**).

- **Who are connected persons** – Individuals, trustees, business partners, and resulting clogged losses (see **3.16–3.21**).

- **Delayed or deferred consideration** – Contingent or unascertainable consideration, contingent liabilities, election to carry back loss, and payment of tax by instalments (see **3.22–3.34**).

- **What is allowable expenditure** – Costs of acquisition, disposal and enhancement. *Mansworth v Jelley* losses, the market value rule, costs met out of public funds, part disposals, and assets derived from other assets (see **3.35–3.46**).

- **Calculation and use of losses** – Order of set-off, claims, non-residents, trading losses, and restrictions due to capital allowances (see **3.47–3.56**).

- **Deduction of reliefs** – Entrepreneurs' relief, indexation, 'no gain, no loss' transactions, double taxation and foreign tax credit (see **3.57–3.69**).

COMPUTATIONAL RULES

Currency, rebasing and indexation

3.1   All chargeable gains must be computed in sterling, as established in *Bentley v Pike* [1981] 53 TC590 (see HMRC Capital Gains Manual at CG25391, CG78314), codified in *CTA 2010, s 5*, for companies.

3.1 *Computation of gains and losses*

Where the sale takes place in a currency other than sterling, each entry in the computation of the gain must be converted into sterling using the spot exchange rate applying at the date that that part of the transaction (purchase, sale, improvement cost) occurred. This means that part of the assessed gain may be attributable to the movement between the currencies (see Example 3.1). There is no relief for the assessment of this exchange gain for individuals, but some relief has been introduced for companies that have a functional currency other than sterling (see **9.46**).

Example 3.1

Christine is resident and domiciled in the UK. She purchased a cottage in France in April 1999 for €120,000. In April 2000, she added improvements costing €70,000.

She sold the cottage on 30 April 2013 for €320,000. Christine has made a capital gain of €130,000, which may be subject to capital gains tax in France, but there may be different computational deductions under French law.

In the UK she will be taxed on the equivalent of €177,155 (£150,771), although any French CGT she pays should be available to set-off against her UK liability (see **3.66**). Up to €47,155 of the gain assessed in the UK is attributable to the movement in exchange rates between 1999 and 2013.

2013/14	€	£
Proceeds (€1.175:£1)	320,000	272,340
Less cost in 1999 (€1.5051:£1)	(120,000)	(79,728)
Less improvements in 2000 (€1.673:£1)	(70,000)	(41,841)
Gain before reliefs and exemptions	130,000	150,771

The indexation allowance, designed to compensate the taxpayer for the effect of inflation, does not apply to disposals by individuals and trustees from 6 April 2008, but continues to apply to corporate disposals from that date (see **3.60**). The calculation of indexation allowance is discussed at **9.15**.

From 6 April 2008, assets held by individuals and trustees are automatically rebased to 31 March 1982, meaning that the value at that date is used in place of the original cost where the asset was acquired earlier (see **3.58**). Assets held by companies are not automatically rebased, unless a global rebasing election has been made. Rebasing to 31 March 1982 simplifies the calculation of gains on long-held assets for non-corporate taxpayers, as the 'kink test' and 'halving relief'(see **9.12**) are removed. These tests and the rebasing election are discussed in **Chapter 9**, as they now only apply to companies.

Example 3.2

Colin inherited a cottage in April 1980 when it was worth £12,000. Its value on 31 March 1982, after some improvements had been made, was £40,000. Colin sold the cottage on 21 June 2012 for £310,000. The legal and estate agents' fees associated with the purchase and sale were £5,000. Colin has a capital loss brought forward of £15,000 but no other CGT reliefs apply; and he makes no other disposals in 2012/13. He is a higher rate taxpayer, so he pays CGT at 28%. His CGT liability for 2012/13 is calculated as follows:

2013/14	£
Proceeds	310,000
Rebased value at 31 March 1982	(40,000)
Legal and estate agents' fees	(5,000)
Gross gain	265,000
Loss brought forward	(15,000)
Net chargeable gain	250,000
Annual exemption	(10,900)
Taxable gain	239,100
CGT due at 28%	66,948

Interaction with VAT

3.2   The acquisition and enhancement costs of an asset for CGT purposes exclude any VAT, where the VAT represents deductible input tax and thus can be reclaimed by the VAT-registered taxpayer. In any other case, the cost for CGT purposes includes the VAT suffered.

If the taxpayer charges VAT on the proceeds of disposal of a chargeable asset, the consideration for the disposal (see **3.4**) excludes the VAT. The treatment of any VAT suffered on expenses relating to the disposal follows the treatment of acquisition and enhancement costs (HMRC Statement of Practice D7).

Exceptions for corporate transactions

3.3   **Chapter 9** discusses the specific computational rules and reliefs that only apply to companies.

A company generally calculates its chargeable gains on the same basis as individuals although indexation allowance is deductible for all periods an asset has been held since 31 March 1982 (see **9.12**), and assets held on that date are not automatically rebased (see **9.4**).

The company pays corporation tax rather than CGT on those gains. There are a number of special corporation tax rules that treat gains falling in the following regimes as income for corporation tax rather than as gains:

- loan relationships (*CTA 2009, Part 5*);
- derivative contracts (*CTA 2009, Part 7*); and
- intangible fixed assets (*CTA 2009, Part 8*).

In addition, non-natural persons (which may be companies, trusts or partnerships) can be liable to CGT on the disposal after 5 April 2013 of residential property which is also subject to the ATED (see **4.39**).

CONSIDERATION FOR THE DISPOSAL

3.4   The first step in the computation is to determine the consideration for the disposal. The consideration may be receivable some time after the date of the disposal, but the full amount must be brought into account without any discount for postponement of the right to receive it, or for the risk that not all of the consideration may be recovered (see **3.22**).

Consideration includes money or money's worth (see **2.14**) and any assumption by the purchaser of a liability of the person making the disposal. The items listed in **3.5** as receipts can also be taken into account for CGT, regardless of the exclusion for sums chargeable as income. Consideration also includes the value of any asset received in exchange for the asset disposed of, and the capitalised value of:

- the right to receive income or payments in the nature of income;
- relief from liability, eg to repay a loan;
- the benefit of loans on non-commercial terms; and
- the benefit of rights to obtain goods or services on favourable terms.

Sums chargeable as income

3.5   Sums that are chargeable to tax as income, or taken into account in computing income or profits or gains or losses for income tax purposes, are excluded from CGT. Income or profits taxable by deduction at source are treated as chargeable to income tax for this purpose (*TCGA 1992, s 52(2), (3)*). This rule does not preclude the following receipts being taken into account for CGT:

- receipts giving rise to balancing charges or certain other adjustments to income tax capital allowances;

- the capitalised value of a rent charge, or ground annual, or feu duty;

- the capitalised value of a right of any other description to income, or to payments in the nature of income over a period, or to a series of such payments (*TCGA 1992, s 37*); and

- amounts charged to income under profit-sharing schemes (*TCGA 1992, s 238*).

A profit on the disposal of trading stock is included in trading profits and charged to income tax. HMRC consider that the disposal of an asset not normally regarded as trading stock may mark the end of 'an adventure in the nature of trade', in which case any profit is chargeable to income tax (CG10260). However, see **4.36** to **4.38** regarding assets appropriated to or from trading stock.

An income tax liability may arise under anti-avoidance rules on the disposal of land, including buildings, or an interest in land, or assets such as shares which derive their value from land; or on the sale by an individual of income derived from personal activities (*ITA 2007, ss 755, 756*, CG14340–CG14342). In such a case, the gain is not charged to CGT, as the sum is charged to income tax. See also **2.13** regarding the question whether compensation received is chargeable to income tax (*TCGA 1992, ss 15, 16; ITA 2007, s 778*).

Other amounts excluded from consideration for CGT purposes are profits made from the sale of trees from woodlands managed on a commercial basis (*TCGA 1992, s 250*).

Market value rule for disposals

3.6   The market value (see **3.7**) of an asset is substituted for the actual consideration for the disposal where the taxpayer disposes of the asset:

(a)   otherwise than by way of a bargain made at arm's length (see below), and in particular where he disposes of it by way of gift, or on a transfer into a settlement by the settlor, or by way of distribution from a company in respect of shares in the company;

(b)   wholly or partly for a consideration that cannot be valued;

(c)   in connection with his own or another's loss of office or employment or diminution of emoluments; or

(d)   otherwise in consideration for (or in recognition of) his or another person's services or past services in an office or employment, or any other service rendered to another person (*TCGA 1992, s 17(1)*).

The market value may be substituted even if there is no corresponding acquisition, eg when a debt is repaid. HMRC regard a bargain as made 'at arm's length' if it is a normal commercial transaction in which all of the parties involved try to obtain the best deal for themselves in their particular circumstances. They accept that both a 'bad bargain', and a deal that is made when one party to the transaction has better information than another party, can be a bargain made at arm's length. HMRC provide the following examples at CG14541:

- Mr A may wish to sell his property quickly so that he can go and live in Malta. Mr B knows that Mr A wants to sell his property quickly so he offers him a low price for a quick sale. No-one else makes an offer. Mr A accepts the price Mr B has offered. This may not have been the best possible price which Mr A could have achieved if he had left the property on the market for longer, but he was still trying to achieve the best deal possible for himself. It was a bargain made at arm's length.

- Mrs S sells a picture from her attic to Mr T for £500. Mr T, who is an art dealer, knows that the picture is worth £5,000. There has been a bargain with both people trying to get the best deal for themselves. Again, this is a bargain made at arm's length, even if the price paid is not the 'market value' of the asset.

A disposal is treated as made not at arm's length – so that the market value rule above applies – if the person acquiring the asset is 'connected' with the person making the disposal (see **3.11**). Other disposals are treated as made not at arm's length, where there is some gratuitous intention on behalf of one of the parties to the bargain (CG14542).

Ascertaining market value

3.7   It is the taxpayer's responsibility to obtain a valuation of market value if one is required, in order to complete a return of chargeable gains. See **1.35** regarding the valuation checking service provided by HMRC, and the information that needs to be provided with the tax return concerning the valuation.

HMRC may challenge a value used in a CGT computation in a tax return. In which case the taxpayer can ask the Tax Tribunal to decide what value would be reasonable. The value decided upon by the Tribunal may be neither of the values put forward by the taxpayer or HMRC, but may be a compromise. See, for example, the outcome in *SAS Marks v HMRC* [2011] UKFTT 1086 (TC).

The general rule is that the 'market value' of an asset is the price that it might reasonably be expected to fetch on a sale in the open market. No reduction is made to take account of the possible impact of all of the assets concerned (eg a holding of shares) being placed on the market at one time (*TCGA 1992, s 272(1), (2)*).

Where the value of an asset has been 'ascertained' for inheritance tax purposes, that valuation fixes its market value for CGT as at the date of death (*TCGA 1992, s 274*).

Focus

- The probate value reported by the executors is not necessarily the 'ascertained' value, particularly where no IHT was payable for the estate (CG32222).

- A value cannot be ascertained unless the specialists in the PT-IHT office of HMRC (formerly Capital Taxes) have used that value to arrive at the final IHT liability, and the amount of that liability was dependent on that valuation (CG32224).

Quoted shares and securities

3.8   The market value of shares or securities quoted on the Stock Exchange Daily Official List ('quoted' or 'listed' shares) is generally taken to be the lower of the figures found in (a) and (b) below, or the figure found in (a) where there were no recorded bargains on the relevant date:

(a)   the 'quarter-up value', ie the lower of the two prices quoted on the relevant date plus a quarter of the difference between them;

(b)   the midpoint between the highest and lowest prices at which bargains were recorded for that date, ignoring bargains at special prices.

This measure of market value does not apply where 'special circumstances' have affected the quoted prices. If the London Stock Exchange is closed on the relevant date, the above exercise is to be done for both the latest previous date and the earliest subsequent date on which it is open. The lower of the two measures found in this way is taken to be the market value (*TCGA 1992, s 272(3), (4)*).

Example 3.3

Sarah gifts 1,000 quoted shares on 18 June 2013. The price of the shares quoted on the Stock Exchange daily list for that day are 100–120 pence, and bargains are marked at 98p (special), 102p, 118p, 115p, and 109p. The market value for CGT purposes is the lower of:

- ¼ up rule: $100 + ¼ (120 - 100) = 105p$; and

- the average of the highest and lowest bargains, ignoring the 'special': $½ (102 + 118) = 110p$.

The value is $105p \times 1,000$ shares = £1,050.

Unit trust holdings

3.9   Where the buying and selling prices of units in unit trusts are published regularly, the market value is the lower published price (ie the price that the managers will pay to someone wishing to sell units). If no prices were published on the relevant date, the lower of the latest prices published before the disposal is taken (*TCGA 1992, s 272(5)*).

Unquoted shares and securities

3.10   The market value of shares and securities that are not listed on a 'recognised stock exchange' (see below) is the price that the shares etc might reasonably be expected to fetch on a sale in the open market. For this purpose it is to be assumed that, in such an open market, any prospective buyer would have available all the information that a prudent prospective buyer might reasonably require if he were proposing to buy it from a willing vendor by private treaty and at arm's length (*TCGA 1992, s 273*).

The shares and assets valuation division (SAV) of HMRC is responsible for checking and negotiating the valuation of unquoted shares and certain other assets including the goodwill and intellectual property. The District Valuer at the Valuation Office Agency deals with the valuation of land and buildings in the UK.

The HMRC Capital Gains Manual (CG59540–CG59632) cautions HMRC Inspectors not to agree valuations of unquoted shares without reference to SAV, even if a very small amount of tax is at stake, as the share value given may bind HMRC when negotiating with other shareholders in the same company. The value of different sizes of shareholdings in the same unquoted company will vary considerably, due to the varying ability of majority and minority shareholders to control or influence the running of the company. For example the value per share of a 75% shareholding may be £100, whereas the value of a 10% shareholding in the same company may be £20 per share. SAV will require details of the entire shareholding of the taxpayer, even where only a small proportion of his shares have been disposed of (CG59562).

A 'recognised stock exchange' means any stock exchange which is designated as a recognised stock exchange by HMRC for the purpose of *ITA 2007, s 1005* (*TCGA 1992, s 288(1)*). This includes the London Stock Exchange and many overseas stock markets (see www.hmrc.gov.uk/fid/rse-recognised-exchanges. htm#3).

Disposals to connected persons

3.11   A disposal is treated as made otherwise than by way of a bargain made at arm's length – so that the market value rule in **3.7** applies – if the person acquiring the asset is 'connected' (see **3.16**) with the person making the disposal.

There are special rules for transactions between spouses and civil partners (see **3.63**) and for assets disposed of in a series of transactions (see **3.12**).

There must be both a disposal and a corresponding acquisition for the 'connected persons' rule to apply. It cannot apply, for example, to an issue of shares by a company, or the purchase by a company of its own shares (*TCGA 1992, s 18(1), (2)*; CG14570).

The market value of the asset, to be used in place of the actual consideration, is adjusted where the asset is subject to a right or restriction such as a restrictive covenant (*TCGA 1992, s 18(6)–(8)*).

Assets disposed of in a series of transactions

3.12 If assets are disposed of in a series of transactions to one or more connected persons, anti-avoidance rules may operate to increase the deemed consideration for one or more of the disposals. The rules are designed to prevent the taxpayer from gaining an advantage where the total value placed on a number of separate gifts (for instance, of shares to relatives) would be less than the value that would apply to a single gift of all of the shares (*TCGA 1992, ss 19, 20*).

The rules apply where:

- a person disposes of assets, to a person (or persons) connected with him, by means of a series of linked transactions, within six years ending on the date of the last disposal; and

- the 'original market value' of the assets disposed of by any of those transactions is less than the 'appropriate portion' of the 'aggregate market value' of the assets disposed of by all the transactions (see **3.13–3.15**).

In these circumstances, the consideration for the disposal effected by any linked transaction is deemed to be equal to the appropriate portion of the aggregate market value (see CG14740). However, this rule does not affect the operation of the no gain, no loss rule for transfers between spouses or civil partners (see **3.63**) (*TCGA 1992, s 19(1), (2)*).

This rule applies when a series of linked transactions is created by a second material transaction and it applies again, with any necessary adjustments being made, when an existing series is extended by a further material transaction. An adjustment may be required if an earlier transaction ceases to form part of the series because of the six-year rule (*TCGA 1992, s 19(4)*).

Original market value

3.13   The original market value is determined as follows where there is a series of linked transactions:

(a)   if the transaction is the most recent in the series of transactions, the 'original market value' of the assets disposed of is the market value that would be deemed to be the consideration in the absence of *TCGA 1992, s 19*; and

(b)   for any other transaction in the series, the original market value of the assets disposed of is the value which, prior to the transaction in (a), was (or would have been) deemed to be the consideration for that transaction, whether as a result of *TCGA 1992, s 19* applying or under any other provision (*TCGA 1992, s 20(3)*).

Appropriate portion

3.14   The 'appropriate portion' of the aggregate market value (see **3.15**) of the assets disposed of by all the transactions in a series is the portion of that value that it is reasonable to apportion to the assets actually disposed of by the particular transaction (*TCGA 1992, s 20(4)(b)*).

Aggregate market value

3.15   The aggregate market value of the assets disposed of by all the transactions in a series of linked transactions is the market value that would have been attributed to all of those assets if, considering all of them together, they had been disposed of by one disposal occurring at the time of the transaction (*TCGA 1992, s 20(4)(a)*).

When the assets are considered 'together' they are considered as a group, holding or collection of assets each of which retains its separate identity. However, they are also considered as brought together to form a single asset (or number of assets) distinct from the assets comprised in the individual transactions, where this would give a higher market value (*TCGA 1992, s 20(5)*).

Some of the assets disposed of in a series of linked transactions may have been acquired after the time of the first transaction. In such a case the aggregate market value is apportioned to each transaction without regard to assets acquired after the time of that transaction, unless the assets were acquired by means of a no gain, no loss transfer within *TCGA 1992, s 171*.

The number of assets taken into account is limited to the maximum number held by the taxpayer at any time in the period covered by the series, ie beginning immediately before the first of the transactions and ending immediately before the last. This is modified where a company disposed of any assets on a no gain, no loss transfer to a company in the same group before the time of the first transaction in the series. In that event, the maximum number of assets taken into account is determined as if that transfer had occurred after the first transaction in the series (*TCGA 1992, s 20(6), (7)*).

If the assets disposed of are securities – including any assets of a nature to be dealt in without identifying the particular assets disposed of or acquired – they are identified with assets acquired on an earlier date (rather than with assets acquired on a later date) on the occasion of each disposal (*TCGA 1992, s 20(8), (9)*).

Example 3.4

Richard owned 10,000 shares in an unquoted company. He made two gifts of shares to his son over four years which in total amounted to 6,000 shares. The market value of each gift is calculated as follows:

Transferred in	Number of shares gifted	Value of 6,000 shares at date of gift	Portion of market value at date of gift
October 2009	2,000	£12,000	£4,000
October 2013	4,000	£36,000	£24,000
Total	6,000		

The appropriate portion of the aggregate market value is computed thus:

October 2009: 2,000 / 6,000 × £12,000 = £4,000

October 2013: 4,000 / 6,000 × £36,000 = £24,000

If the company is Richard's personal company, he may be able to claim hold-over relief against the gains arising on the gifts to his son (see **Chapter 13**) or entrepreneurs' relief (see **Chapter 11**).

CONNECTED PERSONS

3.16   The rules for determining whether one person is connected with another for CGT purposes are set out in *TCGA 1992, s 286* and CG14580–CG14623.

Individuals

3.17   A person is connected with an individual if that person is:

● the individual's spouse or civil partner;

● a relative of the individual (see below);

● the spouse or civil partner of a relative of the individual;

● a relative of the individual's spouse or civil partner; or

● the spouse or civil partner of a relative of the individual's spouse or civil partner.

A 'relative' for this purpose is a brother, sister, ancestor or lineal descendant. The term excludes, for example, uncles, aunts, nephews and nieces (*TCGA 1992, s 286(8)*).

HMRC's Capital Gains Manual provides a diagram showing all of the people who are connected with an individual. It points out that death, divorce or the dissolution of a civil partnership can lead to persons other than the former spouse or civil partner ceasing to be connected with an individual (CG14580).

Trustees

3.18   The trustees of a settlement are connected with:

● any individual who is a settlor in relation to the settlement;

● any person connected with such an individual; and

● any body corporate that is connected (see below) with that settlement.

A body corporate is connected with a settlement if it is a close company (or would be a close company if it were UK resident) and its participators include the trustees of the settlement; or it is controlled by such a company. Any connection between the trustee and the settlement other than in his capacity as trustee is ignored (*TCGA 1992, s 286(3), (3A)*).

The trustees are treated as a single and continuing body, distinct from the persons who are actually serving as trustees, so the identity of the trustees is disregarded. 'Settlement' has the same meaning as in *ITTOIA 2005, s 620* and does not include will trusts or approved or registered pension funds (CG14590, CG14596).

A person who transfers assets into a registered pension fund is not regarded as connected with that pension fund, even if that person is also a beneficiary of the fund. However, HMRC require the transfer to be valued at open market value for CGT purposes, as the bargain may not have been made at arm's length (see **3.6**). In any case, the pension scheme rules would normally demand the contribution of an asset to be independently valued at the open market value.

Business partners

3.19   A person is connected with:

- any person with whom he is in partnership; and

- the spouse or civil partner or a relative of any individual with whom he is in partnership.

However, this rule does not apply in relation to acquisitions or disposals of partnership assets pursuant to bona fide commercial arrangements (*TCGA 1992, s 286(4)*). Partnerships are examined further in **Chapter 6**.

Companies

3.20   A company is connected with another company:

- if the same person has control of both companies, or a person has control of one and persons connected with him (or he and persons connected with him) have control of the other company; or

- if a group of two or more persons has control of each company, and the groups either consist of the same persons or could be regarded as consisting of the same persons by treating (in one or more cases) a member of either group as replaced by a person connected with him.

A company is connected with another person if that person has control of it, or that person and persons connected with him together have control of it.

In addition, any two or more persons acting together to secure or exercise control of a company are treated as connected with one another in relation to that company, and connected with any person acting on the directions of any of them to secure or exercise control of the company. HMRC consider that it is not sufficient for the persons to have control of the company – they have to 'act in some way' to control it – but exercising control could include refraining from voting in a particular way. Directors who are connected with each other under this rule are 'connected persons' only in relation to their transactions with the company. The question whether they are connected in relation to transactions between themselves is a separate issue (*TCGA 1992, s 286(5), (6), (7)*; CG14622–CG14623).

Losses between connected parties

3.21   A loss accruing on the disposal of an asset by the taxpayer (A) to a connected person (B) is not deductible from A's chargeable gains generally, under the normal rules for allowable losses (see **3.47**). It is deductible only from a chargeable gain accruing to A on another disposal to B at a time when A and B are connected. HMRC guidance refers to such losses as 'clogged losses' (*TCGA 1992, s 18(3)*; CG14561).

The application of clogged losses between companies was tested in *Kellogg Brown & Root Holdings (UK) Ltd v Revenue and Customs Comrs* [2010] EWCA Civ 118. The Court of Appeal decided the company was not entitled to capital gains loss relief on the loss realised on the sale of its subsidiaries, as it was connected to the company to which it sold the subsidiaries. The connection was through common shareholders.

This restriction on the use of losses is waived for a gift into a settlement if the gift – and the income from it – is wholly or primarily applicable for educational, cultural or recreational purposes, so long as the persons benefiting are confined to members of an association and most of them are not connected persons. The restriction does not affect the transfer of trustees' unused losses to a beneficiary on the occasion of the beneficiary becoming absolutely entitled to the settled property (*TCGA 1992, s 18(4)*; CG37207).

If A's first disposal to B in the above scenario is the grant of an option to enter into a sale or other transaction, and the option holder (B) disposes of the option, any loss accruing to B on the disposal of the option is allowable only if the disposal is made at arm's length to a person who is not connected with B (*TCGA 1992, s 18(5)*). See **4.6** for further discussion of options.

DELAYED OR DEFERRED CONSIDERATION

3.22   The consideration for a disposal is taken into account:

- without any discount for postponement of the right to receive any part of it; and

- in the first instance, without regard to either a risk of any part of the consideration being irrecoverable, or the right to receive any part of it being contingent.

An adjustment is made, by way of discharge or repayment of tax or otherwise, if any part of the consideration taken into account in this way proves later to be irrecoverable, (*TCGA 1992, s 48(1)*; CG14933).

> **Focus**
>
> The taxpayer must make a claim within four years of the end of the tax year for which the tax reduction is to apply, including the following details:
>
> - the disposal and the tax charge to which the claim relates;
> - the event which gave rise to the consideration becoming permanently irrecoverable;
> - the amount of the consideration that is irrecoverable; and
> - the adjustment in tax to be made in favour of the claimant.

Contingent liabilities

3.23 When an asset (typically, a holding of shares in a company) is sold, the vendor may provide warranties or representations to compensate the purchaser if, for example, there are tax liabilities in addition to those disclosed to the purchaser at the time of the disposal. The liability is contingent on there being a breach of the warranty etc. It is specifically provided that no allowance is made to the vendor in the first instance, when the gain is computed, for:

(a) any liability, remaining with or assumed by the person (B) assigning a lease, that is contingent on the assignee's (C's) default in respect of liabilities assumed by C either at the time of the assignment or subsequently – eg where the original lessee B may remain liable to account to his immediate lessor (A) in the event of a breach of covenant by C;

(b) any contingent liability of the person making the disposal in respect of a covenant for quiet enjoyment or other obligation as vendor of land (or of any estate or interest in land) or as a lessor; or

(c) any contingent liability in respect of a warranty or representation made on a disposal (by way of sale or lease) of any property other than land.

If such a contingent liability is enforced, the payment made is deducted from the consideration for the disposal and the vendor must make a claim for the appropriate adjustment to his CGT computation (see Example 3.5). This claim must be made within four years of the end of the tax year in which the disposal was made, or four years from the end of the accounting period that contained the disposal for corporate taxpayers (*TCGA 1992, s 49*).

If the contingent liability ultimately paid exceeds the consideration received on the disposal, the consideration is reduced to nil and no relief is available to the vendor for the excess. In practice, HMRC accept that this treatment may be extended to a payment made under an indemnity (as opposed to a warranty or representation) given by the vendor to the purchaser (ESC D33, para 13; CG14805, CG14807).

By concession, where the disposal is a sale of shares in exchange for an issue of shares or debentures other than qualifying corporate bonds and the new asset is treated as acquired at the same time as the old asset, HMRC allow the vendor to treat his payment as consideration given for the new shares or debentures. The purpose of the concession, which applies only to cases within (c) above, is to provide relief for the payment where there is no disposal of the old asset because of the way in which the rules concerning share reorganisations in *TCGA 1992, ss 135* and *136* operate (see **4.4**; ESC D52; CG14818–CG14825).

Example 3.5

David sold all the shares in his own software company for £555,000 on 24 July 2013. The disposal qualifies for entrepreneurs' relief (see **11.9**), and he has used his annual exemption for 2013/14 against other gains. Under an indemnity included as part of the deal, David agrees to pay the purchaser £250,000 if the software product produced by the company proves to be defective within two years. David's shares have a base cost of £1,000. His CGT liability, before and after the indemnity comes into effect, is calculated as:

2013/14	£	£
Disposal proceeds		555,000
Less cost		(1,000)
Gain		554,000
CGT payable at entrepreneurs' relief rate of 10%:		55,400
2013/14		
After indemnity is paid and claim submitted:		
Disposal proceeds	555,000	
Less indemnity payment	(250,000)	
	305,000	
Less cost	(1,000)	
Gain	304,000	
CGT payable at entrepreneurs' relief rate of 10%	30,400	

No adjustment for other contingent liabilities

3.24   Where the disposal is made subject to a contingent liability to which (a)–(c) in **3.23** do not apply, the consideration for the disposal is reduced by the value of the contingent liability and there is no adjustment if and when the liability is enforced. This was established in *Randall v Plumb* (1975) 50 TC 392, Ch D.

The purchaser

3.25   So far as the purchaser is concerned, his receipt under the terms of the warranty etc represents a capital sum derived from an asset (see **2.12**). HMRC guidance indicates that, in practice, the purchaser's acquisition cost may be reduced by the amount received, but any excess over that cost will be taxable (CG14807).

Deferred or contingent consideration

3.26   As indicated in **3.22**, the consideration for a disposal must be brought into account without any discount for postponement of the right to receive it. The first step to consider, in the event that part of the consideration is to be deferred, is whether the amounts to be received by the vendor in the future are 'ascertainable'.

Ascertainable deferred consideration

3.27   The full amount of any deferred consideration, the amount of which can be ascertained, is treated as part of the consideration for the disposal, without any discount for postponement of payment (*TCGA 1992, s 48(1)*). However, the CGT may be paid in instalments where the consideration is payable over a period exceeding 18 months (beginning not earlier than the time of the disposal) (see **3.35**).

The amount of any deferred consideration is ascertainable if it is either known at the time of disposal, or is capable of being calculated by reference to information known and events that have occurred by that time. HMRC provide the following examples of ascertainable deferred consideration at CG14882:

- The agreement for the disposal provides for a consideration of £300,000, of which £100,000 is payable on completion and £200,000 will be payable in four annual instalments of £50,000.

- The agreement for the disposal of a business provides for a consideration of £100,000 and a sum equal to half of the taxable profits of the business for the year ended on the date of disposal payable nine months after the date of the contract.

Payments that are ascertainable but contingent, ie they depend on the occurrence of some future event, are treated in the same way as ascertainable amounts that are not contingent (*TCGA 1992, s 48(1)*). Terms stipulating a ceiling on the amount of deferred consideration do not make the amount of that consideration ascertainable (CG14883, CG14889).

Unascertainable deferred consideration

3.28 Where the amount of deferred consideration cannot be ascertained, the value of the right to receive that consideration is treated as part of the consideration for the disposal, as established in *Marren v Ingles* (1980) 54 TC 76, HL. The House of Lords held that the right to the deferred consideration was a *chose in action* and that when the deferred consideration was received there was a disposal of an asset, namely the *chose in action*, within *TCGA 1992, s 22* (capital sums derived from assets, see **2.12**). The amount of any deferred consideration is unascertainable if the events or circumstances fixing that amount do not occur or exist at the time of the disposal.

The *Marren v Ingles* treatment may be found when a business is sold and part of the consideration is received as a deferred 'earn-out'. The earn-out the vendor receives is based on the post-sale profits of the business, and it may be paid in the form of cash, shares or loan notes issued by the purchasing company. The net present value of the earn-out is taxed upfront with the sale of the business and the disposal of the earn-out right is taxed when the earn-out is received.

Focus

Where the original disposal qualifies for entrepreneurs' relief, the present value of the deferred consideration will also qualify for the relief, subject to the life-time limit (see **11.5**).

It will benefit the taxpayer to maximise the present value of the deferred consideration, so that as much as possible of the ultimate proceeds from the deal are subject to the entrepreneurs' relief rate of 10%.

Example 3.6

Ben sold his company B&J Ltd for £750,000 on 1 July 2011, which he formed in 1990 and subscribed £1,000 for the shares at that time. This disposal qualifies for entrepreneurs' relief. Ben was also entitled to deferred earn-out consideration, based on the profits for the two years to 30 June 2013, payable on 31 October 2013. The value of this earn-out as at 1 July 2011 has been agreed at £250,000 with HMRC's SAV. Ben's initial gain taxable in 2011/12 and the final gain taxable in 2013/14 are calculated as follows:

2011/12	£
Sale proceeds	750,000
Present value of earn-out	250,000
Total assessable proceeds	1,000,000
Less original cost of shares	(1,000)
Chargeable gain	999,000
Less annual exemption	(10,600)
Taxable gain	988,400
CGT payable at entrepreneurs' relief rate of 10%	98,840
2013/14	
After the earn-out is paid:	
Earn-out consideration paid in cash	400,000
Less cost assessed in 2011/12	(250,000)
Chargeable gain	150,000
Less annual exemption	(10,900)
Taxable gain	139,100
CGT due at 28%	38,948

The earn-out right disposed of in 2013/14 in Example 3.6 is not a disposal of shares, so it does not qualify for entrepreneurs' relief. Where the earn-out is paid in the form of shares or loan-notes (commonly QCBs), the upfront taxation of the earn-out right can be avoided, if the exchange of the original shares for the new shares or loan notes can meet the conditions for a share exchange in *TCGA 1992, s 135* (see **4.4**). For a further discussion of the application of entrepreneurs' relief to gains deferred on share for share exchanges or share for QCB exchanges, see **Chapter 11**.

The earn-out payment may be made in stages, in which case each separate payment occasion gives rise to a part disposal of the right to future consideration. The value of the right acquired at the time of the original disposal is taken to be the acquisition value for the purpose of the CGT computation; and, in the case of any part disposal, it is necessary to value the right to the remaining future consideration (following the rules for part disposals described in **2.4**).

If any part of the unascertainable deferred consideration becomes 'irrecoverable', no relief is available under *TCGA 1992, s 48(1)* (see **3.21**) because, instead of receiving quantifiable consideration at the time of the disposal, the vendor in this situation received a right which was valued at that time in computing the gain on that disposal. However, a loss may arise on the disposal of the right (see **3.29**).

Election to carry back loss on disposal of a right

3.29   A loss may accrue on the disposal of the right to unascertainable deferred consideration (see **3.28**) where the value of the right – which forms the acquisition value in the CGT computation – exceeds the consideration ultimately received. The taxpayer may elect to carry back such a loss and set it against the gain accruing on the disposal of the asset for which the right was received. This option is only available to taxpayers within the charge to CGT; it is not available to companies subject to corporation tax (*TCGA 1992, s 279A*).

The form of the election, which is irrevocable, is set out in *TCGA 1992, s 279D*. In many cases, the effect of an election will be reasonably straightforward, but several complications can arise, and detailed HMRC guidance is provided at CG15080–CG15130. The election is available if:

(a)   the right was acquired wholly or partly by the taxpayer as the whole or part of the consideration for a disposal (the 'original disposal') by him of another asset (the 'original asset');

(b)   the year of the original disposal was earlier than the year of disposal of the right;

(c)   when the taxpayer acquired the right there was no corresponding disposal of it; and

(d)   the right is a right to unascertainable consideration (*TCGA 1992, s 279A(2)*).

Where the taxpayer disposes of the right and an allowable loss accrues (under the normal rules) on that disposal, and the disposal takes place in a tax year in which the taxpayer is within the charge to CGT (the 'year of loss'), then – subject to the two conditions described in **3.30** and **3.31** – he may elect for the loss to be treated as accruing in the year of the earlier disposal (*TCGA 1992, s 279A(1)*).

Condition 1

3.30   A chargeable gain accrued to the taxpayer (or would have accrued to him, but for a claim to deferral relief under either the enterprise investment scheme or the venture capital trust scheme) on any one or more of the following events:

●   the original disposal;

●   an earlier disposal of the original asset by the taxpayer in the year of the original disposal; and

●   a later disposal of the original asset by the taxpayer in a year earlier than the year of disposal of the right to future consideration.

This condition is modified where the right was acquired in consideration for more than one disposal (*TCGA 1992, s 279A(3), (4)*).

Condition 2

3.31   A chargeable gain accrued to the taxpayer as described in either (a) or (b) below in the 'eligible year' (ie a tax year earlier than the 'year of loss' but not earlier than 1992/93), and a residual amount of gain remains chargeable to CGT for that year:

(a)   a chargeable gain meeting condition 1 above; or

(b)   a chargeable gain that would have met condition 1 if it had not been deferred under the reliefs for investment in the enterprise investment scheme or the venture capital trust scheme, where that gain was treated as accruing at a later time by virtue of a chargeable event – such a gain is called a 'revived gain'.

There is a residual gain remaining for a tax year if there remains (ignoring the effect of the election) an amount on which the taxpayer is chargeable to CGT after taking account of any previous elections made by the taxpayer and after excluding certain trust gains assessed on the taxpayer (against which losses cannot be set) (*TCGA 1992, s 279A(5), (6), (7)*).

Definitions

3.32   Various definitions and further conditions are set out in *TCGA 1992, s 279B*. A key condition is that a right is a right to unascertainable consideration if, and only if:

●   it is a right to consideration the amount or value of which is unascertainable at the time when the right is conferred; and

●   that amount or value is unascertainable at that time because it is referable, wholly or partly, to matters which are uncertain at that time because they have not yet occurred.

Effect of election

3.33   The rules surrounding the election are designed to ensure that any losses already set against gains accruing in the earlier year are not disturbed. The taxpayer cannot elect to carry back only part of the losses, even if this results in a loss of the annual exemption for the earlier year.

Focus

All of the loss must go back and, if this exceeds the chargeable gain in the earlier year, the unused loss is carried forward.

Any carried-forward loss is set against the next eligible tax year, as described in condition 2 in **3.31**. If there is no other eligible year, the loss is carried forward to be used in the year after the year of the loss, or a later year (*TCGA 1992, s 279C*). The election must be made by the first anniversary of 31 January following the end of the tax year in which the loss occurred.

Example 3.7

Sandra sold all the shares in her own soft toy company in July 2010, and realised a gain before entrepreneurs' relief of £90,000. Sandra had losses brought forward of £40,000 to set against her gains in 2010/11. In July 2013, she disposed of a right connected with the sale of her company in 2010 which generated a capital loss of £18,000. Sandra made no other capital gains in 2013/14, so she elects under *TCGA 1992, s 279A* for the loss to be set against her gains in 2010/11:

2010/11	**£**
Gains before losses	90,000
Less losses brought forward:	(40,000)
Gain	50,000
Annual exemption	(10,100)
Chargeable gain	39,900
CGT due at 10%:	3,990
After loss from 2013/14 is carried back:	
Gains before losses	90,000
Less losses brought forward:	(40,000)
	50,000
Less loss carried back:	(18,000)
Gain before entrepreneurs' relief:	32,000
Annual exemption	(10,100)
Chargeable gain	21,900
CGT due at 10%	2,190

Payment of CGT in instalments

3.34   The general rules for payment of CGT are set out in **1.38**. However, CGT may be paid in instalments if all or part of the consideration taken into account in the computation of the gain is payable by instalments over a period longer than 18 months and beginning not earlier than the time of the disposal. If the taxpayer opts for payment by instalments, HMRC may allow payment of CGT over a period of up to eight years, ending not later than the time when the last of the instalments of consideration is payable. The taxpayer does not need to demonstrate hardship in order to pay CGT in instalments (*TCGA 1992, s 280*; CG18601).

Due dates for payment

3.35   HMRC normally expect the taxpayer to pay instalments of CGT equal to 50% of each instalment of consideration due (without any deduction for incidental costs of disposal) until the total CGT liability has been paid.

- Where instalments of consideration fall due on or before the normal due date for the payment of the tax, the corresponding instalments of tax are payable on that normal due date.

- The instalments of tax relating to later instalments of consideration will be payable at the time when the vendor is contractually entitled to receive that consideration, but HMRC are likely to seek to agree a schedule whereby the instalments of tax are paid at intervals of at least six months (CG14912).

Example 3.8

Simon enters into a contract for the sale of intellectual property rights on 1 May 2012. The consideration is £6.6 million payable in six annual instalments of £1.1 million commencing 1 August 2012. The gain realised of £6 million does not qualify for entrepreneurs' relief. The total CGT payable on the deal is £1,680,000 (28% × £6 million), which would normally all be due to be paid by 31 January 2014. Simon asks for *TCGA 1992, s 280* to apply. Using this instalment option, the tax is payable on the following dates:

	Payable:	£ Tax
50% of the consideration due on 1 August 2012	31 January 2014	550,000
50% of the consideration due on 1 August 2013	31 January 2014	550,000
50% of the consideration due on 1 August 2014	1 August 2014	550,000
Balance of tax due from the consideration payable on 1 August 2015		30,000
		1,680,000

ALLOWABLE EXPENDITURE

3.36   Three categories of expenditure are allowable as a deduction from the consideration in computing a chargeable gain or loss. These are:

- the costs of acquiring (or providing) the asset, including certain incidental costs (see **3.39**);

- the costs of enhancing the asset's value, and any costs of establishing, preserving or defending title to it (see **3.41**); and

- certain incidental costs of disposal (see **3.42**).

No payment of interest may be deducted. Any deemed disposal and reacquisition of an asset cannot give rise to a deduction for assumed incidental costs. No deduction is allowed more than once in the computation of a gain (*TCGA 1992, ss 38(1), (3), (4), 52(1)*).

Expenditure that is, or would be, allowable in computing trading income chargeable to income tax is not allowable (see **3.43**). Special rules apply to 'wasting assets' (see **4.27**).

Costs of acquisition

Consideration for the acquisition

3.37   This is the amount or value of the consideration, in money or money's worth, given by the taxpayer, or on his behalf, wholly and exclusively for the acquisition of the asset. If the taxpayer created rather than purchased the asset, for example where goodwill or copyright is created, the allowable expenditure is any expenditure wholly and exclusively incurred by him in providing the asset (*TCGA 1992, s 38(1)(a)*).

Mansworth v Jelley losses

3.38   Confusion arose in 2003 concerning the base cost for shares acquired by way of unapproved share options. The case, *Mansworth v Jelley* [2003] STC 53, was interpreted by HMRC as meaning that the base cost of such shares was the market value of the shares at the date when the shares were acquired, plus the amount charged to income tax when the option was exercised and the shares were acquired. For example, share options exercised for £100 would incur an income tax charge on £100. When the shares were sold shortly after exercise for £100, a capital loss of £100 would be created.

This interpretation meant that many shares acquired through unapproved share options stood at a loss for CGT purposes. This situation applied for all unapproved share options exercised before 10 April 2003, when *TCGA 1992, ss 144ZA–144ZD* were introduced to change the position back to what most people thought applied all along.

On 12 May 2009, HMRC changed their opinion about the base cost of shares acquired through pre-10 April 2003 share options (R&C Brief 30/09), with further information issued as R&C Brief 60/09. These Briefs assert that the base cost for such shares comprises only the market value of those shares at the date they were acquired, so no capital loss would generally arise. Any capital losses already claimed by taxpayers under the previous HMRC guidance should stand, but taxpayers submitting loss claims on or after 12 May 2009 need to consider the new HMRC guidance on this matter.

Focus

The last year for which claims for capital losses under *Mansworth v Jelley* were possible was 2005/06.

Claims for 2005/06 had to be submitted by 31 January 2012.

In February 2012, HMRC wrote to all taxpayers who had open claims relating to a *Mansworth v Jelley* loss (ie pre-10 April 2003 losses), asking them to withdraw the claim. If the taxpayer was not prepared to withdraw the loss claim, they were asked to explain the basis on which they believed that the loss claim was valid. The professional bodies have argued that taxpayers could assert 'legitimate expectation' based on the HMRC guidance issued in January 2003. HMRC have confirmed that their February 2012 letter on this issue was not an appealable decision. For HMRC guidance, see CG12396.

Incidental costs of acquisition

3.39   These are the incidental costs to the taxpayer of the acquisition, as specified below:

(a)   expenditure wholly and exclusively incurred by him for the purposes of the acquisition, being the costs (including stamp duties) of the transfer or conveyance of the asset, and any fees, commission or remuneration paid for professional services of a surveyor, valuer, auctioneer, accountant, agent or legal adviser; and

(b)   the costs of advertising to find a seller (*TCGA 1992, s 38(1)(a), (2)*).

Reasonable costs incurred in ascertaining the market value of the asset for CGT purposes can be deducted, for example where the asset was acquired before 31 March 1982. No deduction is allowed for expenditure by the purchaser in transporting assets from the point of acquisition (CG15260).

Market value rule for acquisitions

3.40   The market value of an asset (determined as set out in **3.7**) is substituted for the actual consideration given for the acquisition where the taxpayer acquires the asset:

(a)   otherwise than by way of a bargain made at arm's length (see **3.6**), and in particular where he acquires it by way of gift, or on a transfer into a settlement by a settlor, or by way of distribution from a company in respect of shares in the company;

(b)   wholly or partly for a consideration that cannot be valued;

(c)   in connection with his own or another's loss of office or employment or diminution of emoluments; or

(d)   otherwise in consideration for (or in recognition of) his or another person's services or past services in an office or employment, or any other service rendered to another person (*TCGA 1992, s 17(1)*).

However, market value is not substituted on an acquisition if there is no corresponding disposal of the asset and:

- there is no consideration in money or money's worth; or

- the amount or value of the consideration is less than the asset's market value (*TCGA 1992, s 17(2)*).

Where a company issues its own shares, there is no disposal corresponding to the shareholder's acquisition. The above exception applies only if no consideration is given or the consideration is less than market value. The market value is substituted, therefore, if the consideration given is higher than the market value. The effect of this rule is that the lower of the actual consideration and market value is taken in a case where there is an acquisition but no corresponding disposal (CG14550).

Costs of enhancement and preservation

3.41   These are the amounts of expenditure wholly and exclusively incurred by the taxpayer (or on his behalf) for:

(a)   the purpose of enhancing the asset's value, which must be reflected in the asset's state or nature at the time of the disposal (see below); or

(b)   establishing, preserving or defending the taxpayer's title to, or to a right over, the asset (*TCGA 1992, s 38(1)(b)*).

The improvements in (a) must affect the state of the asset, and not just be payments made in connection with supporting the value of the asset (see

CG15182). HMRC regard the time of the disposal for this purpose as the date of completion and not the date of the contract (CG15185), although the disposal date for calculating the CGT due would be the date on which contracts were agreed or exchanged (see **2.8**).

TCGA 1992, s 38(1)(b) does not refer (in the way that *TCGA 1992, s 38(1)(a)* refers) to consideration in money or money's worth, but the High Court held in *Chaney v Watkis* (1986) 58 TC 707 that money's worth given (in the form of an agreement to provide a tenant with rent-free accommodation) for the purpose of enhancing the value of an asset was allowable as a deduction.

However, HMRC may seek to challenge a deduction for money's worth where the recipient is connected with the taxpayer or there are other grounds for suspecting that enhancing the asset's value may not have been the only purpose of the transaction. *Oram v Johnson* (1980) 53 TC 319 established that 'expenditure' means money, or money's worth, in the sense of something which diminishes the total assets of the person making the expenditure. It does not include the value of an individual's own skill and labour (CG15211).

Incidental costs of disposal

3.42   These are the incidental costs incurred by the taxpayer for the purposes of the disposal as set out in *TCGA 1992, s 38(1)(c), (2)*:

(a)   the costs (including stamp duties) of the transfer or conveyance of the asset, and any fees, commission or remuneration paid for professional services of a surveyor, valuer, auctioneer, accountant, agent or legal adviser;

(b)   the costs of advertising to find a buyer; and

(c)   costs reasonably incurred in making any valuation or apportionment required in computing the gain, including establishing the market value, where required.

The cost of the transfer or conveyance of an asset would include the vendor's costs of transporting it to the point of sale (CG15260). The costs mentioned in (c) include costs incurred for the purposes of rendering a tax return or for the purposes of a post-transaction valuation check (see **1.35**) in advance of submission of the return, but they exclude costs of resolving valuation disputes with HMRC (CG15261).

Expenditure allowable in computing income

3.43   When computing the chargeable gain, no deduction is available for any of the following categories of expenditure:

3.43 *Computation of gains and losses*

(a) expenditure allowable as a deduction in computing the profits or losses of a trade, profession or vocation for income tax purposes;

(b) expenditure allowable as a deduction in computing any other income or profits or gains or losses for income tax purposes; or

(c) expenditure that would be allowable as a deduction in computing any losses but for an insufficiency of income or profits or gains (*TCGA 1992, s 39(1)*).

These restrictions apply irrespective of how the benefit of the expense mentioned has been obtained. Point (c) was illustrated in *Raha v HMRC* [2010] UKFTT 590 (TC), when Raha was denied a deduction in her CGT computation for various expenses that she incurred while her let property was empty before the sale, including service charges, furniture clearance and council tax.

Expenditure that would have been deductible in computing the profits or losses of a trade, had the asset disposed of been a fixed asset used for that trade, is not deductible in computing a chargeable gain (*TCGA 1992, s 39(2)*).

Example 3.9

Mrs Gold inherited two adjoining cottages in 1981. In 1985, she converted the properties into one property and let it as a furnished property until August 2013, when it was sold. She incurred the following expenses which are treated as deductions from the rental income (for income tax purposes) or from the proceeds of the sale (for CGT purposes) as shown:

Expenditure	Income tax £	CGT £
Market value at 31 March 1982 (in place of inherited value)		1,000
Legal costs to establish the property boundary		2,500
Planning permission to convert cottages to one		200
Conversion costs		40,000
Drawing up tenancy agreements	500	
Commission to letting agent	25,000	
Decoration of interior	4,000	
Replacement of front door (a repair)	400	
New conservatory (an improvement)		10,000
New carpets and curtains (sold with the property)		3,000
Estate agents' fees and commission on sale		5,000
Replacement of central heating boiler (a repair)	1,400	

In *Emmerson v Computer Time International Ltd (in liquidation)* (1977) 50 TC 628, CA, a payment of arrears of rent, made in order to obtain the landlord's consent to an assignment of a lease, was held to be rent paid in respect of a fixed asset of the trade and was not deductible in computing the chargeable gain.

Sums are regarded for this purpose as chargeable to (or taken into account for) income tax if they would be so chargeable (or taken into account) but for the fact that the profits or gains concerned are not chargeable to income tax or that losses are not allowable. Income or profits taxable by deduction at source are treated as chargeable to income tax (*TCGA 1992, s 52(2), (3)*).

These rules do not deny a deduction for expenditure qualifying for capital allowances, but any capital loss arising may be restricted by reference to such allowances (see **3.55**).

Expenditure reimbursed out of public funds

3.44   Any expenditure met (or to be met) directly or indirectly by the Crown or UK or other government, public or local authority is to be excluded from the computation of a gain (*TCGA 1992, s 50*). If, on a disposal of the asset, the taxpayer is required to repay all or part of a grant out of the proceeds of sale, or can demonstrate that there has been a corresponding reduction in the amount of a later grant, then, by concession (ESC D53), HMRC allow the consideration received on the disposal to be reduced by the amount of the repayment (CG15289).

Part disposals

3.45   A part disposal may occur where the disposal itself creates an interest in, or a right over, the asset; for example, the grant of a lease by the person who holds the freehold interest in land. Other part disposals involve the grant of a licence to exploit a copyright, or a patent, or to remove minerals from land, tip rubbish, cut down trees or exercise sporting rights over a particular piece of land, or simply the disposal of part of a large plot of land (*TCGA 1992, s 21(2)*). For further discussion of part disposals, see **2.4**.

Special rules apply to part disposals of land and small disposals (see Examples 2.1 and 2.2).

The apportionment of allowable expenditure is made before applying any restriction of capital losses by reference to capital allowances (provided by *TCGA 1992, s 41*). On a subsequent disposal of the part of the asset retained, the capital allowances to be taken into account (in the event that a loss accrues on that disposal) include such allowances relating to expenditure both before and after the part disposal, but in order to avoid double counting they exclude any allowances that were applied in restricting the capital loss on the first part disposal (*TCGA 1992, s 42(3)*).

This apportionment (and all similar apportionments of expenditure provided for elsewhere) is also made before – and without regard to – any of the following rules in *TCGA 1992*:

- transfers between spouses and civil partners – *s 58*;
- transfers within a group of companies – *s 171*;
- roll-over relief on replacement of business assets – *ss 152–158*; and
- any other rule providing for neither a gain nor a loss to accrue on the disposal (*TCGA 1992, s 42(5)*).

Assets derived from other assets

3.46   The value of an asset may be derived from another asset in the same ownership where:

- assets have been merged or divided or have changed their nature; or
- rights or interests in or over assets have been created or extinguished.

In such a case, it is necessary to apportion the allowable expenditure incurred on the 'old' asset and then apply the appropriate proportions to the old asset (if it is retained) and the new asset. The apportionment is to be made on a 'just and reasonable' basis (*TCGA 1992, ss 43, 52(4)*).

CALCULATION AND USE OF LOSSES

3.47   Where a particular type of transaction will produce a chargeable gain, it will generally also produce an allowable capital loss. The loss is computed in the same way as gains, but the indexation allowance cannot increase or create a loss (see **3.60**). If a gain that arises on a disposal would not be chargeable because it is exempt from CGT, any loss arising from the disposal is not allowable (*TCGA 1992, s 16(1), (2)*).

A loss would not normally arise on the non-recovery or write-off of a debt or unsecured loan (see **4.34**), but a capital loss may be available under the loan to trader provisions (see **17.11–17.15**).

There are special rules for the use of capital losses arising in the following circumstances:

- in the tax year the taxpayer dies (see **7.3**);

- between connected parties (see **3.21**);

- on the disposal of a right to unascertainable deferred consideration (see **3.29**);

- incurred outside the UK by a UK-resident non-domiciliary (see **3.51**);

- where the asset disposed of is a chattel (see **4.25**);

- on the deemed disposal of assets to a beneficiary (see **8.19**);

- where arrangements exist to create a tax advantage (see **10.2**); or

- as part of the disposal of a business qualifying for entrepreneurs' relief (see **11.6**).

In addition, a capital loss sustained by the subscriber of certain unquoted trading company shares on the disposal or loss of those shares may be set off against that taxpayer's income (see **17.14**). In certain circumstances, a trading income loss may be treated as a capital loss (see **3.52** and **3.53**).

Order of set-off of losses

3.48   The allowable capital losses arising in the tax year are normally set off against any capital gains arising in the same tax year, before the annual exemption is deducted (see **1.20**). Where the taxpayer has gains that are chargeable to CGT at more than one rate, the taxpayer can choose which gains their losses are set against, such that the CGT liability for the year is reduced to the lowest possible charge (*TCGA 1992, s 4B*) (see Example 3.10).

Allowable losses brought forward from an earlier tax year are set against the taxpayer's adjusted net gains, which are broadly the gains for the current tax year less the allowable losses for that year. However, the allowable brought-forward losses can be restricted to preserve the annual exemption. The brought-forward losses may also be allocated against gains in such a way that minimises the tax charge for the year (CG21600).

A peculiar feature of entrepreneurs' relief is that it demands aggregation of all the gains and losses arising from a qualifying business disposal, before entrepreneurs' relief for that disposal is calculated (*TCGA 1992, s 169N(1)*) (see **11.7**).

Example 3.10

Nick's taxable income for 2013/14 is £50,000 after his personal allowance and all tax-allowable expenses have been deducted. He sold his business in May 2013, realising a net gain of £72,000 which qualifies for entrepreneurs' relief. In July 2013, he sold a let property for a gain of £100,000, and quoted shares for a loss of £40,000. Nick made a Gift Aid donation of £24,000 net (£30,000 gross) in December 2013. The CGT on those gains is calculated as follows:

2013/14	May 2013 gain	July 2013 gain	CGT payable
	£	£	£
Higher rate threshold	32,010		
Expanded by Gift Aid donation	30,000		
Total basic rate band	62,010		
Taxable income	(50,000)		
Available basic rate band	12,010		
Gross gains	72,000	100,000	
Losses relieved		(40,000)	
Less annual exemption	–	(10,900)	
Net taxable gains	72,000	49,100	
Basic rate band deemed used	12,010	–	
Taxed at 28%		49,100	13,748
Gain taxable at 10%	72,000		7,200
Total CGT payable			20,948

Nick has chosen to set his loss and annual exemption of £10,900 against his later gain, as that gives him tax relief at 28%. Although the first gain is subject to entrepreneurs' relief and is thus taxable in full at 10%, it is deemed to take priority before other gains over the available basic rate band.

Claims

3.49 A loss must be 'claimed' before it can be set against gains. It is not an allowable loss unless the taxpayer gives a notice to HMRC for the tax year in which the loss accrued. The notice, which must quantify the amount of the loss, is treated as a claim within *Taxes Management Act 1970 (TMA 1970), ss 42* and *43 (TCGA 1992, s 16(2A))*.

Where the taxpayer is required to submit a self-assessment tax return, he or she should include the allowable capital losses on the capital gains pages of that return. A computation of the loss must be attached to the return, as the tax return pages only have room for a summary. The HMRC notes to the capital gains pages (SA108 – notes) advise the taxpayer to make it clear on the computation that a claim for losses is being made.

Claims under *TMA 1970, ss 42* and *43* must be submitted by non-corporate taxpayers no more than four years after the end of the tax year to which the claim relates, and for companies within four years of the end of the relevant accounting period. For example, an individual taxpayer must claim capital losses that arose in 2009/10 by 5 April 2014.

Non-residents

3.50　　If the taxpayer is not resident in the UK for any part of the tax year (ie there is no part of the tax year for which he is resident in the UK), a loss accruing to him in that tax year is not an allowable loss. There is an exception where a gain accruing on the relevant disposal would be chargeable on the non-resident taxpayer under *TCGA 1992, ss 10* or *10B* (non-residents with a UK branch, agency or permanent establishment) (see **5.33–5.36**; *TCGA 1992, s 16(3)*).

Non-domicile UK residents

3.51　　Where an individual is resident, but not domiciled, in the UK (a 'non-dom'), and has gains accruing from the disposal of assets situated outside the UK, those gains can escape CGT if the individual claims the remittance basis (*ITA 2007, s 809B*) and those gains are *not* remitted to the UK. Not all non-dom individuals will want to, or need to, claim the remittance basis; see **5.37–5.50**.

From 6 April 2008, non-domiciled individuals who claim the remittance basis can make a one-off irrevocable election to obtain UK tax relief for losses realised on foreign-situated assets (see **5.49**) (*TCGA 1992, s 16ZA(2)*). The election will be effective for the first tax year for which the taxpayer claims the remittance basis, and all subsequent tax years. Some non-domiciled individuals are entitled to use the remittance basis without making a claim under *ITA 2007, s 809B* (see **5.39**); and, in those cases, the taxpayer's offshore losses can be set against their offshore gains remitted to the UK.

Non-domiciled individuals who do not use the remittance basis are taxed on all their worldwide gains and losses just like other UK residents, so do not need to make an election in respect of foreign losses.

Trading losses set against chargeable gains

3.52   Where the taxpayer makes a claim under *ITA 2007, s 64* or *s 128* to set trading or employment losses against income for income tax purposes, he may also make a claim for an amount – the 'relevant amount' – to be treated as an allowable loss for CGT purposes (*TCGA 1992, s 261B*).

The relevant amount for the tax year to which the claim relates is the part of the trading loss that cannot be set off against his income for the year and has not already been relieved for any other year under *ITA 2007, s 64*, or otherwise. However, if the relevant amount exceeds the 'maximum amount' (see below), the excess is not treated as a capital loss.

The 'maximum amount' is the amount on which the taxpayer would be chargeable to CGT disregarding the annual exemption (see **1.17**), and the loss to be relieved under *TCGA 1992, s 261B*. It is calculated without regard to any event occurring after the relevant amount has been determined, which would otherwise reduce the maximum amount.

In the absence of this limitation, a claim to CGT roll-over relief (on the replacement of business assets, for example) could reduce the maximum amount so that part of the trading loss could no longer be treated as a capital loss. Instead, the maximum amount is unchanged and the effect of the roll-over relief claim is to create unrelieved losses available to carry forward and set against future chargeable gains.

Focus

From 2013/14, the loss arising under *ITA 2007, s 64* or *s 128* may be restricted to the greater of £50,000 and 25% of the taxpayer's adjusted total income (*ITA 2007, s 24A*).

There is uncertainty as to whether the restricted loss (ie the excess over £50,000 or 25% of income) can be converted into a CGT loss under *TCGA 1992, s 261B* or whether it must be carried forward as an income tax loss.

HMRC guidance should be applied for under CAP1 to confirm the treatment of such losses (see **10.21**).

Post-cessation expenditure

3.53   Where the taxpayer claims relief for post-cessation expenditure under *ITA 2007, s 96* or *s 125*, he may specify that any amount of that expenditure that cannot be set off against his income is to be treated for CGT purposes as an allowable loss (*TCGA 1992, ss 261D–261E*). The relief under *s 96* is denied from 12 January 2012, where the payment or event that gave rise to the relief is in consequence of, or in connection with, relevant tax avoidance arrangements (*ITA 2007, s 98A*).

Focus

Where the restriction on the set-off of income tax losses under *ITA 2007, s 24A* applies for 2013/14 or later years, it is uncertain whether that restriction will also affect the amount of post-cessation expenditure which can be treated as a CGT loss.

This relief is not available to companies within the charge to corporation tax as the relief only applies to income tax losses.

Former employees: employment-related liabilities

3.54   Where income tax relief is available for liabilities related to a former employment under *ITEPA 2003, s 555*, and the deduction exceeds the taxpayer's total income, the excess relief may be treated as an allowable loss accruing to the former employee (*TCGA 1992, s 263ZA*). However, this excess relief may be restricted from 2013/14 under *ITA 2007, s 24A* to the greater of £50,000 and 25% of the taxpayer's adjusted total income.

Restriction by reference to capital allowances

3.55   Although expenditure allowable as a deduction in computing trading profits etc is not deductible in computing chargeable gains (see **3.43**), there is no general exclusion of expenditure for which a 'capital allowance' or 'renewals allowance' (see **3.56**) is made. If a loss accrues on the disposal, it may be restricted by reference to capital allowances claimed in respect of the same asset (*TCGA 1992, s 41*; CG17430). However, this restriction does not apply in two broad circumstances:

(a)   where the base cost of the asset for capital gains purposes is not the same as the qualifying expenditure for capital allowance purposes; and

(b)   where the sale of the plant or machinery asset denies the seller capital allowances on the asset.

Situation (a) may apply in the following circumstances:

●   the asset is sold to a connected party (eg on incorporation) for less than market value without an election under *CAA 2001, s 266* for the tax written down value to apply (see Example 3.11);

87

- the asset is sold to a connected party at market value, which is not the same as the tax written down value, and an election under *CAA 2001, s 266* is made; or

- the asset was acquired before 31 March 1982. On sale of the asset, the 1982 value is treated as the base cost for CGT purposes (see **3.58**). However, *TCGA 1992, Sch 3, para 3* requires the cost for capital allowance purposes to be the deemed 1982 acquisition cost; so, in this case, the restriction to the capital loss by *TCGA 1992, s 41* will apply.

Example 3.11

Milton traded as a printer as a sole trader from 1995 to 2003, when he incorporated his business into Keynes Ltd. The printing press that originally cost Milton £410,000 was transferred to Keynes Ltd for £200,000 when its market value was £300,000, and its capital allowance written down value was £250,000. Milton used the £50,000 balancing allowance against his final profits as a sole trader. There was no election under *CAA 2001, s 266*.

In May 2013, Keynes Ltd sold the printing press for £80,000 to an unconnected person. The capital allowances and capital loss due to Keynes Ltd are calculated as follows:

Capital allowances calculation:		£
Cost of the asset (transfer value)		200,000
Less disposal proceeds		(80,000)
Capital allowances claimed by Keynes		120,000
Gains calculation:		
Disposal proceeds		80,000
Deduct base cost (market value)	300,000	
Indexation (ignored, as it cannot increase a loss)	nil	
Capital allowances (ignored, as *s 41* does not apply)	(nil)	300,000
Capital loss		220,000

How does the restriction apply?

3.56 The restriction is applied by excluding – from the sums allowable as a deduction in the CGT computation – any expenditure to the extent that a capital allowance or renewals allowance has been (or may be) made for that expenditure. This rule can have the effect of reducing the capital loss to nil, but it cannot turn that loss into a gain (*TCGA 1992, s 41(1), (2), (4), (5)*).

The capital allowances to be taken into account are any allowances under the *Capital Allowances Act 2001 (CAA 2001)*, including any balancing allowances and balancing charges available on disposal of the asset (*TCGA 1992, s 41(6)*).

Crucially, the capital allowances must be claimed by the same person that made the capital loss on the disposal of the asset. Any allowances claimed by a previous owner of the asset, even if that previous owner was a connected party to the final seller of the asset, are generally ignored. There are three circumstances where the allowances claimed by the previous owner are considered:

• the trade including the asset was transferred on death and *CAA 2001, s 268* applies;

• the business was transferred to a company resident in another EU country, so *TCGA 1992, s 140A* applies; or

• the asset was transferred within a group of companies, so *TCGA 1992, s 171* applies.

If the taxpayer acquired the asset, and it was treated for capital allowances purposes as a transfer made at its written-down value (*CAA 2001, s 266*), this restriction takes account of capital allowances made to the transferor (and the previous transferor in relation to any earlier transfers) as well as the taxpayer (*TCGA 1992, s 41(3)*; CG15411).

On a disposal of plant or machinery that has attracted allowances under *CAA 2001, Pt 2* without restriction for either non-qualifying use or partial depreciation subsidies (*CAA 2001, ss 205–212*), the allowances taken into account for the purpose of this restriction are taken to be the difference between the capital expenditure incurred (or treated as incurred) on providing the asset and the asset's disposal value for capital allowances purposes (*TCGA 1992, s 41(7)*).

Example 3.12

Luton Ltd bought a printing press to use in its trade in April 1998 for £220,000. In May 2013, Luton Ltd sold the printing press for £20,000 to an unconnected person. The capital allowances and capital gains are calculated as follows:

Capital allowances calculation:		£
Cost of the asset		220,000
Less disposal proceeds		(20,000)
Capital allowances to be taken into account		200,000
Gains calculation:		
Disposal proceeds		20,000
Deduct cost of asset	220,000	
Less capital allowances:	(200,000)	20,000
Net gain or loss:		Nil

It is important to determine exactly which asset the capital loss arises on. In *Revenue & Customs v Smallwood* [2007] EWCA Civ 462, the taxpayer invested £10,000 in 1989 in an enterprise zone property unit trust. In 1999, he realised a loss on a part disposal of his investment. During that ten-year period, the trustees of the unit trust invested in buildings in the enterprise zone that attracted industrial buildings allowances (IBAs). The taxpayer received the benefit of a portion of those IBAs, but HMRC argued that the loss that he made on his investment should be restricted by the benefit of the capital allowances that he enjoyed, and so the loss should be restricted by *TCGA 1992, s 41*. The Court of Appeal held that the loss arose on the disposal of the units in the property unit trust, and not on the disposal of the buildings that the trustees had invested in, and thus the loss was allowed to stand without restriction.

DEDUCTION OF RELIEFS

Entrepreneurs' relief

3.57 Entrepreneurs' relief is available for certain gains made on or after 6 April 2008 by individuals, and by trustees of interest in possession trusts where there is also a qualifying beneficiary. The relief is restricted to the net gains made on the disposal of a business or part of a business, shares in a personal company, or business assets that are disposed of after the cessation of a business, or in association with the disposal of a business. For gains made on or after 23 June 2010, entrepreneurs' relief is applied as a separate rate of CGT, rather than as a relief that reduces the taxable gain; see further discussion in **Chapter 11**.

Rebased assets

3.58 Assets held by individuals and trustees on 31 March 1982 and disposed of on or after 6 April 2008 are automatically rebased to their value at 31 March 1982 by *TCGA 1992, s 35*. The effect is to substitute the 31 March 1982 value for the actual cost of the asset and any enhancement expenditure incurred prior to that date. If the value of the asset being disposed of is derived from another asset held on 31 March 1982, rebasing may apply by reference to the original asset's value on that date (*TCGA 1992, s 35(1), (2), Sch 3, para 5*).

Rebasing to 31 March 1982 eliminates all the inflationary gains made prior to that date, and this was achieved by a rebasing election made prior to 6 April 2008. In some cases, the March 1982 value would be lower than the original cost of the asset, so a rebasing election would not be advantageous. Where the asset has been rebased to 31 March 1982, the indexation allowance (see **3.60**) is based on the market value at that date.

Companies can still choose whether to have their assets rebased to 31 March 1982 by making a rebasing election (see **Chapter 9**).

Assets held on 6 April 1965

3.59 The rules for assets held on 6 April 1965 only apply to companies in respect of disposals made on or after 6 April 2008, as all assets held by individuals and trustees are automatically rebased to 31 March 1982 (see **3.58**). The valuation rules for assets held at 6 April 1965 will also only apply where a universal rebasing election has not been made, so in practice will be very rarely encountered.

The special rules that apply for different types of assets held at 6 April 1965 are discussed at **9.18–9.21**.

Indexation allowance

3.60 The indexation allowance was introduced in 1982 in order to eliminate 'paper gains' attributable to inflation. Combined with the rebasing of CGT by reference to 31 March 1982 values (see **3.58**) with effect from April 1988, indexation provided 'inflation-proofing' of gains.

The allowance was frozen with effect from April 1998 for individuals, trustees and personal representatives, and was withdrawn completely for these taxpayers from 6 April 2008. The allowance could be obtained in addition to taper relief where appropriate; but, from 30 November 1993, indexation cannot increase a loss, so it does not apply in the case of a capital loss. Companies chargeable to corporation tax continue to be eligible for indexation allowance (*TCGA 1992, s 52A*). The calculation of indexation allowance is discussed in **Chapter 9**.

No gain, no loss transfers

3.61 Where the indexation allowance is available (see **3.60**) and the disposal is treated as a disposal on which neither a gain nor a loss accrues, the consideration for the disposal is taken to be the amount that would give rise to an unindexed gain equal to the indexation allowance available on the disposal. The effect of this rule is that, after deducting the indexation allowance, there is no chargeable gain and no allowable loss. An adjustment to the deemed consideration may be required in some cases, to prevent a loss accruing on a subsequent disposal by the transferee (*TCGA 1992, s 56*).

Example 3.13

Elton bought an investment property in May 1982 for £100,000, which he transferred to his civil partner David in February 2008. David acquires the property as a no gain, no loss transfer after deducting the indexation allowance, which was frozen at a factor of 1.59 for the period to 5 April 1998. David sold the property in August 2013 for £650,000, and the capital gain was calculated as follows:

2013/14

		£
Proceeds from sale of property		650,000
Original cost in 1982	100,000	
Add indexation at 1.59 to April 1998:	159,000	
Cost acquired for no gain, no loss		259,000
Net gain before annual exemption:		391,000

Spouses and civil partners

3.62   Transfers of assets between spouses or registered civil partners living together are treated as 'no gain, no loss' transfers.

Where an individual is living with their spouse or civil partner in a tax year and during that year one of them disposes of an asset to the other, both the transferor and transferee are treated as if the asset was transferred for a consideration that would give rise to neither a gain nor a loss in the hands of the transferor (*TCGA 1992, s 58(1)*).

Spouses or civil partners are treated as living together unless they are either:

•   separated under an order of a court of competent jurisdiction, or by deed of separation; or

•   in fact separated in such circumstances that the separation is likely to be permanent (*TCGA 1992, s 288(3)* applying *ITA 2007, s 1011*).

The no gain, no loss rule described above applies regardless of the rules substituting market value for transfers between connected persons (see **3.11**). This point was misunderstood by Mrs Godfrey who acquired a half-share in a property from her husband in 2005. The property was sold in 2006 and Mrs Godfrey calculated her gain on the basis that she had acquired her half share at market value in 2005, rather than at half the cost her husband had acquired the property for in 1986 (*Mrs A Godfrey v HMRC* [2010] UKFTT 611 (TC)).

The no gain, no loss rule also applies to appropriations to and from trading stock (see **4.36**) and regardless of any other rule fixing the amount of the consideration deemed to be given on the disposal or acquisition of an asset.

However, it does not apply if:

- the asset formed part of the taxpayer's trading stock until the disposal;

- the asset is acquired, by a person carrying on a trade, as trading stock; or

- the disposal is by way of *donatio mortis causa* (see **2.9**) (*TCGA 1992, s 58(2)*).

Charities and CASCs

3.63   Gifts to charities are generally treated such that no gain, no loss arises on the transaction for the donor. This also applies for gifts of assets out of settlements (*TCGA 1992, s 257(3)*).

However, gifts of qualifying assets (listed below) will generate income tax relief or corporation tax relief for the donor, unless the gift is a tainted donation or an associated donation (*ITA 2007, s 431*; *CTA 2010, s 203*). The qualifying assets are:

- listed shares or securities;

- units in an authorised unit trust;

- shares in an open-ended investment company;

- interests in an offshore fund; and

- qualifying interest in land.

A charity for this purpose includes all of the following:

- Trustees of the National Heritage Memorial Fund;

- Historic Buildings and Monuments Commission for England;

- National Endowment for Science, Technology and the Arts; and

- registered Community Amateur Sports Clubs (CASCs).

Double tax relief

3.64   Relief for foreign tax suffered on gains that are chargeable to UK CGT or corporation tax may be obtained under the terms of a double taxation agreement between the UK and the relevant overseas territory (see **3.65**); or by means of a 'unilateral' tax credit granted under UK domestic tax law (see

3.66); or by means of a deduction in computing the gain chargeable to UK tax (see **3.69**). See **5.48** with regard to the application of double tax relief where gains are assessed on the remittance basis. Anti-avoidance provisions were introduced in 2005 to counter schemes designed to create tax credit relief (*TIOPA 2010, ss 83–88*).

Double taxation agreements

3.65   The UK has more than a hundred double tax agreements or treaties with overseas territories, designed to limit the taxing rights of the contracting states in order to prevent double taxation, and to assist in countering evasion by means of exchange of information between tax authorities. The agreements contain articles to determine the residence status of persons who are resident in both territories under their respective domestic tax law. Many agreements have articles setting out how capital gains are to be taxed. Where a UK-resident taxpayer suffers foreign tax on a gain that is subject to CGT or corporation tax, the agreement itself may provide for a credit in respect of the foreign tax to be given against any UK liability (*TIOPA 2010, s 6*).

Unilateral foreign tax credit relief

3.66   Where chargeable gains are subject to tax in a territory that has no double taxation agreement with the UK, credit for any foreign tax liability is given 'unilaterally' unless the taxpayer elects for a deduction instead (see **3.69**) (*TIOPA 2010, s 18*). The provisions are also applied to corporation tax on chargeable gains (*TIOPA 2010, s 42*).

The UK tax and the foreign tax must be chargeable on the same chargeable gain, although there is no requirement that the respective liabilities arise at the same time or are charged on the same person (*TIOPA 2010, s 9*). A liability may arise in the UK, but not in the overseas territory.

In some cases it may be difficult to ascertain the amount of the gain that is subject to 'double taxation' in the absence of any relief. HMRC practice in this regard is set out at CG14380–CG14427 and summarised below.

(a)   Where the whole period of ownership of the asset is considered in arriving at both the UK tax assessment and the foreign tax assessment, and the amount of the UK tax assessment is equal to or greater than the foreign tax assessment, the whole of the foreign tax is allowable for foreign tax credit relief. However, the credit cannot exceed the amount of the UK tax liability arising on the gain, and no deduction is available in the computation for any foreign tax that is not allowed as a tax credit.

(b)   Where the whole period of ownership is considered for both tax assessments as stated in (a), but the amount of the UK tax assessment is less than the foreign tax assessment, the whole of the gain is treated as doubly taxed, but the foreign tax credit is restricted to the fraction A/B, where A is the amount of the UK tax assessment and B is the amount of the foreign tax assessment.

(c)   Relief for the foreign tax paid is restricted when the same period of ownership is considered in arriving at both assessments but the amount of the UK tax assessment is less than the foreign tax assessment, and when the foreign tax assessment relates to a longer period of ownership than the period forming the basis of the UK assessment (eg as a result of the March 1982 rebasing of UK CGT; see **3.58**).

HMRC also provide a working sheet to assist taxpayers to calculate their UK tax liability, which is contained within the tax return helpsheet HS261: Foreign tax credit relief: capital gains.

3.67   HMRC consider that foreign tax credit relief is available in the following circumstances:

●   the foreign tax liability charges capital gains as income;

●   foreign tax is payable on a no gain, no loss disposal between group companies (within *TCGA 1992, s 171*) and a UK tax liability arises on a subsequent disposal;

●   an overseas trade carried on through a branch or agency or permanent establishment is domesticated (ie transferred to a non-resident subsidiary), relief is given under *TCGA 1992, s 140*, a later event gives rise to a UK liability, and foreign tax is charged wholly or partly by reference to the gain accruing at the date of domestication; or

●   foreign tax is payable by reference to increases in the value of assets, although there is no disposal for UK tax purposes, and a UK liability arises on a later disposal (HMRC Statement of Practice 06/88).

HMRC have listed in their Double Taxation Relief Manual (at DT2140 onwards) the double taxation agreements for each country, which in turn list the taxes that they consider to be admissible (or inadmissible) for tax credit relief. New agreements or treaties are added or revised at regular intervals, and the latest information can be found on the Tax Treaty News section of the HMRC website at www.hmrc.gov.uk/taxtreaties/news.htm.

Statement of Practice 07/91 (revised in August 2005) sets out how HMRC interpret the requirement in *TIOPA 2010, ss 8, 9, 29, 30* and *129* that the foreign tax must 'correspond' to the UK tax in order for relief to be available. Broadly, the question is to be determined by examining the tax within its legislative context in the foreign territory and deciding whether it serves the same function as the UK tax.

EU Savings Directive: special withholding tax

3.68   Where the consideration for the disposal of an asset giving rise to a chargeable gain consists of or includes an amount of 'savings income', and 'special withholding tax' is levied in respect of that consideration (or a part of it), credit relief is available for the amount found by the formula:

$$SWT \times [GUK / (G - SWT)]$$

where:

- SWT is the special withholding tax levied;

- GUK is the amount of the chargeable gain received in the UK; and

- G is the amount of the chargeable gain accruing on the disposal.

'Special withholding tax' means a withholding tax (however described) levied under the law of an EU member state territory outside the UK implementing *article 11* of the *EU Savings Directive*, or levied under a 'corresponding provision of international arrangements' in the case of a territory other than an EU member state (*TIOPA 2010, s 32*).

'Savings income', in the case of special withholding tax levied under the law of an EU member state, has the same meaning as 'interest payment' has for the purposes of the *EU Savings Directive*. If the tax is levied elsewhere, 'savings income' has the same meaning as the corresponding expression has for the purposes of the relevant international arrangements. To the extent that it cannot be set off, special withholding tax is repayable (*TIOPA 2010, s 135(2)*).

Relief by deduction

3.69   Relief for foreign tax may be given by deduction if no foreign tax credit relief is available, or the taxpayer elects to forgo any credit (as provided in *TIOPA 2010, s 27*). The effect of the election may be to create or increase an allowable loss. Where foreign tax is suffered on a gain that is the subject of a UK roll-over relief claim (see **Chapter 14**), no foreign tax credit relief is available because there is no UK liability, but relief by deduction reduces both the gain accruing and the amount to be deducted from the acquisition cost of the replacement asset as a result of the roll-over relief claim (*TIOPA 2010, s 113*).

Chapter 4

Particular assets

SIGNPOSTS

This chapter discusses particular types of asset to which special rules apply:

- **Shares and securities** – Identification rules for non-corporates, including employee shares and reorganisations (see **4.1–4.5**).

- **Options and deposits** – Including exercise and abandonment of options (see **4.6–4.9**).

- **Land** – Including part disposals, leases, compulsory purchase and exchange of joint interests in land (see **4.10–4.21**).

- **Furnished holiday lettings** – The various CGT reliefs applicable on the disposal of FHL properties (see **4.22–4.24**).

- **Chattels** – Including sets (see **4.25–4.26**).

- **Wasting assets** – The exemption and capital allowances (see **4.27–4.33**).

- **Finance arrangements** – Gains on debts are exempt, tax treatment of Islamic finance arrangements (see **4.34–4.35**).

- **Assets appropriated to and from trading stock** – Election available (see **4.36–4.38**).

- **Enveloped dwellings** – Annual charge, valuations, reliefs and the CGT charge (see **4.39–4.43**).

Various exemptions for certain assets, gains or persons are examined in **Chapter 1**. Reliefs for the main residence are examined in **Chapter 12**.

SHARES AND SECURITIES

4.1 The taxation of gains arising on the disposal of shares has been considerably simplified for disposals made after 5 April 2008 by individuals, trustees and personal representatives. The 'pooling' rules for identifying shares continue to apply for companies, and these are discussed in **Chapter 9**. For illustrations of how the identification rules applied to shares and securities disposed of by non-corporate taxpayers between 5 April 1998 and 6 April 2008, please refer to *Capital Gains Tax 2007/08* (Tottel Publishing).

'Securities' means shares or securities (ie loan capital) of a company and any other assets (eg units in a unit trust) that are dealt in without identifying the particular assets concerned. These are 'fungible' assets in that they all answer to the same definition; the separate components of a holding cannot be identified and distinguished from each other. This definition of 'securities' is separate from – and wider than – the definition in *TCGA 1992, s 132*, which determines whether loan capital is a chargeable asset (see **4.35**).

Shares or securities of a company are treated as being of the same class only if they are treated as such by a recognised stock exchange, or would be so treated if they were dealt in on a recognised stock exchange (*TCGA 1992, s 104(3)*).

Securities held by a person who acquired them as an employee (of any company) on terms that restrict his right to dispose of them are treated as being of a different class from other securities (*TCGA 1992, s 104(4)*), which do not have such restrictions. Shares with these restrictions are known as 'clogged shares' (HMRC Capital Gains Manual at CG50575).

Shares may be held in wrappers known as a depositary receipts (DRs) or American depositary receipts (ADRs). For capital gains purposes, the DR is looked through, and the shareholder is taxed as if he holds the underlying shares (see R&C Brief 14/12 and CG50240).

Share identification: general rules for CGT

4.2 The general rules that apply for CGT (not corporation tax) purposes are summarised below. These rules apply to disposals after 5 April 2008, when all assets held at 31 March 1982 are automatically rebased to their market value at that date (see **3.59**). All shares of the same company and class, held by the same person in the same capacity, are generally treated as a single pool of shares that expands or contracts with additions and disposals. This is known as the *TCGA 1992, section 104* pool or holding. The base cost of each share contained in the *section 104* pool is calculated as an average cost for the entire holding.

Special rules apply to shares acquired through:

- the enterprise management incentive scheme or other approved share option scheme (see **4.3**);

- the employee shareholder scheme where those shares are exempt from CGT (see **Chapter 17**);

- enterprise investment scheme (see **16.7**);
- seed enterprise investment scheme (see **16.37**); and
- venture capital trusts (see **16.45**).

'Shares' in the following summary includes securities that are within the definition of 'securities' set out in **4.1**. Shares disposed of are identified with shares of the same class acquired by the person making the disposal. The shares disposed of are identified with acquisitions in the following order:

(a) any shares acquired on the same day as the disposal (*TCGA 1992, ss 105(1)(b), 106A(9)*);

(b) any shares acquired in the period of 30 days after the disposal, taking earlier acquisitions first (*TCGA 1992, s 106A(5)*); and

(c) all other shares in the *section 104* pool which are not acquisitions under (a) or (b) (*TCGA 1992, s 106A(6)*).

With regard to (a), shares of the same class that are acquired (or disposed of) by the same person on the same day and in the same capacity are treated as acquired (or disposed of) in a single transaction. The 30-day rule in (b) was introduced in March 1998 to remove the tax advantage gained by 'bed and breakfasting' shares (see **10.12**) in order to realise losses or utilise the CGT annual exemption.

If there are more shares or securities disposed of than are identified using the rules in (a)–(c) above, the excess is identified with the acquisitions made after the disposal and after the 30-day rule in (b), taking earlier acquisitions in priority to later ones. This could happen where shares have been sold 'short', ie sold before they are acquired.

The date of disposal for share transactions will normally be clear from the broker's statement. In the case of a private sale, the principles discussed in **Chapter 2** should be referred to.

Example 4.1

Judith sold 500 ordinary shares in BBH Ltd on 1 December 2013 for £68,000 and had the following share history for ordinary shares in that company:

Date	Transaction	Holding	Cost
1 May 1998	bought	5,000	£5,000
1 September 2007	bought	500	£50,000
	Total:	5,500	£55,000

The 500 shares disposed of on 1 December 2013 are assumed to be 500/5,500 of the complete holding of her BBH shares, which collectively has a base cost of £55,000. The gain on the disposal of 500 shares is calculated as:

2013/14		£
Proceeds		68,000
Cost	(500 / 5,500) × £55,000	(5,000)
Taxable gain		63,000

To summarise, the *section 104* pool may contain shares of the same class from the same company from the following former share pools and holdings:

- the existing *section 104* pool from 6 April 2008;

- the old 1982 pool;

- shares acquired between 6 April 1998 to 5 April 2008 which were not previously pooled; and

- shares acquired prior to 6 April 1965.

EMI and approved share schemes

4.3   The taxpayer may elect for rule (a) in **4.2** to be modified, for acquisitions made after 5 April 2002, where shares are acquired under an approved employee share option scheme or an enterprise management incentive (EMI) scheme. The approved share scheme shares are then treated as a separate acquisition, and are treated as disposed of after the non-scheme shares. This election may be beneficial if the allowable expenditure relating to the scheme shares is higher than the average cost computed under the 'same day' rule (*TCGA 1992, ss 105(1)(a), 105A, 105B*). See **4.6** for discussion of EMI options.

Reorganisations and stock dividends

4.4   There are special rules to cater for reorganisations and stock dividends (*TCGA 1992, ss 127–131*). Broadly, shares issued on the occasion of a bonus or rights issue are treated as acquired at the same time as the original shares.

Where a company offers its shareholders a dividend in the form of additional shares (ie a stock or scrip dividend) as an alternative to cash, the new shares are treated as a free-standing acquisition – they are not related back to the time when the original shares were acquired (*TCGA 1992, s 142*).

Example 4.2

Duncan bought 500 shares in Anybank Plc for £5,000 on 17 May 2000. Anybank Plc announced a one-for-one rights issue of new ordinary shares at £1 each in May 2013. Duncan sold his rights when they were worth £600 and the original holding of 500 shares was worth £8,000:

2013/14	Total	Sold	Retained
	£	£	£
Proceeds of sale of rights	600	600	
Market value of shares retained	8,000		8,000
	8,600		
Cost allocated in proportion: (600 / 8,600) × £5,000	(5,000)	(349)	(4,651)
	3,600		
Gain on disposal of rights chargeable to CGT:		251	

Where company A is taken over or merges with company B, the shares of company A may be exchanged for new shares issued by company B. In this case, the new company B shares are treated as standing in the shoes of the old company A shares, such that there is no disposal for CGT purposes on the exchange of the company A shares (*TCGA 1992, s 135*). When the new company B shares are disposed of, the entire gain, as accrued from the acquisition of the company A shares, becomes taxable.

A similar treatment applies on a reorganisation of share capital, when shares in company A are exchanged for securities issued by company B. The exchange of shares for securities or debentures is not treated as a disposal for CGT (*TCGA 1992, s 136*).

For a detailed discussion of the reliefs under *TCGA 1992, ss 135–136*, refer to *Capital Gains Tax: Roll-over, Hold-over and Deferral Reliefs 2013/14* (Bloomsbury Professional).

Relevant securities

4.5   There is a further exception to the general pooling rule for relevant securities, which are:

- securities and loan stock identified by the accrued income scheme rules (*ITA 2007, Part 12, Ch 2*);

- qualifying corporate bonds (QCBs); and

- securities which are interests in a non-reporting fund, within the meaning of *Offshore Funds (Tax) (Amendment) Regulations 2011 (SI 2011/1211), reg 44(1), (4).*

These relevant securities are matched with other relevant securities of the same company, type and class acquired at a later time rather than at an earlier time (*TCGA 1992, s 106A(6)*).

OPTIONS AND DEPOSITS

4.6   An option is an offer to acquire, or dispose of, an asset, which is the subject of the option. It is made clear in *TCGA 1992, s 21* that options are also assets in their own right. When an option is granted the grantor has disposed of an asset (ie the option itself) and the person who acquired the option (the grantee) has acquired an asset. This applies even in the case where the option is abandoned. In many cases the grant of the option will be treated as part of a larger transaction (see below). The basic rules relating to the grant, exercise and abandonment of options are set out below (see CG12300–CG12399; *TCGA 1992, ss 144–148*).

So far as the person who granted the option is concerned, the time of the asset's disposal for CGT purposes is the time of the following disposal:

- if the option binds the grantor to sell, the disposal made in fulfilment of the grantor's obligations under the option; or

- if the option binds the grantor to buy, the disposal made to the grantor in consequence of the exercise of the option.

The date the option is exercised, a separate contract is made in relation to the asset under the option and the actual option is disposed of. The date of exercise of the option is thus the disposal date for the option.

For taper relief, the holding period for shares acquired by the exercise of options granted under an enterprise management incentive (EMI) scheme began on the date when the option was granted (*TCGA 1992, Sch 7D, para 15*). However, for entrepreneurs' relief, the holding period for shares acquired under EMI was set to begin when the option was exercised and the shares were acquired, not when the option was granted. This rule is amended by *FA 2013, Sch 24* for EMI options exercised from 6 April 2012, and within ten years of the date when the option was granted. In this case, the holding period for the purposes of entrepreneurs' relief includes the period when the option is held, as well as the period when the shares are held (*TCGA 1992, s 169I(7A), (7B)*).

To qualify for entrepreneurs' relief, the EMI option or shares acquired must be held for at least a year before the shares are disposed of (or the trade ceases), and that disposal date must fall on or after 6 April 2013. Shares acquired as replacements for EMI shares may also qualify for entrepreneurs' relief (see **Chapter 11**).

Focus

Shares acquired through qualifying EMI options held for a year and exercised on and after 6 April 2013 can qualify for entrepreneurs' relief, as the personal company condition (see **11.10**) is ignored, if the other conditions for that relief are met (*TCGA 1992, s 169I(7A)–(7R)*).

Exercise of an option

4.7   If an option is exercised, the grant of the option and the transaction taking place on its exercise are merged into a single transaction. Where the option binds the grantor (A) to sell, the consideration for the grant is added to the sale consideration in A's CGT computation. Where the option binds the grantor (A) to buy, the consideration received by A for that option is deducted from the cost of A's acquisition (*TCGA 1992, s 144(2)*).

Where the person (B) who is entitled to exercise an option does so, there is no disposal by him. The acquisition of the option and the transaction taking place on its exercise are treated as a single transaction. Where the option binds the grantor (A) to sell, the cost of acquiring the option forms part of B's allowable expenditure on acquisition of the asset. Where the option binds the grantor (A) to buy, the cost of the option is treated as a cost incidental to B's disposal to A (*TCGA 1992, s 144(2)*).

Abandonment of an option

4.8   The abandonment of an option by the person entitled to exercise it is not generally a disposal of an asset by him (*TCGA 1992, s 144(4)*). However, in the following situations the abandonment of the option is a disposal when the option is:

- a quoted option to subscribe for shares in a company, a traded option or financial option (these are options listed on a recognised stock exchange or recognised futures exchange); or

- an option to acquire assets to be used for trade purposes by the person who acquired them.

Forfeited deposits

4.9   Where a deposit of purchase money for a prospective purchase is forfeited because the transaction is abandoned, there is no disposal by the prospective purchaser and no capital loss can arise. The prospective seller, however, is treated as disposing of an option (*TCGA 1992, s 144(7)*).

LAND AND LEASES OF LAND

4.10   Land (including any building situated on it), or an interest in or right over land, is an asset for CGT purposes. However, in certain circumstances land transactions can give rise to a charge to income tax (or corporation tax) as trading or other income. This may apply where the land is acquired with the intention of selling it for profit, or holding it as trading stock, or developing it prior to disposal at a profit. See Chapter 7 of *Income Tax 2013/14* (Bloomsbury Professional) for a discussion of the relevant anti-avoidance provisions.

The legal owner of land will not always be the person who has the beneficial interest in it. In most cases, it is the beneficial owner who is chargeable to CGT. HMRC regard the following factors as indicative of beneficial ownership, although each case is considered on its particular facts:

- legal title (in the absence of any contrary evidence the legal owner will normally also be the beneficial owner);
- occupation of the land;
- receipt of any rental income from the land;
- provision of the funds used to purchase the land; and
- receipt of the sale proceeds from a disposal of the land (CG70230).

The case of *Y Lawson v HMRC* [2011] UKFTT 346 (TC) demonstrates how a couple can be judged to be joint beneficial owners of a property, even though only one of the couple may be named on the mortgage deed.

Part disposals of land

4.11   The special rules that apply to small part disposals of land are discussed in **2.5**. Where the conditions are satisfied, the taxpayer may claim that the part disposal does not constitute a disposal for CGT purposes. The disposal proceeds are instead deducted from the cost of the land when calculating a gain on its subsequent disposal.

The grant of a lease is a part disposal and the CGT treatment depends on the term of the lease (see **4.16**).

Leases of land

4.12　It is important to distinguish between the grant of a new lease by a landlord, and the assignment of an existing lease. A leasehold interest entitles the holder to exclusive possession of the property for a fixed term. For HMRC guidance on CGT arising from the grant, merger or disposal of leases, see CG70700–CG71400. A lease includes, for this purpose:

- an underlease, sublease, tenancy or licence;

- an agreement for a lease, underlease, sublease, tenancy or licence; and

- a corresponding interest in land outside the UK (*TCGA 1992, Sch 8, para 10(1)(a)*).

There are special rules to determine the duration of a lease for these purposes, for example, where the terms of the lease include a provision that either allows the landlord to terminate the lease before the end of the stated term, or allows the tenant to extend the term.

Any term of a lease that makes it unlikely that it will continue beyond a certain time – for example, a provision for an increase in rent to an amount greatly in excess of a commercial rent – is treated as granted for a period ending at that time (*TCGA 1992, Sch 8, para 8*).

Assignment of a lease

4.13　The assignment of a lease is treated as a disposal (not a part disposal) of an interest in the property. The calculations involved in such a disposal can be complex (see CG71100–CG71304).

The CGT treatment depends on how long the lease has to run at the time of the assignment:

- the assignment of a long lease is subject to the normal CGT rules; and

- the assignment of a short lease (ie one that has no more than 50 years to run at the time of the disposal) is a disposal of a 'wasting asset', and only a percentage of the original cost is allowable for CGT purposes, as set out below.

A lease does not become a wasting asset until its duration does not exceed 50 years. Once it has become a wasting asset, its value does not waste away at a uniform rate (as described in **4.27** in relation to other wasting assets). The rate of decline in the value of the lease increases towards the end of its term, and the allowable expenditure is restricted by reference to the formula in note 1 below using the percentages in the following depreciation table.

4.13 *Particular assets*

Leases which are wasting assets–depreciation table

(TCGA 1992, Sch 8, para 1)

Years	%	Monthly increment*	Years	%	Monthly increment*
50 or more	100	–	24	79.622	0.123
49	99.657	0.029	23	78.055	0.131
48	99.289	0.031	22	76.399	0.138
47	98.902	0.032	21	74.635	0.147
46	98.490	0.034	20	72.770	0.155
45	98.059	0.036	19	70.791	0.165
44	97.595	0.039	18	68.697	0.175
43	97.107	0.041	17	66.470	0.186
42	96.593	0.043	16	64.116	0.196
41	96.041	0.046	15	61.617	0.208
40	95.457	0.049	14	58.971	0.221
39	94.842	0.051	13	56.167	0.234
38	94.189	0.054	12	53.191	0.248
37	93.497	0.058	11	50.038	0.263
36	92.761	0.061	10	46.695	0.279
35	91.981	0.065	9	43.154	0.295
34	91.156	0.069	8	39.399	0.313
33	90.280	0.073	7	35.414	0.332
32	89.354	0.077	6	31.195	0.352
31	88.371	0.082	5	26.722	0.373
30	87.330	0.087	4	21.983	0.395
29	86.226	0.092	3	16.959	0.419
28	85.053	0.098	2	11.629	0.444
27	83.816	0.103	1	5.983	0.470
26	82.496	0.110	0	0	0.499
25	81.100	0.116			

Notes

(1)   **Formula:** Fraction of expenditure disallowed:

$$\frac{A - B}{A}$$

where:

- A is the percentage for duration of lease at acquisition or expenditure; and

- B is the percentage for the duration of the lease at disposal.

(2) *** Fraction of years:** Add one-twelfth of the difference between the percentage for the whole year and the next higher percentage for each additional month. Odd days under 14 are not counted; 14 odd days or more are rounded up to and treated as a month.

Exclusion from acquisition expenditure

4.14 A fraction of the acquisition expenditure (within *TCGA 1992, s 38(1)(a)*) that is equal to:

$$\frac{P(1) - P(3)}{P(1)}$$

is excluded, where:

- P(1) is the percentage shown in the table for the duration of the lease at the beginning of the period of ownership; and

- P(3) is the percentage shown in the table for the duration of the lease at the time of the disposal (*TCGA 1992, Sch 8, para 1(4)*).

- See example at CG71146.

Exclusion from enhancement expenditure

4.15 A fraction of the enhancement expenditure (within *TCGA 1992, s 38(1)(b)*) that is equal to:

$$\frac{P(2) - P(3)}{P(2)}$$

is excluded, where:

- P(2) is the percentage shown in the table for the duration of the lease at the time when the expenditure is first reflected in the nature of the lease; and

- P(3) is the percentage shown in the table for the duration of the lease at the time of the disposal (*TCGA 1992, Sch 8, para 1(4)*).

- See example at CG71148.

Grant of a lease

4.16 The owner of a freehold interest may grant a lease, or a leaseholder may grant a sublease for all or a part of the remaining term of his leasehold interest (see CG70800–CG70850).

The grant of a lease out of a freehold or longer lease is treated as an asset derived from another asset (see **3.46**), and a chargeable gain or loss will arise. Generally, a premium will be paid on the grant of a sublease, but in some cases no premium will be paid as the market rent fully compensates the landlord. In times of recession, the landlord may pay a tenant to take on the lease, a practice known as a 'reverse premium'.

Focus

Normally, a reverse premium will not be subject to CGT as it does not derive from an asset in the tenant's hands, but it may be taxable as part of the tenant's trade (CG70835).

The grant of a lease or sublease is a part disposal because the taxpayer retains an interest in the property. Part of the lease premium is chargeable to income tax as additional rent if the lease is for 50 years or less (see **4.18** and **4.19**). The part of the lease premium that is not treated as rent represents the proceeds of a part disposal for CGT purposes.

If a lease is granted to a connected person, or otherwise granted in a transaction not made at arm's length (see **3.6**), the market value is taken to be the premium received (*TCGA 1992, ss 17, 18*).

Grant of a long lease

4.17 Where a long lease is granted out of either a freehold interest or a long lease, the computation of the gain accruing follows the normal part disposal rules, using the formula [A/(A + B)] (*TCGA 1992, s 42*), as described in **2.4**. In this situation:

- A is the amount of the premium received; and

- B is the value of the interest retained by the landlord plus the value of the right to receive rents payable under the lease (*TCGA 1992, Sch 8, para 2; CG70952*).

Grant of a short lease out of freehold or long lease

4.18 Where a short lease is granted out of a freehold interest, or a short sublease is granted out of a long lease, the following rules apply.

First, part of the premium is treated as rent and is chargeable to:

- income tax under *ITTOIA 2005, s 276*; or

- corporation tax under *CTA 2009, s 217*.

This amount is excluded from the consideration for the disposal (*TCGA 1992, Sch 8, para 5(1)*). It is calculated using the formula set out in the relevant income tax or corporation tax provision.

Secondly, the [A/(A+B)] part disposal formula in **4.17** is modified so that:

- A in the numerator is not the whole of the premium received but only the part of it that is not treated as rent, but

- A in the denominator (A + B) is unchanged, because (A + B) has to represent the value of the whole interest before the lease was granted (*TCGA 1992, s 42(2)*; CG70962).

Grant of a short sublease out of a short lease

4.19   Where a short sublease is granted out of a short lease, the part disposal formula in *TCGA 1992, s 42* does not apply. A short lease is a wasting asset, and the allowable expenditure to be set against the premium in computing the gain is restricted so as to allow, as a deduction, the expenditure that will waste away during the term of the sublease (*TCGA 1992, Sch 8, para 4*).

The amount of the premium that is treated as rent is, in this case, deducted in arriving at the chargeable gain. It is not excluded from the consideration for the disposal (as shown in **4.18**) (*TCGA 1992, Sch 8, para 5(2)*; CG71004).

Compulsory purchase of land

4.20   Where land is purchased by or on behalf of an authority that has compulsory purchase powers, and the proceeds are reinvested in acquiring new land, a form of CGT roll-over relief may be available under *TCGA 1992, s 247*. The taxpayer – who may be an individual, trustee or company – may claim to defer the gain by setting it against allowable expenditure on replacement land acquired within one year before and three years after the disposal.

This relief operates in a broadly similar manner to roll-over relief for replacement of business assets (see **Chapter 14**). However, the roll-over relief is restricted where the original proceeds are only partly reinvested. Relief will also be denied where:

- the landowner advertised the land for sale, or otherwise indicated a willingness to sell; or

- the replacement property attracts main residence relief (see **Chapter 12**) within six years following its acquisition.

Focus

- The land does not have to be acquired by the authority under a compulsory purchase order.

- It may be acquired by a third party under contract to the authority, if that authority retains compulsory purchase powers.

This point was argued by the taxpayer in *Abdul Ahad v Commissioners for HMRC* [2009] UKFTT 353 (TC). However, Ahad failed to show that the Commissioner for New Towns in Milton Keynes did have compulsory purchase powers to acquire the land in question, so the taxpayer lost the case.

For further discussion of this relief, see *Capital Gains Tax: Roll-over, Hold-over and Deferral Reliefs 2013/14* (Bloomsbury Professional).

Example 4.3

David owns freehold land with an agreed 31 March 1982 value of £98,000. Part of the land is made the subject of a compulsory purchase order, and compensation of £70,000 is agreed on 10 August 2013. The market value of the remaining land is £175,000. The chargeable gain accruing on the disposal is £42,000, computed as shown below. David acquires new land for £80,000 in December 2012, and claims roll-over relief:

2013/14	£	£
Disposal consideration August 2013		70,000
Market value in March 1982:		
£98,000 × [70,000 / (70,000 + 175,000)]		(28,000)
Chargeable gain		42,000
Consideration for disposal		70,000
Allowable cost of land compulsorily purchased	28,000	
Deemed consideration for disposal		(28,000)
Roll-over relief		42,000
Allowable cost of replacement land £80,000 – £42,000		38,000

Exchange of joint interests in land

4.21   Relief is given on similar lines to the relief described in **4.20** where there is an exchange of interests in land that is in joint ownership (*TCGA 1992, ss 248A–248E*). The relief is available where:

- a holding of land is held jointly and, as a result of the exchange, each joint owner becomes the sole owner of part of the land formerly owned jointly; or

- a number of separate holdings of land are held jointly and, as a result of the exchange, each joint owner becomes the sole owner of one or more holdings.

There are no restrictions on the use of the land, either before or after the exchange. However, the relief is denied or restricted where land acquired on the exchange is, or becomes subsequently, a dwelling house (or part of a dwelling house) eligible for the main residence relief within *TCGA 1992, ss 222–223* within six years of the date of the exchange (*TCGA 1992, s 248C*). See **Chapter 12** for a detailed discussion of the main residence relief.

However, the relief may be claimed where, as a result of the exchange, individuals who were joint beneficial owners of two or more main residences become sole owners of just one home each, providing that any gain accruing on a disposal of each dwelling house immediately after the exchange would be exempt by virtue of main residence relief (*TCGA 1992, s 248E*). For further discussion of this relief, see *Capital Gains Tax: Roll-over, Hold-over and Deferral Reliefs 2013/14* (Bloomsbury Professional).

FURNISHED HOLIDAY LETTINGS

4.22   Letting property is not regarded as a trade for income tax purposes, so property used for a letting business does not qualify for the various capital gains and inheritance tax reliefs that apply to business assets that are used for a trade. However, from 6 April 1984 the 'commercial letting of furnished holiday accommodation' in the UK has been treated as a trade (*TCGA 1992, s 241*). This allows a number of special tax reliefs to apply (see **4.23**). *FA 2011, Sch 14* amended the tax treatment of commercial furnished holiday lettings (FHL) as follows:

- property situated in other EEA countries can qualify for FHL, with retrospective effect, but profits/losses from a UK holiday lettings business cannot be offset against profits/losses from FHL properties based in other EEA countries;

- from 6 April 2011 (or 1 April for companies), losses from the FHL businesses can only be set against other FHL profits, not against other income (sideways relief) or even against property letting profits which are not from an FHL;

- from April 2012, each property must be available for letting to the public for 210 (previously 140) days per year; and

- each property must be actually let to the public for 105 (previously 70) days in a year. If this actual letting requirement is not met, a period of grace election can be made to allow a property to continue to qualify as FHL for up to two years. The days let can also be averaged across the FHL properties held by the same person, so every property is deemed to qualify.

For a discussion of the qualifying conditions for FHL properties, see Chapter 7 of *Income Tax 2013/14* (Bloomsbury Professional).

Focus

Where the FHL business becomes an ordinary lettings business (because, for instance, the FHL letting conditions are not met), the FHL business is treated as ceasing.

If the property ceases to qualify as FHL, the owner may wish to dispose of it quickly, to take advantage of one or more of the CGT reliefs (see **4.23**).

The CGT reliefs

4.23   A property business that consists of FHL properties is treated as a trade, and all such lettings made by a particular person (or partnership or body of persons) are treated as one trade, for all of the following purposes:

(a)   roll-over relief on replacement of business assets (*TCGA 1992, s 152*);

(b)   hold-over relief for gifts of business assets (*TCGA 1992, s 165*);

(c)   relief for loans to traders (*TCGA 1992, s 253*);

(d)   entrepreneurs' relief (*TCGA 1992, ss 169H–169S*); and

(e)   the substantial shareholdings exemption for companies (*TCGA 1992, Sch 7AC*).

As long as the FHL conditions are met for the tax year, or accounting period for a company, the accommodation is taken to be used only for the purposes of the lettings trade in that tax year. This applies even if the accommodation is let out of season for longer than the prescribed 31 days to one tenant (CG73503).

However, if the property is neither let commercially nor available to be so let for a part of the period, and it is not prevented from being so let by construction or repair work, the trade is not treated as carried on during that part of the period (*TCGA 1992, s 241(3)–(5)*).

A 'just and reasonable' apportionment is to be made where accommodation is let and only a part of it is holiday accommodation (*TCGA 1992, s 241(7)*).

Where roll-over relief is obtained on a disposal under *TCGA 1992, s 152*, and the main residence relief is available on a disposal of the replacement asset, the gain eligible for main residence relief is reduced by the amount of the reduction in allowable expenditure to take account of the roll-over relief claim. The effect is that the main residence relief is restricted to the part of the gain that exceeds the amount of the earlier gain that was rolled over (*TCGA 1992, s 241(6)*; CG61452).

Application of entrepreneurs' relief

4.24   Entrepreneurs' relief can be claimed when the gain arises from the disposal of the whole or part of a business (see **11.3**), and the other ownership conditions are met. When the FHL business consists of just one property that is sold, clearly the FHL business has ceased and the whole business has been disposed of. Where the FHL business contains several let properties and only some of the properties are disposed of, HMRC are reluctant to accept there has been a disposal of part of the business (see **11.22**), so entrepreneurs' relief may not apply.

The FHL business may cease trading, or cease qualifying as FHL, so effectively become an ordinary letting business, some months before the disposal of the property. Entrepreneurs' relief can be claimed where the assets are disposed of up to three years after the date an unincorporated business has ceased trading (see **11.27**). As long as the property was used for the FHL business at the date the FHL business ceased it should qualify for entrepreneurs' relief (see **11.30**). There is no restriction on the relief if the properties are used for some other purpose between the cessation of the FHL business and the sale, for example if the properties are let but do not qualify for FHL (see **11.31**).

The conditions for claiming entrepreneurs' relief after the disposal of a partnership business are more restrictive than those that apply after the cessation and disposal of a sole-trader business (see **11.33–11.38**). Although the FHL properties may be owned in joint names, this does not mean that HMRC will consider that a partnership existed. In their Property Income Manual they advise: 'Jointly letting does not, of itself, make the activity a partnership' (PIM1030). Where the owners provide significant additional services to the FHL customers, a partnership may exist. A claim for entrepreneurs' relief may be more easily established if the FHL business is not judged to be a partnership.

Example 4.4

Three brothers jointly purchased a property in 2002 and let it initially on an assured shorthold tenancy. The property was then let as FHL from 1 January 2005 to 31 December 2012. The property remained empty until it was sold on 30 June 2013 realising a gain of £270,000. Does entrepreneurs' relief apply to the gain made in June 2013 and does the gain need to be apportioned before the relief is applied?

The brothers had an FHL business from 2005 to 2012, but this business will not be considered to be a partnership, based on the HMRC guidance in PIM1030. The property was disposed of within three years of the cessation of the FHL business, so entrepreneurs' relief will apply to the gain assessed on each brother. Assuming they held equal shares in the property, each brother will be taxed on £90,000 of gain before deduction of their annual exemptions.

As the FHL business was not a partnership, the disposal of the property is not an associated disposal, and the gain does not have to be time-apportioned for the period when the property was not used for the FHL business.

CHATTELS

4.25   An asset is a chattel if it is tangible, moveable property, ie a physical object that is not permanently attached to land or a building and can be moved easily without damaging its surroundings. Examples would include paintings and small items of plant and machinery.

A gain accruing on the disposal of a chattel that is not a wasting asset (see **4.27**) is not a chargeable gain if the amount or value of the consideration is £6,000 or less (*TCGA 1992, s 262(1)*).

Where the consideration exceeds £6,000, a marginal relief is deducted in arriving at the chargeable gain. The chargeable gain is restricted to five-thirds of the amount by which the consideration exceeds £6,000 (*TCGA 1992, s 262(2)*).

If a loss accrues on the disposal and the consideration does not exceed £6,000, the allowable loss is restricted by substituting £6,000 for the actual consideration. There is no such restriction if the consideration exceeds £6,000 (*TCGA 1992, s 262(3)*).

The chattels exemption does not apply to disposals of currency of any description, or disposals of commodities dealt with on a terminal market (*TCGA 1992, s 262(6)*).

Example 4.5

Hannah sells an Olympic torch for £7,215 in July 2012 which she acquired for £215. The gain accruing, before deduction of the chattels exemption, is £7,000. Marginal relief is available, so that the chargeable gain is restricted to 5/3 × (£7,215 – £6,000) = £2,025.

Parts of a set

4.26   Anti-avoidance rules prevent the taxpayer splitting a set of articles worth more than £6,000 into individual assets and selling them for less than £6,000 in order to secure the chattel exemption.

They apply where the taxpayer has disposed of two or more assets that have formed part of a set of articles, all of which he has owned at one time, and the disposals were made (either on the same occasion or on different occasions) to:

(a)   the same person;

(b)   persons acting 'in concert' (see below); or

(c)   persons who are connected persons (see **3.16**).

In these circumstances, the transactions are treated as a single transaction disposing of a single asset. The chattels exemption, as described in **4.25**, is applied to the deemed single transaction and apportioned accordingly among the various assets (*TCGA 1992, s 262(4)*).

HMRC take the view that a number of articles will form a set only if they are essentially similar and complementary, and their value taken together is greater than their total individual value (CG76632).

With regard to (b) above, HMRC consider that, if persons not connected with each other acquire assets forming part of a set, the fact that they have done so is not sufficient. There must be evidence that they have previously agreed to act together to acquire the assets, such as a number of dealers acting together at an auction (CG76631).

WASTING ASSETS

Exemption for wasting chattels

4.27   As a general rule, no chargeable gain accrues on a disposal of a 'wasting chattel', ie an asset that is both tangible moveable property (see **4.25**) and a wasting asset (see **4.28**). Where an asset has been used for business purposes and has qualified for capital allowances, the gain may be taxable if the disposal consideration was more than £6,000; see **4.29** (*TCGA 1992, s 45(1)*).

Wasting asset: definition

4.28   A 'wasting asset' is generally an asset with a predictable life of no more than 50 years, as determined at the time the asset was acquired (CG76700). In the case of tangible moveable property, 'life' means useful life having regard to the taxpayer's purpose in acquiring or providing the asset. Freehold land is never a wasting asset, irrespective of the nature of the land itself or the buildings on it.

Plant and machinery is always regarded as having a predictable life of less than 50 years. It is assumed, in estimating its predictable life, that:

- the asset's life will end when it is finally put out of use as being unfit for further use; and

- the asset will be used in the normal manner and to the normal extent throughout its estimated life.

A life interest in settled property is not regarded as a wasting asset until the predicted life expectancy of the life tenant is 50 years or less. The HMRC Policy Business (Life Assurance) department will provide an estimate of the predictable life of such life interests (*TCGA 1992, s 44*; CG38022).

Wasting assets qualifying for capital allowances

4.29   All items of plant and machinery are wasting assets, but unless the item is also a chattel the wasting chattels exemption (see **4.27**) does not apply. However, the allowable expenditure deducted in the CGT computation may be restricted (see **4.30**) if the taxpayer:

(a)   claimed capital allowances for the cost of the asset, which is also the base cost in the CGT computation (see **3.55**); or

(b)   incurred any expenditure on the asset (or interest in it) that has otherwise qualified in full for capital allowances (*TCGA 1992, s 45(2)*).

Separate CGT computations are required where:

- the taxpayer has used the asset partly for the purposes of the business and partly for other purposes;

- he has used it for business purposes for only part of the period of ownership; or

●   the asset has qualified in part only for capital allowances.

In these circumstances, both the consideration for the disposal and the allowable expenditure are apportioned by reference to the extent to which the expenditure qualified for capital allowances, and the exemption is not given for the part of the gain apportioned to the use or expenditure described in (a) or (b) above (*TCGA 1992, s 45(3)*).

The exemption does not apply to a disposal of commodities that is made by a person dealing on a terminal market (*TCGA 1992, s 45(4)*).

Example 4.6

Victor bought an aircraft on 31 May 2003 at a cost of £90,000 for use in his air charter business. It has been agreed that Victor's non-business use of the aircraft amounts to 1/10th, on a flying hours basis, and capital allowances and running costs have accordingly been restricted for income tax purposes.

On 1 June 2013, Victor sells the aircraft for £185,000. The aircraft is agreed as having a useful life of 20 years at the date it was acquired. Only the business use part of the gain arising on the disposal of the aircraft is taxable:

2013/14	£
Relevant portion of consideration 9/10 × £185,000	166,500
Relevant portion of expenditure 9/10 × £90,000	(81,000)
Taxable gain	85,500

Restriction of allowable expenditure

4.30   The gain accruing on the disposal of a wasting asset that is not exempt (see **4.27**) is computed on the assumption that an equal amount of expenditure on the asset is written off every day. This restriction does not apply, however, to certain wasting assets qualifying for capital allowances (see **4.34**).

Acquisition costs

4.31   The asset's residual or scrap value is deducted from the amount of expenditure incurred on its acquisition (including incidental costs) and the balance remaining is written off – from its full cost down to nil – at a uniform rate from the time of the acquisition of the asset to the end of its life. The residual or scrap value in this calculation is adjusted for any enhancement expenditure (see below) that increases that value.

This writing down of the allowable expenditure is achieved by excluding from the acquisition costs the fraction:

$$\frac{T(1)}{L}$$

where:

- L is the predictable life of the asset at the time when it was acquired or provided by the person making the disposal; and

- T(1) is the period from that time to the time of disposal (*TCGA 1992, s 46(2)(a)*).

Enhancement costs

4.32 Enhancement expenditure is written off, in the same way, from the time when it is first reflected in the asset's state or nature to the end of the asset's life (*TCGA 1992, s 46(1), (3)*).

The allowable expenditure to be excluded from the enhancement costs is given by the fraction:

$$\frac{T(2)}{L - [T(1) - T(2)]}$$

where

- L is the predictable life of the asset at the time when it was acquired or provided by the person making the disposal; and

- T(1) is the period from that time to the time of disposal (*TCGA 1992, s 46(2)(a)*).

- T(2) is the period from the time when the enhancement expenditure is first reflected in the state or nature of the asset to the time of disposal (*TCGA 1992, s 46(2)(b)*).

Residual or scrap value

4.33 The 'residual or scrap value' of a wasting asset is the value that the asset is predicted to have at the end of its predictable life. Where the nature of an asset does not determine immediately its predictable life and its residual or scrap value, such questions are determined on the basis of facts that were known or ascertainable at the time when the person making the disposal acquired or provided the asset (*TCGA 1992, s 44(2), (3)*).

FINANCE ARRANGEMENTS

Debts

4.34   A debt is an asset for CGT purposes. However, where a person (A) incurs a debt to another person (B), no chargeable gain accrues to the original creditor (B) on a disposal of the debt. A gain may arise, however, where the disposal is of a debt on a security (*TCGA 1992, ss 21(1), 251*).

For individuals, trustees and personal representatives, a debt is, therefore, not normally subject to CGT unless it is a 'debt on a security' (meaning, broadly, marketable loan stock). See *Taylor Clark International Ltd v Lewis* [1998] STC 1259 for a full definition of a debt on a security. Most loan stock is a type of 'qualifying corporate bond' (QCB), which is an exempt asset (*TCGA 1992, s 115*).

Gains on simple debts (which are not debts on securities) are exempt from CGT, and no relief is available for losses. However, capital loss relief is available for losses incurred (or guarantee payments made) in respect of loans made after 11 April 1978 to UK traders, where the loan has become irrecoverable and certain conditions are met. This relief is discussed at **17.09**.

Profits and losses on loans by companies are generally dealt with under the 'loan relationship' rules. Corporate debt is, therefore, outside the scope of corporation tax on chargeable gains but is otherwise included in the calculation of profits chargeable to corporation tax. Refer to Chapter 15 of *Corporation Tax 2013/14* (Bloomsbury Professional) for a discussion of the loan relationship rules.

Islamic finance arrangements

4.35   'Alternative finance arrangements' is the term used in *TCGA 1992, Pt IV, Ch IV*, which defines the tax treatment for specific types of Islamic finance arrangements that generally avoid the payment or receipt of interest. Under many of these arrangements, an asset is sold from one party to another, and the return on the deal is taxed as if it were interest rather than a capital gain.

The following Islamic finance structures are defined, and the tax treatment applies from 2010/11 or from 1 April 2010 for corporation tax purposes:

- purchase and resale known as *Murabahah* (*TCGA 1992, s 151J*);
- deposit arrangements known as *Modaraba* (*TCGA 1992, s 151I*);
- profit-share agency known as *Wakala* (*TCGA 1992, s 151M*);
- diminishing share ownership also known as a diminishing *Musharaka*,

which is specifically not treated as a partnership for CGT purposes (*TCGA 1992, ss 151K, 151Y*); and

- investment bond arrangements known as *Sukak*, which are treated as securities for CGT purposes but are not unit trust schemes or offshore funds (*TCGA 1992, s 151N*).

ASSETS APPROPRIATED TO OR FROM TRADING STOCK

Assets appropriated to trading stock

4.36   If the taxpayer appropriates a valuable asset that he has owned personally into his business where it is categorised as a stock item, then, in the absence of any election (see **4.37**), he is treated as if, at the time of the appropriation, he sold the asset for its market value. This is the case, provided that a chargeable gain or allowable loss would have accrued on an actual sale at market value (*TCGA 1992, s 161(1)*). Note that entrepreneurs' relief will not apply on such a deemed disposal, as it will not be a qualifying business disposal (*TCGA 1992, s 169H(2)*).

Election

4.37   This deemed disposal rule does not apply where the asset is appropriated for the purposes of a trade carried on wholly or partly in the UK, the income of which is chargeable to income tax or corporation tax, and the taxpayer makes an election (*TCGA 1992, s 161(3)*).

The effect of the election is that the asset's market value at the time of the appropriation is treated as reduced, in computing the trading income, by the amount of the chargeable gain that would have accrued on the deemed sale mentioned in **4.36**. If an allowable loss would have arisen, the market value is increased by the amount of that loss. An election made by a person carrying on a trade in partnership at the time of the appropriation is effective only if the other partners concur in the election (*TCGA 1992, s 161(3), (4)*).

The election must be made by the first anniversary of 31 January following the tax year in which the accounting period ended that contained the appropriation to stock. For corporation tax purposes, the election must be made within two years after the end of the accounting period in which the appropriation took place (*TCGA 1992, s 161(3A)*).

Note this election apparently works independently of the requirement to value the stock item within the trade as if it had been acquired at market value (*ITTOIA 2005, s 172C* for income tax; *CTA 2009, s 158* for corporation tax). The combination of the capital gains and the income tax/corporation tax provisions could wipe out all the taxable profit on an item of stock.

> **Example 4.7**
>
> Trulove purchased an antique desk for his personal use some years ago for £600. In May 2013, he transfers the desk into his own business (Trulove Antiques) to sell at the market value of £1,600. The gain in Trulove's hands is £1,000; but, as he has a number of other gains arising in 2013/14, he makes an election under *TCGA 1992, s 161(3)* to transfer the desk at a value of £600, reducing his taxable gain to nil. Trulove Antiques immediately sells the desk for £1,600. However, *ITTOIA 2005, s 172C* requires the desk to be valued at its market value of £1,600 as it enters the business, so the taxable profit on the sale of the desk is nil.

Assets appropriated from trading stock

4.38   If the taxpayer appropriates for another purpose an asset forming part of his trading stock, or he retains the asset on the cessation of his trade, he is treated as having acquired it at that time for a consideration equal to the amount brought into the accounts as a trading receipt (*TCGA 1992, s 161(2)*). The provisions in *ITTOIA 2005, s 172B* and *CTA 2009, s 157* require the amount brought into the accounts to be the open market value of the item, where the stock is appropriated on or after 12 March 2008.

ENVELOPED DWELLINGS

What is charged?

4.39   An enveloped dwelling is an interest in a single residential property located in the UK, owned by a non-natural person, which includes companies, collective investment schemes and partnerships with corporate members. Such structures have been used in the past to avoid stamp duty land tax (SDLT) and capital gains on the transfer of the residential property.

To discourage such tax avoidance, the government introduced three measures which all apply to enveloped dwellings with a value exceeding £2 million:

- SDLT on purchase at 7%, or 15% where the purchase is a non-natural person;
- annual tax on enveloped dwellings (ATED); and
- CGT charge on disposal.

The definition of the enveloped dwelling, the interest in the dwelling, the reliefs and exemptions are the same for all three charges. Thus, where a dwelling is subject to the ATED from 1 April 2013, part or all of the gain on disposal of that dwelling occurring on or after 6 April 2013 will be subject to the CGT charge on ATED-related gains, known as the 'CGTED' (see **4.43**).

Focus

Any tax planning concerning the ATED and associated CGTED should consider all other relevant taxes including SDLT, IHT, pre-owned assets tax, benefit-in-kind charges, offshore trust and close company imputation rules, and the transfer of assets code.

Annual tax on enveloped dwellings

4.40   The annual tax on enveloped dwellings (ATED) is based on the capital value of the property at the valuation date. Its structure is similar to the locally assessed council tax, paid by all home owners in the UK. However, the ATED is administered by HMRC centrally and is charged in addition to any council tax due for the property. The ATED rules are contained in *FA 2013, ss 94–174* and *Schs 25* and *33–35*. Basic guidance on the ATED is given on the HMRC website at www.hmrc.gov.uk/ated/index.htm.

The ATED has effect for properties under the ownership of a non-natural person on or after 1 April 2013, ie if the dwelling is owned, acquired, built or converted from a non-residential property from that date.

The ATED payable for 2013/14 for a single dwelling is shown in Table 4.1. The ATED rates will be increased according to the consumer prices index (CPI) each year, but the property bands will not be changed, so more properties will be drawn into the ATED net as property values rise.

Table 4.1	
Taxable value of property on relevant day	Annual charge for 2013/14
Up to £2,000,000	£Nil
£2,000,001–£5,000,000	£15,000
£5,000,001–£10,000,000	£35,000
£10,000,001–£20,000,000	£70,000
Over £20,000,000	£140,000

The ATED applies by the day, but it is paid annually (see below). If the taxpayer holds the property interest for only part of the chargeable period, as it was acquired part way through the year or a relief applies for part of the year (see **4.42**), the ATED is charged pro rata for the chargeable part of the year. The chargeable periods run for 12 months commencing 1 April each year.

For the first chargeable period to 31 March 2014, the ATED returns must be made by 1 October 2013, and payments made by 31 October 2013 (*FA 2013, Sch 35, Pt 2*). However, for subsequent chargeable periods, the ATED return and payment are both due by 30 April within the year. Where a dwelling first falls within ATED, returns and payments are due within 30 days from the purchase date, or 90 days if the dwelling is newly built (*FA 2013, ss 159–161, 163*).

As the ATED payment date falls close to the beginning of the chargeable period, in practice the ATED will be paid for the full year on that date. If there is an ownership change or the application of a relief in a later part of the year, a repayment of the charge can be made to the taxpayer.

Valuation issues

4.41   The value of a property interest for ATED purposes is generally its market value on 1 April 2012 (or when acquired, if later). For a new property, or an existing property which has been altered to be a dwelling, the valuation date is broadly the date of entry on the council tax valuation lists (or Northern Ireland valuation list) – or when it is first occupied, if earlier.

The value of the property only needs to be accurate enough to place the property within one of the bandings set-out in **4.40**. Where the property value is considered to be within 10% of one of the band boundaries, eg within £1.8 million to £2.2 million for the first band, the taxpayer can ask HMRC for a pre-return banding check (PRBC), see: www.hmrc.gov.uk/ated/pre-return-banding-checks.htm. HMRC will confirm, or reject, the banding proposed by the taxpayer, but they will not provide a specific valuation of the property. The PRBC cannot be used to establish the base value of the property at April 2013 for the gains assessed for the CGT charge on ATED-related gains (CGTED).

The initial banding will be used for up to five ATED return periods. Thus, all properties within the ATED will need to be revalued on 1 April 2017, to assess the banding to be used for the five ATED return periods starting on 1 April 2018.

Focus

Where the property owner is a partnership that includes a corporate member, the ATED applies to the whole value of the property, irrespective of the size of the corporate partner's interest in the property. This does not apply for the CGTED (see **4.43**).

Reliefs from ATED

4.42   Reliefs from ATED are provided for in *FA 2013, ss 132–155*. These include dwellings which are:

- let to an unconnected third party on a commercial basis and are not occupied by anyone connected with the owner;

- held by property development companies or as trading stock;

- used for charitable purposes;

- open to the public for at least 28 days a year;

- classified as farmhouses and occupied by qualifying farm workers;

- used for the employees of the company where the employee does not have an interest of more than 5% in the owning company.

Where a relief applies, the taxpayer must claim that relief by submitting an ATED return.

CGT charge on ATED-related gains (CGTED)

4.43   Where a property is subject to the ATED, and it is disposed of on or after 6 April 2013, the ATED-related gain will be subject to a CGT charge (known as the 'CGTED') set at 28%. The rules for this new CGT charge are introduced by *FA 2013, s 65* and *Sch 25*.

The ATED-related gain accrues from 6 April 2013 onwards. Any gain or loss accruing for an earlier period of ownership is subject to corporation tax or CGT in the usual way. An ATED-related loss can only be set against an ATED-related gain in the same or later tax year. If the property originally cost more than £2 million, but it is sold for less than that value, it is treated as being sold for £2 million for the purposes of the CGTED, to restrict the loss.

Any period for which the ATED is not due post 1 April 2013 because a relief applies, or the property was worth less than £2 million at the valuation date, will reduce the ATED-related gain.

Anti-fragmentation rules apply so that, if the whole property is worth over £2 million, but only a part is sold, the CGTED will apply to each individual part that is sold.

Where the property owner is a UK company within the charge to UK corporation tax, the CGTED (rather than corporation tax) applies to the ATED-related gain. Certain persons are excluded from the CGTED, such as individuals, trustees and PRs who are members of the partnership which holds the enveloped property.

In a partnership which includes corporate and individual members, the CGTED will only apply to the corporate partner's interest in such a partnership, measured in the normal way using the capital profit-sharing ratio. However, to judge whether the £2 million threshold is passed, the full value of the property is considered, and not just the corporate partner's interest.

A taper relief applies to ATED-related gains between £2 million and £3.2 million. Taxpayers can choose to pay the CGTED on the actual gain or on the 5/3rds of the proceeds which exceed £2 million.

Focus

Where the property is held by a company entirely, the CGTED may be avoided by selling the company rather than selling the property.

Chapter 5

Foreign issues

SIGNPOSTS

- **Territorial limits** – The location of assets, domicile and residence of the taxpayer determine whether and to what extent a taxpayer is liable for CGT (see **5.1–5.2**).

- **New tax charge on high-value UK residential properties** – Residential properties valued above £2m and owned by non-natural persons will be subject to a new annual tax charge and new CGT charges (see **5.3–5.4**).

- **Territorial limits of CGT – residence** – For residence issues up to 5 April 2013, the interpretation of 'resident' and 'ordinarily resident', which is mainly based on decisions in the courts and HMRC's interpretation of the case law, will be relevant. This has been replaced by a statutory residence test as of 6 April 2013 (see **5.5–5.6**).

- **Territorial limits to CGT – domicile** – The definition of 'domicile' is based on the general law, and a good understanding of case law is required. Domicile remains a key factor to determine a person's liability to CGT (see **5.7–5.11**).

- **Residence – the pre-6 April 2013 rules** – These rules will prevail for residence issues relating to the period to 6 April 2013. Under ESC D2, HMRC will apply split-year treatment for the year of arrival and departure, unless the taxpayer entered into an arrangement to use ESC D2 for tax avoidance. If someone comes to the UK as a student but remains in the UK for less than four years, he will be resident but not ordinarily resident in the UK (see **5.12–5.20**).

- **Residence – the new statutory residence test** – These rules apply from 6 April 2013 and introduce the 'automatic overseas' test, the 'automatic UK' test and the 'sufficient ties' test (see **5.21–5.23**).

- **Visiting armed forces and diplomatic and European Union staff** – Special rules apply, making such individuals exempt from CGT (see **5.24–5.25**).

- **Non-residents doing business in the UK** – Non-resident individuals and businesses are charged to CGT in certain circumstances (see **5.28–5.32**).

- **Anti-avoidance – temporary non-residence** – Anti-avoidance legislation was introduced in *TCGA 1992, s 10A* to tax individuals who realise capital gains during a period of temporary absence from the UK (see **5.33–5.36**).

- **Foreign assets of non-UK domiciled individuals** – Following *FA 2008*, non-UK domiciled individuals may be charged to offshore gains unless the remittance basis applies (see **5.37–5.50**).

- **Penalty regime in *FA 2010, Sch 10*** – Three penalty levels, depending on the territories where the gain arises, have been introduced to strengthen the existing penalty regime (see **5.61**).

This chapter focuses on the CGT implications of an individual's residence and domicile status. The residence status of trustees is examined in **Chapter 8**. For companies, see **Chapter 9** and *Corporation Tax 2013/14* (Bloomsbury Professional).

This chapter only sets out an initial guide to foreign issues. For a more detailed analysis on the treatment of foreign income and gains, see *Booth & Schwarz: Residence, Domicile and UK Taxation*, 17th edition (Bloomsbury Professional).

Finance Act 2013 introduced a new statutory test of residence in the UK and has abolished the test for 'ordinary residence' from 6 April 2013. Transitional rules apply.

Finance Act 2013 also introduced two new forms of tax payable by persons who use UK or offshore intermediary structures to hold residential property valued at over £2 million:

- a new annual tax on enveloped dwellings (ATED) applies to high-value residential properties owned by non-natural persons (see **5.3**); and

- CGT will apply to corporate entities that are also liable to the ATED, subject to certain exemptions (see **5.4**).

BASIS OF THE CHARGE TO CGT

5.1   A person is chargeable to CGT in respect of chargeable gains accruing to him on the disposal of assets in a tax year:

- during any part of which he is 'resident' in the UK; or

- during which he is 'ordinarily resident' in the UK (*TCGA 1992, ss 1, 2(1)*).

'Accruing' here means realised or deemed to be realised, rather than accumulated over a period.

5.2 *Foreign issues*

Where an individual is not domiciled in the UK but resident or ordinarily resident in the UK, the remittance basis applies for CGT (see **5.37**).

Anti-avoidance rules provide for a person to be chargeable to CGT on gains accruing to others in certain circumstances. For example:

- a non-resident person carrying on a business in the UK through a branch or agency (or through a permanent establishment, in the case of a company) is chargeable to CGT (or corporation tax) on gains arising from assets in the UK that are used for the purposes of the business (see **5.28**);

- a person who is a 'temporary non-resident' of the UK may be chargeable on gains accruing during years of non-residence (see **5.22**); and

- the gains of a non-resident trust (see **8.44**) or company (see **5.51**) may be attributed to a UK-resident individual.

LOCATION OF ASSETS

5.2 It is often unnecessary to establish the location of an asset for CGT purposes, but in some circumstances the asset's location will determine the extent of any liability. For example:

- non-residents are chargeable to tax on gains arising on the disposal or deemed disposal of UK assets used to carry on a business in the UK (see **5.28**); and

- a remittance basis applies to non-domiciled individuals, but only in relation to non-UK assets (see **5.33**).

The territorial limits of the UK are set out in **5.3**. Most of the rules fixing the location of assets for CGT purposes are contained in *TCGA 1992, s 275* and the main rules are summarised briefly in Table 5.1. Note also the changes enacted in *F(No 2)A 2005* as summarised below.

Table 5.1

Asset	Location
1. Immovable property	Where the property is situated
2. Tangible movable property or chattels	Where the property is situated
3. Debts (secured or unsecured)	Where the creditor resides
4. Shares or securities of a local or governmental authority	The country of that authority
5. Other shares or securities	See below

6. Ships or aircraft	The country in which the owner is resident
7. Goodwill	Where the trade etc is carried on
8. Patents, trademarks and registered designs	Where they are registered
9. Copyright, design right and franchises	Where the right or design is exercisable
10. A judgment debt	Where the judgment is recorded
11. Futures, options and intangible assets	See below

With regard to item 5, anti-avoidance legislation applies to assets such as bearer shares in a UK company with effect from 16 March 2005. Shares in, or debentures of, a company incorporated in the UK (other than shares etc within item 4) are treated as situated in the UK. Subject to that rule, registered shares or debentures are situated where they are registered. If they are registered in more than one register, they are situated where the principal register is situated (*TCGA 1992, s 275(1)*, as amended by *F(No 2)A 2005, s 34, Sch 4, para 4*).

Rules for determining the location of futures, options and underlying intangible assets (item 11) were also introduced with effect from 16 March 2005. The basic rule is that such assets are located in the UK if they are subject to UK law (*TCGA 1992, ss 275A–275C*, inserted by *F(No 2)A 2005, s 34, Sch 4, para 5*).

HIGH-VALUE UK RESIDENTIAL PROPERTY – NEW ANNUAL TAX ON ENVELOPED DWELLINGS AND NEW CGT CHARGE

Annual tax on enveloped dwellings (ATED)

5.3 High-value UK residential properties owned by non-natural persons (NNPs) will be subject to a new regime of taxation from April 2013.

In addition to an annual tax on enveloped dwellings (ATED) and the increased rate for stamp duty land tax of 15%, a charge to CGT is imposed. The level of ATED is set as follows:

- £15,000 per annum for properties valued at between £2m and £5m;
- £35,000 per annum for properties valued at between £5m and £10m;
- £70,000 per annum for properties valued at between £10m and £20m; and
- £140,000 per annum for properties valued at more than £20m.

A valuation will be required at 1 April 2012 to determine which charging band applies to the property. The ATED takes effect from 1 April 2013 and, in most cases, is payable on or before 31 October 2013 for 2013/14, and on or before 30 April in each subsequent year. If the taxpayer is not chargeable for the full year, a later repayment claim can be made.

There are a number of exemptions for:

- property development businesses where the property is not occupied by a 'connected person';

- property rental businesses subject to the 'connected person' qualification;

- property trading businesses subject to the same requirement as to 'connected persons';

- employee accommodation provided the occupier is not too closely connected with the company;

- properties open to the public for at least 28 days a year;

- most dwellings owned by charity;

- farmhouses occupied by a working farmer subject to certain conditions;

- diplomatic and publicly owned properties; and

- properties that are conditionally exempt from inheritance tax.

The exemption must be claimed on the tax return, and failure to make a return will incur penalties.

Following representation by a number of professional bodies, trusts and trustees which directly own relevant UK properties will not be subject to these new charges.

CGT charge on ATED-related gains

5.4   From 6 April 2013, a CGT charge, at a rate of 28%, will apply to non-natural persons who are subject to the ATED. Individuals, trustees who are members of a partnership and PRs of deceased members of a partnership are excluded from the charge to CGT by new *TCGA 1992, s 2B*.

Only or main residence relief under *TCGA 1992, s 222* does not apply to the CGT charge on ATED-related gains (known as 'CGTED'), because this relief applies only to individuals and trustees, and not to non-natural persons.

The new CGTED only applies to gains from 5 April 2013 onwards, which means that the base value of a property subject to the new charge will receive a tax-free uplift to that date.

> **Focus**
>
> Owners of residential properties subject to the ATED and the CGTED will require two valuations.
>
> The ATED will be based on the value of the property on 1 April 2012.
>
> The rebasing under the CGTED will require a professional valuation as of 6 April 2013.

TERRITORIAL LIMITS OF CGT

5.5   The UK comprises Great Britain and Northern Ireland. It includes the UK's territorial seas but excludes the Isle of Man and the Channel Islands. However, CGT is not limited to gains on the disposal of UK assets.

Meaning of residence and domicile

Overview

5.6   Up to 5 April 2013, 'resident' and 'ordinarily resident' were the determining factors and they had the same meanings in *TCGA 1992* as they had in the *Income Tax Acts* (ie the enactments relating to income tax, including any provisions of the *Corporation Tax Acts* which relate to income tax) (*TCGA 1992, s 9(1); ICTA 1988, s 831(1)*). In each case the legislation was revised by *FA 2008, s 24*, as shown below. The interpretation of 'residence' and 'ordinary residence' was largely based on decisions made in the courts and the interpretation of these decisions adopted by HMRC, so uncertainty therefore prevailed.

For residence queries relating to periods to 5 April 2013, guidance in HMRC6 – Residence, Domicile and Remittance Basis (replacing IR20, which ceased to apply from 6 April 2009) will remain relevant. HMRC6 was published to update guidance in light of the changes brought about by *FA 2008, s 24* and *Sch 7*. Following criticism from professional bodies, Part 5 of HMRC6, which deals with the remittance basis, was updated in February 2010, with further revision in December 2010. However, caution still needs to be exercised in relation to HMRC6, which is couched in such general terms that it is difficult to apply to more complex situations. The residency rules are difficult to interpret, and therefore careful consideration needs to be given to case law, established practice and HMRC6.

Legislation introduced in *Finance Act 2013* tried to address these uncertainties and introduced a statutory test to determine an individual's tax residence. The statutory residence test includes two levels: the 'automatic overseas' test, which dictates whether an individual will automatically be resident in the UK; and the 'sufficient ties' test, which an individual will have to look at if the 'automatic overseas' test does not apply.

The 'sufficient ties' test includes a sliding scale, based on the following:

- the 'family tie' test;
- the 'accommodation tie' test;
- the 'work tie' test;
- the '90-day' test; and
- the 'country tie' test.

The new guidance note for the statutory residence test was published in May 2013 (see www.hmrc.gov.uk/international/rdr3.pdf). The complexity of the new rules is evidenced by the fact that the guidance note runs to 101 pages.

HMRC have also published a new toolkit (the Tax Residence Indicator) to assist individuals in determining their residence status (see http://tools.hmrc. gov.uk/rift/screen/SRT+-+Combined/en-GB/summary?user=guest).

An individual's domicile is also a key factor in determining a person's liability to CGT. An individual who meets the residence tests outlined below, and is domiciled in any part of the UK, is chargeable to CGT on gains accruing on the disposal of assets situated anywhere in the world. However, the liability of a non-domiciled individual in respect of gains accruing on the disposal of non-UK assets was formerly limited to gains remitted to the UK (see 5.37), although that general rule has been severely cut down by *FA 2008, s 25* and *Sch 7*. In this chapter, any reference to '*Sch 7*' is to *FA 2008, Sch 7*.

The Treasury and stakeholders are currently working together to produce a statutory residence test, which is expected to take effect from April 2013.

HMRC's Centre for Non-Residents handles matters relating to a taxpayer's residence status (see www.hmrc.gov.uk/cnr).

Domicile

5.7   Under UK law, every individual has a domicile, but only one domicile. For capital gains tax purposes, a person is domiciled in the state in which he is domiciled under the general law. The deemed domicile rules for inheritance tax in *IHTA 1984, s 267* have no application to capital gains tax. It is difficult to acquire a domicile of choice which will displace a domicile of origin, difficult to know if this has indeed been achieved, and it requires fairly drastic lifestyle changes. Change of domicile is a matter of fact and generally requires a detailed analysis of the individual's circumstances. Those who do have, or can with determination acquire, a non-UK domicile could until recently use this to minimise the impact of capital gains tax on their assets, even whilst retaining some assets and presence here, but that has now changed.

5.8   HMRC6 (at pp 16–19) includes a number of flowcharts and examples to assist the understanding of domicile. However, HMRC6 has been superseded by the Guidance on Statutory Residence for matters arising after 6 April 2013. Therefore, it is uncertain whether HMRC6 continues to apply in relation to domicile.

Under the general law, there are three different types of domicile:

- domicile of origin;
- domicile of dependence; and
- domicile of choice.

They are described as different *types* of domicile because they can be acquired and lost in different ways. The country in which a person is domiciled is sometimes described as his permanent home (see *Winans v Attorney General* [1904] AC 287). This can be a useful description, and it is certainly true that domicile requires a degree of permanence which residence, by contrast, does not. Remember, though, that both domicile of origin and domicile of dependence are acquired by operation of law rather than by choice: it is possible for a person to be domiciled in a place where he has never been, let alone had a home or lived permanently.

Domicile of origin

5.9   Everyone acquires a domicile of origin at birth and this remains his domicile until it is replaced by a domicile of dependence or a domicile or choice. It is important to identify a person's domicile of origin because it can revive when a domicile of choice is lost. A person's domicile of origin is:

- his father's domicile at the time of his birth; unless
- his parents were not married; or
- his father died before he was born.

In those other cases, his domicile of origin will be his mother's domicile. Although as a matter of fact it will often be the country in which he was born, this need not be so.

> **Example 5.1**
>
> A child might be born in California to parents who had lived there for 20 years and who were married at the time of its birth. Suppose that the father had an English domicile of origin and that this had not been displaced by a domicile of choice. In that case, the child would acquire an English domicile of origin at birth, despite the fact that it might never come to England.

A domicile of origin is the most clinging, tenacious form and will be displaced only if a person acquires a domicile of choice or a domicile of dependence.

Domicile of dependence

5.10 Domicile of dependence now only affects children under 16 and persons of unsound mind. Prior to 1 January 1974, this category included married women. Before that date, a woman acquired her husband's domicile on marriage and her domicile changed when his did. This rule was abolished by the *Domicile and Matrimonial Proceedings Act 1973*, but has some relevance to women who were married before 1 January 1974. The rule has no relevance to women married on or after 1 January 1974.

Domicile of choice

5.11 A domicile of choice is acquired by both physical presence in another country *and* the intention of settling there permanently. It will not be acquired if, for example, that intention is conditional; nor will it be acquired by going to a country for work, even for an extended period, unless there is a definite intention to stay there permanently once the employment has ceased.

A domicile of choice can be lost by leaving the country without any definite intention of returning. A person will acquire a new domicile of choice if he goes to another country with the intention of settling there permanently. If no new domicile of choice is acquired, his domicile of origin will revive.

A person seeking to establish that a domicile of origin has been lost and a domicile of choice acquired has to discharge a heavy burden of proof. This is equally so whether it is the taxpayer whose domicile of origin is in the UK and who is arguing that it has been superseded by the acquisition of a domicile of choice; or HMRC arguing that a taxpayer whose domicile of origin is outside the UK has lost that domicile and acquired a domicile of choice in the UK.

For example, the Revenue argued in favour of acquisition of domicile of choice before the Special Commissioners in *F and another (personal representatives of F deceased) v IRC* [2000] STC (SCD) 1, but failed to prove that the deceased had lost his Iranian domicile of origin and acquired a UK domicile of choice. In *IRC v Bullock* [1976] STC 409, the taxpayer had been brought up in Canada but had come to live in England in 1932. He married in England and lived there virtually constantly thereafter, but was held to have retained his Canadian domicile of origin because his intention, in the event of surviving his wife, was to return to Canada permanently. This meant that he could not be described as having a settled intention of remaining in England permanently.

In *Re Furse, Furse v IRC* [1980] STC 596, on the other hand, the taxpayer had been born in Rhode Island in 1883 and was a US citizen but had a close connection with England throughout his life. He and his wife had a family house in New York and visited it regularly but they also had a farm in Sussex. It had been bought by the wife in 1924 and the taxpayer lived there until his death in 1963. Unlike the taxpayer in *Bullock*, there was evidence that this taxpayer was happy on the Sussex farm. The only suggestion that he might ever leave England was if and when he was no longer fit enough to lead an active life on the farm. He did not really wish to leave and was quite settled in England. The court accordingly found that he died domiciled in England.

The case of *Re Clore (No 2)* [1984] STC 609 shows how important it is, if there is a settled intention of acquiring a domicile of choice in another jurisdiction, that there is plenty of clear written evidence of that intention and that matters are not just left to the recollections of friends and acquaintances after the death of the individual.

The effect on domicile, as it happens in a non-tax context, of the acquisition of British citizenship was illustrated in the case of *Re Bheekhun deceased* (CA, 2 December 1998, unreported). Mr Bheekhun had a domicile of origin in Mauritius. He came to the UK to find work in 1960 at the age of 29. When Mauritius became independent he had to choose whether to take British citizenship or Mauritian citizenship. He chose British citizenship, although he retained business links with Mauritius, acquired properties there and later acquired a Mauritian passport. At all times, he continued to live and work in the UK. When he renewed his UK passport, it described him as resident in the UK. After his death, his separated spouse claimed under the *Inheritance (Provision for Family and Dependants) Act 1975* and her claim depended upon establishing that he died domiciled in the UK. The Court of Appeal upheld the decision that he had acquired a domicile of choice in the UK by the time of his death.

We should not conclude from this decision that citizenship is a determinant of domicile. It is not. The case remains unreported, so we have to assume that Mr Bheekhun's choice of a UK passport was simply one fact taken into account as evidence of his intention to settle permanently in the UK. The question ultimately remains one of fact and that the weight attached to any particular fact will depend on all the circumstances.

Allen and Hateley (as executors of Johnson deceased) v HMRC [2005] STC (SCD) 614 concerned Mrs Johnson, who was born in England in 1922, but moved abroad with her husband in 1953. She was diagnosed as suffering from Parkinson's disease in 1975. The couple settled in Spain in 1982 and bought a house there. Following her husband's death in 1996, Mrs Johnson moved to England to live with family as a 'visitor' (as she described it) in order to receive the care and support her illness demanded. Apart from clothes and jewellery she left her possessions (including pets) in the Spanish property, which was maintained ready for her occupation. In 2001 she bought the house next door to the family residence, with the intention of renovating it for her needs. However, she was admitted to hospital and died in August 2002 without occupying the property. Mrs Johnson retained the property in Spain until her death, and regarded it as her home.

On the executors' appeal from the notice of determination by HMRC that Mrs Johnson was domiciled in the UK at the time of her death the Special Commissioner held that the Revenue had failed to establish that she ceased to intend residing permanently in Spain. Mrs Johnson had maintained her house there. The purchase of a UK property had been the alternative to moving into a residential care home. The appeal was allowed.

In *Mark v Mark* [2006] 1 AC 98, the House of Lords held, inter alia, that unlawful presence is not necessarily a bar to the establishment of a domicile of choice.

In *Cyganik v Agulian* [2006] EWCA Civ 129, the Court of Appeal held that an individual born in Cyprus but who had lived and worked in England for about 43 years between the age of 19 and his death at the age of 63, had not lost his Cypriot domicile of origin and had not acquired a domicile of choice in England.

The recent case of *Holliday v Musa* [2010] WTLR 839 reiterated the threefold approach applied in *Fuld* [1968] P 675. The issue in this case was whether a Turkish Cypriot individual had acquired a domicile of choice in England or whether the domicile of origin was retained. The *ratio* of this case is as follows: first, domicile of origin adheres until displaced by evidence of acquisition and continuance of domicile of choice; secondly, domicile of choice is only acquired if there is evidence of an independent intention to reside there indefinitely; and, thirdly, if evidence is lacking about the individual's state of mind or if his mind is not made up, the domicile of origin adheres. In this case, a vague intention to retire to Cyprus, which had disappeared at the time of his death, indicated that he had his permanent home in the UK.

Revenue and Customs Brief (RCB) 34/10 details changes to the circumstances in which HMRC will consider an individual's domicile (see www.hmrc.gov.uk/

briefs/inheritance-tax/brief3410.htm). In essence, HMRC will only consider opening an enquiry where there is a significant risk of loss of UK tax.

Residence and ordinary residence prior to 6 April 2013

5.12   An individual can be resident in one or more countries for tax purposes. Prior to 6 April 2013, it was possible to be resident in the UK but not ordinarily resident. There was no statutory definition of 'residence' or 'ordinary residence', and the rules, despite the introduction of the guidance in HMRC6, contained uncertainties. If an individual was in the UK for 183 days or more in a tax year, he was resident in the UK for tax purposes. If someone was in the UK for less than 183 days in a tax year, HMRC6 introduced a number of factors which were taken into account to determine whether that person was resident. These included family ties, social ties, business ties and property ties. It also stated that, if a person had previously resided in the UK, then, in order to become non-resident, they had to leave the UK, either by making a definite break or by taking up full-time employment abroad.

Ordinary residence, in contrast, was where an individual resided in the UK for a sufficient period on a habitual basis. Following the case of *Genovese v Revenue and Customs Commissioners* [2009] SpC 741, that period was held to be three years. However, this clarity was displaced by the First-tier Tribunal case of *Tuczka v HMRC* [2010] UKFTT 53 (TC), which seemed to indicate that, if a person became resident in the UK and took up employment in the UK, he would become ordinarily resident immediately on his arrival, even if his intention was not to stay very long. It is difficult to see how these two cases could be reconciled.

Further uncertainty was introduced by the case of *R (on the application of Davies, James & Gaines-Cooper) v HMRC* [2010] EWCA Civ 38, which suggested that mere day-counting was not conclusive, but that other factors were taken into account.

This seemed to indicate a more subjective approach to determining residence – see 5.22. This has to be contrasted with the decision in *Philip George Turberville v HMRC* [2010] UKFTT 69 (TC), which found in favour of the taxpayer. A great deal of uncertainty surrounded the concepts of 'residence' and 'ordinary residence', and the higher court authority rests with the *Gaines-Cooper* decision. The new statutory residence test introduced in *Finance Act 2013* is supposed to clarify the determination of residence from 6 April 2013.

Presence in UK for temporary purposes only

5.13   As a general rule, an individual who is present in the UK for some temporary purpose only, and not with any intent to establish his residence here, is charged to CGT on chargeable gains accruing in a tax year if (and only) if he is resident in the UK in that tax year for a period (or periods) amounting to more than 183 days. The day-counting rules have been altered or clarified by *FA 2008, s 24(7)*. The new rules apply for 2008/09 and onwards. A day is spent in the UK if the person is present at the end of the day: see new *TCGA 1992, s 9(5)*. However, the day of arrival as a passenger 'just passing through' is ignored if the passenger leaves the next day and, in effect, does not use the time in the UK:

- for business;
- to see friends; or
- to visit a property in the UK owned by that person.

See *TCGA 1992, s 9(6)(b)*, which refers to not engaging 'in activities that are to a substantial extent unrelated to the individual's passage through the United Kingdom'. It may prove difficult to police.

Any living accommodation available in the UK for the individual's use is disregarded for this purpose. For years prior to 1993/94, an individual who had living accommodation available to him in the UK was generally treated as UK resident in any tax year during which he visited the UK, regardless of the length of his visit (*TCGA 1992, s 9(3), (4)*).

In *HMRC v Grace* [2009] STC 213, it was decided that a South African airline pilot was not in the UK for only temporary purposes, as he fulfilled duties under an indefinite contract of employment in the UK.

In *Kimber v HMRC Commissioners* [2012] UKFTT 107 (TC), Mr Kimber's claim, that his presence in the UK was for temporary purposes only, was rejected once he had made plans for his family to permanently move to the UK.

Coming to the UK as a student

5.14   If an individual comes to the UK as a student and remains in the UK for less than four years, he will be resident in the UK, but not ordinarily resident if:

- he does not own or buy accommodation here; or
- he does not acquire accommodation on a lease of three years or more; and
- when leaving the UK, he does not plan to return for regular visits which average 91 days or more in a tax year.

Calculation of average visits

5.15   The formula to be applied is (see HMRC6):

$$\frac{\text{Total days visiting the UK}}{\text{Tax years you have visited (in days)}} \times 365 = \text{annual average visits}$$

If the annual average visits exceed 91 days over a four-year period, the individual will become resident and ordinarily resident in the UK, even if he never exceeded the normal 183 days rule.

ARRIVING IN OR LEAVING THE UK

Arriving in the UK

5.16   An individual who is not ordinarily resident in the UK and arrives in the UK with the intention of settling here is treated as UK resident from the date of arrival. He is, therefore, resident for a part of the tax year in which he arrives and is chargeable to CGT for that year (see **5.1**).

An individual who is present in the UK for a temporary purpose only (see **5.13**), but spends at least 183 days in the UK in a tax year becomes chargeable to CGT on the basis that he is resident for that part of the year in which he is present here.

The rule set out in **5.1** means that, strictly speaking, an individual who is resident in the UK during any part of the tax year is chargeable to CGT on all chargeable gains accruing during that year, including those accruing before he became resident.

By concession, however, for an individual (but not a trustee), HMRC will split the year in which UK residence begins, so that gains accruing before the change of status are not chargeable, so long as the taxpayer has not been resident or ordinarily resident here at any time during the five preceding tax years (HMRC concession ESC D2, reproduced below, CG25791).

HMRC will consider withholding the benefit of this concession where the taxpayer 'has entered into arrangements in an attempt to use the terms of ESC D2 to avoid liability to CGT which would otherwise arise'. See, for example, **5.18** with regard to *R v HM Inspector of Taxes, Reading ex parte Fulford-Dobson* (1987) 60 TC 168 (CG25981).

'HMRC concession ESC D2

Residence in the UK: year of commencement or cessation of residence: CGT

1. An individual who comes to live in the United Kingdom and is treated as resident here for any year of assessment from the date of arrival is charged to capital gains tax only in respect of chargeable gains from disposals made after arrival, provided that the individual has not been resident or ordinarily resident in the United Kingdom at any time during the five years of assessment immediately preceding the year of assessment in which he or she arrived in the United Kingdom.

2. An individual who leaves the United Kingdom and is treated on departure as not resident and not ordinarily resident here is not charged to capital gains tax on gains from disposals made after the date of departure, provided that the individual was not resident and not ordinarily resident in the United Kingdom for the whole of at least four out of the seven years of assessment immediately preceding the year of assessment in which he or she left the United Kingdom.

3. This concession does not apply to any individual in relation to gains on the disposal of assets which are situated in the United Kingdom and which, at any time between the individual's departure from the United Kingdom and the end of the year of assessment, are either:

    (i)   used in or for the purposes of a trade, profession or vocation carried on by that individual in the United Kingdom through a branch or agency; or

    (ii)   used or held for, or acquired for use by or for the purposes of, such a branch or agency.

4. This concession does not apply to the trustees of a settlement who commence or cease residence in the United Kingdom or to a settlor of a settlement in relation to gains in respect of which the settlor is chargeable under Sections 77-79 TCGA 1992, or Section 86 and Schedule 5 TCGA 1992.

5. This revised concession applies to any individual who ceases to be resident or ordinarily resident in the United Kingdom on or after 17 March 1998, or becomes resident or ordinarily resident in the United Kingdom on or after 6 April 1998.'

The split-year treatment provided by paragraph 1 of the concession does not apply, therefore, where a taxpayer arriving in the UK was previously resident here and there are less than five complete tax years between the time of his departure and his return to the UK. In this situation, gains accruing at any time in the tax year of arrival are chargeable.

Leaving the UK

5.17   An individual leaving the UK during a tax year may be treated as not resident and not ordinarily resident in the UK from the day after his departure. However, his UK-resident status for the period up to the date of departure means, as indicated in **5.1**, that strictly speaking he is chargeable to CGT on all chargeable gains accruing during the year, including those accruing after he became not resident and not ordinarily resident.

By concession, HMRC will split the year of departure so that gains accruing after the change of status are not chargeable, so long as the taxpayer has been not resident and not ordinarily resident in the UK for the whole of at least four out of the seven preceding tax years (HMRC concession ESC D2, reproduced in **5.16**).

The split-year treatment provided by paragraph 2 of the concession does not apply, therefore, where a taxpayer leaving the UK has been UK resident or ordinarily resident in any part of four or more of the seven preceding tax years. In this situation, gains accruing at any time in the tax year of departure are chargeable.

HMRC guidance indicates that cases will be examined where the date of disposal of an asset appears to be soon after the date of emigration, with a view to establishing whether a CGT liability arises, because:

- there was a binding agreement or contract for sale on or before the date of emigration;

- a business was carried on in the UK through a branch or agency in the period from the date of emigration to the date of disposal; or

- an attempt has been made to use ESC D2 for tax avoidance (CG25805).

HMRC's approach has been supported by the case of *Dr Broome v HMRC* [2011] UKFTT 760 (TC), where HMRC went to great lengths to gather evidence that Dr Broome remained resident in, and retained links with, the UK for at least part of the year of assessment.

See **5.30** regarding the exception in paragraph 3 of the concession for gains on the disposal of assets used in or for the purposes of a trade etc carried on in the UK through a branch or agency.

5.18   As indicated above, HMRC may seek to withhold the concession if the taxpayer tries to use it for tax avoidance purposes. In *R v HM Inspector of Taxes, Reading ex parte Fulford-Dobson* (1987) 60 TC 168 (QB), the taxpayer's wife (W) inherited a farm in 1977. She was considering selling it during 1980, at a time when the taxpayer (H) was negotiating employment with a German firm. H's contract of employment was signed on 18 August, requiring him to live and work in Germany and to commence work on 15

141

September. W transferred the farm to H by deed of gift on 29 August; H left for Germany on 13 September; and the farm was sold by auction on 17 September.

H admitted that one of the reasons for W's transfer of the farm to him was to ensure that the sale would be outside the scope of CGT by virtue of ESC D2, because at the time of the sale he would not be UK resident. HMRC took the view that there was an attempt to use the concession for tax avoidance and denied the benefit of the concession. The taxpayer sought a judicial review of that decision and the High Court held that:

- concession D2 was lawful, falling within the proper exercise of managerial discretion;

- HMRC were entitled, in giving a concession, to take reasonable steps to prevent its abuse; and

- the transactions undertaken by the taxpayers amounted to tax avoidance within the terms of HMRC's general 'health warning' about the use of concessions for tax avoidance.

HMRC do not regard a genuine postponement of the disposal on its own as an attempt to use the concession for avoidance, although they may regard it as such if it is combined with other arrangements (CG25982).

They accept that the benefit of the no gain, no loss rule for transfers between spouses and civil partners (under *TCGA 1992, s 58*, see **3.61**) is available on the transfer to a non-resident spouse or civil partner (i) after that spouse or civil partner has become non-resident, and (ii) in a year throughout the whole of which that spouse or civil partner is non-resident. This reflects the majority decision of the House of Lords in *Gubay v Kington* (1984) 57 TC 601, HL. HMRC guidance says (CG22300):

> 'There is no longer any authority to treat a non-resident spouse as separated from a resident spouse merely because of their residence status. Similarly a non-resident civil partner may not be treated as separated from a resident civil partner merely because of their residence status. So the possibility of passing assets outside the UK tax net remains.'

A taxpayer who becomes neither resident nor ordinarily resident in the UK may become chargeable to CGT, as a result of his change of status, on a gain that was held over following a claim to hold-over relief for gifts of business assets (see **13.2**) or gifts immediately chargeable (or exempt from) inheritance tax (see **13.35**).

'Clean break'

5.19   The decision in *R (on the application of Davies, James & Gaines-Cooper) v HMRC* [2010] EWCA Civ 38 seems to confirm that a mere day-counting test is not sufficient. The case determined that the act of leaving indefinitely will not automatically lead to non-resident status because HMRC will look, among other factors, at the connections that are retained with the UK. Severing of ties sufficient to divest a taxpayer of residence status will remain a key factor. This approach has been confirmed in the recently updated version of HMRC6.

In the case of Mr Gaines-Cooper, the fact that his wife and son remained living in the UK and that his son attended school in the UK determined that he did not leave the UK 'permanently or indefinitely'. Mr Gaines-Cooper was granted leave to take the case to the Supreme Court, alleging unreasonable behaviour by HMRC. The Supreme Court rejected Mr Gaines-Cooper's arguments. However, the battle may not be over, as Mr Gaines-Cooper issued a statement indicating that he is considering an appeal to the European Court of Justice.

STATUTORY RESIDENCE TEST TO DETERMINE RESIDENCE FROM 6 APRIL 2013

5.20 The basic rule is that a person will be resident in the UK for a tax year if he does not meet any of the 'automatic overseas' tests but meets the 'automatic UK' or 'sufficient ties' tests.

The first 'automatic overseas' test determines that a person is automatically non-resident if:

- he was resident in the UK for one or more of the three years preceding the tax year; and

- he spent less than 16 days in the UK in the tax year.

The second 'automatic overseas' test determines that a person is automatically non-resident if:

- he was not resident in the UK for any of the three years preceding the tax year; and

- he spent less than 46 days in the UK in the tax year.

The third 'automatic overseas' test, subject to a number of qualifications, determines that a person is automatically non-resident if:

- he works full-time overseas over the tax year without any significant breaks; and

- he spends less than 91 days in the UK in the tax year; and

- the number of days in the tax year on which he works for more than three hours in the UK is less than 31 days.

If none of the 'automatic overseas' tests apply, one has to look towards the 'automatic UK' test or the 'sufficient ties' test.

The first 'automatic UK' test determines that a person is resident in the UK for a tax year if he spends 183 days or more in the UK in the tax year.

The second 'automatic UK' test determines that a person is resident in the UK for a tax year if:

- he has or had a home in the UK during all or part of the tax year; and

- there is at least one period of 91 consecutive days, at least 30 days of which fall in the tax year, when the person has a home in the UK in which he spends more than 30 days, and either he:

  - has no overseas home; or

  - he has an overseas home or homes in each of which he spends fewer than 30 days.

The third 'automatic UK' test determines that a person is resident in the UK for a tax year if he works full-time in the UK for any period of 365 days with no significant break from UK work, and:

- all or part of that 365-day period falls within the tax year;

- more than 75% of the total number of days are days when a person does more than three hours of work; and

- at least one day in the tax year is a day on which he does more than three hours of work in the UK.

The third 'automatic UK' test does not apply if a person works on board a vehicle, aircraft or ship, and at least six of the trips that he makes during the tax year as part of his job are cross-border trips that begin and/or end in the UK.

If a person does not meet the 'automatic overseas' tests or the 'automatic UK' tests, one has to ascertain whether the 'sufficient ties' test applies.

If a person was not UK resident for any of the three years before the tax year under consideration, it will be necessary to consider whether any of the following UK ties apply:

- a family tie, which means that a person's husband, wife or civil partner (unless separated) is UK resident; a partner, if living together as husband and wife or civil partners, is UK resident; or the person has a child below the age of 18 and spends fewer than 61 days in the UK in the tax year concerned;

- an accommodation tie, which means that a person has a place to live in the UK for a continuous period of 91 days or more; and the person spends one or more nights there during the tax year; or spends 16 nights or more at the home of a close relative (parents, siblings and issue aged 18 or over);

- a work tie, which means that a person does more than three hours of work a day in the UK on at least 40 days in that tax year;

- a 90-day tie, which means that a person spends more than 90 days in the UK in either or both of the previous two tax years; or

- a country tie for a tax year, if the UK is the country in which a person is present at midnight for the greatest number of days in that year.

5.21 The number of days spent in the UK in a tax year determines the number of ties required to be UK resident. There are complex rules to determine the number of days – see HMRC Guidance Note RDR3, pages 29–39.

Table 5.2: UK ties needed to be UK resident for one or more of the three tax years before the tax year under consideration

Days spent in the UK in the tax year under consideration	UK ties needed
16–45	At least 4
46–90	At least 3
91–120	At least 2
Over 120	At least 1

Table 5.3: UK ties needed if a person is non-UK resident in any of the three preceding tax years before the tax year under consideration

Days spent in the UK in the tax year under consideration	UK ties needed
46–90	All 4
91–120	At least 3
Over 120	At least 2

Temporary periods of non-residence under the statutory residence test

5.22 If a person leaves the UK to live or work abroad, or comes to the UK from abroad, the tax year will be split into two parts if certain requirements are satisfied. The HMRC Guidance Note RDR3 sets out eight sets of circumstances which satisfy the split year treatment:

Case 1:

If in a tax year a person takes up full-time work overseas and:

●   is UK resident for the tax year in question;

●   is UK resident for the previous tax year;

●   is non-UK resident in the following tax year because he meets the third 'automatic overseas' test; and

●   satisfies the overseas work criteria during the relevant period.

Case 2:

If in a tax year the person's partner (husband, wife or civil partner, or someone they live together with as husband, wife or civil partner) meets the conditions in Case 1 and the taxpayer accompanies that person to live with them overseas, and the taxpayer:

●   is UK resident for the tax year being considered for split year treatment;

●   is UK resident for the previous tax year;

●   is non-UK resident for the tax year following the tax year being considered for split year treatment;

●   has a partner whose circumstances fall within Case 1 for the tax year or previous tax year;

●   has been living together in the UK either at some point in the tax year or the previous tax year;

●   moves overseas so they can live together while the partner is working overseas; and

●   in the period beginning on the deemed departure day and ending on the first day of the tax year, either:

       –   has no home in the UK or (if they have homes in both countries) spends the greater part of the time in the overseas home; or

       –   spends less than the permitted limit of days in the UK (see Table on page 50 of the Guidance Note).

Case 3:

A person may benefit from the split year treatment if he moves abroad and no longer has a home in the UK and:

●   is UK resident for the tax year being considered for split year treatment;

●   is UK resident for the previous tax year;

●   is non-UK resident for the tax year following the tax year being considered for split year treatment; and

- has one or more homes in the UK at the start of the tax year and, at some point in the year, ceases to have any home in the UK for the rest of the tax year.

Case 4:

A person may benefit from the split year treatment if for a tax year he did not meet the 'only home' test at the beginning of the year but, at some time during the year, the test is satisfied and he:

- is UK resident for the tax year being considered for split year treatment;
- is non-UK resident for the previous tax year;
- did not meet the 'only home' test at the beginning of the tax year but this changed during the tax year in question; and
- did not meet the 'sufficient UK ties' test at the beginning of the tax year, which may need to be reconsidered by reducing the day count limit, as per Table F in the Guidance Notes.

Case 5:

A person may benefit from the split year treatment if for a tax year he starts full-time work in the UK and the third 'automatic test' is satisfied over a period of 365 days and he:

- is UK resident for the tax year being considered for split year treatment;
- is non-UK resident for the previous tax year; and
- did not meet the 'sufficient ties' test for the part of the tax year before meeting the third 'automatic UK' test.

Again, the day count limit (mentioned in Case 4) needs to be considered.

Case 6:

A person may benefit from the split year treatment if he ceases full-time employment abroad and:

- is UK resident for the tax year being considered for split year treatment;
- has not been UK resident for the previous tax year because he satisfied the third 'automatic overseas' test;
- is UK resident in the following tax year; and
- satisfies the overseas work criteria for a relevant period.

Case 7:

A person may benefit from the split year treatment if he has lived abroad but is returning or relocating with his partner who was in full-time employment overseas and:

- is UK resident for the tax year being considered for split year treatment;

- has not been UK resident for the previous tax year;

- has a partner who satisfies the Case 6 criteria;

- moves together with the partner to the UK to continue living together; and

- is UK resident in the following tax year.

Case 8:

A person may benefit from the split year treatment if he starts having a home in the UK at some time during the tax year and:

- is UK resident for the tax year being considered for split year treatment;

- has not been UK resident for the previous tax year;

- is UK resident in the following tax year;

- has no home in the UK at the beginning of the tax year but starts having a home at some point during the tax year; and

- does not have sufficient UK ties until he starts having a home in the UK.

Visiting armed forces

5.23   A member of the visiting armed force of a designated country is not treated as resident in the UK for CGT purposes, and is not treated as changing his residence or domicile status, for any period to which the income tax exemption in *ITEPA 2003, s 303(1)* applies solely because he is a member of that force (*TCGA 1992, s 11(1)*).

Diplomatic and European Union staff

5.24   UK-resident '*agents-general*' (representatives of certain foreign governments) and certain members of their staff are entitled to the same immunity from CGT as that conferred on a UK-resident head of a diplomatic mission under the *Diplomatic Privileges Act 1964* (*TCGA 1992, s 11(2)–(4)*).

The relevant section in HMRC6 was amended in October 2011. It now states that a UK-resident and ordinarily resident individual who takes up employment with the European Union institutions will remain ordinarily resident in the UK for income tax purposes (but not for CGT purposes) and will remain resident for any year in which he visits the UK, no matter how short his stay.

Disputes as to residence etc status

5.25   Any decision as to whether a person is (or has been) ordinarily resident or domiciled in the UK for CGT purposes can be appealed within 30 days. However, under the appeals procedure introduced on 1 April 2009, if a taxpayer disagrees with a decision, he should first write to the person who made the decision. If matters cannot be resolved, the taxpayer can request an internal review by the HMRC review team, or this can be offered by HMRC. Where the taxpayer does not agree with the conclusion of this review, or declines the offer of an internal HMRC review, he can ask the First-tier Tax Tribunal to determine the question. HMRC have no power to refer cases directly to the Tribunal.

Practicalities

5.26   If leaving (or arriving in) the UK, individuals, in addition to day-counting, may wish to consider any of the following actions to show that they are leaving indefinitely or are arriving, in order to take advantage of the split-year treatment discussed in **5.22**.

For an individual who is leaving:

- File P45 and P85 to obtain a tax refund for year of departure and inform HMRC of their intention of leaving the UK.

- Sever all ties with the UK (for example, cease employment, move family abroad and change postal address).

- Sell accommodation or lease it on a long lease, to convince HMRC that there is no intention to return in the near future.

- Generate permanent ties with their new home country: buy a house, open bank accounts and join local clubs.

- Remain outside the UK for a full tax year or make sure that, over a four-year period, no more than 90 days are spent in the UK.

- Obtain an overseas employment contract covering at least a whole tax year.

For an individual who is arriving in the UK:

- Collate evidence to establish presence at a particular home (for example, utility bills, local parking permits, memberships of clubs, address on a driving licence etc).

- Where residence status is determined by the automatic tests relating to working full-time in the UK or overseas, keep a detailed work diary, contracts of employment and evidence of travel arrangements.

Focus

HMRC will look at all the facts, evidence and the settled pattern of an individual's life.

Detailed record-keeping is vital to counter an attack by HMRC.

Transitional provisions

5.27   The residence status for the tax years 2013/14 and the following two tax years, under the 'automatic overseas' test and the 'sufficient ties' test, is based on the residence status for one or more of the three tax years preceding 2013/14, which is before the statutory residence test was introduced.

HMRC have confirmed that, for tax years prior to 6 April 2013, the rules outlined in HMRC6 continue to apply.

However, for the purpose of determining the UK residence status for tax years 2013/14, 2014/15 and 2015/16, the taxpayer can elect to determine his residence status by reference to the statutory residence test. Such election will not change the residence status for the pre-commencement years.

Election must be made either on the self-assessment tax return or in writing in a letter addressed to HMRC. It must be made no later than the first anniversary of the end of the relevant tax year to which it applies, and the election is irrevocable.

NON-RESIDENTS DOING BUSINESS IN THE UK

5.28   Non-residents are, broadly, chargeable to tax on gains arising (i) on the disposal of UK assets used to carry on a business in the UK (see **5.30**), or (ii) on a deemed disposal when the assets are removed from the UK or the business ceases (see **5.31**).

Individuals

5.29   A person who is neither resident nor ordinarily resident in the UK in a tax year remains chargeable to CGT in respect of certain gains accruing to him in that year if he is carrying on a trade, profession or vocation in the UK through a branch or agency in that year. See **5.32** regarding companies chargeable to corporation tax.

Disposal of assets

5.30   The charge applies to gains accruing on the disposal of any of the following assets, where the disposal is made at a time when the person is carrying on the trade etc in the UK through a branch or agency:

- assets situated in the UK and used in, or for the purposes of, the trade etc either at the time when the capital gain accrued or before that time;

- assets situated in the UK and used, or held, for the purposes of the branch or agency either at or before that time; and

- assets situated in the UK and acquired for use by, or for the purposes of, the branch or agency (*TCGA 1992, s 10(1), (2), (5)*).

'Branch or agency' means any factorship, agency, receivership, branch or management. There is no charge under this rule if the taxpayer is exempt from income tax on the profits or gains of the branch or agency by virtue of double tax relief arrangements (*TCGA 1992, s 10(4), (6)*).

The split-year concession ESC D2, discussed in **5.19**, and the split-year treatment under the statutory residence test, discussed in **5.22**, do not apply (see paragraph 3 of the concession) to an individual in relation to gains on the disposal of assets situated in the UK that are used as set out in (a) or (b) below at any time between his departure from the UK and the end of the tax year:

(a)   used in or for the purposes of a trade, profession or vocation carried on by that individual in the UK through a branch or agency; or

(b)   used or held for, or acquired for use by or for the purposes of, such a branch or agency.

For an individual seeking to sell a UK business as a going concern and emigrate from the UK, the combined effect of *TCGA 1992, s 10* and HMRC's denial of concession ESC D2 is broadly as set out below:

- Delaying the contract until after the taxpayer's departure is likely to involve making arrangements for the business to continue in his absence – HMRC consider that, in most cases such as this, they could argue that the activity is carried on in the UK through a branch or agency in the period between departure and the date of the contract.

- A disposal after the date of emigration but before the end of the tax year would be within the charge to CGT as set out in *TCGA 1992, s 2* and ESC D2 would not apply (as already indicated).

- A disposal in the tax year following the year of emigration would also be within the charge to CGT, by virtue of *TCGA 1992, s 10* (CG25900–CG25903).

151

Deemed disposals

5.31   A chargeable gain is deemed to accrue in the circumstances described below. This rule was introduced to prevent a taxpayer avoiding the charges on an actual disposal, described in **5.30**, by (i) transferring assets abroad before the disposal, or (ii) discontinuing the branch activities in one tax year and disposing of the assets in the following tax year.

There is a deemed disposal and reacquisition at market value where 'chargeable assets' (see below) are:

(a)   transferred abroad (*TCGA 1992, s 25(1)*); or

(b)   cease to be 'chargeable assets' because the individual ceases to carry on the trade etc in the UK through a branch or agency (*TCGA 1992, s 25(3)*).

For this purpose, assets are 'chargeable assets' only if the individual is not resident and not ordinarily resident in the UK and a chargeable gain on their disposal would be chargeable under *TCGA 1992, s 10(1)* as described above (*TCGA 1992, s 25(7)*).

There is no deemed disposal within (a) if:

•   the transfer occurs on the cessation of the trade etc; or

•   the asset is an exploration or exploitation asset, as defined (*TCGA 1992, s 25(2)*).

There is no deemed disposal within (b) if the asset is used, before the end of the chargeable period in which the cessation occurs, in another trade etc carried on by the same individual in the UK through a branch or agency (*TCGA 1992, s 25(5)*).

Companies

5.32   A company that is not resident in the UK is nonetheless chargeable to corporation tax in respect of chargeable gains accruing to it if the company is carrying on a trade (including for this purpose a vocation, office or employment) in the UK through a permanent establishment in the UK (*TCGA 1992, s 10B*). See **Chapter 9** and *Corporation Tax 2013/14* (Bloomsbury Professional).

ANTI-AVOIDANCE: TEMPORARY NON-RESIDENCE

5.33   Special rules apply to individuals who realise capital gains during a period of temporary absence from the UK, during which their residence status would otherwise mean that they escaped CGT (*TCGA 1992, s 10A*). Broadly, an individual who leaves the UK and subsequently returns is chargeable to CGT on gains arising during his absence on the disposal of assets owned prior to departure, if:

- he was UK resident for at least four of the seven tax years prior to departure; and

- the period of non-residence is less than five complete tax years.

Gains arising in the year of departure are chargeable in that year and gains arising during the period of absence are chargeable in the year in which UK residence is resumed (*TCGA 1992, s 2*). Gains on assets acquired abroad that are realised in the intervening years of non-residence are outside the charge, subject to certain anti-avoidance provisions.

The following summary relates to the provisions of *TCGA 1992, s 10A* as amended by *F(No 2)A 2005*. These apply, broadly, where the 'year of departure' (see below) is 2005/06 or later (or, in some cases, 2004/05).

5.34 The charge arises in the following circumstances, a 'year' being a tax year:

(a) the taxpayer satisfies the 'residence requirements' (ie broadly speaking, he is resident or ordinarily resident in the UK, see below) for a year (the 'year of return');

(b) he did not satisfy the residence requirements for one or more years immediately preceding the year of return, but there are prior years for which he did satisfy them;

(c) there are fewer than five 'intervening years', ie years falling between the year of departure (see below) and the year of return; and

(d) he satisfied the residence requirements for at least four out of the seven years immediately preceding the year of departure (*TCGA 1992, s 10A(1)*).

All of these conditions must be met before the charge can arise. If any of these conditions is not met, no charge arises on any gains accruing in the intervening years (and any losses accruing in those years are not allowable).

With regard to (a), the taxpayer satisfies the residence requirements for a tax year:

- if he is resident in the UK and not 'treaty non-resident' (see below) during any part of that year; or

- if he is ordinarily resident in the UK during that year (unless he is treaty non-resident during that year) (*TCGA 1992, s 10A(9)*).

The 'year of departure' in (c) is the last tax year, before the year of return, for which the taxpayer satisfied the residence requirements. An 'intervening year', where conditions (a) to (d) above apply, is a tax year falling between the year of departure and the year of return (*TCGA 1992, s 10A(8)*).

An individual is 'treaty non-resident' at any time if, at that time, he is regarded as resident in a territory outside the UK for the purposes of double taxation relief arrangements (*TCGA 1992, ss 10A(9A), 288(7B)*).

Gains etc treated as accruing in year of return

5.35   In the circumstances outlined above, the taxpayer is chargeable to CGT as if the following gains or losses accrued to him in the year of return:

(a)   all the chargeable gains and losses which, apart from this rule, would have accrued to him – had he been resident and ordinarily resident in the UK – in an intervening year;

(b)   all the chargeable gains which, under *TCGA 1992, s 13* or *s 86* (see **8.1**), would be treated as accruing to him in an intervening year if he had been resident in the UK throughout that intervening year; and

(c)   any losses which, by virtue of *TCGA 1992, s 13(8)*, would have been allowable in an intervening year if he had been resident in the UK throughout that intervening year (*TCGA 1992, s 10A(2), (6)*).

Chargeable gains and allowable losses are not to be brought into account in the year of return if they are gains or losses accruing in an intervening year and they fall to be taken into account under *TCGA 1992, s 10* or *s 16(3)* (non-residents carrying on a trade etc through a UK branch or agency, see **5.22**) (*TCGA 1992, s 10A(5)*).

In order to simplify computations for 2010/11 onwards, transitional provisions were introduced in the *Finance (No 2) Act 2010*. Therefore, where a taxpayer has been temporarily non-resident but resumes UK residence during 2010/11, any gains that become chargeable under *TCGA 1992, s 10A* are treated as arising before 23 June 2010.

The normal time limits for assessments are modified where *TCGA 1992, s 10A* applies. Any assessment for the year of departure may be made at any time up to two years after the 31 January following the year of return (*TCGA 1992, s 10A(7)*).

Exclusion for assets acquired after departure from UK

5.36   The legislation must be read with care, to take account of double negatives. The gains and losses treated as accruing to the taxpayer in the year of return (see **5.35**) exclude (except as mentioned below) any gain or loss accruing on his disposal of an asset if:

(a)   he acquired the asset at a time in the year of departure or any intervening year when (i) he was neither resident nor ordinarily resident in the UK, or (ii) he was resident or ordinarily resident in the UK but was 'treaty non-resident' (see below);

(b)   the acquisition did not take place by means of a 'relevant disposal' (see below) treated as a no gain, no loss transfer by virtue of *TCGA 1992, ss 58, 73* or *258(4)* (transfers between spouses or civil partners, property reverting to settlor on the death of a life tenant, and transfers of heritage property);

(c)   the asset is not an interest created by or arising under a settlement; and

(d)   the amount or value of the consideration for the taxpayer's acquisition of the asset is not reduced by any of the CGT roll-over reliefs provided by *TCGA 1992, ss 23(4)(b), (5)(b), 152(1)(b),*or *153(1)(b)* (with effect for disposals after 15 March 2005), *162(3)(b), 247(2)(b)* or *247(3)(b).*

The 'relevant disposal' above is a disposal of an asset acquired by the person making the disposal at a time when he was resident or ordinarily resident in the UK and was not 'treaty non-resident' (*TCGA 1992, s 10A(3), (8)*).

However, a gain is not excluded from the charge (ie it is chargeable as described in **5.35**) if:

●   it has accrued or would have accrued on the disposal of any asset (the 'first asset');

●   it is treated as accruing on the disposal of the whole or part of another asset (the 'other asset') by virtue of *s 116(10), (11), 134* or *154(2), (4)* (reorganisations, compensation stock and roll-over relief for depreciating assets); and

●   paragraphs (a)–(d) above apply to that other asset but not to the first asset (*TCGA 1992, s 10A(4)*).

The exclusion for assets acquired after departure from the UK applies only to the special charge under *TCGA 1992, 10A*. It does not have any bearing on any liability under the basic charging provision of *TCGA 1992, s 2*, which may give rise to a liability in the year of departure or the year of return to the UK where the split-year concession (ESC D2) is not available.

Nothing in any double tax relief treaty is to be read as preventing the taxpayer from being chargeable to CGT in respect of chargeable gains treated as accruing to him in the year of return (*TCGA 1992, s 10A(9C)*).

155

Example 5.2

Sergio came to live permanently in the UK on 5 January 1996. He left the UK to live in Cuba on 1 April 2008 and returned on 16 March 2012. During the period of absence he sold shares he acquired in a UK company in 1997 and made a gain of £40,000. Sergio is treated as being a temporary non-resident, as the period of non-residence amounted to less than five complete tax years, and he was UK resident for at least four of the seven tax years before he left on 1 April 2008. The gain of £40,000 realised while he was living in Cuba is chargeable to CGT in 2011/12 and the CGT due is payable on 31 January 2013.

FOREIGN ASSETS OF NON-UK DOMICILED TAXPAYERS

The remittance basis

5.37   Until enactment of *FA 2008*, CGT was not charged (except as stated below) on gains accruing on the disposal of assets situated outside the UK to an individual who was:

- resident or ordinarily resident in the UK (ie within the charge to CGT); but

- not domiciled in any part of the UK.

Where this exemption applied but amounts were remitted to the UK in respect of such gains, CGT was charged on the amounts received in the UK. Remittances were treated as gains accruing when they were received in the UK. The remittance basis did not apply, however, to remittances of gains that accrued before the individual became resident or ordinarily resident in the UK (*TCGA 1992, s 12(1)*).

HMRC take the view that, if a non-domiciled individual acquires a UK domicile, the remittance basis applies to gains accruing before the change of domicile that are remitted to the UK after the change (CG25311).

A non-domiciled individual who meets the residence tests in **5.1** remains chargeable on all gains accruing on the disposal of UK assets. The location of assets is examined in **5.3**.

This structure has been overhauled by *Sch 7*, which taxes the gains of non-UK domiciliaries even if not remitted to the UK and which tightens up considerably the meaning of remittance. Following representations by various professional bodies, amendments were made to the remittance basis in *FA 2009*.

Remittances

5.38   For years up to 5 April 2008, the remittance basis applied by default. From 6 April 2008 it applies only by election. The entitlement to the remittance basis has not changed by *FA 2008*, but it is now available only on the making of an annual claim and payment of the RBC.

HM Treasury's 'clamp-down' on non-UK domiciled individuals is evident by the increase of the remittance basis charge (RBC) from £30,000 to £50,000 as of 6 April 2012 for non-UK domiciled individuals who have been resident in the UK for 12 of the previous 14 tax years. The £30,000 RBC will remain for those who have been resident for at least seven of the past nine years and fewer than 12 years.

To encourage overseas investment, it was further announced that, from 6 April 2012, non-UK domiciled individuals will be able to remit foreign income or capital gains where they are for the purposes of a 'qualifying investment'. A 'qualifying investment' is an investment in unlisted companies, or those listed on exchange regulated markets, which carry out trading activities on a commercial basis or undertake the development or letting of commercial property. There will be specific anti-avoidance provisions to ensure the investment is made on proper commercial terms.

The general rule is that an amount is treated as received in the UK in respect of a gain if it is:

- an amount paid, used or enjoyed in the UK; or
- an amount transmitted or brought in any manner or form to the UK.

It is also provided that the anti-avoidance rules in *ITTOIA 2005, ss 833* and *834* (dealing with the repayment of UK-linked debts) apply as they would apply for the purpose of *ITTOIA 2005, s 832* if the gain were 'relevant foreign income' (*TCGA 1992, s 12(2)*). These rules are designed to counter arrangements involving loans, the proceeds of which are used or enjoyed in the UK, that are repaid out of gains that are not otherwise remitted to the UK.

There is no CGT charge on a gain that is remitted before the person making it comes to the UK. Where a gain is not remitted directly but is invested in other assets, the gain is traced through those assets in order to establish whether the gain has been remitted to the UK. HMRC take the view that such tracing can take place through 'any number of investments, deposits to bank accounts, transfers between accounts etc' (CG25352).

Whether to choose the remittance basis or pay CGT on an arising basis will very much depend on the scale of the unremitted gains that an individual made during the period in question.

'Small income or gains' rule

5.39   If a taxpayer has a combined total of unremitted offshore income and gains of less than £2,000 in a tax year, the old rules still apply, and tax will be charged only on UK gains and on any offshore gains that are remitted in the UK (*ITA 2007, s 809D*). Such a person will keep the advantages of the annual exempt allowance (£10,900 for 2013/14) and need not pay the RBC. No remittance basis claim will need to be made in such circumstances.

If the offshore income and gains exceed £2,000 and the taxpayer does not wish to pay the RBC, he must pay UK tax on the offshore gains (and income) on an arising basis.

Unremitted gains of more than £2,000

5.40   If the unremitted gains (and income) exceed £2,000, a claim has to be made if the taxpayer wishes to rely on the remittance basis. Care needs to be taken, as in addition to the RBC the taxpayer may lose his entitlement to UK personal allowances including the annual exempt amount for CGT. There are double taxation agreements between the UK and a number of countries (such as France, Germany, Sweden and Switzerland) which allow UK personal allowances to be used for dual residents who rely on the remittance basis. Any decision will turn on the facts of each individual case, and it is important to see whether any double taxation agreements apply.

'Stay away' rule

5.41   If a person has no UK income or gains, has remitted neither income nor gains to the UK, and has not been resident in the UK either in the year under consideration or in at least seven of the last nine years, he need not complete a self-assessment return, even if the offshore income and gains in that year exceed £2,000. See *ITA 2007, s 809E*: in the seventh year of residence in the UK, the remittance basis must be claimed under *ITA 2007, s 809B*.

Election for the remittance basis

5.42   The claim may be made, under *ITA 2007, s 809B*, by a person resident in the UK who is either not ordinarily resident or who is not domiciled here. If the claimant:

- is over 18 in the tax year; and

- has been resident in the UK for at least seven of the last nine tax years,

the RBC is due and the taxpayer must nominate the income or the gains that are subject to the RBC. These are the 'nominated gains' and will usually be of at least £107,142 so that, ignoring the annual exempt amount, which by *ITA 2007, s 809H* is not available, the tax on the gains is at least £30,000, rising to £178,571 for those who will be charged the £50,000 RBC.

The intended structure of the RBC is that it franks the tax on the relevant income or gains, which can thereafter be remitted in the UK free of a further tax charge. This may also help the taxpayer to claim double taxation relief but there is no guarantee of that. Payment of the RBC is not itself a remittance of income or gains. Once the claim is made, *TCGA 1992, s 12* operates to tax on the remittance basis any gains over the nominated gains that are brought to the UK. CGT adopts the income tax rules as to what constitutes a remittance. As always, there are exceptions: offshore life bonds are taxed on the arising basis, and gains from offshore companies and trusts attract special rules.

In order to simplify computations for 2010/11, transitional provisions were introduced in *F(No 2)A 2010*. Therefore, where an individual pays the remittance basis charge for the year and, as a result, gains are deemed to be remitted under *ITA 2007, s 809J*, those gains are deemed to arise in the UK before 23 June 2010.

In each year, resident non-domiciled individuals have a choice whether to pay the RBC or to be liable to UK tax on their worldwide income and capital gains. They are able to opt in and out of the remittance basis from year to year, and not choosing the remittance basis in one year will not preclude claiming the remittance basis in the following year.

'Remittance' under the new rules

5.43   Gains are remitted to the UK where conditions A and B are met, or where condition C or D is met (see *ITA 2007, s 809L*):

- Condition A: money etc is brought to the UK; or received in the UK; or used in the UK; or services are bought in the UK; and is so brought, or is received by a 'relevant person'.

- Condition B: the property or value involved is:
    - part of the gain; or
    - belongs to a 'relevant person' or is consideration given by such a person and is derived in some way from the gains; or
    - the gains are used outside the UK in connection with a 'relevant debt'; or
    - anything derived from the gains is used in some way in connection with a relevant debt.

- Condition C: a gift is enjoyed by the relevant person, being property that would have been within condition A or B above but is remitted in the UK by way of gift. (This closes a long-established loophole, illustrated by *Carter v Sharon* [1936] 1 All ER 720.)

- Condition D: there is a remittance by connected operations as defined in *ITA 2007, s 809O(3)*.

Where a transaction is caught by condition C or D, it is remitted when the person first enjoys the benefit, so there are no ongoing charges: *ITA 2007, s 809L(6)*.

Definitions for the remittance rules

5.44   'Relevant debt' (see *ITA 2007, s 809L(7)*) means, in relation to the relevant person, any debt that relates to:

- money brought, received or used in the UK;

- services provided in the UK;

- qualifying property as a gift that is brought, received, used or enjoyed in the UK;

- the like property which is consideration for a service enjoyed in the UK;

- property of a third party, brought, received or enjoyed in the UK, where connected operations apply; or

- property of a third party where there are connected operations and a service is enjoyed in the UK.

Paying interest can be a remittance under these rules.

'Relevant person' (see *ITA 2007, s 809M*) means:

- the person himself;

- that person's spouse, civil partner or (see *ITA 2007, s 809M(3)(a)*) cohabitee;

- that person's child or grandchild, if under 18;

- the close company in which any person mentioned here is a participator;

- the trustees of a settlement that can benefit any person mentioned here; or

- a body connected with such a settlement.

The inclusion of cohabitees under *ITA 2007, s 809M(3)* is a bold step that some will welcome as tending to prevent avoidance. Few relatives escape the definition, but parents and adult children are unaffected by the new rules.

'Gift recipients' are defined by *ITA 2007, s 809N* as those to whom property (wholly or partly) derived from chargeable gains is given, so defined at the time the gift is made. If the recipient becomes a relevant person, as where she gives him a red sports car and he later moves in with her, he changes status. Gifts may be outright or transfers at an undervalue; if the latter, the remittance is of the discount only: *ITA 2007, s 809N(6)*. Where a gift is made from which the relevant person derives no benefit or enjoyment; or pays a high price to enjoy; or gets no greater benefit than any member of the public could; such enjoyment as he gets is disregarded. This overrules the decision in *Carter v Sharon* (above).

How much is remitted?

5.45 The proceeds of sale will usually include the original cost as well as the gain. The old rule was usually that any remittance was pro rata the gain. The new rule is harsher: the remittance is first of any gain, see *ITA 2007, s 809P*, but limited to gains that are subject to the remittance basis, so pre-residence gains are not taxable when brought in the UK. That makes it important for taxpayers to keep such funds separate from gains realised after they reach the UK.

It may even be wise to keep each gain separate from others, especially where losses have been made. The proceeds of a small gain on a large sum allow greater sheltered remittances of the original stake than where a small investment has done very well; but beware remittances of small gains that are derived from earlier, larger, unremitted gains. The proceeds of any nominated gains should sit in a 'tax paid' fund so that they can be remitted later. Note, however, the effect of anti-avoidance legislation in *ITA 2007, s 809S*, described in the next paragraph.

Order of remittances

5.46 Although this account of the changes introduced by *FA 2008* is concerned with capital gains, the treatment of sums remitted must be put in the context of income as well. Where the taxpayer has already nominated either income or gains but, over and above that, has both income and gains offshore that have not yet been remitted, once there is a remittance, *ITA 2007, ss 809I* and *809J* set out this deemed order (see *ITA 2007, s 809J(2)*):

5.46 *Foreign issues*

(1)   foreign earnings not subject to foreign tax;

(2)   foreign specific employment income not taxed offshore;

(3)   foreign income not taxed overseas;

(4)   foreign gains not taxed offshore;

(5)   foreign earnings subject to foreign tax;

(6)   foreign specific employment income taxed overseas;

(7)   foreign income taxed overseas; and finally

(8)   foreign gains taxed abroad.

Previously, the approach of HMRC to remittances from 'mixed' funds was set out in CG25380–CG25440. It was not statutory. With effect from 6 April 2008, *ITA 2007, ss 809Q* and *809R* deem remittances from a mixed fund to be broadly as set out below. Where an item falls within two categories, it may be allocated on a 'just and reasonable' basis (see *ITA 2007, s 809R(3)*):

(1)   employment income, unless within (2), (3) or (6) below;

(2)   'relevant foreign earnings', unless within (6) below;

(3)   foreign specific employment income, unless within (6) below;

(4)   relevant foreign income, unless within (7) below;

(5)   foreign gains, unless within (8) below;

(6)   employment income taxed abroad;

(7)   relevant foreign income taxed abroad;

(8)   foreign gains taxed abroad; then

(9)   any other income or capital.

ITA 2007, ss 809R and *809S* will require detailed examination in difficult cases. They trace indirect payments and seem to override careful bank account planning, so as to treat the fund, not as containing, say, a foreign tax credit, or some other non-taxable item but as subject to the allocation rules just described. Some property is exempt, to keep the rules slightly simpler than they would otherwise have been. There are six categories (see *ITA 2007, s 809X*):

•   heritage items;

•   personal items;

•   items for repair;

•   temporary imports;

- items under £1,000; and

- certain foreign services.

Heritage items must meet the rules as to public access, viz:

- works of art, antiques or *objets de vertu*;

- access at an approved establishment such as a museum or gallery;

- transit to or from storage at an approved establishment, or available on request for educational use;

- in the UK for at least two years; and

- they qualify for relevant VAT relief.

Personal items such as clothing and jewellery must belong to a 'relevant person' and be for the use of a 'relevant individual': see *ITA 2007, ss 809M* and *809Z2*.

Restoration items must be at, or in transit to or from, defined premises: see *ITA 2007, s 809Z3*.

Temporary importation means in the UK for 275 days or fewer, including any public access days: see *ITA 2007, s 809Z4*.

For items to come within the 'under £1,000' rule, the test is the amount of income that would be caught under the remittance rules. Cash never comes within this rule. The import of only part of a set of items triggers an apportionment based on what actually comes to the UK.

The 'foreign services' exception, see *s 809W*, arises where the service, though provided in the UK, relates mainly to property abroad, and is paid for from foreign income or gains. This could relate to legal fees for advice on foreign assets and may thus protect a niche sector of the UK economy.

Anti-avoidance: temporary non-residence

5.47   A rule similar to that described at **5.33** is introduced by *TCGA 1992, s 10A(9ZA)* to catch the non-UK domiciled taxpayer living in the UK who wishes to go offshore briefly so as to set up pre-entry tax-free remittances. The new subsection deems the remittances made in the 'year away' to be made in the year of return, catching any gains made during the period of non-residence on assets that had been held at the time of departure if those gains are remitted in the UK, either whilst the taxpayer is still abroad or after return. This is slightly harsher than the income tax treatment of short absences; but it mirrors the previous difference between income and gains in this respect.

Remittance basis: computation of gains

5.48   Once gains remitted to the UK have been identified, the computation of the chargeable gain (in sterling) follows the normal rules applying at the time of the disposal, with indexation allowance (frozen at April 1998) being given where appropriate. Any delay between the time of the disposal and the remittance to the UK does not change the qualifying holding period for taper relief (see Example 5.3). HMRC practice regarding the application of double tax relief where gains are assessed on the remittance basis is explained at CG14385–CG14427.

> **Example 5.3**
>
> Arno is a non-UK domiciled but UK-resident taxpayer. He acquired shares in ABC, a foreign quoted company, in May 2003 and disposed of them in August 2008. The gain was remitted to the UK in December 2012. Depending on the amount of capital gain, Arno now needs to decide whether to pay the £50,000 RBC, or pay CGT on an arising basis. Detailed calculations are required.

A loss accruing on the disposal of non-UK assets to an individual who is resident or ordinarily resident but not domiciled in the UK was not formerly an allowable loss (*TCGA 1992, ss 12(1), 16(4)*). That has changed. If a non-UK domiciliary never claims the remittance basis, he is effectively taxed in the UK like a UK taxpayer; he will therefore be able to use such losses. *TCGA 1992, s 16(4)* has been amended to achieve this. From 6 April 2008, foreign losses can be set against any gain, but subject to anti-avoidance carry-forward rules as for UK losses. There is no need to remit anything: this might not always be possible anyway.

It is more complicated where the taxpayer claims the remittance basis after 6 April 2008. The rules look at the year to which the claim relates and depend on whether, in that year, the remittance basis or the arising basis applied (*ITA 2007, s 809B*). As might be expected, allowance of losses is less generous in years to which the remittance basis applied. The first claim under *ITA 2007, s 809B* to the remittance basis closes the door forever to the use of losses as they arise, even though there may later be a year when the remittance basis no longer applies.

The rules for making an election to offset losses under *TCGA 1992, s 16ZA* are strict. Often the taxpayer will not wish to claim, as where relief is available under *TCGA 1992, s 16* as revised. Where the new election is in force, there are difficult identification rules: see *TCGA 1992, ss 19ZB* and *19ZC*, which are beyond the scope of this book.

Losses and the remittance basis

5.49   An individual who claims the remittance basis can make a one-off irrevocable election to obtain UK tax relief for losses realised on foreign situated assets (*TCGA 1992, s 16ZA*). The election will be effective for the first tax years for which the taxpayer claims the remittance basis and all subsequent tax years. As this election will impact on both UK and foreign losses, detailed advice should be taken.

If no such election is made, 'foreign losses' are not allowable losses.

Detailed rules on how to determine the capital gain chargeable to capital gains tax can be found in the legislation:

Step 1

Deduct any allowable losses from the chargeable gains in the following order:

(1)   foreign chargeable gains accruing and remitted to the UK in that year;

(2)   foreign chargeable gains accruing but not remitted in that year; and

(3)   all other chargeable gains arising in that year (other than gains treated as accruing on the remittance to the UK of foreign chargeable gains arising in a previous year).

Chargeable gains accruing under *TCGA 1992, s 87* or *89(2)*, ie gains treated as accruing to the beneficiary are not taken into account.

If the losses do not exhaust the available chargeable gains within (2) above, the losses are deducted first from the last of the gains to accrue.

Step 2

Therefore, the actual chargeable gain will be all the gains arising within that year, less the losses mentioned in Step 1 from the gains within (1) and (3), but not (2).

Where a loss has been deducted from an unremitted foreign chargeable gain, the loss relief will continue if the gain is subsequently remitted to the UK.

Liability to CGT on the remittance basis

5.50   Table 5.4 (based on HMRC6, para 5.4) summarises the effect of an individual's residence, ordinary residence and domicile status and the location of assets in determining CGT liability. It is necessarily of general application, and the detailed provisions should be examined in each case.

Table 5.4

Residence and domicile	UK resident and domiciled	UK resident but not domiciled
UK ordinarily resident	Not eligible to use the remittance basis (RB)	Eligible to use RB
	All UK and foreign income and gains are liable to UK tax on the arising basis (AB)	If RB is used, all UK income and gains are liable to UK tax on the AB
		Foreign income and gains are liable to UK tax on the RB
UK not ordinarily resident	Eligible to use RB	Eligible to use RB
	If RB is used, all UK income and gains are liable to UK tax on the AB	If RB is used, all UK income and gains are liable to UK tax on the AB
	Foreign gains are liable to UK tax on the AB	Foreign income and gains are liable to UK tax on the RB
	Foreign income is liable to UK on the RB	

APPORTIONMENT OF NON-RESIDENT COMPANY'S GAINS

5.51   Chargeable gains accruing to certain non-UK resident companies may be treated as accruing to UK-resident individuals who have an interest in the company. The rules in *TCGA 1992, s 13* apply to chargeable gains accruing to a company that is not resident in the UK but would be a close company if it were UK resident. HMRC guidance on the application of these rules is set out in CG57200–CG57411.

Following a challenge by the EU Commission, new relaxations of the attribution of gains to members of non-resident companies were introduced in *Finance Act 2013*. The draft legislation includes the following reliefs:

●   for gains from a disposal of an asset used for the purposes of an economically significant activity carried on outside the UK; and

- where avoiding a liability to tax was not one of the main motives behind the acquisition, holding or disposal of the asset.

It remains to be seen whether the EU Commission will be satisfied.

Apportionment to UK-resident participator

5.52 When a chargeable gain accrues to the company, a part of it is treated as accruing to every person who:

- is resident or ordinarily resident in the UK when the chargeable gain accrues to the company;

- is (in the case of an individual) domiciled in the UK; and

- is a participator in the company.

There is no 'motive test': the rules are absolute. The company's gain is computed as if the company were within the charge to corporation tax on capital gains. Transfers between members of a group of non-resident companies are treated as if the group was UK resident for this purpose. The part of the gain that is attributed to each participator is based on the extent of his interest as a participator in the company. However, there is no charge where the amount apportioned to the taxpayer and to persons connected with him is not more than 10% of the gain (*TCGA 1992, ss 13(1)–(4), (11A), 14*).

If the company to which the gain accrues pays the participator's tax liability, that payment is ignored for the purposes of income tax, CGT and corporation tax but is not allowable as a deduction in computing the participator's gain on a disposal of shares (*TCGA 1992, s 13(11)*).

'Participator' and 'close company' take their meaning from *ICTA 1988, ss 417* and *414* respectively (*TCGA 1992, ss 13(12)* and *288(1)*), but see also **5.58** regarding participators.

Exceptions

5.53 There is no charge in respect of a chargeable gain:

- accruing on the disposal of an asset used only for the purposes of (i) a trade carried on by the company wholly outside the UK, or (ii) the part carried on outside the UK of a trade carried on by the company partly within and partly outside the UK;

- accruing on the disposal of either currency or a debt within *TCGA 1992, s 252(1)*, where the currency or debt is (or represents) money in use for the purposes of a non-UK trade carried on by the company; or

- in respect of which the company is chargeable to tax under *TCGA 1992, s 10B* (see **5.32**) (*TCGA 1992, s 13(5)*).

The assets of a pension scheme are ignored in determining a person's interest as participator for this purpose, if a gain accruing on disposal of the scheme's assets would be exempt from CGT (*TCGA 1992, s 13(10B)*).

Set-off on distribution of gain

5.54 Where a charge arises (see **5.52**) and tax is paid accordingly, and there is a distribution in respect of the chargeable gain within a specified period (see below), the tax is set against the taxpayer's liability to income tax, CGT or corporation tax on the distribution.

The distribution may be made by means of a dividend or distribution of capital, or on the dissolution of the company. The set-off is reduced to the extent that the tax is reimbursed by the company or applied as a deduction (see below).

The specified period is the period of three years from the earlier of:

- the end of the company's period of account in which the chargeable gain accrued; or
- the end of the period of 12 months from the date when the chargeable gain accrued (*TCGA 1992, s 13(5A), (5B)*).

Deduction on disposal of interest in the company

5.55 If the taxpayer pays the CGT charged as mentioned in **5.52** and the tax is neither reimbursed by the company nor set off as mentioned in **5.54**, it is allowable as a deduction in computing a gain accruing on his disposal of any asset representing his interest as a participator in the company (*TCGA 1992, s 13(7)*).

Calculation of the income tax or CGT chargeable

5.56 For the purpose of calculating any income tax or CGT chargeable for any year on the distribution or disposal, the following rules apply:

(a) a distribution treated as the person's income for that year forms the highest part of his chargeable income;

(b) a gain accruing in that year on the person's disposal of any asset representing his interest as a participator forms the highest part of his chargeable gains;

(c)   where a distribution falls to be treated as a disposal giving rise to a chargeable gain, the gain forms the next highest part of his chargeable gains, after any gains within (b); and

(d)   a gain apportioned to him as mentioned in **5.52** and treated as accruing to him in that year is regarded as the next highest part of his chargeable gains, after any gains within (c) (*TCGA 1992, s 13(7A)*).

Losses

5.57   Losses accruing to the non-resident company are not attributed to participators. However, in arriving at the amount of gains accruing to a company that can be apportioned to participators, a loss may be deducted if it would be an allowable loss in the hands of a UK-resident company (*TCGA 1992, s 13(8)*).

Participators

5.58   'Participator' takes its meaning from *CTA 2010, s 454*. Broadly, any person who has a share or interest in the capital or income of the company is a participator. However, it is also provided, for the purpose of the apportionment of gains under *TCGA 1992, s 13*, that:

(a)   a person's interest as a participator in a company is the interest in the company that is represented by all the factors contributing to his treatment as a participator; and

(b)   the 'extent' of that interest is the proportion of all participators' interests that the person's interest represents.

The apportionment in (b) is made on a just and reasonable basis and takes account of interests of participators who are neither resident, nor ordinarily resident, in the UK (*TCGA 1992, s 13(13)*).

Any appeal as to the extent of a person's interest as a participator for this purpose is made to the First-tier Tax Tribunal (*TCGA 1992, s 13(15)*).

If a person's beneficial interest under a settlement is a factor in determining whether he has an interest as a participator in a company, the interest as a participator is deemed to be the trustees' interest to the extent that it is represented by the beneficial interest (*TCGA 1992, s 13(14)*).

Corporate participators

5.59   If the participator (A) in the non-UK resident company (B) is itself a non-UK resident company, but would be a close company if it were UK resident, the amount apportioned to A is further apportioned among A's participators according to the extent of their respective interests as participators. Since A's participators may include companies, and those companies' participators may also include companies, the rule is applied through any number of companies (*TCGA 1992, s 13(9)*).

Trustees

5.60 Gains may be attributed to trustees of a settlement who are participators in the company, even if they are neither resident nor ordinarily resident in the UK. Such gains may be attributed to UK-resident beneficiaries under the provisions of *TCGA 1992, Ch II* (see **8.1**) (*TCGA 1992, s 13(10)*; *FA 2006, Sch 12, para 8*).

DOUBLE TAX RELIEF

5.61 Double tax relief is described in detail at **3.64**. Relief may be available by virtue of double tax relief arrangements to taxpayers who are not resident in the UK but are chargeable to UK tax under any of the provisions discussed in this chapter. See, however, **5.36** regarding double tax relief arrangements to be disregarded in relation to gains accruing in a period of temporary non-residence, and **5.48** regarding the application of double tax relief where gains are assessed on the remittance basis.

NEW PENALTIES TO TACKLE OFFSHORE TAX EVASION

5.62 HMRC issued a press release on 31 January 2011. This outlined the penalty regime which came into force from 6 April 2011. In April 2012, a factsheet was published (www.hmrc.gov.uk/compliance/cc-fs17.pdf) which summarises the legislation that can be found in *FA 2010, Sch 10*.

The new offshore penalty regime strengthens existing penalties for:

- failure to notify;
- inaccuracy on a return; and
- failure to file a return in time.

There are three penalty levels, which depend on the territory in which the income or gain arises:

- Where the income or gain arises in a territory in 'Category 1' (which includes most of Europe and the United States), the penalty regime will be the same as under the existing legislation and the maximum penalty is 100% of the tax.

- Where the income or gain arises in a territory in 'Category 2', the penalty rate will be 1.5 times that in the existing legislation, up to 150% of tax.

- Where the income or gain arises in a territory in 'Category 3', the penalty rate will be double that in the existing legislation, up to 200% of tax.

There are no penalties for those who have taken reasonable care or have a reasonable excuse for the failure to notify taxable income and gains.

Chapter 6

Partnerships

HOW CGT APPLIES TO PARTNERSHIPS

Fiscal transparency

6.1 Partnerships, including limited liability partnerships (LLPs), and Scottish partnerships are treated as transparent entities for CGT purposes. This means that:

(a) a disposal of a chargeable asset owned by the partnership is treated as a disposal by the partners, and not as a disposal by the partnership itself; and

(b) CGT is charged on each partner separately in respect of any chargeable gain accruing to him on the disposal of a partnership asset, and that gain is charged in the same way as other chargeable gains accruing to him in the same chargeable period (and if a loss accrues on the disposal each partner's share of the loss becomes an allowable loss which he can set against his own chargeable gains) (*TCGA 1992, s 59*).

A partner making such a disposal may be eligible for hold-over relief (see **Chapter 13**) or roll-over relief for replacement of business assets (see **Chapter 14**). A disposal of a partnership share, or asset used by the partnership may be eligible for entrepreneurs' relief (see **11.23**).

A partner treated as disposing of a partnership asset (or a share in it) can roll-over a chargeable gain accruing against the acquisition of an asset used for the purpose of another trade, whether that trade is carried on by him as a sole trader or by a partnership in which he is a partner.

What is a partnership?

6.2 The CGT legislation does not define 'partnership', but the *Partnership Act 1890* defines it as 'the relationship which subsists between persons carrying on a business in common with a view to profit'. A partnership is a separate legal person in Scotland, but this rule is overridden for CGT purposes so that there is no difference in treatment between, for example, a Scottish partnership and an English one (*TCGA 1992, s 59(1)(a)*).

Although a partnership's dealings are treated as dealings by the partners and not by the partnership itself, the partnership is required to provide details of disposals of partnership property. For this purpose the partnership tax return is to include the particulars that would be required if the partnership itself were liable to tax on a chargeable gain accruing on the disposal (*TMA 1970, s 12AA(7)*).

It may not always be clear whether, for CGT purposes, arrangements amount to a partnership or merely joint ownership of the assets concerned. Joint ownership of a let property will not by itself mean a partnership exists, even where the property is let as furnished holiday lettings. HMRC provide their opinion on jointly held property in their Property Income Manual (PIM1030). General guidance on whether a business is operated as a partnership is provided in their Business Income Manual (BIM72005–BIM72015).

Legislation and HMRC practice

6.3 The only tax legislation, which is specifically written for dealing with the capital gains of partners and partnerships, is contained in *TCGA 1992, s 59* (and *s 59A* for LLPs). This is inadequate to deal with all the complexities that can arise with partnership gains, so HMRC issued Statement of Practice D12 (set out in full at **6.26**) in 1975. This was supplemented by Statements of Practice 1/79 and 1/89. These statements of practice apply, in principle, to corporate partners as well as individuals, although companies are generally chargeable to corporation tax on their chargeable gains (see **Chapter 9**). For the CGT charge on ATED-related gains (known as the CGTED), which can apply to companies and partnerships with corporate members, see **4.43**.

SP D12 was extended following the creation of LLPs as bodies corporate in 2001 (see **6.24**). See **6.4** regarding partnerships residing outside the UK or carrying on a business controlled and managed outside the UK. In addition to SP D12, the following Revenue & Customs Briefs deal with aspects of CGT for partnerships:

- Brief 3/08: the contribution of assets to a partnership, overruling SP D12, para 4 (see **6.18**); and

- Brief 9/09: the rebasing rules as they apply to partnership assets (see **6.12**).

Guidance on the taxation of partnership gains, and gains made by partners, is found in the HMRC Capital Gains Manual at CG27000–CG28420. The operation of CGT for partners largely relies on HMRC practice rather than legislation; and, without a legislative framework, this practice can be changed at any point, sometimes with retrospective effect.

In 2013 the government consulted on proposals to change two aspects of partnership tax law relating to:

- the allocation of profits and losses in partnerships and LLPs containing corporate members; and

- the presumption of self-employed status for members of LLPs who would otherwise be treated as employees.

These changes, if introduced, will not affect the taxation of gains within partnerships, but they may force businesses operating as LLPs or partnerships with corporate members to change their structure.

Residence and domicile

6.4   A partnership's fiscal transparency (see **6.1**) means that special rules applying to partnerships controlled abroad are (with the exception mentioned below) no longer relevant. Each partner's CGT position depends on his own residence and domicile status (see **Chapter 5**). For example:

- a partner who is resident and domiciled in the UK is chargeable on gains accruing to him on the disposal of partnership assets irrespective of where they arise; and

- a partner who is not resident in the UK is chargeable only in relation to gains accruing on the disposal of assets used for the purpose of a trade carried on via a UK branch or agency (see **5.30**).

Any double taxation agreement providing relief from CGT in the UK for a partnership's capital gains does not affect the CGT liability on a UK-resident partner's share of those gains where the partnership carries on a trade, profession or business whose control and management are situated outside the UK (*TCGA 1992, s 59(2), (3)*).

PARTNERSHIP ASSETS AND 'OTHER' ASSETS

6.5   A 'partnership asset' is an asset owned by all of the partners. An asset that is owned by only some of the partners but used by the partnership is not a partnership asset – HMRC guidance refers to such assets as 'other assets'. The distinction between partnership assets and 'other' assets used by the partnership may not affect the CGT payable on disposal, but it will make a difference to the IHT payable on the death of a partner where business property relief (BPR) is claimed. BPR will give 100% relief from IHT for the value of partnership assets, but only 50% relief for 'other' assets held outside the partnership (*IHTA 1984, s 105 (1)(d)*). For further discussion of BPR, see Chapter 11 of *Inheritance Tax 2013/14* (Bloomsbury Professional).

It may be difficult to determine whether an asset is a partnership asset if it is not included within the partnership accounts or referred to in the partnership agreement, in which case the intentions of the partners will be taken into account. *Partnership Act 1890, s 20* defines partnership property as:

> 'All property and rights and interests in property originally brought into the partnership stock or acquired, whether by purchase or otherwise, on account of the firm, or for the purposes and in the course of the partnership business, must be held and applied by the partners exclusively for the purposes of the partnership and in accordance with the partnership agreement.'

The identification of partnership property was examined in *I H Bhatti v HMRC* [2013] UKFTT 355 (TC). I Bhatti was in partnership with his two brothers (M and A Bhatti), trading as Central Properties. Various properties were acquired and disposed of, with the names of M and A Bhatti as the registered proprietors but not that of I Bhatti. However, a trust deed signed by all three brothers indicated that the properties were held as partnership assets. The Tribunal concluded that the properties were partnership assets.

Assets held by a member firm of the Scottish Stock Exchange Association are not regarded as partnership assets (CG27200). HMRC indicate in their Inheritance Tax Manual (IHTM25104) that an asset included on the balance sheet of the partnership accounts is almost certainly a partnership asset, but this guidance may not be followed by the Shares and Assets Valuation (SAV) division of HMRC on disposal of the asset on the death of a partner, or otherwise.

Focus

Where it is intended that an asset should be treated as a partnership asset, the partnership deed should make it clear that the asset is partnership property.

This is particularly important in the case of family farms, where certain partners may develop specific areas of the farm business as part of a diversification project.

Roll-over relief for replacement of business assets (see **Chapter 14**) is available to the owner of assets that are let to a partnership in which he is a partner, if those assets are used for the purposes of the partnership's trade or profession and the other conditions for the relief are met (SP D11). Entrepreneurs' relief is available on the disposal of a share in the partnership assets, either on the introduction of a partner or when a partner reduces their interest in the partnership (see **Chapter 11**).

Fractional share in a partnership asset

6.6   When a partnership buys an asset, each partner is treated as acquiring a fractional share in it. In order to compute the gain or loss accruing to a partner on either the disposal of a chargeable asset owned by the partnership (see **6.9**) or a change in asset surplus-sharing arrangements (see **6.13**), it is necessary to calculate each partner's disposal consideration and allowable expenditure by reference to his fractional share in the partnership asset.

HMRC guidance sets out a series of tests to determine a partner's fractional share of a partnership asset. Where there is actual consideration for the disposal, HMRC will apply the following tests in the order shown:

- any specific written agreement setting out the allocation of capital assets;
- any agreement or other evidence setting out how capital profits are to be shared; and
- any agreement or other evidence setting out how income profits are to be shared.

If none of the above evidence exists (eg treatment in the accounts), the assets should be treated as held in equal proportions by all the partners as provided for by *Partnership Act 1890, s 24(1)* (CG27220).

Where the market value of a partner's share in a partnership asset is to be ascertained for CGT purposes it is taken as a fraction of the value of the partnership's entire interest in the asset. There is no discount to take account of the size of the partner's share. For example, if a partner has a one-tenth share in the partnership assets and the partnership owns all of the shares in a company, the value of the partner's interest in the shareholding is one-tenth of the partnership's interest (SP D12, para 1; see **6.26**).

Allowable expenditure: multiple acquisitions

6.7   Where a partner has built up his fractional share in the partnership assets (including goodwill) in stages over a period of time, his acquisition cost of the latest fractional share of those assets is calculated by pooling the expenditure relating to each acquisition (CG27300).

Where all or a part of the partner's share was acquired before 6 April 1965, the disposal will normally be identified with shares acquired on a 'first in, first out' basis, but HMRC may accept a different approach where this produces an unreasonable result (eg where there is a temporary change in the shares in a partnership due to a delay between the departure of one partner and the arrival of a new one) (SP D12, para 10; see **6.26**).

Partnership goodwill

6.8   The value of goodwill generated by a partnership is not generally recognised in the balance sheet, and it is customary not to place a value on that goodwill in dealings between the partners. In such cases, the HMRC practice on a disposal of a partner's interest in the goodwill for actual consideration, is to regard that interest as the same asset as was acquired by the partner when he first became entitled to a share in it (CG68100).

Where the partnership goodwill was previously recognised in the accounts but the value has been written down to zero for whatever reason, HMRC will resist claims for a share of that goodwill to be treated as becoming of negligible value (*TCGA 1992, s 24(2)*). Such a claim, if successful, would create a capital loss for the claimant partner (see **2.10**). HMRC will only accept a capital loss on goodwill has arisen where the entire goodwill of the partnership has become of negligible value (CG28000).

Purchased goodwill may also not be recognised in the balance sheet at a value greater than cost, and may not otherwise be taken into account in dealings between partners. However, this purchased goodwill is treated as a separate asset for CGT purposes from the partnership's self-generated goodwill. The interest in purchased goodwill is, therefore, treated as acquired on the later of:

- the date of purchase by the partnership; or

- the date when the disposing partner first became entitled to a share in that purchased goodwill (SP D12, para 12; see **6.26**).

DISPOSAL OF PARTNERSHIP ASSETS

6.9   When a partnership disposes of an asset to an outside party, each partner is treated as making a disposal of his fractional share (see **6.6**) in that asset. The proceeds of disposal are allocated to the partners in the ratio of their share in asset surpluses (capital profits) at the time of disposal.

If this ratio is not specifically laid down, the allocation follows the destination of the surplus as shown in the partnership accounts, but regard is also given to any agreement outside the accounts. If the surplus is put to a common reserve, the asset surplus-sharing ratio is used to divide the proceeds. If no such ratio is specified, the ordinary income profit-sharing ratio will be used (SP D12, para 2; see **6.26**).

Example 6.1

Each of the following partnerships disposes of its chargeable asset to outside parties at arm's length, realising a gain of £90,000. The gain is apportioned among the partners as follows:

Arthur & Co

The partnership agreement states that each of the three partners shall be entitled to share equally in any surplus arising from assets disposed of by the partnership. Each partner is therefore treated as if he had made a gain of £30,000.

Binder & Co

The three partners in Binder & Co have no formal agreement, but interest on capital contributed to the partnership is shown in the accounts at the same sum for each. The inference is that the capital has been equally contributed and can be equally withdrawn, so that the apportioned gain is £30,000 to each partner.

Cooper & Co

The three partners, Abby, Chris and Kate, have no formal agreement and the capital is shown in the accounts as a global sum. The profit-sharing ratio is 3:2:1. Thus the gain is apportioned as follows:

- Abby: £45,000;

- Chris: £30,000; and

- Kate: £15,000.

Part disposals

6.10   If a partnership makes a part disposal, the part disposal rules (see **2.4**) are applied before the gain is divided among the partners. Where the relief for small part disposals of land is available (see **2.5**), the conditions are applied separately in relation to each partner. However, the normal part disposal rules do not apply to changes in fractional partnership shares between the partners (see **6.15**).

Partnership assets distributed in kind

6.11   Where a partnership asset is distributed to one or more partners (eg on a dissolution of the partnership), the disposal is treated as being made for a consideration equal to the market value of the asset. Partners who do not receive a share of the asset are treated as having disposed of their fractional share in the asset at the time of the distribution (CG27400).

The gain accruing to each individual partner is computed but the gain accruing to the partner receiving the asset is deducted from his allowable expenditure on a subsequent disposal of the asset. The same principle applies where a loss arises (SP D12, para 3; see **6.26**).

Rebasing rule for disposal of partnership assets

6.12   All assets held by individual partners at 31 March 1982 which are disposed of after 5 April 2008 are rebased at the March 1982 value for CGT purposes. Statement of Practice 1/89 deals with the indexation allowance in relation to no gain, no loss transfers between partners (CG28100–CG28290). For disposals made after 5 April 2008, SP 1/89 only applies to corporate partners whose capital gains are subject to corporation tax (see **Chapter 9**).

Where an individual partner has previously acquired an asset on a no gain, no loss basis, the base cost of that asset may include indexation allowance from 31 March 1982 or the month in which the partner acquired the asset, to the date of disposal or April 1998 if earlier (*TCGA 1992, s 35A*). This will occur in the following circumstances:

- the partner acquired the asset between 31 March 1982 and 5 April 1998 as a no gain, no loss transaction;

- any previous disposal and acquisition of the asset since 31 March 1982 has been on a no gain, no loss basis; and

- the asset was not rebased on the transfer to the partner.

Example 6.2

Alistair and Tony formed a partnership in March 1979, sharing all profits equally. They immediately acquired a building for use in the partnership business for £100,000, which was valued at £120,000 on 31 March 1982. On 1 May 1999, Gordon joined the partnership and the profit-sharing ratios were changed to: Alistair 25%, Tony 50%, Gordon 25%, although Gordon made no payment towards his acquisition of a share in the partnership-owned building. This building was not revalued in partnership accounts from the historical cost of £100,000 and the partners did not make rebasing elections in their capacity as partners. The building was sold on 30 June 2013 for £660,000.

Alistair is treated as disposing of 25% of the value of the partnership building to Gordon in 1999/00 at a no gain, no loss transfer. When the building is sold in 2013, all three partners are treated as disposing of their fractional shares in the property. The gains are calculated as follows:

Alistair: 1999/2000		£	£
Deemed disposal value	100,000 × 25%		25,000
Indexation allowance to April 1998 on 1982 value of £120,000	120,000 × 25% = 30,000 × 1.047		31,410
			56,410
Less cost – historical			(25,000)
Unindexed gain			31,410
Indexation allowance			(31,410)
No gain, no loss:			Nil

Under the practice set out in SP 1/89, Gordon acquires his share in the building for £56,410 (see **6.16**).

All partners: 2013/14	£		£
Alistair			
Disposal consideration	25% × 660,000		165,000
Less 1982 value	25% × 120,000		(30,000)
Gain:			135,000
Tony			
Disposal consideration	50% × 660,000		330,000
Less 1982 value:	50% × 120,000		(60,000)
Gain:			270,000

Gordon		
Disposal consideration	25% × 660,000	165,000
Less cost per *TCGA 1992, s 35A*	25% × £120,000 = 30,000	
Market value at 31 March 1992	+ 30,000 × 1.047 = 31,410	
plus indexation from 1992 to 1998		61,410
Gain:		103,590

Under *TCGA 1992, s 35A*, Gordon acquires his interest in the partnership building at the indexed cost of the 1982 value. The provisions in *s 35A* supersede the result of the capital gains calculation in 1999/2000 based on SP 1/89 (see Revenue & Customs Brief 9/09).

Market value rule

6.13 Partners are connected persons (see **3.19**) for CGT purposes. However, where an interest in a partnership asset is transferred between partners on a commercial basis, market value is not substituted for the actual consideration passing unless the partners are otherwise connected.

HMRC guidance makes it clear that this practice applies to:

- 'normal disposals and acquisitions' of fractional shares in partnership assets carried out on a commercial basis between partners who are otherwise acting at arm's length and connected solely by partnership; and

- acquisitions made by an incoming partner and disposals made by the existing partners, carried out under genuine commercial arrangements (*TCGA 1992, s 286(4)*; CG27800).

HMRC may seek to apply the market value rule where the partners are connected otherwise than by partnership (such as relatives), or where they are not so connected but the transaction is not conducted at arm's length. HMRC will consider whether any consideration passing is of an amount that might reasonably have been expected to pass had they been unconnected except by partnership, and acting at arm's length (CG27800; SP D12, para 7).

CHANGE IN FRACTIONAL SHARE OF ASSETS

6.14 A reduction in an individual partner's fractional share of a partnership asset is a disposal for CGT purposes, and an increase in that share is an acquisition. Such a change can arise from:

- the actual disposal or acquisition of a partnership asset (see **6.9**);

- the partners varying the terms of the partnership agreement or reaching a separate agreement with regard to the asset concerned (see **6.15**); or

- a partner joining or leaving the partnership (see **6.18**).

Transfers of fractional shares between spouses or civil partners living together are, however, subject to the no gain, no loss rule laid down for such transfers and outlined in **3.62** (*TCGA 1992, s 58*).

Change in asset surplus-sharing ratios

6.15   An individual may introduce capital when joining a partnership, which is credited to his capital account (see **6.19**). The partnership's retained profits may subsequently increase his capital account balance. No CGT liability arises when those amounts of capital are subsequently withdrawn, for example, on retirement.

However, if consideration in money or money's worth passes between the partners on a change in asset surplus-sharing ratios, that consideration represents:

- the disposal consideration received by the partner whose share is reduced; and

- acquisition expenditure incurred by the partner whose share is increased.

In those circumstances a chargeable gain may well arise.

The CGT treatment of a merger between two or more partnerships to form one partnership follows the treatment for a change in partnership asset surplus-sharing ratios. Roll-over relief on replacement of business assets (see **Chapter 14**) may be available where a partner disposes of part of his share in the assets of the old partnership and acquires a share in other assets put into the merged partnership (SP D12, paras 4, 9; see **6.26**).

Consideration within the accounts

6.16   If there is no direct payment of consideration outside the partnership, the consideration for the disposal is the fraction of the asset's current balance sheet value that corresponds to the fractional share passing between the partners. The normal part disposal rule (see **2.4**) is not applied in this situation.

If the firm's assets have not been revalued, a reduction in an existing partner's capital profit-sharing ratio is treated as a disposal on which no gain or loss arises. This no gain, no loss treatment also applies for the purpose of the 31 March 1982 rebasing rules (*TCGA 1992, Sch 3*) and the partial relief for deferred charges on gains accrued before 31 March 1982 (*TCGA 1992, Sch 4*).

Where indexation allowance is available, the consideration for the disposal is calculated on the assumption that an unindexed gain equal to the indexation allowance accrued, so that there is no gain and no loss after deducting the indexation allowance (SP 1/89). If the disposal occurred before 6 April 2008, it does not attract taper relief as there has been no gain.

Example 6.3

Ben and Jerry are in partnership and the only chargeable asset is a property. If the fractional shares change from 50:50 to 40:60, Ben has disposed of a 10/50 of his share in the assets and Jerry has acquired a 10/50 share.

The current balance sheet value of the property is £50,000. Ben's disposal proceeds, and Jerry's acquisition cost, will be $(10/50 \times £50,000) \times 1/2 = £5,000$.

Ben's disposal gives rise to no gain and no loss, so long as the asset has not been revalued – see below – because his acquisition cost is also $(10/50 \times £50,000) \times 1/2 = £5,000$.

If assets (such as land and buildings) are revalued to a higher amount, the surplus is credited to the existing partners' capital accounts. No chargeable gain accrues on that event. However, the partner has effectively realised a proportion of the partnership's assets. A chargeable gain therefore arises upon a subsequent disposal, which results in all or part of the capital account being paid to him (see CG27500).

In summary, an upward revaluation of the partnership asset in the balance sheet gives rise to a potential gain on a future change in asset surplus-sharing ratios, although the revaluation itself does not represent a disposal for CGT purposes (SP D12, para 5; see **6.26**).

Consideration outside the accounts

6.17   Any payment made outside the partnership accounts on a change of asset surplus-sharing ratios represents consideration for the disposal of the whole or part of a partner's share in partnership assets. This consideration is in addition to the consideration by reference to balance sheet value (see **6.16**). It may be paid directly to the partners or via a transfer between capital accounts.

Such a payment may represent consideration for goodwill that is not included in the balance sheet. In such cases:

●   the partner receiving the payment will have no allowable expenditure to set against it unless he made a similar payment for his share in the asset; and

- the partner making the payment will only be allowed to deduct it in computing gains or losses on a subsequent disposal of his share in the asset (CG27500; SP D12, para 6).

Example 6.4

David, Edward and Fiona are partners in a firm of accountants who share all profits in the ratio 7:7:6. George is admitted as a partner in May 2013 and pays the other partners a total of £10,000 for the partnership goodwill. The new partnership shares are: David 6/20, Edward 6/20, Fiona 5/20 and George 3/20. The book value of goodwill is £18,000, being its cost on acquisition of the practice from the predecessor in 1990. The table below shows the calculation of the chargeable gains accruing to David, Edward and Fiona and George's acquisition costs. The capital gains accruing to David, Edward and Fiona could be reduced by entrepreneurs' relief if the other conditions for that relief also apply (see **Chapter 11**).

David	£	£
Fractional share disposed of 7/20 – 6/20 = 1/20		
Disposal consideration for partnership goodwill:		
Notional reduction in book value: 1/20 × £18,000	900	
Actual disposal paid by new capital: 7/20 × £10,000	3,500	
		4,400
Allowable expenditure, reduction in book value 1/20 × £18,000		(900)
Gain		3,500

Edward		
Fractional share disposed of 7/20 – 6/20 = 1/20		
Gain (computed as for David)		3,500

Fiona		
Fractional share disposed of 6/20 – 5/20 = 1/20		
Disposal consideration for partnership goodwill:		
Notional reduction in book value: 1/20 × £18,000	900	
Actual disposal paid by new capital: 6/20 × £10,000	3,000	
		3,900
Allowable expenditure, reduction in book value 1/20 × £18,000		(900)
Gain		3,000

George		£	£
Allowable expenditure on share of goodwill:			
Actual consideration paid			10,000
Notional consideration transferred:	from David: 1/20 × £18,000	900	
	from Edward: 1/20 × £18,000	900	
	from Fiona: 1/20 × £18,000	900	
			2,700
Total consideration			12,700

Partners joining and leaving the partnership

6.18   Until 21 January 2008, it was thought that changes in asset surplus-sharing arrangements on the occasion of one or more partners joining or leaving the partnership would be treated for CGT purposes in a similar way to the changes outlined in **6.14**. However, the Revenue & Customs Brief 3/08 changed the approach where capital is contributed to the partnership (see **6.19**).

The CGT treatment is different where a partner leaves the partnership and reduces his share to nil. The capitalised value of an annuity paid to a retiring partner may represent consideration in money's worth, but HMRC practice is to disregard annuities meeting certain conditions (see **6.20**).

Capital introduced to a partnership

6.19   Revenue & Customs Brief 03/08 clarified HMRC practice in relation to capital gains arising on the introduction of a capital asset to a partnership. When the asset is introduced on forming a new partnership, or where a new partner joins an existing partnership, this can generate a chargeable gain (CG27900).

Example 6.5

Martin owns music rights worth £600,000, which he has acquired from various music creators over time. These rights are the major asset of his sole-trader business. He joined the B&H partnership as an equal one-third partner and introduced the music rights to the partnership by way of his capital contribution. Martin's sole-trader business ceases when he joins the B&H partnership, and he is treated as making a disposal of two-thirds of the music rights at their current value: £600,000 × 2/3 = £400,000. Martin's gain could be reduced by entrepreneurs' relief as it arises from the disposal of assets used in his sole-trader business, which ceased within three years of that disposal (see **11.27**).

When a new partner introduces cash as his capital contribution to the partnership, rather than an asset, no gain can arise, as the gift or transfer of cash into the partnership is not a disposal for CGT purposes.

The application of the ruling in Revenue & Customs Brief 3/08 may not be entirely clear for every situation. Where genuine uncertainty exists and the issue is commercially significant, the taxpayer can apply to HMRC for a ruling using the non-statutory business clearance process as detailed in the HMRC Non-statutory Business Clearance Guidance Manual.

Focus

Where HMRC have advised the taxpayer (or his agent) based on the pre-21 January 2008 interpretation of SP D12, they will stand by that advice, and not disturb the agreed tax treatment.

Where no ruling was given on the case, which has not been finalised through the self-assessment system, the tax treatment could be disturbed and a chargeable gain may arise where none was thought to exist. In these cases, it may also be prudent to seek a ruling from HMRC under the clearance procedure mentioned above.

Annuities to retiring partners

6.20   The capitalised value of an annuity paid to a retiring partner represents consideration in money's worth for the disposal of the retiring partner's share of the partnership assets. This is the case whether or not the partnership buys a life annuity for the benefit of the retiring partner. The potential CGT charge on this consideration is not precluded by the general exclusion of money or money's worth charged to income tax from the consideration for a disposal of assets (*TCGA 1992, s 37(3)*).

However, HMRC practice is to treat that capitalised value as consideration only if the amount of the annuity is 'more than can be regarded as a reasonable recognition of the past contribution of work and effort made by the partner to the partnership' (CG28400). HMRC's measure of 'reasonable' recognition is based on a fraction of the partner's share of the partnership's profits. That fraction depends on how long the taxpayer has been a partner, as indicated below. See **6.23** regarding the treatment of a lump sum paid in addition to an annuity.

Partner for at least ten years

6.21   A reasonable recognition of the partner's contribution will be no more than two-thirds of their average share of profit in the 'best three' of the last seven years of assessment in which he devoted substantially the whole of their time to acting as a partner. The share of profit is computed before deducting any capital allowances, charges, or losses (CG28400).

Partner for less than ten years

6.22   If the retiring partner was a partner for less than ten years, the fraction of his average share of profit – to be used instead of two-thirds in **6.21** – is set out in the table in para 8 of SP D12 (see **6.26**). The annuity may be stated as a percentage of future partnership profits. HMRC guidance indicates that they are unlikely to spend time enquiring about the level of future payments in cases that are 'clearly marginal'. In most cases, a reasonable estimate of the amount likely to be paid would fall within the above limits (CG28400).

However, the full capitalised value of the annuity is taken as consideration for the partner's disposal (and will represent allowable acquisition expenditure on the part of the remaining partners) if it exceeds the limits. HMRC will take advice from the HMRC Actuarial Team where necessary, but their guidance indicates that the response to any request from the taxpayer for an advance clearance will be limited to providing a general outline of their published practice (CG28400).

Lump sum paid in addition to annuity

6.23   Where a lump sum is paid in addition to an annuity:

*   the lump sum is treated as consideration for the disposal; and

*   one-ninth of the lump sum is added to the capitalised value of the annuity and, if the total exceeds the fraction of the retired partner's average share of the profits (ie the fraction given in either **6.21** or **6.22**), the capitalised value of the annuity is treated as additional consideration (SP 1/79; CG28420).

LIMITED LIABILITY PARTNERSHIPS

Taxed as other partnerships

6.24   A limited liability partnership (LLP) carrying on a trade or business with a view to profit is treated in the same way as a conventional partnership for CGT purposes, ie it is 'fiscally transparent'. Although an LLP is a corporate body, for CGT purposes its assets are treated as held by its members as partners, and the LLP's dealings are treated as dealings by the members in partnership rather than by the LLP itself. Tax is charged on the members of the LLP separately, in respect of chargeable gains accruing to them as members, on a disposal of any of the LLP's assets (*TCGA 1992, s 59A(1)*).

The CGT provisions applying to partnerships other than LLPs are generally extended to LLPs, and it is provided that references to members of a partnership include members of an LLP. However, references to a company or its members do not include an LLP or its members (*TCGA 1992, s 59A(2)*).

The members of an LLP are entitled to the same reliefs as partners in a conventional partnership. All HMRC concessions and statements of practice currently apply to an LLP in the same way as they apply to a conventional partnership while it is carrying on a trade or business (but see **6.3**). However, they do not apply to the members of an LLP that has ceased to be 'fiscally transparent' (see **6.25**) (SP D12, introduction; CG27050).

End of transparency

6.25 The 'transparency' treatment outlined in **6.24** continues on the temporary cessation of a trade or business carried on with a view to profit. It also continues during a period of winding up following a permanent cessation of the trade or business, so long as that period is not unreasonably prolonged and the winding up is not done for reasons connected with tax avoidance. Transparency ceases to apply, however:

- on the appointment of a liquidator; and
- where a court makes a winding-up order or there is a corresponding event under the law of an overseas territory (*TCGA 1992, s 59A(3), (4)*).

Where transparency does end, and tax is charged on the LLP as a company in respect of chargeable gains accruing on a disposal of its assets (or on the members in respect of chargeable gains accruing on a disposal of their capital interests in the LLP), the liability is computed and tax is charged as though the rules outlined above never applied (*TCGA 1992, s 59(5)*).

There is no deemed disposal of assets by the LLP or any member as a result of transparency beginning or coming to an end (*TCGA 1992, s 59(6)*).

However, when transparency ends and a member of the LLP holds an asset that he acquired for a consideration that was treated as reduced by virtue of a claim to roll-over relief (under *TCGA 1992, s 152* or *s 154*), he is treated as if a gain equal to the amount of that reduction accrued at that time. There is a similar provision for clawback of hold-over relief on gifts under *TCGA 1992, s 165* or *s 260* (*TCGA 1992, ss 156A, 159A*).

HMRC STATEMENT OF PRACTICE D12

6.26 The full text of the statement of practice is reproduced below:

'This statement of practice was originally issued by the Commissioners for Her Majesty's Revenue and Customs on 17 January 1975 following discussions with the Law Society and the Allied Accountancy Bodies on the capital gains tax treatment of partnerships. This statement sets out a number of points of general practice which have been agreed in respect of partnerships to which *TCGA 1992, s 59* applies.

The enactment of the *Limited Liability Partnerships Act 2000*, has created, from April 2001, the concept of limited liability partnerships (as bodies corporate) in UK law. In conjunction with this, new capital gains tax provisions dealing with such partnerships have been introduced through *TCGA 1992, s 59A*. *TCGA 1992, s 59A(1)* mirrors *TCGA 1992, s 59* in treating any dealings in chargeable assets by a limited liability partnership as dealings by the individual members, as partners, for capital gains tax purposes. Each member of a limited liability partnership to which *s 59A(1)* applies has therefore to be regarded, like a partner in any other (non-corporate) partnership, as owning a fractional share of each of the partnership assets and not an interest in the partnership itself.

This statement of practice has therefore been extended to limited liability partnerships which meet the requirements of *TCGA 1992, ss 59, 59A(1)*, such that capital gains of a partnership fall to be charged on its members as partners. Accordingly, in the text of the statement of practice, all references to a 'partnership' or 'firm' include reference to limited liability partnerships to which *TCGA 1992, ss 59, 59A(1)* applies, and all references to 'partner' include reference to a member of a limited liability partnership to which *TCGA 1992, ss 59, 59A(1)* applies.

For the avoidance of doubt, this statement of practice does not apply to the members of a limited liability partnership which ceases to be 'fiscally transparent' by reason of its not being, or its no longer being, within *TCGA 1992, ss 59, 59A(1)*.

1. Valuation of a partner's share in a partnership asset

Where it is necessary to ascertain the market value of a partner's share in a partnership asset for capital gains tax purposes, it will be taken as a fraction of the value of the total partnership interest in the asset without any discount for the size of his share. If, for example, a partnership owned all the issued shares in a company, the value of the interest in that holding of a partner with a one-tenth share would be one-tenth of the value of the partnership's 100% holding.

2. Disposals of assets by a partnership

Where an asset is disposed of by a partnership to an outside party each of the partners will be treated as disposing of his fractional share of the asset. In computing gains or losses the proceeds of disposal will be allocated between the partners in the ratio of their share in asset surpluses at the time of disposal. Where this is not specifically laid down the allocation will follow the actual destination of the surplus as shown in the partnership accounts; regard will of course have to be paid to any agreement outside the accounts. If the surplus is not allocated among the partners but, for example, put to a common reserve, regard will be had to the ordinary profit sharing ratio in the absence of a specified asset-surplus-sharing ratio. Expenditure on the acquisition of assets by a partnership will be allocated between the partners in the same way at the time of the acquisition. This allocation may require adjustment, however, if there is a subsequent change in the partnership sharing ratios (see paragraph 4).

3. Partnership assets divided in kind among the partners

Where a partnership distributes an asset in kind to one or more of the partners, for example on dissolution, a partner who receives the asset will not be regarded as disposing of his fractional share in it. A computation will first be necessary of the gains which would be chargeable on the individual partners if the asset has been disposed of at its current market value. Where this results in a gain being attributed to a partner not receiving the asset the gain will be charged at the time of the distribution of the asset. Where, however, the gain is allocated to a partner receiving the asset concerned there will be no charge on distribution. Instead, his capital gains tax cost to be carried forward will be the market value of the asset at the date of distribution as reduced by the amount of his gain. The same principles will be applied where the computation results in a loss.

4. Changes in partnership sharing ratios

An occasion of charge also arises when there is a change in partnership sharing ratios including changes arising from a partner joining or leaving the partnership. In these circumstances a partner who reduces or gives up his share in asset surpluses will be treated as disposing of part of the whole of his share in each of the partnership assets and a partner who increases his share will be treated as making a similar acquisition. Subject to the qualifications mentioned at 6 and 7 below the disposal consideration will be a fraction (equal to the fractional share changing hands) of the current balance sheet value of each chargeable asset provided there is no direct payment of consideration outside the partnership. Where no adjustment is made through the partnership accounts (eg by revaluation of the assets coupled with a corresponding increase or decrease in the partner's current or capital account at some date between the partner's acquisition and the reduction in his share) the disposal is treated as made for a consideration equal to his capital gains tax cost and thus there will be neither a chargeable gain nor an allowable loss at that point. A partner whose share reduces will carry forward a smaller proportion of cost to set against a subsequent disposal of the asset and a partner whose share increases will carry forward a larger proportion of cost.

The general rules in *TCGA 1992, s 42* for apportioning the total acquisition cost on a part-disposal of an asset will not be applied in the case of a partner reducing his asset-surplus share. Instead, the cost of the part disposed of will be calculated on a fractional basis.

5. Adjustment through the accounts

Where a partnership asset is revalued a partner will be credited in his current or capital account with a sum equal to his fractional share of the increase in value. An upward revaluation of chargeable assets is not itself an occasion of charge. If, however, there were to be a subsequent reduction in the partner's asset-surplus share, the effect would be to reduce his potential liability to capital gains tax on the eventual disposal of the assets without an equivalent reduction of the credit he has received in the accounts. Consequently at the time of the reduction in sharing ratio he will be regarded as disposing of the fractional share of the partnership asset represented by the difference between his old and his new share for a consideration equal to that fraction of the increased value at the revaluation. The partner whose share correspondingly increases will have his acquisition cost to be carried forward for the asset increased by the same amount. The same principles will be applied in the case of a downward revaluation.

6. Payments outside the accounts

Where on a change of partnership sharing ratios payments are made directly between two or more partners outside the framework of the partnership accounts, the payments represent consideration for the disposal of the whole or part of a partner's share in partnership assets in addition to any consideration calculated on the basis described in 4 and 5 above. Often such payments will be for goodwill not included in the balance sheet. In such cases the partner receiving the payment will have no capital gains tax cost to set against it unless he made a similar payment for his share in the asset (eg on entering the partnership) or elects to have the market value at 6 April 1965 treated as his acquisition cost. The partner making the payment will only be allowed to deduct the amount in computing gains or losses on a subsequent disposal of his share in the asset. He will be able to claim a loss when he finally leaves the partnership or when his share is reduced provided that he then receives either no consideration or a lesser consideration for his share of the asset. Where the payment clearly constitutes payment for a share in assets included in the partnership accounts, the partner receiving it will be able to deduct the amount of the partnership acquisition cost represented by the fraction he is disposing of. Special treatment, as outlined in 7 below, may be necessary for transfers between persons not at arm's length.

7. Transfers between persons not at arm's length

Where no payment is made either through or outside the accounts in connection with a change in partnership sharing ratio, a CGT charge will only arise if the transaction is otherwise than by way of a bargain made at arm's length and falls therefore within *TCGA 1992, s 17* extended by *TCGA 1992, s 18* for transactions between connected persons. Under *TCGA 1992, s 286(4)* transfers of partnership assets between partners are not regarded as transactions between connected persons if they are pursuant to genuine commercial arrangements. This treatment will also be given to transactions between an incoming partner and the existing partners.

Where the partners (including incoming partners) are connected other than by partnership (eg father and son) or are otherwise not at arm's length (eg uncle and nephew) the transfer of a share in the partnership assets may fall to be treated as having been made at market value. Market value will not be substituted, however, if nothing would have been paid had the parties been at arm's length. Similarly if consideration of less than market value passes between partners connected other than by partnership or otherwise not at arm's length, the transfer will only be regarded as having been made for full market value if the consideration actually paid was less than that which would have been paid by parties at arm's length. Where a transfer has to be treated as if it had taken place for market value, the deemed disposal will fall to be treated in the same way as payments outside the accounts.

8. Annuities provided by partnerships

A lump sum which is paid to a partner on leaving the partnership or on a reduction of his share in the partnership represents consideration for the disposal by the partner concerned of the whole or part of his share in the partnership assets and will be subject to the rules in 6 above. The same treatment will apply when a partnership buys a purchased life annuity for a partner, the measure of the consideration being the actual costs of the annuity.

Where a partnership makes annual payments to a retired partner (whether under covenant or not) the capitalised value of the annuity will only be treated as consideration for the disposal of his share in the partnership assets under *TCGA 1992, s 37(3)* if it is more than can be regarded as a reasonable recognition of the past contribution of work and effort by the partner to the partnership. Provided that the former partner had been in the partnership for at least ten years an annuity will be regarded as reasonable for this purpose if it is no more than two-thirds of his average share of the profits in the best three of the last seven years in which he was required to devote substantially the whole of this time to acting as a partner. In arriving at a partner's share of the profits regard will be had to the partnership profits assessed before deduction of any capital allowances or charges. The ten-year period will include any period during which the partner was a member of another firm whose business has been merged with that of the present firm. For lesser periods the following fractions will be used instead of two-thirds:

Complete years in partnership	Fraction
1–5	1/60 for each year
6	8/60
7	16/60
8	24/60
9	32/60

Where the capitalised value of an annuity is treated as consideration received by the retired partner, it will also be regarded as allowable expenditure by the remaining partners on the acquisition of their fractional shares in partnership assets from him.

9. Mergers

Where the members of two or more existing partnerships come together to form a new one, the capital gains tax treatment will follow the same lines as that for changes in partnership sharing ratios. If gains arise for reasons similar to those covered in 5 and 6 above, it may be possible for roll-over relief under *TCGA 1992, ss 152–158* to be claimed by any partner continuing in the partnership insofar as he disposes of part of his share in the assets of the old firm and acquires a share in other assets put into the 'merged' firm. Where, however, in such cases the consideration given for the shares in chargeable assets acquired is less than the consideration for those disposed of, relief will be restricted under *TCGA 1992, s 153*.

10. Shares acquired in stages

Where a share in a partnership is acquired in stages wholly after 5 April 1965, the acquisition costs of the various chargeable assets will be calculated by pooling the expenditure relating to each asset. Where a share built up in stages was acquired wholly or partly before 6 April 1965 the rules in *TCGA 1992, Sch 2, para 18* will normally be followed to identify the acquisition cost of the share in each asset which is disposed of on the occasion of a reduction in the partnership's share; that is, the disposal will normally be identified with shares acquired on a 'first in, first out' basis. Special consideration will be given, however, to any case in which this rule appears to produce an unreasonable result when applied to temporary changes in the shares in a partnership, for example those occurring when a partner's departure and a new partner's arrival are out of step by a few months.

11. Elections under *TCGA 1992, Sch 2, para 4*

Where the assets disposed of are quoted securities eligible for a pooling election under *TCGA 1992 Sch 2, para 4* partners will be allowed to make separate elections in respect of shares or fixed interest securities held by the partnership as distinct from shares and securities which they hold on a personal basis. Each partner will have a separate right of election for his proportion of the partnership securities and the time limit for the purposes of *Schedule 2* will run from the earlier of:

(a)   the first relevant disposal of shares or securities by the partnership; and

(b)   the first reduction of the particular partner's share in the partnership assets after 19 March 1968.

12. Partnership goodwill and taper relief

This paragraph applies where the value of goodwill which a partnership generates in the conduct of its business is not recognised in its balance sheet and where, as a matter of consistent practice, no value is placed on that goodwill in dealings between the partners. In such circumstances, the partnership goodwill will not be regarded as a 'fungible asset' (and, therefore, will not be within the definition of 'securities' in *TCGA 1992, s 104(3)*) for the purpose of capital gains tax taper relief under *TCGA 1992, s 2A*. Accordingly, on a disposal for actual consideration of any particular partner's interest in the goodwill of such a partnership, that interest will be treated as the same asset (or, in the case of a part disposal, a part of the same asset) as was originally acquired by that partner when first becoming entitled to a share in the goodwill of that partnership.

The treatment described in the preceding paragraph will also be applied to goodwill acquired for consideration by a partnership but which is not, at any time, recognised in the partnership balance sheet at a value exceeding its cost of acquisition nor otherwise taken into account in dealings between partners. However, such purchased goodwill will continue to be treated for the purpose of computing capital gains tax taper relief as assets separate from the partnership's self-generated goodwill. On a disposal or part disposal for actual consideration of an interest in such purchased goodwill by any particular partner, that interest shall be treated for taper relief purposes as acquired either on the date of purchase by the partnership or on the date on which the disposing partner first became entitled to a share in that goodwill, whichever is the later.'

Chapter 7

Administration of an estate

INTRODUCTION

7.1   In the event of death, the property included in the deceased's estate does not automatically pass to the beneficiaries, but passes to the personal representatives or executors whose duty it is to administer the estate. The executors' or personal representatives' duty includes getting in the property, discharging the deceased's debts and finally distributing the assets to the beneficiaries under the will or according to the rules of intestacy.

In relation to CGT, the personal representative will be concerned with:

- capital gains arising in the period to the date of death; and

- capital gains arising in the administration of the estate.

Legislation was included in the *Finance (No 2) Act 2010* which introduced a rate of 28% for personal representatives of deceased persons. This had the effect that, during 2010/11, there were two rates of capital gains tax. Capital gains triggered prior to 23 June 2010 were charged at 18%, while gains triggered on or after 23 June 2010 were charged at 28%.

CAPITAL GAINS TAX IN THE PERIOD TO THE DATE OF DEATH

General provisions

7.2   Generally, the deceased will be liable to tax on any capital gains made in the period up to the date of death and it is the duty of the personal representative to ensure that this tax liability is discharged or provisions are made prior to the distribution of the estate. The normal self-assessment procedure has to be followed; however, *TMA 1970, s 40(1)* extends the self-assessment time limits and the assessment must now be made by the end of the third year after 31 January following the tax year in which the death took place. From 1 April 2010 the time limit has changed to the end of four years.

> **Example 7.1—Time limits**
>
> John died on 1 July 2012. The tax return for the period from 6 April 2012 to the date of death has not yet been completed.
>
> The date of death occurred in the tax year ending 5 April 2013, for which the filing date is 31 January 2014 for returns filed online. Paper returns need to be filed by 31 October 2013. Therefore, assessment in respect of the period to date of death may be made at any time up to 31 January 2017.

CGT losses of the deceased

7.3   Special provisions in relation to capital losses made in the tax year in which a person dies are introduced by *TCGA 1992, s 62(2)*. These rules provide that allowable losses sustained by an individual in the tax year in which he dies may, so far as they cannot be deducted from chargeable gains accruing in that year, be deducted from chargeable gains accruing to the deceased in the three tax years preceding the tax year in which his death occurs, taking chargeable gains accruing in a later year before those accruing in an earlier year.

> **Example 7.2—Capital losses**
>
> John (see Example 7.1), in the period from 6 April 2012 to the date of death, made capital losses of £10,000. In 2011/12, he made capital gains of £12,000, on which CGT was paid.
>
> His executors can make a claim under *TCGA 1992, s 62(2)* and obtain a tax refund, which will fall into John's estate for IHT purposes.

Otherwise, the normal capital gains tax principles apply when calculating any CGT charges to date of death.

CAPITAL GAINS TAX IN THE ADMINISTRATION OF AN ESTATE

General provisions

7.4 The general rule is that the 'assets of which a deceased person was competent to dispose' are deemed to have been acquired by his personal representatives for a consideration equal to their market value at the date of death. These assets are not deemed to be disposed of by the deceased on death, and therefore there is no charge to CGT on the deceased's unrealised gains (*TCGA 1992, s 62(1)*).

'Assets of which the deceased was competent to dispose' are defined in *TCGA 1992, s 62(10)* as assets of the deceased, which he could, if of full age and capacity, have disposed of by will, assuming that the assets were situated in England, and, if he was not domiciled in the UK, that he was domiciled in England, and include references to his severable share in any assets to which, immediately before his death, he was beneficially entitled as joint tenant.

Focus

There are problems with tax-free uplifts on death if there is a double death.

If husband dies first, leaving all his estate to his wife absolutely, and his wife dies at a time when the husband's estate is still unadministered, her interest in the husband's estate is only a *chose* in action.

Therefore, if the value of his estate assets increases between the two deaths, there will be no CGT-free uplift on the wife's death under *s 62*, despite being subject to inheritance tax at the higher value.

The provisions of *TCGA 1992, s 73* extend the general rule to settlements with an interest in possession created prior to 22 March 2006, immediate post-death interests (IPDI), transitional serial interests (TSI), disabled person's trust (DT) and bereaved minor trusts (BMT), with the effect that, on the death of a life tenant, the gains within the fund will be exempt from CGT. Following *FA 2006*, these provisions do not apply to interest in possession settlements which fall under the relevant property regime, as the assets within such trusts no longer form part of the estate of the deceased life tenant.

If, on death, the property within the trust reverts to the settlor, the disposal and reacquisition are deemed to be for such consideration that neither a loss nor a gain accrues to the trustee (*see TCGA 1992, s 73(1)(b)*).

The exception to the rule in *s 73* is that, where gains were held over on the transfer of assets into a trust, such held-over gains are chargeable to CGT on the death of the life tenant (see *TCGA 1992, s 74*).

Example 7.3—Tax-free uplift on death

John's estate includes a seaside cottage, which he purchased in 1990 for £50,000. The property is now worth £250,000.

On John's death, the gain of £200,000 on the seaside cottage is not chargeable to tax; instead, John's executors acquire the seaside cottage at a new base value of £250,000.

John was also the life tenant of a pre-22 March 2006 interest in possession trust which was valued at £150,000 at date of his death. The settlor of the trust was John's father, who transferred shares in X Ltd valued at £50,000 into the trust in 1982. The gain held over in 1982 was £20,000.

On John's death, the held-over gain on the shares of £20,000 becomes chargeable. If X Ltd is a trading company, it is possible to make another hold-over claim (*TCGA 1992, s 165*). John's estate, therefore, includes the value of the interest in possession trust at date of death (£150,000) less any held-over gain (£20,000), namely £130,000.

Personal representatives

7.5   Personal representatives are treated as a single and continuing body of persons, and they are treated as having the deceased's residence, ordinary residence and domicile at the date of death (*TCGA 1992, s 62(3)*). They are liable to capital gains tax on disposals made by them during the administration of the estate. For the tax year in which the death occurs and the following two years of assessment, the personal representatives are entitled to the same annual exempt amounts as individuals with the same general provisions applying (*TCGA 1992, s 3(7)*).

As personal representatives are deemed to take the deceased's residence status, UK personal representatives of a non-resident deceased are not chargeable to CGT. However, this exception does not apply to trustees, and therefore if there are ongoing trusts, for example, because there are minor beneficiaries, the residence status of the trustees will determine whether the trust is UK resident for CGT purposes (see **8.43**).

Valuation of chargeable asset at the date of death

7.6 When considering a potential charge to CGT during the administration of an estate, any computation of a capital gain must start with a consideration of the market value, ie 'the price which the asset might reasonably be expected to fetch on a sale in the open market' (*TCGA 1992, s 272(1)*).

Where, on the death of any person, IHT was chargeable on the value of the estate immediately before death and where the value of an asset as part of that estate has been 'ascertained' for the purposes of IHT, that value is taken to be the market value for CGT purposes unless the value has only been ascertained to establish the amount of transferable nil rate band between spouses or civil partners from 9 October 2007 (*TCGA 1992, s 274*).

Care has to be taken in cases where the deceased's estate does not attract a charge to IHT, as the value of the asset will not be 'ascertained' for IHT, and so the personal representatives' base value will not be fixed. This can happen in the following situations:

- All the assets pass to a surviving spouse and the entire estate is IHT exempt.

- All the assets pass to charities or political parties and the estate is thus IHT exempt.

- The estimated value of the estate is well below the threshold on which tax is to be payable and therefore the estate is not subject to IHT charges.

- The assets of the estate are all subject to agricultural and business property relief for IHT at the rate of 100%.

- Some combination of the above factors and/or other exemptions makes the estate non-taxpaying.

If the value of an asset is not ascertained for inheritance tax, the normal rules of *TCGA 1992, s 272* will apply to determine the capital gains tax acquisition value of the beneficiary. The acquisition cost of each asset must be negotiated with HMRC when the asset is sold. The taxpayer *must* supply information about the transactions to which the valuations relate, as specified on CG34, together with any relevant tax computations. The taxpayer *may* use form CG34, but this is not mandatory. Costs *may* be subject to negotiations if HMRC decide to open an enquiry.

HMRC Capital Gains Manual in CG32210–CG32271 explains the procedure to be adopted when either: values have been ascertained for IHT and there are queries; or the values have not been ascertained.

Focus

If PRs require valuations, HMRC offer a free service to help them to complete the relevant tax returns. However, this service does not extend to provide probate valuations for executors.

If valuations for probate purposes are required, see *Inheritance Tax 2013/14* (Bloomsbury Professional).

If it transpires during the administration of an estate that the market value on death of an asset for IHT is too high, relief from IHT may be available. The personal representatives may substitute a lower figure for the market value on death where property valued on death as 'related property' is sold within three years after the death (*IHTA 1984, s 161*), or if quoted securities are sold within 12 months of death for less than their market value on death (*IHTA 1984, ss 178 et seq*) and land is sold within four years for less than its market value on death (*IHTA 1984, s 190 et seq*). See Chapter 10 of *Inheritance Tax 2013/14* (Bloomsbury Professional). This lower figure will then also be used to form the personal representatives' base value for CGT.

Alternatively, it may be advantageous for the personal representatives to claim a CGT loss on the disposal. The example below illustrates this point:

Example 7.4—IHT revaluation

William died on 1 July 2013. His main asset is his home which is valued at £250,000. He also owns (quoted) shares in Green Ltd which on his death were valued at £100,000. His estate is worth £350,000 and the executors paid IHT of £10,000 ((£350,000 – £325,000) @ 40%).

During the first year of administration, it transpires that the shares in Green Plc have fallen in value and are now only worth £35,000. The executors decide to sell. At the same time, the value of the property, following a successful planning application, has increased by £110,000. The executors could consider claiming relief under *IHTA 1984, s 178* to reduce the estate below the nil rate band threshold for IHT of £325,000. A repayment of IHT would be £10,000, while at the same time a CGT charge of £27,748 (28% of £110,000 less annual exemption of £10,900) will be payable on the sale of the property.

This will result in an additional tax charge of £17,748 (CGT payment of £27,748 less repayment of IHT of £10,000).

Alternatively, the executors could claim the CGT loss of £65,000 on the sale of the shares against the £110,000 gain on the property, thereby returning a net taxable gain of £45,000. Taking into account the annual exemption of £10,900, an additional CGT charge of £9,548 will be due ((£45,000 – £10,900) @ 28%).

The executors, if they decide to use the capital loss on the shares against the gain on the property rather than reclaiming IHT, save tax of £8,200 (£17,748 less £9,548).

Transactions during the administration period

7.7   Sales of assets comprised in the deceased's estate by the personal representatives are disposals for capital gains tax purposes. Capital gains tax, subject to the deductions and allowances mentioned below, will have to be paid on the difference between the sale consideration and the market value at the date of death. The rates of tax are as follows:

- Transactions until 5 April 2004   34%
- Transactions between 6 April 2004 and 5 April 2008   40%
- Transactions after 5 April 2008 but before 23 June 2010   18%
- Transactions on or after 23 June 2010   28%

Allowable expenses

7.8   Following the decision in *IRC v Richards' Executors* [1971] 1 All ER 785, 46 TC 626, HL, personal representatives can deduct an appropriate proportion of the cost of acquiring the assets from the testator (ie legal and accountancy costs that are involved in preparing the inheritance tax account and obtaining the grant of probate) from the sales proceeds.

HMRC Statement of Practice 02/04 has suggested a scale for deaths after 5 April 2004. (For deaths prior to 6 April 2004, see HMRC Statement of Practice 8/94.)

Table 7.1—Statement of Practice 02/04 – Allowable expenditure	
Gross value of estate	**Allowable expenditure**
A. Up to £50,000	1.8% of the probate value of the assets sold by the personal representatives
B. Between £50,001 and £90,000	A fixed amount of £900, to be divided between all the assets in the estate in proportion to the probate values, and allowed in those proportions on assets sold by the personal representatives

Gross value of estate	Allowable expenditure
C. Between £90,001 and £400,000	1% of the probate value of all assets sold
D. Between £400,001 and £500,000	A fixed amount of £4,000, divided as at B above
E. Between £500,001 and £1,000,000	0.8% of the probate value of the assets sold
F. Between £1,000,001 and £5,000,000	A fixed amount of £8,000, divided as at B above
G. Over £5,000,000	0.16% of the probate value of the assets sold, subject to a maximum of £10,000

Personal representatives may claim to deduct more, when higher expenses have been occurred. Note that this relief is available only to the personal representatives, and not, for example, to a beneficiary to whom the asset may have been appropriated.

Taper relief and indexation

7.9   The application of business asset taper relief and indexation allowance in relation to disposals by personal representatives prior to 6 April 2008 is explained in *Capital Gains Tax 2011/12* (Bloomsbury Professional) and earlier editions of this book.

Following *FA 2008*, disposals by personal representatives after 5 April 2008 but before 23 June 2010 are charged at the single rate of 18% irrespective of the type of asset disposed of. The single rate of 18% was increased to 28% in *F(No 2)A 2010* for disposals on or after 23 June 2010.

Annual exemption

7.10   Personal representatives have the same annual exemption from CGT as individuals (£10,900 for 2013/14) in the tax year of death, and in each of the two following tax years (*TCGA 1992, s 3(7)*).

Focus

It may be advantageous to transfer assets to legatees prior to a sale and use the legatees' annual exemptions to reduce the CGT burden. Personal representatives need to consider carefully the tax consequences of any sale (see **7.11**).

Compare Examples 7.5 and 7.6.

Administration of an estate   7.11

Example 7.5—Sale of property by personal representatives

Alice died on 29 June 2013, leaving a property worth £1,000,000 at date of death. Alice's will leaves her estate equally to her six children, Alfie, Ben, Claire, David, Emily and Freddie. The personal representatives have sold the property for £1,100,000.

	£
Sale proceeds	1,100,000
Probate value	1,000,000
Capital gain	100,000
Allowable expenses (0.8% of probate value)	(8,000)
Annual exemption	(10,900)
Taxable gain	81,100
Tax @ 28%	22,708

The personal representatives' liability to CGT will be £22,708 on the disposal of the property.

Transfers to legatees

7.11   Where a person disposes of an asset to which he became absolutely entitled as legatee, any incidental expenditure incurred by that person or by the personal representative in relation to the transfer of the asset to him is allowable as a deduction in the computation of the gain arising on the disposal (*TCGA 1992, s 64(1)*).

A 'legatee' includes any person taking under a testamentary disposition or on intestacy or partial intestacy, whether he takes beneficially or as trustee (*TCGA 1992, s 64(2)*).

On a transfer of an asset to a legatee, the personal representatives neither make a gain nor a loss for capital gains tax purposes. The legatee acquires the asset at the personal representative's base cost, which is usually the probate value. If there is more than one legatee receiving an asset, the base costs will have to be apportioned accordingly.

Where the asset disposed of is a dwelling house that has at some time in the period of administration been a residence of a person who is a legatee in respect of that dwelling house, private residence exemption may, in certain circumstances, be available under the terms of Extra-statutory Concession D5 and, for disposals after 9 December 2003, *TCGA 1992, s 225A* (see **12.36**).

A *donatio mortis causa* (a gift in anticipation of death) is treated as a testamentary disposition and not a gift, so that the donee acquires the asset at its market value on the date of death and the asset is therefore subject to a tax-free uplift on death (*TCGA 1992, s 62(5)*).

CGT may be saved by using each legatee's annual exemption. In addition, further tax can be saved if any of the legatees are not resident or ordinarily resident in the UK for tax purposes.

Example 7.6—Sale of property by legatees

The facts are the same as in Example 7.5, but the personal representatives recognise that a sale by the legatees may be advantageous.

Alfie and Ben live in Switzerland and are not resident or ordinarily resident in the UK for tax purposes.

Claire and David's income is modest and is just above the personal allowance of £8,105 and they are both basic rate taxpayers.

Emily's taxable income, after all allowable deductions and the personal allowance, is £31,000. The upper limit of the income tax basic rate band is £32,010 during 2013/14.

Freddie is a higher rate taxpayer with taxable income of £90,000.

	£
1/6th share in sale proceeds	183,333
Proportionate probate value	166,667
Capital gain on 1/6th share	16,666
Alfie and Ben's CGT position	
They escape a charge to CGT, as they are not UK resident	
Claire and David's CGT position	
Capital gain (each)	16,666
Annual exemption (each)	10,900
Taxable gain (each)	5,766
Tax @ 18% (each)	1,037

	£
Emily's CGT position	
Capital gain	16,666
Annual exemption	10,900
Taxable gain	5,766
Tax @ 18% on £1,010 (£32,010 − £31,000)	181
Tax @ 28% on £4,756 (£5,766 − £1,010)	1,331
CGT payable by Emily	1,512
Freddie's CGT position	
Capital gain	16,666
Annual exemption	10,900
Taxable gain	5,766
Tax @ 28% payable by Freddie	1,614

The total CGT liability on the sale of the property by the legatees will be £5,200. This represents an overall tax saving of £17,508.

Exempt legatees

7.12   As mentioned above, certain legatees are exempt from capital gains tax and the personal representative therefore has to consider carefully the capital gains tax position prior to selling any assets within the estate which are subject to a capital gain. The following legatees are exempt:

- UK charities under *TCGA 1992, s 256*; and

- legatees who are not resident or ordinarily resident in the UK.

Problems may arise in situations where the estate is divided among several charities or where the personal representatives need part of the sale proceeds to cover administration expenses. In order for the charity exemption or the non-resident exemption to apply, the personal representatives should consider the following options:

- appropriate the assets to the charities or to the non-UK resident individual in partial or total satisfaction of their entitlement and then, having received instructions from the beneficiary, sell the assets as bare trustees for those charities; or

- appropriate the assets to charities or to the non-UK resident individual subject to a lien in favour of the personal representative.

LEGATEE OR BENEFICIARY

7.13   It is often difficult to determine whether someone receives assets as a legatee or as a beneficiary absolutely entitled under the terms of a trust. If assets are appointed by trustees of a trust, this will be a deemed disposal under *TCGA 1992, s 71* and a charge to CGT may arise (see **8.11**). In contrast, as explained above, there will not be any CGT consequences under *TCGA 1992, s 62* if personal representatives pass assets to legatees.

If a trust is created by a will or on intestacy, the trustees of that trust are legatees in precisely the same way as, for example, an individual taking an absolute interest in an asset. This is confirmed by *TCGA 1992, s 64(2)*. As a result the personal representatives are not liable to capital gains tax for disposals after assets have vested in the trustees, and the trustees acquire the assets at market value.

Problems often arise in situations where the same persons are appointed as executors and trustees under a will or on intestacy. The question then arises in what capacity those persons acted. In order to answer this question it is important to consider whether the administration period has come to an end. This will be the case once all the assets of the estate have been determined and the liabilities have been discharged or adequate provisions have been made. It will then be possible to ascertain the residue, ie the assets which will pass to the residuary beneficiaries, which signals the end of the administration period. Once the administration period has ended, it is likely that the beneficial interests have vested in trustees rather than being retained by the personal representatives. Any acts carried out after that time will therefore be carried out by those persons acting as trustees rather than the personal representatives (CG31123).

DEEDS OF APPOINTMENT, VARIATIONS OR DISCLAIMERS

7.14   The devolution of the estate may be varied in a number of ways:

- *Deeds of appointment*: if a will directs that after completion of the administration period, some or all of the assets of the estate are to be held on trust and that trust contains powers enabling the trustees to appoint assets out of the trust, a deed of appointment may be executed so that those assets pass direct to the appointee on vesting rather than entering the trust. For a discussion of the capital gains tax consequences of deeds of appointment, see **8.11**.

- *Disclaimers*: if a legatee wishes to give up his or her entitlement to assets of the estate without directing how those assets should be dealt with thereafter, a deed of disclaimer may be executed.

- *Deeds of variation*: if a legatee wishes to give up his or her entitlement to certain assets of the estate but wishes to direct to whom those assets should devolve in place of that legatee, a deed of variation may be executed.

Disclaimers

7.15   A disclaimer operates in much the same way as a deed of variation, although it is a much simpler document. A legatee can terminate his entitlement to an inheritance by executing a disclaimer. However, unlike with a variation, the legatee cannot redirect his interest. The benefit disclaimed will pass in accordance with the terms of the will relating to the residue in an estate or on intestacy.

Therefore, if the disclaimed interest was an absolute interest, either in specific assets or in residue, after the disclaimer those assets are added to the remaining residual entitlements. The residue is then distributed in accordance with the pre-existing terms of the will. If an interest in residue has been disclaimed, residue is divided between the other persons entitled to residue ignoring the bequest to the disclaimer, or if there are no other residuary beneficiaries, according to the rules of intestacy.

If, under the terms of a will, a person would have received a life interest, a disclaimer by that person will result in the acceleration of the interests of other persons having successive interests.

Example 7.7—Disclaimer

Alice's will leaves her husband William a pecuniary legacy of £50,000 with a life interest in the residue. The life interest will pass, on William's death, to their children, Hannah and Imogen, absolutely in equal shares.

William is elderly and financially secure, and he wishes to help Hannah and Imogen, who are both in the process of purchasing their first property. He therefore wishes to disclaim his interest in the pecuniary legacy and the life interest. If he executes a disclaimer, the estate will pass to Hannah and Imogen in equal shares absolutely.

Deeds of variation

7.16   A person who executes a deed of variation gives up his or her rights to receive an interest that he or she would otherwise have received under the terms of a will or intestacy. However, in contrast to disclaimers, the person who decides to vary his interest gives directions as to how the assets subject to the variation shall devolve. Variations are very flexible tools which usually remove certain clauses from the will and replace them with other clauses redirecting the original legatee's interest. For intestacies, variations deem to pass assets under a will having clauses containing the new conditions.

A deed of variation may be used to:

- vary certain clauses in a will;

- create a trust that was not in the original will, which is often used in estate planning to create a nil rate band discretionary trust to utilise the IHT nil rate band of a deceased spouse;

- vary the terms of a trust created by the will without varying the assets passing from the estate to the trustees;

- delete a trust that was in the will; or

- sever a joint tenancy to allow jointly held assets to pass under the terms of the will or the variation.

Example 7.8—Deed of variation

Using the scenario in Example 7.7, William is worried about passing the assets to Hannah and Imogen absolutely. Hannah is about to get married. William does not like her future husband, who has poor job prospects and spends most of his spare time gambling. He is worried that Hannah's inheritance will rapidly be whittled away.

Under a deed of variation, William could consider passing some of the assets to the two daughters outright to help them to purchase a property, while leaving the remainder on trust to retain some control over the use of those assets.

Effect of disclaimers and deeds of variations

7.17 A variation or disclaimer shall not constitute a disposal for capital gains tax purposes and it will be treated as if the dispositions have been effected by the deceased if:

- the variation or disclaimer was made within the period of two years after a person's death; and

- the variation or disclaimer was made by an instrument in writing made by the persons who benefit or would benefit under the dispositions (*TCGA 1992, s 62(6)*).

In other words, the effects of the disclaimer or variation are treated as being retrospective to the date of death. The assets are therefore deemed to have been acquired by the person at market/probate value at the date of death. A future gain therefore is calculated by reference to the probate value and not to the value at the time the variation or disclaimer was executed. It may sometimes be beneficial not to elect for *s 62(6)* to apply, as is discussed at **7.18**.

The provisions of *s 62(6)* do not apply to a variation or a disclaimer that is made 'for any consideration in money or money's worth other than consideration consisting of the making of a variation or disclaimer in respect of another of the dispositions' *(TCGA 1992, s 62(8))*.

FA 2002, s 52 amended *s 62(7)* in that, for a variation to be effective for capital gains tax purposes, the deed of variation has to contain a statement by the persons making the instrument to the effect that they intended *s 62(7)* to apply to the variation. This in effect means that, for deeds executed after 31 July 2002, it will not be necessary to give notice to HMRC, within six months of the date of execution of the instrument, for *s 62(6)* to apply. As long as the variation expressly states that the provisions of *s 62(6)* are to apply to the deed of variation, the provisions automatically apply without further notices to HMRC. Note, however, that although for the purposes of trust law, a deed of variation may give effect to many changes, as described at **7.16**, it will be retrospective for CGT only if it varies the dispositions of the estate of the deceased.

Care has to be taken if the variation creates a settlement as, following the case of *Marshall v Kerr* [1994] 3 All ER 106, [1994] STC 638, HL, the settlor for the purposes of CGT is the original beneficiary who made the variation and not the deceased. Prior to 6 April 2008, if the variation established a UK settlement, *TCGA 1992, s 77* provided that, if the settlor retains an interest, he is taxed on all gains realised by the trustees. This would be the case where a surviving spouse executed a deed of variation to create a nil rate band discretionary trust to utilise the nil rate band of the deceased spouse, but is included in the list of beneficiaries. Following the introduction of a single CGT rate of 18% for individuals, trustees and personal representatives from 6 April 2008, *s 77* was no longer considered necessary, and was therefore abolished in *FA 2008*. However, the corresponding anti-avoidance rule for non-UK resident settlements *(s 86)* continues to apply after 5 April 2008.

FA 2006 inserted a new section to determine the identity of the settlor of a trust following a *s 62(6)* election. These new rules apply to variations occurring on or after 6 April 2006 irrespective of the date on which the deceased person died. Therefore, the person who gives up part or all of their entitlement to property under the will or intestacy will be regarded as a settlor for capital gains tax purposes *(TCGA 1992, s 68C)*.

Advisers need to be aware of the case of *Mrs Margaret Lau (The Executor of Werner Lau Deceased) v Her Majesty's Revenue & Customs* [2009] UK VAT SpC 00740 (18 March 2009). The deceased left, among others, a legacy of £665,000 to his stepson, with the residue passing to his widow. The stepson subsequently disclaimed this legacy but, following the administration of the estate, the widow paid £1 million to him. The widow contended that the payment of £1 million was unconnected with her son's disclaimer – the payment was made in fulfilment of an earlier promise to fund her son's business ventures. The Special Commissioner decided that evidence overwhelmingly demonstrated that the disclaimer was made in return for the payment of the £1 million and therefore it was ineffective for *Inheritance Tax Act 1984, s 142(3)*, as it was made for consideration.

To elect or not to elect?

7.18   As explained above, if the deed of variation or disclaimer expressly elects for *s 62(6)* to apply, the new beneficiaries are deemed to acquire the assets at market/probate value at the date of death.

Focus

Sometimes, there may be capital gains tax advantages in not electing for *s 62(6)* to apply, and for the new beneficiary to acquire the assets based on the market value at the date of execution of the variation or disclaimer, rather than at probate value.

The consequences of an election can best be illustrated by the following examples.

Example 7.9—To elect or not to elect?

Scenario 1

Isabella's will, among other assets, leaves shares worth £100,000 to her daughter Julie. Julie wishes to vary her mother's will and to pass the shares to her son Stuart. The value of the shares has now increased to £108,000.

If Julie decides not to elect for *s 62(6)* to apply, Julie will be subject to a capital gain of £8,000. This will be covered by her annual exemption and Stuart will acquire the shares at the higher base cost of £108,000, which may reduce a potential future capital gains tax liability when he decides to sell the shares.

Scenario 2

Alice's estate includes shares which have a probate value of £400,000. Alice's son James, the sole legatee, wishes to pass these shares to his daughter Isabella. In the meantime, the shares have risen in value to £440,000. James will have to decide whether to elect for *s 62(6)* to apply. If James elects for *s 62(6)* to apply, the shares pass to Isabella at the base cost of £400,000 and therefore will escape a charge to CGT on the capital gain of £40,000. If James has personal losses, he may decide not to elect for *s 62(6)* to give Isabella a higher base value. This may be advantageous in a rising market if Isabella wishes to sell the shares in the near future.

SALES BY LEGATEES

7.19   During the administration period, until assets are vested in the beneficiaries or residue has been ascertained, the legatee only holds a *'chose in action'*, ie a right to have the estate properly administered (see *Cochrane's Executors v CIR* (1974) 49 TC 299 and *Prest v Bettinson* (1998) 53 TC 437, Ch D).

The disposal of such a *'chose in action'* by the legatee is the same as when the legatee executes a deed of variation for full consideration which is not retrospective to the date of death. The disposal consideration is the price received rather than the market value of the expectation.

Chapter 8

Capital gains tax – settlements

SIGNPOSTS

- **Settlements** – Some arrangements may look like settlements, but for tax purposes are not treated as settlements (see **8.2–8.4**).

- **Transfer of assets into a settlement** – A settlor and his advisers need to consider the potential CGT consequences of transferring assets into a settlement (see **8.5–8.6**).

- **Actions by trustees** – An actual or deemed disposal by trustees may incur a charge to CGT, which under certain circumstances may be mitigated or deferred (see **8.7–8.13**).

- **Disposals of interests in trust property** – A charge to CGT arises, in certain circumstances, on the disposal of beneficial interests in trust property (see **8.14–8.17**).

- **Tax rate** – The tax rate for trustees has been increased from 18% to 28% for disposals on or after 23 June 2010 (see **8.18**).

- **Allowable trust expenses and losses** – Certain costs of acquisitions and disposals can be deducted from gains accruing to trustees (see **8.19–8.21**).

- **Insurance policy gains** – The term 'chargeable event gain' is misleading, as these gains are assessed to income tax (see **8.22**).

- **Exemptions and relief** – Both individuals and trustees may benefit from certain exemptions and reliefs (see **8.27–8.42**).

- **Offshore settlements** – This is a complex area of tax legislation which includes a number of anti-avoidance provisions. This chapter can give only a brief synopsis and flag some of the issues involved (see **8.43–8.45**).

- **Trusts and vulnerable beneficiaries** – The tax regime for trusts for vulnerable beneficiaries may offer CGT advantages in certain circumstances (see **8.46–8.49**).

INTRODUCTION

8.1   *FA 2008*, apart from introducing a single rate of CGT of 18%, made sweeping changes to CGT by abolishing indexation and taper relief. These rules also apply to settlements.

The generous tax rate of 18% was increased to 28% in *F(No 2)A 2010* for disposals by trustees on or after 23 June 2010.

Trustees of certain settlements are liable to capital gains tax on disposals and deemed disposals. The legislation distinguishes between UK-resident trusts and non-resident trusts. In addition, there are separate rules for bare trusts which charge any capital gains tax arising on the beneficiary.

FA 2006 introduced a new tax regime for interest in possession trusts and accumulation and maintenance trusts with the effect that such settlements are now chargeable transfers for inheritance tax. Therefore, in relation to interest in possession trusts, it will be necessary to ascertain whether the settlement was created prior to 22 March 2006, or is an immediate post-death interest (IPDI), transitional serial interest (TSI), bereaved minor trust (BMT) or disabled person trust. In relation to accumulation and maintenance trusts, it will be necessary to ascertain whether a beneficiary has become entitled to an interest in possession prior to 22 March 2006.

FA 2006 also introduced changes to the definition of settlor-interested settlements in *TCGA 1992, s 169F* by extending these provisions to parental trusts for minor children who are unmarried, or not in a civil partnership. Capital gains tax hold-over relief for settlements where children or stepchildren are potential beneficiaries is not available from 22 March 2006.

FA 2008 has removed some of the rules for settlor-interested trusts found in *TCGA 1992, ss 77–79*, because the new single rate of CGT means that these rules became superfluous.

When determining the tax position of a settlement, it is important to determine whether one deals with the creation of a settlement, a disposal or deemed disposal by the trustees. In addition, it will be necessary to determine whether the trustees will be assessed on any capital gains tax arising or whether one of the special rules, listed below, apply:

- *TCGA 1992, s 60* provides for a number of situations in which the 'settled property' is treated for tax purposes as belonging to the beneficiary and taxed as such (see **8.2**).

- In settlor-interested settlements, gains accruing to the trustees up to 5 April 2008 are not chargeable on them, but are treated as accruing to the settlor (see **8.40**).

- Special capital gains tax rules apply to overseas resident settlements (see **8.44**).

- *FA 2005* created a new trust tax regime for 'vulnerable persons' (see **8.46–8.49**).

DEFINITION OF 'SETTLEMENT' AND 'SETTLED PROPERTY'

General considerations

8.2   Prior to *FA 2006*, the legislation did not define the term 'settlement'. *TCGA 1992, s 68* provided that 'settled' property meant any property held in trust other than property to which *s 60* applies. *FA 2006, Sch 12* introduced a group of changes which had the effect that, from 6 April 2006, the definitions of 'settled property', 'settlement', 'settlor' and the tests as to residence of trustees are the same for income tax and CGT.

In outline:

- *s 68A* defines 'settlor';

- *s 68B* looks at transfers of property between settlements, to determine who is the settlor of them;

- *s 68C* introduces rules in relation to instruments of variation to determine who is the settlor;

- *s 69* has been substantially revised by the insertion of subsections *(1)*, *(2)* and *(2A)–(2E)* which address residence issues; and

- *s 169F* has been substantially amended so as to widen the concept of 'settlor-interest' to include benefits for minor dependent children (including stepchildren) who are unmarried and do not have a civil partner.

'Bare trusts' and 'absolute entitlement'

8.3   *Section 60(1)* provides that, although there is a trust of property, the property is not 'settled property' and is treated as belonging to the beneficiary where:

- assets are held by a person as nominee for another person, or as trustee for another person absolutely entitled as against the trustee, which includes nomineeships and simple or bare trusts;

- property is held on trust 'for any person who would be absolutely entitled but for being an infant or other person under a disability'; and

- property is held for two or more persons who are or would be jointly entitled, which, for example, includes joint ownership of land in England or Wales where trustees hold the legal title upon 'trust for sale' for the joint tenants or tenants in common (see *Kidson v Macdonald* [1974] STC 54).

If a person is 'absolutely entitled against the trustee' and he has the 'exclusive right' to direct how that asset shall be dealt with, the property will not be 'settled property' for capital gains tax, and any gains will be assessed on the beneficiary personally (*TCGA 1992, s 60(2)*).

Example 8.1—Bare trust

Sven holds shares for his son Matthew who is 26 years old. As Matthew can direct Sven at any time either to transfer the shares to him or to sell the shares and to pass the proceeds to him, this is a bare trust.

For capital gains tax, the shares will be treated as belonging to Matthew and a transfer of the shares to Matthew will not incur a charge to capital gains tax. Any capital gain on the sale of the shares will be attributed to Matthew personally.

Example 8.2—Minor beneficiaries

Scenario 1

Max is nine years old and therefore is not able to own property in his own name. His parents hold the property for him absolutely. As a minor cannot demand the property from his parents, the trust is not a bare trust. Nevertheless, *s 60(1)* provides that for capital gains tax purposes he is treated as owning the asset absolutely. When he attains the age of 18 and his parents transfer the property to him, the transfer will not trigger a charge to CGT.

Scenario 2

The property was passed to Max under his father's will contingent upon Max attaining the age of 18. Max is only nine years old. As his entitlement is contingent upon his attaining the age of 18, the property will be settled property for capital gains tax purposes and *s 60(1)* does not apply. Therefore, when he attains the age of 18, there will be a disposal by the trustees under *s 71(1)* which will trigger a charge to CGT.

For a time, it seemed that HMRC wished to challenge the status of a bare trust where its terms contained administrative powers, in particular the power to accumulate income. That was logical if the trustees did in fact have a discretion over the application of income, but the professions argued, eventually successfully, that a mere statutory power, such as in the *Trustee Act 1925*, did not turn what was otherwise a bare trust into a substantive trust. The point is more important for IHT than for CGT, and is discussed in *Inheritance Tax 2013/14* (Bloomsbury Professional).

'Exclusive right'

8.4   'The exclusive right … to direct how that asset shall be dealt with' may cause problems where there is more than one beneficiary entitled to the fund and the assets within the fund are indivisible assets like land, a painting, an item of antique furniture or a single share in a company. Therefore, apart from the terms of the settlement, the type of property held will determine when a beneficiary can direct the trustees to deal with his or her share in the trust asset and when such assets may be assessed to capital gains tax. One has to look towards the judgment of Goff J in *Crowe v Appleby* [1976] 2 All ER 914 and HMRC Capital Gains Manual at CG37540 to find the answer to when a beneficiary becomes absolutely entitled in an indivisible asset as against the trustees.

The rule in *Crowe v Appleby* states that, in relation to indivisible assets, a beneficiary, among a group of beneficiaries, might have to wait for his absolute entitlement until the last beneficiary has fulfilled a possible contingency (eg reached a specified age).

Example 8.3—Absolute entitlement to trust assets

Under James' will, his estate passes to his three children Sophie, Max and Saskia contingent upon them attaining the age of 21. James' estate comprises a property and 90,000 shares in Pharmaceuticals Plc. Sophie has just turned 21 and the question arises whether she will be able to claim her one-third share in her father's estate and whether the trustees will be charged to capital gains tax.

Sophie now can claim her one-third share in the shares, as they are divisible assets, and the trustees can pass these shares to her, subject to any capital gains tax charges which may arise.

Following the rule in *Crowe v Appleby*, however, she will only become entitled to her one-third share in the property once all her siblings have turned 21 or die before they are 21. Any capital gain, therefore, will be assessed once the last sibling has become absolutely entitled. The assessment will be on the market value of the property when the last beneficiary turned 21.

The rule in *Crowe v Appleby* ceases to apply if the trustees sell the land in question after the first contingency, even if the proceeds are used to buy further land. Once the sale has taken place, the trust fund, or the relevant part, consists of cash, and the beneficiaries with absolute interests can call upon the trustees to hand over their share of the money. If further land is bought, there is a tenancy in common, with the tenants in common being the trustees of the original settlement and the absolutely entitled beneficiaries.

> **Focus**
>
> HMRC have updated their Capital Gains Tax Trusts and Estates Toolkit in April 2013. The Toolkit highlights areas of risk and provides guidance on commonly found errors – see www.hmrc.gov.uk/agents/toolkits/cgt-trusts-estates.pdf.

THE CREATION OF A SETTLEMENT

General provisions

8.5   *Section 70* provides that a transfer into a settlement, whether revocable or irrevocable, is a disposal of the entire property thereby becoming settled property, notwithstanding that the settlor has some interest as a beneficiary (ie the settlement is settlor-interested) and notwithstanding that he is a trustee, or the sole trustee, of the settlement.

The transfer into the trust is made at market value. If the transfer is a chargeable transfer for inheritance tax purposes, or would be but for the annual inheritance tax exemption (of currently £3,000) or normal gifts out of income exemption under *IHTA 1984, s 21*, the settlor can elect hold-over relief to hold any capital gain over as against the trustees under *s 260* or, in the case of business assets, under *s 165*, unless the trust is settlor-interested, which precludes the application of hold-over relief.

> **Example 8.4—Creation of a settlement**
>
> Alice decides to settle her shares in X Plc on trust for her 19-year-old son, Boris. She acquired the shares in 2000 for £100,000. The market value of the shares now stands at £200,000.
>
> | | |
> |---|---:|
> | Deemed disposal consideration: | £200,000 |
> | Cost | £100,000 |
> | Capital gain | £100,000 |
>
> Alice will be subject to capital gains tax on her gain of £100,000 when she transfers the shares into the settlement. Alice can use her annual exemption to reduce her tax liability. Alternatively, since the creation of a lifetime settlement is now nearly always a chargeable transfer, Alice could elect for hold-over relief under *s 260*, as Boris is not a dependent child under *TCGA 1992, s 169F(4A)*.

The 'connected persons' rule

8.6   If the settlor and the trustees are connected persons, any gains on a transfer from the settlor to the trustees of a settlement can only be offset against losses on a transfer to the same settlement *(TCGA 1992, s 81(3))*. This can best be illustrated by the following example:

Example 8.5—Connected persons

James wishes to benefit his two children, Louis and Lily, who have three children each. Ideally, he would like to set up two trusts – one for each branch of the family. His assets include a property worth £200,000 which he acquired many years ago for £50,000 and a share portfolio which is also worth £200,000, but which he originally acquired for £250,000.

He discusses the capital gains tax position with his accountant. If James decides to create two new settlements, one which will receive the property, the other which will receive the share portfolio, he will not be able to offset the loss on the shares against the gain on the property.

His accountant therefore advises him to transfer his assets into the same settlement. Subsequently, it will be possible to create two sub-funds, one for each branch of the family, which will not be a disposal under *s 71(1)*, unless the trustees elect for the new sub-fund rules to apply (see **8.17**).

The issue of connected persons was examined by the Court of Appeal in *Foulser v MacDougall* [2007] STC 973, where the taxpayer had entered into the following complicated series of transactions designed to shelter from CGT a large gain in company shares.

- They set up trusts in the Isle of Man.

- The trustees bought shelf companies in the Isle of Man.

- The taxpayers took out a personal portfolio bond with an Irish company and assigned it to one of the shelf companies.

- The Irish bond provider bought two shelf companies within the personal portfolio bond.

- The taxpayers then gave their shares in the company that stood at a gain to the shelf companies, claiming hold-over relief under *TCGA 1992, s 165*.

The issue was whether the taxpayers were connected persons who were acting together to control the donee company, within *TCGA 1992, s 167(3)*. If they were, the scheme would fail. The court held that they were, and so the scheme did fail.

Focus

Settlors and trustees can often take advantage of hold-over relief under *TCGA 1992, s 260* or *s 165* to defer a potential CGT liability when transferring assets into a settlement.

However problems may arise many years later when trustees and beneficiaries need to ascertain the held-over gain.

It is therefore advisable to keep records of values transferred.

ACTUAL AND DEEMED DISPOSALS BY TRUSTEES

General considerations

8.7   The general rule is that gains arising from an actual disposal or a deemed disposal of trust assets, whether of assets originally settled or acquired subsequently by the trustees, are chargeable on the trustees. Exceptions to this rule apply to the disposal of trust assets of settlor-interested trusts prior to 5 April 2008 (see **8.40**), non-UK resident trusts (see **8.43–8.45**) and trusts for 'vulnerable persons' (see **8.46–8.49**).

Following *TCGA 1992, s 69(1)*, when new trustees are appointed, this is not treated as a disposal for capital gains tax, as trustees are treated as a single and continuing body. However, care has to be taken when appointing a non-UK resident trustee not inadvertently to export the trust, which may trigger a charge to capital gains tax. Following the *FA 2006* changes to the residence rules of trusts, practitioners are advised to review certain offshore arrangements which may be affected (see **8.46**).

Person becoming absolutely entitled to settled property (s 71)

8.8   There are many ways in which a beneficiary may become absolutely entitled as against the trustee. The main examples are:

- the termination of the trust after a term of years;
- when a beneficiary reaches a particular age;
- the happening of any other contingency;
- the termination of a prior life interest;
- the exercise by the trustee of a discretionary power to release capital;
- an order of the court;
- an agreement by the beneficiaries to terminate the trust; and
- the merger of interests.

Termination of the trust after a term of years and/or happening of a contingency

8.9 *Section 71(1)* provides that there is a deemed disposal by the trustees when the beneficiary of a settlement 'becomes absolutely entitled to any settled property as against the trustees'. The trustees are treated as disposing of that property at market value and immediately reacquiring it for the same value. A charge to capital gains tax may arise on the capital gain.

After the reacquisition of the assets, the trustees will hold the property in question at market value as bare trustees. The beneficiary is then treated as the owner of the property and anything done by the trustees afterwards is treated as if it had been done by the beneficiary. When the trustees actually transfer the property to the beneficiary entitled to it, this is disregarded for capital gains tax purposes. If they sell it on behalf of the beneficiary, that is treated as a disposal by him or her, and the gain or loss is the difference between the sale proceeds and the market value on the occasion of the deemed acquisition.

Example 8.6—See HMRC Capital Gains Manual at CG37040

The case of *Stephenson v Barclays Bank Trust Co Ltd* [1975] STC 151 illustrates the general principles for determining when absolute entitlement occurs.

The facts (simplified) are as follows. Under the will of W, his daughters C, D and E were entitled to annuities of £300 a year during widowhood. Subject to the annuities the property was to be held in trust for such of his grandchildren as should reach the age of 21. There were two grandchildren, A and B, who both reached 21 before CGT was introduced in 1965.

In 1969 the trustees, the daughters and the grandchildren entered into a deed under which specific funds should be set aside to meet the annuities and the rest of the property should be paid over to the grandchildren. In fact, however, the trustees held onto this property.

The Revenue argued that A and B became absolutely entitled only when the deed was executed.

The trustees' arguments were that an individual grandchild merely had to be entitled to specific property, not to possess it. The judge agreed: he considered that the two grandchildren together were entitled to the whole of the settled property prior to 1965. Therefore, they were 'jointly' absolutely entitled as against the trustees when the deed was executed. Thus, there was no charge to capital gains tax on the trustees when the property was handed over to the beneficiary some time later.

Where trustees sell assets after the occasion of charge under *s 71(1)* but before assets are appropriated to the beneficiaries, charges on the beneficiaries should be calculated under *s 60(1)* in proportion to their entitlement on the gain arising between absolute entitlement and sale by the trustees.

Life interest released in favour of remaindermen

8.10   It is very common for a deed to give a person a life interest, with the property going absolutely to one or more individuals, or to the members of a class of persons, on the death of the life tenant. Sometimes, the life interest can be contingent upon the happening of a certain event, ie until the life tenant remarries.

On the termination of the life interest, when the property passes absolutely to one or more beneficiaries (also called the 'remaindermen'), the trustees will be subject to capital gains tax charges on the gain arising on any assets which now pass absolutely to these beneficiaries. *Section 71(1)* also applies where a life tenant releases his or her interest in favour of any remainderman who then becomes entitled to an absolute interest as against the trustees.

If, however, the termination is due to the death of the person entitled to the life interest, which was created prior to 22 March 2006, or an IPDI, TSI, BMT or trust for disabled persons , the trustees may, subject to certain exceptions, escape a charge to capital gains tax under *ss 72* and *73* (see **8.12**).

Exercise of power to advance or appoint capital

8.11   A beneficiary may become absolutely entitled as against the trustees on the following occasions:

- Following a power within the trust document, the trustees pay a capital sum (rather than interest) to a beneficiary of a discretionary trust or they use their overriding powers in an interest in possession trust.

- The trustees exercise their powers under *Trustee Act 1925, s 32* (the statutory power of advancement for England and Wales) which permits trustees to pay or apply one half of a beneficiary's presumptive or vested share for his or her 'advancement' or benefit. In many cases, the deed authorises payment of the full share instead of limiting it to the statutory one half.

Section 71(1) applies to such an advance and/or appointment and the trustees will be chargeable to any capital gains arising on the advanced/appointed assets.

A charge to capital gains tax under *s 71(1)* may also arise when the trustees, in the exercise of their express powers in the trust document, resettle property on a new, different settlement.

221

Termination of life interest on death of the person entitled (s 73)

8.12   For inheritance tax purposes, if a person has a life interest in possession in settled property, which was created prior to 22 March 2006 and this person dies, the value of the settled property in which he or she has the interest is treated as part of his or her property on death.

Section 73 was amended by *FA 2006* to include a new *s 73(2A)*, so that from 22 March 2006 the capital gains tax-free uplift on death applies only to an interest in possession that is:

- an immediate post-death interest (IPDI);

- a transitional serial interest (TSI);

- a bereaved minor trust (BMT); or

- a disabled person trust (DPT).

The expressions IPDI, TSI, BMT and disabled person trust refer to categories of trusts that were formerly treated as interests in possession prior to the coming into force of *FA 2006* and which are still so treated. For a full exposition of the subject, the reader is referred to Chapters 7 and 8 of *Inheritance Tax 2013/14* (Bloomsbury Professional).

Therefore, if a life interest settlement has been created after 22 March 2006 and does not fall into one of the four categories of trusts mentioned above, *FA 2006* provides that the settled property will not be treated as part of the deceased's estate, as the creation of such a life interest is now treated as a chargeable event for inheritance tax.

Following *s 72* for life interests created prior to 22 March 2006, IPDIs, BMTs, TSIs or DPTs, no chargeable gain accrues on the death of the life tenant, unless there was a hold-over election on the acquisition of the property by the trustees (**8.29**), or where the property reverts to the settlor.

> **Example 8.7—Death of life tenant (I)**
>
> Alice has an interest in possession in her husband's estate for life or until she remarries. The remainderman is her son William.
>
> *Scenario 1*
>
> Alice's husband died on 5 June 2005 which was prior to the changes introduced by *FA 2006*.
>
> On Alice's death, there will not be a charge to capital gains tax following *s 73*, but the value of the assets subject to the life interest will form part of her estate for inheritance tax.

If Alice's interest is terminated following remarriage, *s 73* will not apply, and there will be a charge to capital gains tax on William's absolute entitlement following *s 71(1)*.

Scenario 2

Alice's husband died on 5 June 2006 which was after the changes introduced by *FA 2006*. Her life interest therefore will be an 'immediate post-death interest'. Sadly, Alice dies a month later, so William becomes absolutely entitled to the trust assets.

On Alice's death, there will not be a charge to capital gains tax (*TCGA 1992, s 73(2A)(a)*). As in Scenario 1, the value of the assets subject to the life interest will form part of Alice's estate for inheritance tax.

Example 8.8—Death of life tenant (II)

Scenario 1

Alice is the life tenant of an interest in possession trust, which was created by her father during his lifetime on 1 May 2005, which was before the introduction of the *FA 2006* changes. Alice died recently. The fund now passes to William.

This is an 'old-style' interest in possession which is not subject to the relevant property regime for IHT. The life interest therefore forms part of Alice's estate for IHT on her death, and capital gains tax-free uplift on her death therefore applies. Following *s 73*, there will not be a CGT liability when the assets pass absolutely to William.

Scenario 2

Assuming the same facts as in *Scenario 1* but the trust was created by her father during his lifetime on 1 May 2006, which was after the introduction of the *FA 2006* changes. Again, Alice died recently. The fund now passes to William.

Section 73(2A) applies here. Alice's interest in possession does not fall within the restricted class of interests in *s 72(1B)*. As a result, the charge that would have applied under *s 73(1)* or *(2)* is disapplied. Therefore, on her death there will be no capital gains tax-free uplift and it does not form part of her estate for inheritance tax as it is a relevant property trust. If the trust had continued, there would not have been a disposal for CGT; however, as the trust now comes to an end on the vesting of William's interest, any capital gains within the fund will be subject to a charge under *s 71(1)* because the remainderman now becomes absolutely entitled. As the termination of the life interest will be a chargeable transfer for IHT, the trustees ought to consider a hold-over election under *s 260* (see **8.29–8.30** and **Chapter 13** for a discussion on hold-over relief).

Termination of life interest on death of the person entitled (s 72), where settlement continues

8.13   The rule prior to 22 March 2006 was that, where the life interest on the death of the life tenant was terminated and the property continued to be settled property, the trustees were treated as disposing of the settled property and reacquiring it at market value on the date of death, but without any charge to capital gains tax.

In relation to settlements created after 22 March 2006, the rule is that, as noted above, the tax treatment will depend on whether the fund remains with the trustees. The ending of the prior (post-*FA 2006*) life interest is not treated as an occasion of charge, see *s 72(1A)*, because it is not an interest within *s 72(1B)*, ie not an IPDI, TSI, BMT or disabled person trust.

DISPOSAL OF INTERESTS IN SETTLED PROPERTY

General considerations

8.14   The general rule is that there is no charge to CGT when a beneficial interest in trust property is disposed of and the disposal was made:

- by the person for whose benefit the interest was created; or
- by any other person except one who acquired the interest for a consideration in money or money's worth (*TCGA 1992, s 76(1)*).

However, once a beneficial interest has been purchased, a future disposal is chargeable to CGT.

The capital gains tax exemption in *s 76(1)* used to offer CGT planning opportunities for individuals who placed assets in trust subject to a CGT hold-over election, but retaining an interest in the trust asset which was subsequently sold. The sale of the interest did not attract a charge to CGT. However, as of 21 March 2000, trustees of settlor-interested trusts are treated as disposing of the asset and re-acquiring it at market value. Following the changes introduced by *FA 2008* from 5 April 2008, any CGT is charged on the trustees at the trust tax rate. The trustees can then recover the tax charge from the beneficiary who sold his interest (*TCGA 1992, s 76A, Sch 4A*).

Example 8.9—Disposal of beneficial interest

William is the remainderman in a life interest trust set up under his father's will. He sells his interest to his friend, Fred. Under the rule in *s 76(1)*, there is no charge to CGT.

However, Fred's subsequent sale of the beneficial interest in the trust is outside the protection of the rule in *s 76(1)*, and any capital gain therefore will be taxable under general principles.

Purchase by one beneficiary of other beneficiary's interest

8.15   The general rule in *s 76(1)* does not apply where an original life tenant of settled property makes a payment to the original remainderman for the sale of his or her interest to the original life tenant, as the life tenant now becomes absolutely entitled to the property as against the trustees. The gain will be chargeable under *s 71(1)* and the property is deemed to have passed to the original life tenant at market value.

The same applies if the original remainderman acquires a life interest from the original life tenant.

Purchase of life interest and reversion

8.16   Where a person acquires a life interest or remainder interest in settled property for a consideration in money or money's worth and subsequently also acquires the other interest and therefore becomes absolutely entitled as against the trustees to the settled property, a charge to CGT will occur on the trustees under both *ss 71(1)* and *76(2)*.

> **Example 8.10—Purchase of life interest and reversion**
>
> Alice has a life interest in a trust and William is the remainderman; both are original beneficiaries. Fred buys Alice's life interest and, before this interest terminates, he also buys the remainder interest from William.
>
> Fred therefore becomes absolutely entitled to the settled property as against the trustees, and a charge to CGT will arise on the trustees. As Fred is not the original life tenant, a charge under *s 76(2)* will arise on him.

SUB-FUND ELECTIONS

8.17   Where a settlement has been divided into one or more sub-funds which are administered by either the same, or different, trustees for different beneficiaries, the main settlement and any sub-funds are treated as a single settlement for capital gains tax purposes.

FA 2006 introduced provisions which allow trustees of a settlement to elect that a sub-fund or portion of the settlement shall be treated as a separate settlement, called a 'sub-fund' settlement for capital gains tax purposes as of 6 April 2006 (*TCGA 1992, Sch 4ZA*).

Making a sub-fund election will give rise to a charge to capital gains tax, as it is considered to be a deemed disposal under *s 71(1)* (*TCGA 1992, Sch 4ZA, para 20*). This single factor is likely to deprive the facility of any practical use for trustees (see below).

In order to make the election, a number of conditions have to be satisfied:

- Condition 1 is that the principal settlement is not itself a sub-fund (*TCGA 1992, Sch 4ZA, para 4*).

- Condition 2 is that the sub-fund does not comprise the whole of the property of the principal settlement (*TCGA 1992, Sch 4ZA, para 5*).

- Condition 3 is that, if the sub-fund election had taken effect, the sub-fund settlement would not consist of or include an interest in an asset which would be comprised in the principal settlement (*TCGA 1992, Sch 4ZA, para 6*).

- Condition 4 is that, once the sub-fund election had taken effect, no person would be a beneficiary under both the sub-fund settlement and the principal settlement.

As making the election gives rise to a disposal for capital gains tax purposes, the trustees would be in the same position as trustees who had used their powers to transfer property out of the principal settlement into a new settlement, thereby triggering a charge to capital gains tax. A sub-fund election therefore will only be useful in relation to settlements which were drafted without wide powers of advancement. A sub-fund election is unlikely to be attractive where trust assets are subject to substantial gains.

RATES OF TAX

General considerations

8.18   The rate of capital gains tax applicable to the trustees of any settlement who are liable in respect of disposals of settled property is as follows:

From 6 April 1998 to 5 April 2005	34%
From 6 April 2005 to 5 April 2008	40%
From 6 April 2008 to 22 June 2010	18%
From 23 June 2010	28%

Trustees are treated as a single and continuing body of persons, regardless of any changes in the persons acting. Assessments are to be made on those in office at the time of the assessment, not those in office when the gain is made.

If tax assessed on the trustees of a settlement in respect of a chargeable gain accruing to the trustees is not paid within six months from the date when it becomes payable by the trustees, and the asset in respect of which the chargeable gain accrued (or any part of the proceeds of sale of that asset) is transferred by the trustees to a beneficiary, that person may, at any time within two years from the time when the tax became payable, be assessed and charged (in the name of the trustees) to capital gains tax (*TCGA 1992, s 69(4)*).

Actual disposals and losses

8.19   The rules in *TCGA 1992, s 16* in relation to capital losses also apply to trustees. With some exceptions (see **8.20**), trustees can use allowable losses against realised gains made on disposals of trust assets.

Focus

Following the increase in the CGT rate from 18% to 28% for 2010/11, the legislation provides for allowable losses to be used in the most tax advantageous manner, in the same way as the annual exemption.

Losses could be used against gains chargeable at 28% rather than 18%.

8.20   Where a beneficiary becomes absolutely entitled to settled property as against the trustees, any allowable loss which arises on the deemed disposal by the trustees of the asset transferred, and which cannot be deducted from gains accruing to the trustees, is treated as a loss of the beneficiary (*TCGA 1992, s 71(2)*).

Where the beneficiary has become absolutely entitled to an asset on or after 16 June 1999, and he is treated as if he had incurred an allowable loss on that occasion, that loss can only be set against chargeable gains accruing on the same asset or, where the asset is an estate, interest or right in or over land, that asset or any asset deriving from that asset.

Example 8.11—Allowable losses

William becomes absolutely entitled to a trust set up by his late father. The trust assets are a portfolio of shares. The trustees have unused trust losses of £15,000. The share portfolio to which William becomes absolutely entitled to is worth £25,000 less than when it was acquired.

The unused losses of £15,000 belong to the trustees and cannot be passed on to William.

The capital loss of £25,000 on the share portfolio can only be used by William on a future gain of the disposal of the same share portfolio, unless the trustees can use it against gains realised earlier or gains arising on William's absolute entitlement.

Allowable expenditure by trustees

8.21   *TCGA 1992, s 38* sets out the basic types of expenditure regarded as
'incidental costs ... of making an acquisition or disposal' (see **3.39**), which can
be deducted from capital gains. *Section 38* also applies to trustees.

In addition, there are a number of cases which directly refer to allowable
expenses by trustees:

- Expenses in varying and/or ending settlements are allowable and they
  may include the costs of legal and actuarial services including stamp
  duty on transfers and ancillary expenses incurred in varying or ending a
  settlement (see *CIR v Chubb's Trustee* 1972 SLT 81).

- Fees in respect of discharges and commission on the transfer of assets to
  beneficiaries, but not insurance premiums (see *Allison v Murray* [1975]
  3 All ER 561).

Where property is transferred to a person absolutely entitled to that property
as against the trustees of a settlement, then, on any subsequent disposal of that
property, the person to whom the property is transferred may be allowed a
deduction for the expenses involved in the transfer of this asset.

The issue of deductibility of trust expenses was considered by the Special
Commissioners in some detail in *Clay v HMRC* [2007] STC (SCD) 362. The
case was concerned with the rate of income tax applicable to trusts, but has
implications for the allocation of costs to capital. It decided that, in order to
achieve a fair balance between income and capital beneficiaries, a proportion
of all the expenses that were in issue, with the exception of the investment
management fees, was attributable to income for the purposes of what was then
ICTA 1988, s 686(2AA), but is now *ITA 2007, s 484*; and that the accruals basis
that had been adopted by the trustees was a proper way of allocating expenses
to a particular tax year. The law as redrafted does now adopt the accrual basis
and to that extent adopts the decision in *Clay*.

It was clear in that case that the fees of investment managers were attributable
to capital: yet, after such costs have been so allocated, it does not follow that
they may be set against any gains arising on sale of the investments. Such
expenditure is not set against income and is therefore not excluded from offset
by *TCGA 1992, s 39*. Can a gain therefore be reduced by a proportion of the
manager's fee? It is arguable that the work of an investment manager does not
enhance the value of any individual asset, even though it may have a profound
influence on the value of the portfolio as a whole. The advisory element of the
manager's fee is therefore probably not deductible; but custody fees (which
were substantial in *Clay*) should be claimable as incurred for preserving the
title to the trust assets.

HMRC Statement of Practice 2/04, updating Statement of Practice 8/94, lists the amount of expenditure allowable to be deducted for expenses incurred by personal representatives and corporate trustees. Note, however, that this allowance is not available to a beneficiary to whom an asset has been appropriated or assented, because the expenses in question were incurred not by the beneficiary but by the personal representative/trustee, even though in reality it may be the beneficiary who eventually foots the bill.

The deductibility of valuation costs and costs of appeal was reviewed in *Caton's Administrators v Couch* [1997] STC 970 and disallowed by the Court of Appeal, affirming the judgment of the High Court. The costs of the initial valuation were allowable but not the litigation costs, since that would deter taxpayers from 'reaching a sensible agreement with the Revenue as to the quantum of liability'.

Focus

HS392 (www.hmrc.gov.uk/helpsheets/hs392.pdf) gives useful guidance when considering the correct treatment of trust management expenses.

Trust insurance policy gains

8.22   Trustees may decide to invest in a policy so as to avoid both the complication of receipt of income, and having to account for it to the beneficiaries, and its taxation under *ITA 2007, s 493* (formerly *ICTA 1988, s 687*). A chargeable event gain is not a capital gain for tax purposes, but will be treated as income and taxed accordingly. Therefore, if trustees encash a policy, they may trigger a chargeable event gain for income tax under *ITTOIA 2005, s 491*. For trustees of discretionary trusts the question arises what part, if any, of the resultant tax liability goes into the tax pool in *ITA 2007, s 497*. This has been addressed by *FA 2007, s 56*, inserting into *ITA 2007, s 498* an extra category, or type, of income, being the tax arising on life insurance contracts. What goes into the pool is:

- the tax deemed to be paid under *ITA 2007, s 482*, less

- the savings rate under *ITTOIA 2005, s 530*.

Therefore, only the additional tax paid by the trustees (30% from 5 April 2010) will enter the tax pool.

Focus

Care needs to be taken when taking out such policies within interest in possession trusts. The income tax rates for such trusts are 10% for dividend income and 20% for all other income. Chargeable event gains, however, are charged on trustees at the income tax rate applicable to trusts, which is 50% from 6 April 2010, reduced to 45% from 6 April 2013.

As interest in possession trusts do not have tax pools, the additional income tax payable by the trustees (25% from 5 April 2013) cannot enter a tax pool, and therefore does not seem to be reclaimable by the beneficiaries.

Trustees need to consider whether it may be beneficial to assign policies to beneficiaries, who can then sell them and potentially benefit from top-slicing relief.

PARTICULAR TRANSACTIONS AFFECTING TRUSTS

Capital receipts on company purchase of own shares

8.23   *FA 2006, Sch 13, para 3* amended *ICTA 1988, s 686A*, which applies on the purchase by a company of its own shares where a trust is involved. In trust law, ie disregarding any tax treatment, such a purchase is a capital transaction, and the problem for HMRC was that *s 686* caught only income that was subject to the discretion of the trustees. However, the 2006 amendment did not hit its target accurately, making further amendment necessary. The change, backdated to 6 April 2006, is in *FA 2007, s 55* and amends both *ICTA 1988, s 686A* and *ITA 2007, s 482* as necessary.

Single farm payment and 'old' quota entitlements

8.24   Many trusts of farming interests will be affected by the introduction of the entitlement to Single Farm Payment, which has superseded entitlements under 'old' quota arrangements, as for milk etc, making them valueless. Although some were acquired by allocation, some may have been purchased and where this has happened, and the quota in question has ceased to exist, an opportunity may now arise to make a 'negligible value' claim under *TCGA 1992, s 24*, especially when realising a capital gain on the disposal of other assets.

Identifying the source of distributions from a trust IRS

8.25   Although the tax treatment of offshore trusts is outside the scope of this book, cases occasionally throw up principles of wider application. In

Herman v HMRC (2007) SpC 609, the Special Commissioner had to review a scheme that attempted to deal with stockpiled gains that they were not treated as capital payments for the purpose of the charging regime under *TCGA 1992, s 87*. The case is important because the taxation of stockpiled gains troubles many families who perhaps now regret that their wealth is tied up in an offshore structure that is becoming increasingly expensive to maintain.

The precise facts may now be academic; they concerned a 'Mark II flip-flop' scheme, use of which has been curtailed by subsequent legislation: see *TCGA 1992, Sch 4C*. What is still relevant is the way the Commissioners applied the phrase 'directly or indirectly' in *TCGA 1992, s 97(5)(a)*. They decided to work back to see exactly where the money had come from. Had the receipt resulted by accident or through circumstances not originally envisaged, the linkage might not be there; but on the facts there was here a comprehensive tax plan. The husband taxpayer knew exactly what was going on; he was consulted at every stage; on the facts, what they received was indirectly received from the trustees, so it was taxable under *TCGA 1992, s 97*.

Tax advantages using a trust in the light of FA 2007

8.26   What is 'normal' tax planning and what is 'objectionable' tax avoidance? A few years ago, 'bed and breakfast' transactions were considered to be no more than good housekeeping, but were outlawed by the identification rules in *TCGA 1992, s 104 et seq*. Continuing this trend, *FA 2006* introduced targeted anti-avoidance rules (TAARs) for corporation tax to prevent some losses from being allowable. The trend has continued by the anti-avoidance rules in *FA 2007, s 25 et seq* and in particular by *FA 2007, s 27* which inserted into *TCGA 1992 s 16A*, which states that with effect from 6 December 2006, a loss is not allowable if:

- there are 'arrangements';

- the loss accrues to a person directly or indirectly from those arrangements; and

- the main purpose, or one of the main purposes, of the arrangements was to secure a tax advantage.

'Arrangements' is very widely drawn, so as to include:

- agreements;

- understandings;

- schemes; and

- a transaction or series of transactions,

whether or not any such are legally enforceable.

'Tax advantage' means:

- tax relief, or extra tax relief;
- tax refunds or bigger tax refunds;
- avoiding tax or paying less of it; or
- managing to avoid a possible assessment to tax.

It does not matter whether the loss accrues at a time when there happen not to be any gains to set against it; nor whether the tax advantage is for the person who has suffered the loss or someone else.

Naturally, there has been much comment in the professional press and by the learned societies as to the scope of the rules. HMRC have been mildly reassuring: transfers between spouses, where one had made a large gain and the other had the potential to transfer loss-making assets, might not always be caught.

Focus

What of the situation where a beneficiary of an estate has losses brought forward and stands to inherit a house which has appreciated since it was valued for probate, where that value is fixed under *TCGA 1992, s 274*? It would be standard practice to appropriate the house to the beneficiary, so that he may set his loss against his new gain.

Is that 'normal' tax planning and, as such, not caught by the new rule? It probably is, but we must await the clarification of seeing tax returns go through unchallenged before we can be sure.

EXEMPTIONS AND RELIEFS

Annual exemption

8.27   *TCGA 1992, Sch 1*, modified by *FA 2009*, determines the level of the annual exemption.

Trustees of a settlement are entitled to one-half of the annual exemption available to an individual for any tax year during the whole or part of which any property is 'settled property' as defined in *TCGA 1992, s 68*. Thus, the trustees' exemption for 2013/14 is £5,450. Trustees of settled property held for people with disabilities and others are entitled to the full annual exemption.

Where two or more 'qualifying settlements' comprise a 'group' (see definitions below) then each qualifying settlement is entitled to an annual exemption equal to the greater of:

- one-tenth of the annual exemption for an individual (ie £1,090 for 2013/14); or

- one-half of that exemption divided by the number of settlements in the group.

For these purposes:

- a 'qualifying settlement' is any settlement (other than an 'excluded settlement', see below) made after 6 June 1978 where these rules apply to the trustees for the tax year; and

- all qualifying settlements that have the same settlor (see below) comprise a group.

A settlement may feature in more than one group by virtue of having more than one settlor. In such a case, the number by which one-half of the annual exemption for an individual is to be divided is the number of settlements in the largest group.

Following the new sub-fund election rules, *FA 2006* introduced *TCGA 1992, Sch 1, para A1*, which states that, in relation to the annual exemption, the principal settlement and its sub-fund settlements are treated as if no sub-fund election has been made.

8.28   'Settlor' has the meaning given by *ITTOIA 2005, s 620* and includes the testator in the case of a settlement arising under a will and the intestate under an intestacy. Thus a settlor, in relation to a settlement, is any person by whom the settlement was made. A person is treated as having made a settlement if he has made or entered into it directly or indirectly. In particular, he is treated as having made the settlement if he has:

- provided funds directly or indirectly for the purpose of the settlement;

- undertaken to provide funds directly or indirectly for the purpose of the settlement; or

- made a reciprocal arrangement with another person for the other person to make or enter into the settlement.

'Excluded settlement' means:

- any settlement where the trustees are not, for the whole or any part of the tax year, treated under *TCGA 1992, s 69(1)* as resident and ordinarily resident in the UK;

- any settlement where the property comprised in it is held for charitable purposes only and cannot become applicable for other purposes;

- with effect from 6 April 2006, subject to transitional rules, any settlement where the property comprised in it is held for the purposes of a registered pension scheme, a superannuation fund to which *ICTA 1988, s 615(3)* applies or an occupational pension scheme within the meaning of *FA 2004, s 150(5)* that is not a registered pension scheme; or

- prior to 6 April 2006, any settlement where the property comprised in it is held for the purposes of a fund to which *ICTA 1988, s 615(3)* applies, schemes and funds approved under *ICTA 1988, s 620 or s 621,* sponsored superannuation schemes as defined in *ICTA 1988, s 624* and exempt approved schemes and statutory schemes as defined in *ICTA 1988, Pt XIV, Ch I.*

Hold-over relief

8.29 Hold-over relief may, subject to the exceptions discussed below, be available in two circumstances:

- On a transfer of assets into a trust, it may be possible to make a claim for gifts hold-over relief under *TCGA 1992, s 260* where, for the purposes of inheritance tax, there is a chargeable transfer or there would be a chargeable transfer but for the application of an inheritance tax exemption or the availability of the nil rate band.

- Hold-over relief also applies to gifts of business assets to a settlement under *s 165(1)(b)*.

Where both reliefs are available, *s 260* takes priority. A claim has to be made on helpsheet HS295.

Hold-over relief under *s 260*

8.30 Prior to 22 March 2006, hold-over relief under *s 260* used to be available only:

- for gifts to discretionary trusts;

- when a discretionary trust was terminated; or

- when assets were appointed/advanced to beneficiaries of discretionary trusts.

Gifts to accumulation and maintenance trusts and interest in possession trusts used to be potentially exempt transfers rather than chargeable transfers for inheritance tax, so *s 260* hold-over relief did not apply.

FA 2006 changed the inheritance tax treatment of interest in possession trusts and accumulation and maintenance trusts, in that transfers into such settlements are treated as chargeable transfers for inheritance tax. Therefore, all transfers into trusts, whether discretionary or not, allow the election of *s 260* hold-over relief.

A planning opportunity existed for accumulation and maintenance trusts where a beneficiary became entitled to income at the age of 18 and capital at the age of 25. If the beneficiary, once he turned 18, but before the age of 25, resettles his interest away from himself so that he will not become entitled to capital until the age of 25, capital gains tax hold-over relief under *s 260* will be available when he becomes absolutely entitled. Despite the changes introduced by *FA 2006*, this planning opportunity is still available for beneficiaries who have obtained an interest in possession in the accumulation and maintenance trust prior to 22 March 2006. All other beneficiaries are subject to the new inheritance tax charging regime for accumulation and maintenance trusts in any event, which allows for the application of *s 260* hold-over relief, when a beneficiary becomes absolutely entitled to trust assets.

The *s 260* relief extends to actual and deemed disposals of trustees of settlements which are subject to ongoing inheritance tax charges or exit charges, or would be if the value of the assets were above the nil rate band for inheritance tax. Such settlements are as follows:

- discretionary settlements, whether created prior to 22 March 2006 or afterwards; and

- interest in possession trusts and accumulation and maintenance trusts created after 22 March 2006.

Hold-over relief under *s 165*

8.31   *Section 165(1)(b)* extends the application of hold-over relief for business assets (as discussed in detail in **Chapter 13**) to settled property.

Anti-avoidance measures

8.32   There are two main anti-avoidance provisions:

- The first can be found in *TCGA 1992, ss 169B–169G* on a transfer into settlor-interested settlements. For this purpose, a settlor has an interest in a settlement where any property within the settlement may be used for the benefit of the settlor or his spouse. *TCGA 1992, s 169F* extends the settlor-interested definition further to include minor unmarried children who are not in a civil partnership, which also includes stepchildren. Hold-over relief under *s 260* or *s 165* will not be available for trusts set up by a parent where minor children and/or stepchildren are potential beneficiaries. Hold-over relief remains available for grandparents' trusts.

- *Section 226A* has been introduced by *FA 2004* and prevents the application of principal private residence relief under *TCGA 1992, s 223* in cases where hold-over relief has been claimed under *s 260* when property was transferred into the settlement. This measure applies from 9 December 2003, and principal private residence relief is not available from this date, and any subsequent gains will have to be apportioned.

For a case that turned on the meaning of this legislation, especially *s 167(3)*, see *Foulser v MacDougall* at **8.6**.

Taper relief

8.33   Taper relief was abolished by *FA 2008*, but the rules still apply for transactions completed prior to 6 April 2008. For a discussion of the operation of taper relief on disposals by individuals with reference to disposals by trustees please refer to the 2011/12 or earlier editions of this book. While the same principles and definitions apply to taper relief on disposals by trustees, when determining whether business asset taper applies, the rules vary from those applying to individuals.

Disposals of assets after 5 April 2008

8.34   *FA 2008* abolished taper relief and indexation relief for transactions completed after 5 April 2008. Irrespective of the type of asset disposed of, a flat rate of CGT of 18% for disposals prior to 23 June 2010, and 28% thereafter, will apply, replacing the complex taper relief.

Entrepreneurs' relief

8.35   Entrepreneurs' relief may apply to disposals of the whole or part of a business and in some circumstances, disposals of shares. For disposals prior to 23 June 2010, entrepreneurs' relief reduced qualifying gains by 4/9ths and the remaining 5/9ths were then charged at the single rate of 18%. This resulted in qualifying gains being taxed at the effective CGT rate of 18%. The amount of an individual's gain that can qualify for entrepreneurs' relief was subject to a lifetime limit of £2 million from 6 April 2010 to 23 June 2010 (£1 million prior to 6 April 2010).

The increase of the capital gains tax rate for trustees from 18% to 28% means that the 4/9ths reduction will not achieve an effective tax rate of 10%. *F(No 2)A*

2010 amended these provisions, in that capital gains on disposals which qualify for entrepreneurs' relief will be charged at a rate of 10%. The lifetime limit was increased to £5 million for the period from 23 June 2010 to 5 April 2011, and to £10 million with effect from 6 April 2011.

This relief applies to disposals by trustees of interest in possession trusts, but not discretionary trusts, as outlined below.

TCGA 1992, s 169J applies to disposals of trust business assets. Entrepreneurs' relief will apply where three conditions are satisfied:

(1)   The trustees of a settlement dispose of 'settlement business assets', which are defined as shares in or securities of a company, or interests in such shares or securities, or assets that have been used for the purposes of a business, or interests in such business.

(2)   The individual is a 'qualifying beneficiary' of the settlement. This means that the individual must have an interest in possession in the whole of the settled property or in part of the settled property that contains the settlement business asset.

(3)   One of two conditions, called the 'relevant conditions', is satisfied:

- The relevant condition that must be satisfied if the settlement business assets are shares in or securities of a company, or interests in such shares or securities, is that, throughout a period of one year ending within three years up to the date of disposal (defined as the 'material time'):
    - the company is the qualifying beneficiary's personal company (see **11.10** for a definition of 'personal company');
    - the company is a trading company, or the holding company of a trading group (see **11.12** and **11.19** for a definition of 'trading company' and 'holding company'); and
    - the qualifying beneficiary is an officer or employee of the company or of one or more companies that are members of the group.

- If the settlement business assets are assets that have been used for the purposes of the business, the relevant condition is that:
    - throughout the period of one year ending with the three years up to the date of disposal, the settlement business assets are used for the purposes of a trade carried on by the qualifying beneficiary; and
    - the qualifying beneficiary ceases to carry on the business some time during that three-year period.

Trustees are advised to consider the application of entrepreneurs' relief, if the trust assets include business assets, especially if a sale of these assets is anticipated in the future. The relief does not apply to assets held subject to the discretion of the trustees and in some situations it may be beneficial to consider appointing these assets on interest in possession trusts which will allow the application of this relief.

The relief has to be applied for jointly by the 'qualifying beneficiary' and the trustees. In effect, the beneficiary will transfer the unused portion of his lifetime allowance up to a maximum of £5 million to the trustees.

Section 169O introduces special provisions where on a disposal of trust business assets there is in addition to the qualifying beneficiary at least one other beneficiary who, at the material time, has an interest in possession in all the trust assets or the part now disposed of. In such situations the aggregated gains and losses are apportioned by reference to the qualifying beneficiary's interest, at the material time, in the income of that part of the settled property that includes the settlement business assets. The relevant proportion of the aggregated gains and losses so calculated is to be taken into account for entrepreneurs' relief and the remainder of the amount which does not qualify for relief is a chargeable gain.

These special provisions will restrict the availability of entrepreneurs' relief where there is more than one beneficiary in an interest in possession trust.

Roll-over relief

8.36 Trustees may claim reinvestment roll-over relief to roll the gain realised on a business asset into the purchase of another asset (*TCGA 1992, ss 152–158*). The rules are explained in detail in **Chapter 14**.

However, as one of the requirements for the application of roll-over relief is that the asset on which roll-over relief is to be claimed, and the trade in which the asset is used, must be within the same ownership, the availability of roll-over relief to the trustees is likely to be rare. It would only apply where a trust owns the asset and is a partner in the trade.

Example 8.12—Roll-over relief

Julian is a life tenant in a settlement and runs a restaurant from premises owned by the trust. If the premises were sold to purchase bigger premises, roll-over relief will not be available.

Roll-over relief would only be available if the trust was a partner in the restaurant.

Principal private residence relief

8.37   The disposal by trustees of a dwelling house which has been the only or main residence of a beneficiary or beneficiaries entitled to occupy it under a settlement may well give rise to a chargeable gain or allowable loss.

Section 225 extends the scope of private residence relief to gains or losses accruing to trustees on the disposal of settled property. The property must be a dwelling house, and/or its garden or grounds if it has any, which has been occupied as the only or main residence of a person entitled to occupy it under the terms of the settlement during the period of ownership of the trustees.

If these conditions are fulfilled, private residence relief is applied in the same way as it would be applied on a gain accruing to an individual. Further relief may also be available to the trustees under *s 223(4)* if that dwelling house has been let, in the same way as it would be available to an individual.

If a life tenant or other beneficiary, who has satisfied those conditions from the time of acquisition of the house by the trustees, or 31 March 1982 if later, subsequently becomes the absolute owner of the residence, no chargeable gain or allowable loss will arise on that event under *s 71(1)*.

If the asset to which the beneficiary becomes absolutely entitled was previously occupied as an only or main residence by another beneficiary under the terms of the settlement, then *s 225* also may apply.

CGT small disposal rule

8.38   As explained in **4.26** in relation to individuals, a gain is not chargeable if it arises on the disposal of an asset which is tangible moveable property (a chattel) and the consideration does not exceed £6,000.

For the application of marginal relief, where the consideration exceeds £6,000, see **4.24**.

The same rules apply to disposals made by trustees.

SETTLOR-INTERESTED SETTLEMENTS

General considerations

Disposals after 5 April 2008

8.39   *FA 2008* abolished the settlor-interested provisions in *ss 77–78* for disposals made after 5 April 2008, as the new single rate of CGT of 18% removed any tax advantages to higher rate tax-paying settlors.

Any gains, therefore, are returned by the trustees on the trust tax return rather than by the settlor. Settlor-interested trusts are entitled to an annual capital gains tax amount of half the normal amount (ie £5,450 for 2013/14).

Disposals between 5 April 1988 and 5 April 2008

8.40   For disposals after 6 April 1988 but before or on 5 April 2008, special capital gains tax rules deal with the case where the person who made the settlement (the 'settlor'), the settlor's spouse or the settlor's minor unmarried children who are not in a civil partnership retain an interest in the settlement (see *ss 77–78*). Therefore, a settlement is settlor-interested where:

- both the settlor and the trustees are resident in the UK during any part of the year (or ordinarily resident in the UK during the year); and

- the settlor, the settlor's spouse or the settlor's unmarried minor children who are not in a civil partnership, at any time during the tax year have an interest in the settlement, or enjoy a benefit deriving from the settlement income or property (see *ITTOIA 2005, s 625*).

A settlor has an interest in the settlement if the settlor, his spouse or minor children have a present or future interest in income or capital under the settlement, whether vested or contingent, even if they never have received, or will actually receive, any income or capital from the trust.

8.41   'Benefit' is a rather vague concept, but it includes the use of trust income or property on non-commercial terms, which may include a low or nil interest loan, rent-free occupation of trust property, or appointments of trust income or capital (including the writing off of a loan to the settlor).

It is accepted that a small *de minimis* benefit will not bring the settlement within *s 77*.

Following *s 77(3)*, a 'spouse of the settlor' does not include the following:

- a person to whom the settlor is not presently married but might marry later;

- a person of whom the settlor is not for the time being a civil partner but of whom he may later be a civil partner;

- a spouse from whom the settlor is separated under a court order, under a separation agreement or in other circumstances such that the separation is likely to be permanent; or

- a widow or widower of the settlor. (In other words, if the person who is presently the spouse of the settlor can only benefit after the settlor is dead, he or she is disregarded.)

Following *s 77(4)*, certain interests are to be disregarded when determining whether someone has an interest in the settlement if the settlor can only benefit on:

- the bankruptcy of a beneficiary;

- any assignment of, or charge on, the beneficiary's interest in the property or income;

- the failure of a marriage settlement or civil partnership settlement by reason of both parties to the marriage or civil partnership and all or any of the children of the marriage or civil partnership;

- the death of a child of the settlor who had become beneficially entitled to the property or the income at an age not more than 25; or

- so long as a person is alive and under 25, during whose lifetime none of the property or income may become payable to the settlor unless that person becomes bankrupt or assigns etc his interest.

Computation of trust gains

8.42   The chargeable gains of the settlement are computed in the normal way subject to allowable reliefs and exemptions, and if capital gains tax is payable, this has to be paid by the trustees. The trustees' own annual exempt amount is taken into account in these computations.

If a settlor has set up more than one trust, the trustees' annual exempt amount has to be apportioned between the number of settlements set up by the settlor (see **8.27**).

OFFSHORE SETTLEMENTS

General considerations

8.43   The capital gains tax rules applying to offshore settlements are complex and are beyond the scope of this book.

Offshore settlements are used to offer substantial capital gains tax advantages, as they are not liable to capital gains tax on gains accruing to them on disposals of the trust property. Therefore, they were much reviled by the Inland Revenue which tightened the rules and closed many tax-planning loopholes. Consequently, there are special provisions to charge the gains accruing to such trustees to capital gains tax insofar as they are reflected in payments made to beneficiaries resident and/or domiciled within the UK.

While it will be necessary to consult a tax practitioner or a specialist text on offshore tax planning, an inadvertent export of the trust may catch the unwary and trigger a charge to capital gains tax. Practitioners therefore need to have an understanding of the residence rules of trusts and the ensuing consequences of the inadvertent export of a trust. The area is strictly policed by HMRC: see, for example, the decision of the High Court in favour of HMRC on the unsuccessful appeal from the Special Commissioner in *Snell v HMRC* [2006] EWHC 3350 (Ch), where the taxpayer emigrated to the Isle of Man but was still caught. In that case, an exchange of securities was held not to be for *bona fide* commercial purposes.

Residence of trust

8.44   Prior to *FA 2006*, the rules for residence of trustees were different, depending on whether income tax or capital gains tax was under consideration. For capital gains tax, a trust was considered as non-resident if its administration was ordinarily carried on outside the UK and the trustees for the time being, or a majority of them, were neither resident nor ordinarily resident in the UK. A resident professional trustee may be treated for this purpose as not resident in the UK if the settled property was provided by a settlor who was not domiciled, resident or ordinarily resident when he settled the property.

FA 2006 introduced new rules with effect from 5 April 2007, ie only for 2007/08 and later years, which in theory allowed trustees to alter their arrangements if required. The new rules are modelled on the old income tax test, based initially on the residence status of the trustees, and using the residence and domicile status of the settlor as a tiebreaker where the body of trustees contains a mixture of UK-resident and non-UK resident trustees. Therefore:

- If all the persons who are the trustees of the settlement are UK resident, the trust is both UK resident and ordinarily UK resident (*s 69(2A)*).

- If all the persons who are the trustees of the settlement are non-UK resident, the trust is both non-UK resident and not ordinarily UK resident.

- If at least one trustee is UK resident and at least one is non-UK resident, the residence and ordinary residence of the trust are treated as UK resident if a settlor in relation to the settlement meets the conditions specified below (*s 69(2B)*):

  - a settlor in relation to a settlement was UK resident, ordinarily UK resident or domiciled in the UK when the settlement was established;

  - if the settlement arises on the death of the settlor (whether by will, intestacy or otherwise), the settlor was UK resident, ordinarily UK resident or domiciled immediately before his death; or

– in any other case, the settlor was UK resident, ordinarily UK resident or domiciled when the settlor makes, or is treated as making, the settlement.

Thus, if a settlement has both resident and non-resident trustees, irrespective of whether the majority are either resident or non-resident, then if the settlor is UK resident etc at the relevant time, the settlement is UK resident.

Example 8.13—Residence of trustees

A trust has three trustees. All three are resident in the UK; two of them are partners in a firm of solicitors in London. The settlor is resident and domiciled in Switzerland. The administration of the trust is carried out in Guernsey.

Under the old rules, the trustees are resident in the UK because a majority are so resident; however, as two of the trustees are professional trustees, they are treated as non-resident, which means that a majority of the trustees are non-resident. In addition, the administration of the trust was carried on in Guernsey, which makes the trust non-resident under *s 69(1)*. If the administration of the trust had been carried out in London, the trust would have been treated as a resident trust.

Under the new rules, however, all the trustees are treated as resident in the UK: as the professional trustee exemption under *s 69(2)* no longer exists, the trust will be treated as a UK trust for capital gains tax purposes.

The trustees had until 5 April 2007 to introduce a non-UK resident trustee, to ensure that the trust remained offshore.

There were strong representations to HMRC that these new rules seriously damaged the trust provider sector, especially for smaller firms that did not have an international network of offices to which trusts could be redirected. HMRC confirmed the position and advised that there is no alleviating treatment. The point is more likely to have caught non-professional trustees unawares. Presumably, HMRC's position would be that there was a year or so between announcement and the effective date of the new rule during which action could have been taken, in this case for all the non-UK resident trustees to retire in favour of UK residents.

Charge to tax on emigration of trust under s 80

8.45 If the trustees cease to be resident in the UK, even if this happens inadvertently, a charge to capital gains tax may arise on the deemed disposal and reacquisition of the settled property at its market value on the date of emigration (*TCGA 1992, s 80*).

TRUSTS AND VULNERABLE BENEFICIARIES

General considerations

8.46 *FA 2005, ss 23–45* created a new trust tax regime for a 'vulnerable person' which was backdated to 6 April 2004. For CGT, the full exempt amount applies, rather than the 50% exemption given to trustees generally.

A 'vulnerable person' is a 'disabled person' or a 'relevant minor'. A 'vulnerable persons' election' has to be made to HMRC in writing on the requisite form for the beneficial tax treatment to apply (*FA 2005, s 37*).

'Disabled person'

8.47 A 'disabled person' is defined in *FA 2005, s 38* as a person who:

- by reason of mental disorder within the meaning of the *Mental Health Act 1983* is incapable of administering his property or managing his affairs;
- is in receipt of attendance allowance;
- is in receipt of a disability living allowance by virtue of entitlement to the care component at the highest or middle rate; or
- satisfies HMRC that, if he were to satisfy the residence conditions, he would be entitled to either attendance allowance or disability allowance.

Where property is held on trust for the benefit of a disabled person, those trusts are 'qualifying trusts' if any property is applied for the benefit of the disabled person and either the disabled person is entitled to all the income arising from the property or no such income may be applied for the benefit of any other person (*FA 2005, s 34*).

In light of the Welfare Reform Act 2012, the *Finance Act 2013* amended the definition of 'disabled person'.

'Relevant minor'

8.48 A person under the age of 18 is a 'relevant minor' if at least one parent has died (*FA 2005, 39*).

Where property is held on trust for the benefit of a relevant minor, those trusts are 'qualifying trusts' if they are statutory trusts for the relevant minor under the *Administration of Estates Act 1925*, or they are established under the will of a deceased parent of the relevant minor, or they are trusts established by the Criminal Injuries Compensation Scheme (*FA 2005, s 35*).

Finance Act 2013 introduced clauses to allow small payments of income and capital to non-vulnerable beneficiaries without the trust losing its favoured status. Regulations made by the Treasury will determine the amounts. The definition of 'disabled person' has been widened to include those entitled to the daily living component of the new personal independence payment (PIP).

Capital gains tax treatment

8.49   Following *FA 2005, s 30*, special capital gains tax treatment applies for a tax year if:

- chargeable gains accrue in that tax year to the trustees of a settlement from the disposal of settled property which is held on qualifying trusts for the benefit of a vulnerable person;

- the trustees would be chargeable to capital gains tax in respect of those gains;

- the trustees are UK resident; and

- a claim for special tax treatment has been made by the trustees for this tax year.

For disposals prior to 6 April 2008, the special tax treatment determines that a UK-resident vulnerable person will be treated as the settlor of the settlement in that tax year. He is therefore able to use his full annual exemption and will be taxed at his marginal tax rate. The vulnerable person is then able to reclaim any tax paid back from the trustees.

FA 2008 replaced the previous rule, which used the settlor-interested provisions in *s 77*, and which charged the vulnerable person to CGT as though the trust gains arose directly to him. Therefore, where a vulnerable person is resident in the UK, the trustees' liability to CGT for gains realised after 5 April 2008 is reduced to the amount which would have been payable by the vulnerable person if the gains arose directly to him.

If the vulnerable person is not resident in the UK during the tax year, the vulnerable persons' liability has to be calculated according to the formulae described in *FA 2005, ss 32* and *33*, which are complex and beyond the scope of this book.

COMPLIANCE

8.50   One change introduced by *FA 2007, s 89* is to accelerate the filing date for trust and estate tax returns. Paper returns must be filed by 31 October, unless notice to file was given after 31 July, in which case the return must be filed within three months. If notice is given after 31 October, the old filing date of 31 January still applies. For electronic returns, the filing date remains at 31 January, unless the notice to file was made after 31 October, in which case the filing date is three months from the notice.

Chapter 9

Companies

BASIS OF CHARGE

Gains subject to corporation tax

9.1   Companies are chargeable to corporation tax in respect of chargeable gains accruing to them. The relevant legislation is contained in *Corporation Tax Act 2009* (*CTA 2009*), *s 2* and in *TCGA 1992, s 1(2)*.

The rate of corporation tax payable on chargeable gains is the rate appropriate to the accounting period in which the gains accrued. Companies are not entitled to the annual CGT exemption that is generally available to individuals, trustees and personal representatives (see **1.17**).

There is one exception to this rule: where the company holds a residential property subject to the annual tax on enveloped dwellings (ATED). Part or all of the gain arising on the disposal of such a property can be subject to CGT at 28% (see **4.40**).

Amount of chargeable gain

9.2   The gain accruing on the disposal of a company's chargeable asset is computed according to normal capital gains tax principles (see **Chapter 3**). The CGT provisions set out in the *Taxation of Chargeable Gains Act 1992* (*TCGA 1992*) are used to determine questions as to:

- the amounts taken into account as chargeable gains or as allowable losses, or in computing gains or losses, or charged to tax as a person's gain; and

- the time when any such amount is treated as accruing.

These questions are determined as if accounting periods were tax years (*TCGA 1992, s 8(3)*).

The rules that determine the value of the consideration for the disposal (see **3.4**), and the expenditure allowable as deductions (see **3.36**) in the computation, apply to companies, except where otherwise stated.

The amount included in a company's profits for an accounting period in respect of chargeable gains is the total amount of chargeable gains accruing to the company in that accounting period, less:

- any allowable losses accruing to the company in the period; and

- any allowable losses that accrued to the company in earlier periods when it was within the charge to corporation tax, and have not already been allowed as a deduction from chargeable gains (*TCGA 1992, s 8(1)*).

A loss is not an allowable loss if the disposal that generated a loss would be exempt from corporation tax, should that disposal have created a gain. Losses may also be denied by targeted or general anti-avoidance rules (see **9.29**).

Legislative references

9.3   As a general rule, references in CGT legislation to income tax or the *Income Tax Acts* (except those restricted, for example, to individuals) are to be read, in relation to a company, as references to corporation tax or to the *Corporation Tax Acts*. The *Income Tax Acts* are the enactments relating to income tax, including any provisions of the *Corporation Tax Acts* which relate to income tax (*TCGA 1992, s 8(4), (5); ICTA 1988, s 831(1)*).

Transactions with liquidator

9.4 The acts of a liquidator in whom the assets of a company have been vested are treated as if they were the acts of the company, and the assets are treated as remaining vested in the company. Transfers of assets between the liquidator and the company are ignored (*TCGA 1992, s 8(6)*).

Matters covered elsewhere

9.5 *Corporation Tax 2013/14* (Bloomsbury Professional) has detailed coverage of corporation tax on chargeable gains. Various matters relevant to disposals by companies are discussed in this chapter or elsewhere in this book, as shown in Table 9.1.

Table 9.1

Chapter 2	Disposal
2.7	No gain, no loss disposals
2.10	When asset value is lost
2.22	Deemed disposal by non-resident
Chapter 3	**Computation**
3.11	Disposals to connected persons
3.12	Assets disposed of in a series of transactions
3.20	Companies as connected persons
3.22	Delayed or deferred consideration
Chapter 4	**Particular assets**
4.20	Compulsory purchase of land
4.22	Furnished holiday lettings
4.35	Debts and financial arrangements
4.39	ATED and ATED-related gains
Chapter 5	**Residence**
5.28	Non-residents doing business in the UK
5.51	Apportionment of non-resident company's gains
Chapter 6	**Partnerships**
6.25	When transparency ends for an LLP

REBASING

9.6   Assets held by companies at 31 March 1982 are not automatically rebased to that date, as they are for individuals and trustees who make disposals after 5 April 2008 (see **9.7**). Corporate disposals are also eligible for indexation allowance, calculated from the date the asset was acquired, or 31 March 1982 if later, to the month in which the asset was disposed of (see **9.14**).

Rebasing to 31 March 1982

9.7   The discussion in **9.7–9.13** relates to disposals made after 5 April 2008, and as such is restricted to taxpayers that are subject to corporation tax. For the application of rebasing to disposals made by other taxpayers, please see *Capital Gains Tax 2007/08* (Tottel Publishing) or an earlier edition.

The general rebasing rule is that, where a company held an asset at 31 March 1982 and makes a disposal of it after 5 April 1988, the gain or loss accruing is calculated on the assumption that the company sold the asset on 31 March 1982 and immediately reacquired it at its market value on that date. The effect of rebasing is to substitute the 31 March 1982 value for the actual cost of the asset and any enhancement expenditure incurred prior to that date. If the value of the asset being disposed of is derived from another asset held on 31 March 1982, rebasing may apply by reference to the original asset's value on that date (*TCGA 1992, s 35(1), (2), Sch 3, para 5*).

Exceptions to the rebasing rule

9.8   These exceptions do not apply in any case where a rebasing election has been made (see **9.9**). The exceptions to the general rebasing rule are (*TCGA 1992, s 35(3)*):

(a)   where the effect of rebasing is to increase a gain arising under the normal rules, or to turn a loss arising under the normal rules into a gain;

(b)   where the effect of rebasing is to increase a loss arising under the normal rules, or to turn a gain arising under the normal rules into a loss;

(c)   where neither a gain nor a loss would accrue in the absence of rebasing, either on the facts or because of the rules for assets held on 6 April 1965 (*TCGA 1992, Sch 2*) (see **9.21**); or

(d)   where neither a gain nor a loss would accrue on the disposal by virtue of any of the provisions listed in *TCGA 1992, s 35(3)(d)*. Many of those provisions are not relevant for disposals made after 6 April 2008. The ones that remain relevant relate to the following disposals (statutory references being to *TCGA 1992* unless otherwise stated):

–   transfers of assets on company reconstructions – *s 139*;

–   transfers of UK trades by non-resident companies in exchange for securities – *s 140A*;

–   transfers of assets as part of a merger forming a European Company or SE – *s 140E*;

–   transfers within a group of companies – *s 171*;

–   transfers of insurance business – *s 211*;

–   disposals on amalgamations of building societies – *s 215*;

–   transfers of assets from a building society to a company – *s 216*;

–   transfers of assets on incorporation of a registered friendly society – *s 217A*;

–   transfers on the amalgamation of industrial and provident societies – *s 217D*;

–   certain disposals by housing associations – *ss 218–220*;

–   deemed disposals where a charity becomes absolutely entitled to settled property – *s 257(3)*;

–   gifts of heritage property – *s 258(4)*;

–   transfers of land between local constituency associations of political parties on reorganisation of constituencies – *s 264*; and

–   disposals relating to the sharing of transmission facilities between national broadcasting companies – *s 267(2)*.

A disposal is treated as giving rise to neither a gain nor a loss in a case where:

•   the effect of the rebasing rule would be to turn a gain into a loss, or to turn a loss into a gain; but

- that rule has been disapplied by one of the exceptions listed above (*TCGA 1992, s 35(4)*).

Rebasing election

9.9   The company may elect that the rebasing rule will apply to any disposal that company makes of assets that it held at both 31 March 1982 and 5 April 1988, whether or not the disposal is within the list of exceptions at **9.8**. The election, once made, is irrevocable and applies to all such disposals, including those made before the time of the election.

The election is to be made at any time before 6 April 1990 or during the period beginning on the day of the 'first relevant disposal' (see below) and ending two years after the end of the accounting period in which that disposal takes place; and at such later time as HMRC may allow (*TCGA 1992, s 35(6)*).

The 'first relevant disposal' is the first disposal to which the 31 March 1982 rebasing rules apply. HMRC take the view that, strictly, the disposal of any asset, whether chargeable or not, can be the first relevant disposal, but in exercising their discretion to extend the time limit they will disregard certain disposals. These are set out in HMRC Statement of Practice 4/92 and include (HMRC Capital Gains Tax Manual at CG16804):

- disposals on which a gain would not be a chargeable gain by virtue of a particular statutory provision, eg the exemption for gilt-edged securities;
- disposals that do not give rise to a chargeable gain in practice, eg a gift of eligible property for the benefit of the public or to a charity; and
- certain 'excluded disposals' that could not be covered by a rebasing election (see **9.10**).

Excluded disposals

9.10   From 6 April 2008, only companies can make a rebasing election, and that election will exclude disposals of (or disposals of an interest in) plant or machinery, or an asset used in a trade of working mineral deposits, where in either case capital allowances were available. These disposals are also excluded if the person making the disposal acquired the asset on a no gain, no loss transfer, and capital allowances were available to either the last person to acquire the asset other than on such a transfer or to any person who subsequently acquired the asset on such a transfer (*TCGA 1992, Sch 3, para 7*).

As a general rule, a rebasing election to cover assets held by a group of companies on 31 March 1982 may be made only by the group's principal member (*TCGA 1992, Sch 3, paras 8, 9*).

Assets acquired on a no gain, no loss transfer

9.11   Where the company makes a disposal after 5 April 1988 of an asset it acquired after 31 March 1982 by virtue of a no gain, no loss transfer (ie a disposal to which any of the provisions listed in *TCGA 1992, s 35(3)(d)* applies – see (d) in **9.8**), that company is treated as having held the asset on 31 March 1982 (*TCGA 1992, Sch 3, para 1*).

If the company ('the transferee') acquired the asset after 5 April 1988 and the no gain, no loss transfers principles applied to the acquisition (*TCGA 1992, s 171* between group companies), then:

(a)   any rebasing election made by the transferee does not cover the disposal by the transferee of that asset; and

(b)   any rebasing election made by the transferor causes the disposal to fall outside the exceptions listed above, so that rebasing applies on the transferee's disposal whether or not the transferee makes a rebasing election.

If the transferor in this situation acquired the asset after 5 April 1988, and *TCGA 1992, s 171* applied to his acquisition, a rebasing election made by the transferor will not have the effect noted in (b) above. However, an election made by either of the following taxpayers will have that effect:

● the last company to acquire the asset after 5 April 1988 on a transfer outside *TCGA 1992, s 171*; or

● if there is no such taxpayer, the person who held the asset on 5 April 1988 (*TCGA 1992, Sch 3, para 2*).

Halving relief

9.12   Halving relief applies to reduce by half a deferred gain when it crystallises after 5 April 1988 (*TCGA 1992, s 36, Sch 4*). The gain must have been deferred between 31 March 1982 and 6 April 1988, in respect of an asset held on 31 March 1982 when the rebasing rules came into effect.

Assets held on 6 April 1965 and 31 March 1982

9.13   Special rules (set out in *TCGA 1992, Sch 2*; see **9.21**) apply to a disposal of an asset held on 6 April 1965 in a case where:

● the rebasing rule in **9.8** does not apply; and

● the no gain, no loss rule in **9.11** does not apply.

INDEXATION ALLOWANCE

9.14   The discussion in **9.15–9.24** relates to disposals made after 5 April 2008, and as such is restricted to taxpayers that are subject to corporation tax. For the application of the indexation allowance to disposals made by other taxpayers in earlier periods, please see *Capital Gains Tax 2008/09* (Tottel Publishing) or an earlier edition. Guidance on the current application of indexation is found in CG17230–CG17292 and CG17700–CG17880.

The indexation allowance was introduced in 1982 in order to eliminate 'paper gains' attributable to inflation, as measured by the changes in the retail prices index (RPI). Combined with the rebasing of assets by reference to 31 March 1982 values (see **9.7**) with effect from April 1988, indexation provided 'inflation-proofing' of all gains accruing since 31 March 1982. The indexation allowance can only be claimed by organisations subject to corporation tax for disposals made after 5 April 2008 (*TCGA 1992, s 52A*).

Calculation of indexation allowance

9.15   If an 'unindexed gain' accrues on a disposal of an asset, an indexation allowance is allowed against it. No allowance is available where a loss has accrued. The allowance is set against the unindexed gain and the result is the 'gain' for the purpose of *TCGA 1992* (also known as the 'indexed gain').

Where the indexation allowance is equal to or greater than the unindexed gain, the result is that neither a gain nor a loss accrues. The 'unindexed gain' is the gain computed as required by *TCGA 1992, Pt II* (see **Chapter 3**) (*TCGA 1992, s 53(1)*).

The indexation allowance is the aggregate of the 'indexed rise' in each item of 'relevant allowable expenditure'. The 'indexed rise' for each item of expenditure is found by multiplying the amount of the expenditure by the figure (the 'indexation factor') given by the formula:

$$\frac{(RD - RI)}{RI}$$

where:

- RD is the RPI for the month in which the disposal occurs; and

- RI is the RPI for the later of March 1982 and the month in which the expenditure was incurred.

There is no indexed rise if RD is equal to or less than RI. The indexation factor is expressed as a decimal and rounded to the nearest third decimal place, but

HMRC may accept computations prepared using computer software where this rounding adjustment is not made, so long as computations are prepared on a consistent basis that favours neither HMRC nor the taxpayer (CG17274).

HMRC publish tables of the indexation allowance factors for use by companies at www.hmrc.gov.uk/rates/cg-indexation-allowance. The inflation measure used for indexation allowance is the 'all items RPI' – a data set with code name CHAW:RPI on the National Statistics website.

There is no indexed rise where expenditure concerned relates to acquisition of 'relevant securities', as defined in *TCGA 1992, s 108*, and the securities are disposed of within ten days of the expenditure being incurred (*TCGA 1992, 54(2)*). Other aspects of indexation allowance are also modified in relation to disposals of shares, securities and options (see **9.30**).

Relevant allowable expenditure

9.16 'Relevant allowable expenditure' above means any sum allowed as a deduction in computing the unindexed gain, adjusted as necessary for any provision increasing, reducing, writing down or excluding such expenditure (see **3.36**). Any foreign tax charged on a gain is not regarded as relevant allowable expenditure, but it may be deducted from the tax charge as foreign tax credit relief (see **3.66**). Costs of acquisition are taken to have been incurred when the asset was acquired or provided, and costs of enhancement are taken to have been incurred when the expenditure became due and payable (*TCGA 1992, s 54(4)*).

Part disposals

9.17 The apportionment of allowable expenditure on the part disposal of an asset (see **3.45**) takes place before the calculation of indexation allowance. This means there is no indexed rise to be computed for the part of the relevant allowable expenditure that is apportioned to the part retained (*TCGA 1992, s 56(1)*).

Assets held on 31 March 1982

9.18 Where the asset has been rebased to 31 March 1982, the indexation allowance is based on the market value at that date.

The rebased value can only apply where the company has made a rebasing election (see **9.9**). Where the rebasing election has not been made, the indexation will normally be based on the greater of the actual expenditure (or possibly market value at 6 April 1965) and the market value at 31 March 1982.

Assets acquired on a no gain, no loss transfer

9.19   Where the asset has been acquired on a no gain, no loss transfer before 31 March 1988 (see **9.11**):

- in computing the indexation allowance on the disposal, the taxpayer is treated as having held the asset on 31 March 1982 so that the allowance may be based on the market value at that date; but

- in computing the gain or loss accruing on the disposal, any indexation allowance taken into account in fixing the consideration that the taxpayer has deemed to have given for the asset is deducted from that consideration (*TCGA 1992, s 55(5), (6)*).

For this purpose, a no gain, no loss disposal is one on which neither a gain nor a loss accrues by virtue of:

- any of the rebasing provisions listed in *TCGA 1992, s 35(3)(d)* (see **9.8**);

- the rules relating to gifts to charities, registered clubs and relevant housing providers in *TCGA 1992, ss 257(2)* and *259(2)* respectively (*TCGA 1992, s 55(5)*); or

- oil licence-consideration swaps under *TCGA 1992, s 195B, 195C* or *195E*.

Acquisition on a no gain, no loss transfer before 30 November 1993

9.20   As indicated in **9.15**, the indexation allowance can neither create nor increase a loss – it can only reduce the unindexed gain to nil. This was not the case before 30 November 1993. Special rules apply where the person making a disposal on or after that date acquired the asset on a no gain, no loss transfer before that date. Broadly, the effect is that a measure of indexation allowance that accrued on the no gain, no loss transfer – called the 'rolled-up indexation' – may create or increase a loss on the subsequent disposal.

For this purpose, it is necessary to compute the gain under the normal rules and compute the amount of the rolled-up indexation. No adjustment is required if indexation allowance included in the computation exceeds the rolled-up indexation. If it is less than the rolled-up indexation, the full amount of the rolled-up indexation is allowed in computing the chargeable gain or allowable loss (*TCGA 1992, s 55(7)–(11)*; CG17766).

Assets held on 6 April 1965

9.21   The rules for assets held on 6 April 1965 described below only apply to companies where a universal rebasing election has not been made, so in practice will very rarely be encountered.

Quoted shares and securities

9.22   A gain or loss on disposal of quoted shares or securities is computed by reference to both the original cost and the market value of the asset as at 6 April 1965. The lower gain (or loss) arising is taken. If one computation produces a gain and the other produces a loss, the disposal is treated as giving rise to no gain and no loss. An irrevocable election (similar to the 31 March 1982 rebasing election, see **9.9**) can be made to use the 6 April 1965 market value of quoted shares and securities instead of their original cost (*TCGA 1992, Sch 2, Pt I*).

Land reflecting development value

9.23   The gain or loss on the disposal of land reflecting development value that was held at 6 April 1965 is computed as described for quoted shares and securities (see **9.21**) if special provisions relating to development land apply (*TCGA 1992, Sch 2, Pt II*).

Other assets held on 6 April 1965

9.24   Where an asset, other than quoted shares or land with development value, was acquired before 6 April 1965, the general rule is that gains are calculated on the basis of original cost but those gains are then time-apportioned. Only that part of the gain relating to the period falling after 6 April 1965 is chargeable. Any period of ownership before 6 April 1945 is ignored for time-apportionment purposes. The gain is reduced by any indexation allowance before being time-apportioned. However, the rebasing calculation using the 31 March 1982 value (see **9.9**) should normally give rise to a lower gain and this time-apportionment method is now likely to be used only rarely.

The taxpayer may make an irrevocable election to ignore the original cost and compute the gain by reference to the asset's market value on 6 April 1965. Alternatively, where a rebasing election has been made, the asset's market value at 31 March 1982 replaces the original cost and no time-apportionment of the gain is necessary (*TCGA 1992, Sch 2, Pt III*).

Example 9.1

The West End Trading Co Ltd prepares accounts to 31 March each year. The company disposed of an office block in February 2013 for £40 million. The incidental costs of sale were £50,000. The block was purchased in January 2006 for £25.5 million. Costs of acquisition including SDLT amounted to £1.25 million. In January 2007, a new frontage at a cost of £2 million was added to the building that was deemed to be capital expenditure. The chargeable gain to be included within the corporation tax computation for the year ended 31 March 2013 is calculated as follows:

		£000	£000
Feb 2013	Gross sale proceeds		40,000
	Less: Incidental costs of sale		(50)
	Net sale proceeds		39,950
	Less: Relevant allowable expenditure:		
January 2006	Acquisition cost	25,500	
January 2006	Incidental costs of acquisition	1,250	
January 2007	Enhancement expenditure	2,000	
			(28,750)
	Unindexed gain		11,200
	Less: Indexation allowance		
	Cost 26,750 × 0.28	7,490	
	Enhancement 2,000 × 0.228	456	
			(7,946)
	Chargeable gain		3,254

Calculation of indexation factors:

RPI	February 2013	247.6
RPI	January 2006	193.4
RPI	January 2007	201.6
Factor:	Rounded to three decimal places	
Cost	(RPI Feb 2013 – RPI January 2006) ÷ RPI January 2006	0.280
Enhancement	(RPI Feb 2013 – RPI January 2007) ÷ RPI January 2007	0.228

CAPITAL LOSSES

9.25 As a general rule, capital losses may only be set against capital gains of the current accounting period or carried forward to be set against future capital gains. There are no provisions that permit corporate taxpayers to carry back capital losses (see **3.29** and **7.3** for individuals).

In circumstances where the UK or Scottish Government has invested in the company, and that investment has been written off, the losses of the company are reduced by the amount of the government investment written off (*CTA 2010, s 92*). Income losses are reduced before any capital losses.

Capital loss against income

9.26 A capital loss on the disposal by an investment company of shares, for which it subscribed, in an unlisted trading company may be set against the company's income for corporation tax purposes (see **17.18**). A loss made on shares acquired under the corporate venturing scheme (CVS) before 31 March 2010 may also be set against income under certain circumstances (see **9.54**).

Income loss against gains

9.27 The effect of a claim to relief for trading losses under *CTA 2010, s 37* may be to set such losses against chargeable gains, because the losses are set against total profits including chargeable gains.

Loss transferred

9.28 Where losses are made by a company within a group of companies, elections can be made effectively to transfer the loss to another group company (see **9.34** and **9.35**).

Anti-avoidance rules

9.29 A targeted anti-avoidance rule (TAAR) in *TCGA 1992, s 16A* applies to any company that is seeking to make use of a capital loss that is not a genuine commercial loss, which arose from a genuine commercial disposal. A capital loss is not an allowable loss if it accrues directly or indirectly in consequence or in connection with any arrangements of which the main purpose is to secure a tax advantage (*TCGA 1992, s 16A(1)*). This is a very wide-ranging provision, but in practice its scope is limited by the HMRC guidance contained in Appendix 9 to the HMRC Capital Gains Manual; see also **10.20**. There are also three TAARs that apply to companies with effect from 5 December 2005 that seek to target:

- the buying of capital losses and gains (*TCGA 1992, ss 184A, 184B*);

- the conversion of an income stream into capital and the use of capital losses to create a deduction against it (*TCGA 1992, s 184G*); and

- the artificial generation of capital losses (*TCGA 1992, s 184H*).

The detailed rules for these provisions are discussed in Chapter 22 of *Corporation Tax 2013/14* (Bloomsbury Professional).

Losses arising from an abuse of any tax rule can be denied under the GAAR (see **Chapter 10**).

IDENTIFICATION OF SHARES

9.30   The changes made from 6 April 2008 to simplify the calculation of gains on the disposal of shares and securities (see **4.1**) do not apply for corporation tax. This means that the various pools used to identify shares acquired at different times continue for corporation tax.

All shares of the same class in the same company that are acquired after 31 March 1982 are 'pooled', ie treated as a single asset with a single average indexed cost per share. Each disposal of shares out of the pool represents a part disposal of a single asset, and the chargeable gain or allowable loss is computed by reference to the averaged indexed cost of the shares sold.

Shares disposed of are identified with acquisitions in the following order:

(a)   acquisitions on the same day as the disposal;

(b)   securities treated as part of the *section 104* holding where acquisitions were made during the nine days before the disposal date (earlier acquisitions first);

(c)   shares acquired after 31 March 1982 and comprised in the '*section 104* holding' (see **9.31**);

(d)   shares acquired before 1 April 1982 (the '1982 holding'; see **9.32**);

(e)   shares acquired before 6 April 1965 (taking later acquisitions first); and

(f)   acquisitions after the disposal (taking earlier acquisitions first) (*TCGA 1992, ss 105–107*; CG50562).

Special rules apply to 'relevant securities', ie qualifying corporate bonds, securities within the accrued income provisions and material interests in non-reporting offshore funds (*TCGA 1992, s 108*).

Section 104 holding

9.31 The *section 104* holding comprises shares of the same class that were acquired after 31 March 1982. For non-corporate shareholders, this pool was restricted to shares acquired after 5 April 1982 and before 6 April 1998 by the same person in the same capacity. See Chapter 4 of *Capital Gains Tax 2007/08* (Tottel Publishing) for a full description of the share identification rules that applied for 2007/08 and earlier tax years for individuals, trustees and personal representatives.

Shares in the *section 104* holding are treated as indistinguishable parts of a single asset. A disposal of some of the shares in a *section 104* holding is treated as a part disposal of an asset (*TCGA 1992, s 104(1), (3), (6)*).

There are special rules for calculating indexation allowance for shares in this pool (*TCGA 1992, s 110*). The gain is computed by reference to the averaged indexed cost of each share disposed of. The shares in the *section 104* holding are referred to as the 'new holding' by HMRC, and detailed guidance is given at CG50590–CG50801.

Example 9.2

Imperious Capital Ltd holds 1,500 shares in Destroying Angel Ltd, which represents 1.5% of ordinary share capital of that company, so the substantial shareholding exemption does not apply (see **9.48**). The Destroying Angel shares were acquired as follows:

Date	Number of shares	Cost £	Indexed cost £
1 June 2000	1,000	80,000	7,360
Indexed to April 2004, factor: 0.092			87,360
3 April 2004	300	9,000	96,360
Indexed to Dec 2007, factor: 0.136			13,104
7 December 2007	200	1,000	110,464
Indexed to April 2013, factor: 0.183			20,215
	1,500	90,000	130,679
Disposal in April 2013	(500)		(43,560)
Remaining pool:	1,000		87,119

As shown above, Imperious Capital Ltd disposed of 500 of the Destroying Angel shares in April 2013, and the cost of that part disposal is calculated as: 500 / 1,500 × £130,679 = £43,560.

The 1982 holding

9.32   This comprises all shares of the same class in the same company that were acquired between 6 April 1965 and 31 March 1982. The holding is treated as acquired on 31 March 1982 (*TCGA 1992, s 109*).

Where shares are held by a company in a group and are disposed of outside of that group, special treatment applies for indexation or rebasing purposes at 31 March 1982. Where the shares were both acquired:

- by no gain, no loss transfer after that date by a member of a group of companies; and

- out of a holding which another member of the group held at 31 March 1982,

the company making the disposal outside the group may elect that the shares be valued as a proportionate part of the other group member's holding on 31 March 1982 (*TCGA 1992, Sch 3, para 1A*). Such an election may be advantageous where the shares were acquired out of a larger holding of the other group member.

GROUPS OF COMPANIES

Definitions

9.33   Tax charges and reliefs relating to chargeable gains can depend on whether a company is part of a group. For these purposes, a group broadly consists of a company (known as the principal company) and all of its 75% subsidiaries. If any of those subsidiaries have 75% subsidiaries of their own, the group includes them and their 75% subsidiaries. Any subsidiary that is not an effective 51% subsidiary of the principal company of the group is excluded.

A company that is a 75% subsidiary of another company cannot be the principal company of a group. The principal company can be UK or overseas resident, and the inclusion of a non-resident subsidiary does not disturb the group relationship.

Example 9.3

A Ltd owns 75% of the ordinary share capital of B Ltd.

B Ltd owns 80% of the ordinary share capital of C Ltd.

A Ltd and B Ltd are a group, as A Ltd owns 75% of B Ltd.

A Ltd and C Ltd are a group because A Ltd effectively owns 60% (75% × 80%) of C Ltd.

A company cannot be a member of more than one group. Where a company would be a member of two or more groups but for this rule, the group to which it is treated as belonging is determined by reference to its links to the principal company. If the group conditions are not met, the links should then be established with the next group – see Example 9.4 (*TCGA 1992, s 170*).

Example 9.4

A Ltd owns 75% of the ordinary share capital of B Ltd.

B Ltd owns 80% of the ordinary share capital of C Ltd.

C Ltd owns 75% of the ordinary share capital of D Ltd.

D Ltd owns 75% of the ordinary share capital of E Ltd.

A Ltd and B Ltd are a group.

A Ltd and C Ltd are a group.

A Ltd and D Ltd are not a group because A Ltd effectively owns 45% (75% × 80% × 75%) of D Ltd.

D Ltd and E Ltd are a group.

Transfers within a group of companies

9.34   For chargeable gains purposes, intra-group transfers of assets are deemed to be made at a price that results in neither a gain nor a loss accruing to the transferee company (*TCGA 1992, s 171*) (*Innocent v Whaddon Estates Ltd* (1981) 55 TC 476, [1982] STC 115).

This no gain, no loss rule is applied automatically – no claim is required, but it does not apply to a disposal:

- arising on the satisfaction of a debt due from the transferee company;
- arising on the redemption of redeemable shares in a company;
- by or to an investment trust, a venture capital trust (VCT), a qualifying friendly society, or a dual-resident investing company;
- by or to a real estate investment trust; or
- in fulfilment of the company's obligations under an option granted to the transferee company before those companies were members of the group (*TCGA 1992, s 171(2)*).

The effect of this no gain, no loss rule is that, when the transferee company eventually disposes of the asset to a third party, its allowable acquisition expenditure in the chargeable gains computation will comprise the original base cost of the asset to the group, plus indexation allowance for the period to the date of the transfer. The transferee company will be eligible for indexation on this deemed acquisition expenditure as well as any allowable enhancement expenditure that it incurs.

Although a non-UK resident company can be a member of the group, it cannot take part in a no gain, no loss transfer unless it trades in the UK through a permanent establishment in the UK. The asset must be in the UK and be used for the purposes of that trade (*TCGA 1992, s 171(1A)*).

On a company reconstruction involving an exchange of shares or debentures under the conditions set out in *TCGA 1992, s 135*, the no gain, no loss rule in *s 171* does not apply, as the alternative no gain, no loss treatment in *TCGA 1992, ss 127–131* takes preference (*TCGA 1992, s 171(3)*). For further discussion of company reconstructions, refer to Chapter 20 of *Corporation Tax 2013/14* (Bloomsbury Professional).

Election to transfer gains and losses within a group

9.35   Where a capital gain or loss accrues on or after 21 July 2009, group companies can transfer the gain or loss between each other to allow full matching of losses and gains that arise within the group. There is no need actually to transfer the ownership of assets within a group. Losses arising as a result of a negligible value claim (see **2.10**) can be transferred as well as realised losses (*TCGA 1992, ss 171A–171C*). Where a degrouping charge arises on or after 19 July 2011 (see **9.36**), this can also be transferred between group companies.

The gain or loss is transferred by way of a joint election by the two group companies made within two years of the end of the accounting period for the company where the gain or loss is accrued (*TCGA 1992, s 171A*). The companies concerned must both be members of the same group at the time the gain or loss accrues, and the no gain, no loss conditions under s *171* must apply (see **9.34**).

Gains or losses made before 21 July 2009 could only be transferred between group companies where the asset concerned was transferred outside the group. The transfer of the loss or gain was achieved in the same fashion by joint election between the two group companies.

Degrouping charges

9.36   If a company leaves a group within six years of an intra-group transfer of an asset that was treated as a no gain, no loss disposal (see **9.34**) and the company still owns that asset when it leaves the group, a chargeable gain arises on that occasion (*TCGA 1992, s 179*). The gain is calculated on the basis that the company leaving the group sold and repurchased the asset at its market value at the time of the no gain, no loss transfer, but the gain is charged in the accounting period in which the company leaves the group (*TCGA 1992, s 179(3)*). For example, a new subsidiary may be formed to contain the trade and assets of a particular activity that the parent group wants to dispose of. The deemed *s 179* gain would arise in the new subsidiary rather than in the vendor company.

FA 2011, s 45 and *Sch 10* simplified the calculation of the degrouping charge where a company leaves a group as a result of the disposal of its shares. In this situation any degrouping charge under *s 179* is treated as additional consideration for the disposal of the shares and thus will normally qualify for the substantial shareholding exemption (see **9.48**). This simplification generally has effect from 19 July 2011. However, where a company leaves a group on or after 1 April 2011 the group can opt to have the degrouping charge treated as consideration for that departing company's shares. For a detailed discussion of the degrouping charges, refer to Chapter 17 of *Corporation Tax 2013/14* (Bloomsbury Professional).

Example 9.5

In 1988, Nereus Ltd acquired a freehold property for £280,000. On 30 December 2003, when the market value was £500,000, and the indexation to date was £20,000, Nereus Ltd transferred the freehold property to Pontus Ltd (a fellow group member). Pontus Ltd left the group on 31 December 2011. Both companies prepare accounts to 30 June each year.

The *TCGA 1992, s 179* gain for the year ended 30 June 2012 is calculated as follows:

Pontus Ltd	£	£
Market value at date of transfer:		500,000
Original cost	280,000	
Indexation:	20,000	
Indexed cost:		(300,000)
Capital gain		200,000

If Pontus Ltd purchases another qualifying asset, Pontus Ltd will be able to make a roll-over relief claim under *TCGA 1992, s 152*.

If Nereus Ltd and Pontus Ltd jointly elect for the *s 179* deemed gain to be treated as accruing to Nereus Ltd, then Nereus Ltd may be able to make a roll-over relief claim against its acquisition of a qualifying asset.

Value shifting

9.37   The value of shares disposed of by companies can be affected by the value of assets transferred into those subsidiary companies. Where assets were transferred at an undervalue before 19 July 2011, a set of the complex value shifting rules could apply. For details of these rules, refer to *Corporation Tax 2010/11* (Bloomsbury Professional).

For disposals made on or after 19 July 2011, a simple targeted anti-avoidance rule applies if there is an intention to avoid tax (*TCGA 1992, s 31*). This rule applies if:

- arrangements have been made so that the value of those shares or securities or any relevant asset are materially reduced (or increased, if a disposal of shares or securities precedes their acquisition);

- the main purpose, or one of the main purposes, of the arrangements is to obtain a tax advantage, either for the disposing company or for any other person; and

- the arrangements do not consist wholly of the making of an exempt distribution.

Where value shifting does apply, the disposal proceeds are increased by an amount which is just and reasonable, having regard to the arrangements made and the corporation tax charge or relief (CG45450). This anti-avoidance rule does not apply if the substantial shareholdings exemption applies (see **9.48**).

Series of transactions

9.38   A transfer of assets between members of a group of companies is not a material transaction if it is a 'no gain, no loss' transfer by virtue of *TCGA 1992, s 171* (*TCGA 1992, s 19(5)*; see **9.34**).

An anti-avoidance rule applies to prevent a group circumventing the rule concerning the valuation of assets as part of a series of transactions (see **3.12**) by having one company transfer assets to other group companies under the no gain, no loss rule in *TCGA 1992, s 171* and then arranging for the assets to be transferred to connected persons outside the group (*TCGA 1992, s 19(6)*; CG14702).

Transfers of assets to trading stock

9.39   Where one group member acquires a capital asset from another member and appropriates that asset to trading stock, the intra-group asset transfer will be treated as a no gain, no loss disposal (see **9.34**), but as soon as the asset is transferred to stock a chargeable gain will arise in the hands of the transferee. The transferee adopts the transferor's asset base cost and indexation to the date of the transfer (*TCGA 1992, ss 171, 173*).

Alternatively, the transferee can elect under *TCGA 1992, s 161(3)* to treat the asset as acquired at market value less the capital gain arising. The gain will therefore be taken as part of the trading profit on the asset.

Example 9.6

Odin Ltd transfers a fixed asset to its holding company Thor Ltd which has a market value of £20,000, and a cost plus indexation allowance (the indexed cost) of £12,500. Thor Ltd immediately appropriates the asset to its trading stock, and eventually sells the asset to a third party for £30,000.

Without a *TCGA 1992, s 161(3)* election, the position is as follows:

Thor Ltd	£
Market value at time of transfer to stock	20,000
Indexed cost from no gain, no loss acquisition	(12,500)
Capital gain	7,500
Thor Ltd	
Sale proceeds	30,000
Deemed cost (market value)	(20,000)
Trading profit	10,000

With a *TCGA 1992, s 161(3)* election, the position is as follows:

Thor Ltd	£
Sales proceeds	30,000
Indexed cost	(12,500)
Trading profit	17,500

9.40   There is the potential here to turn a capital loss into a trading loss. The loss will only be allowed if there is a true trading intention (*Coates v Arndale Properties Ltd* (1984) 59 TC 516, [1984] STC 637, [1984] 1 WLR 1328, [1985] 1 All ER 15).

Transfers of assets from trading stock

9.41   Where a group company transfers an asset that it holds as trading stock to another group company, and the transferee holds it as a capital asset, the asset is deemed to be transferred at market value giving rise to a trading profit in the hands of the transferor (*CTA 2009, s 157*). When the transferee company sells the asset outside the group, it adopts as its base cost the market value of the asset at the time of the transfer, plus indexation allowance.

Example 9.7

Thor Ltd transfers a chargeable asset from its trading stock to its subsidiary company Odin Ltd. Odin Ltd holds the asset as an investment. The cost of the asset was £10,000 and the market value on transfer is £30,000. Odin Ltd then sells the asset to a third party for £40,000. The indexation from the time of transfer is £500.

Thor Ltd	£	£
Market value		30,000
Cost		(10,000)
Trading profit		20,000
Odin Ltd		
Sale proceeds		40,000
Deemed cost (market value)	30,000	
Indexation	500	
		(30,500)
Capital gain		9,500

Roll-over relief and groups

9.42   Roll-over relief (see **Chapter 14**) is extended to group situations. For this purpose, all trades carried on by the members of a group are treated as a single trade. The new assets must be purchased from outside the group (*TCGA 1992, s 175*).

Losses attributable to depreciatory transactions

9.43   A transfer of assets between group companies for a consideration other than market value may have the effect of deflating the value of a group company. Any capital loss accruing on the sale of the shares in that company may not be an allowable loss to the extent that it is attributable to the 'depreciatory transaction'. The detailed rules are set out in *TCGA 1992, s 176*, and are discussed in greater depth in Chapter 17 of *Corporation Tax 2013/14* (Bloomsbury Professional). HMRC guidance is given at CG46500–CG46580.

Dividend stripping

9.44   The rule in **9.43** may also apply in a non-group situation. Say company (A) owns 10% or more of all holdings of the same class of shares of another company (B), but company A is not part of the same group as company B, and does not hold the company B shares as trading stock. A distribution is made by company B which materially reduces the value of the shares held by company A. Company A then sells its shares in company B, but an adjustment is made for that distribution in calculating the chargeable gain or loss accruing on a disposal of the company B shares (*TCGA 1992, s 177*).

Pre-entry losses and gains

9.45   A pre-entry asset is an asset owned by a company before it joins a group. A loss or gain accruing on the disposal of that asset, either before or after the company joins the group, is a pre-entry loss or gain. Anti-avoidance rules exist to prevent companies from buying other companies which have exiting capital losses in order to use those losses against their own gains.

The rules for treatment of pre-entry capital losses are simplified with effect from 19 July 2011 (*TCGA 1992, Sch 7A*). Losses realised after a change of ownership will be available to offset against any capital gains from assets used in the same business as the company which was carried on before the change in ownership. It is sufficient that this business is carried on somewhere within the group of companies. This is known as capital loss streaming (CG47400–CG47465).

The pre-entry loss rules are supplemented by restrictions on buying losses that apply for accounting periods ending on or after 5 December 2005 (*TCGA 1992, s 184A*), where there is an arrangement to avoid tax. The ability of a group company to set its capital losses against capital gains accruing in another group company (see **9.35**) is denied in the following circumstances:

(a)   where there is a direct or indirect change in ownership of a company;

(b)   where a loss accrues to the company or another company on a pre-entry asset;

(c)   where the main purpose of the change in ownership is to secure a tax advantage; and

(d)   the tax advantage involves the deduction of loses from chargeable gains.

The operation of the anti-avoidance rules in *TCGA 1992, ss 184A–184I* are discussed in greater detail in Chapter 22 of *Corporation Tax 2013/14* (Bloomsbury Professional).

RELIEF ON DISPOSAL OF SHARES

9.46   Three important reliefs are available in relation to a company's disposal of shares. These relate to:

- losses on shares in unlisted trading companies (see **9.47**);

- substantial shareholdings exemption (see **9.48**); and

- corporate venturing scheme losses (see **9.52**).

The computation of all chargeable gains must be made in sterling (see **3.1**). However, for periods beginning on or after 1 April 2011, this rule is modified where the company has a functional currency other than sterling or is an investment company which has made a designated currency election (*CTA 2010, s 9A*).

For such companies, the gain arising on the disposal of shares (but not other assets) can be made using the functional currency. Any chargeable gain or loss will then be translated into sterling using the exchange rate at the date of the disposal.

Losses on shares in unlisted trading companies

9.47   Relief against income is available to an investment company incurring an allowable loss for corporation tax purposes on the disposal of shares, for which it subscribed, in a qualifying trading company (see **17.18**).

Substantial shareholdings exemption

9.48   Where a trading company (the investing company) holds at least 10% of the share capital of another trading company (the investee company), and the other conditions of the substantial shareholdings exemption (SSE) are met, a gain made on the disposal of any investee company shares is not a chargeable gain. Also, a loss accruing on the disposal of any of the investee company shares by the investing company is not an allowable loss (*TCGA 1992, s 192A, Sch 7AC*).

For HMRC guidance on the SSE, see CG53000–CG53240.

SSE relief applies automatically if the conditions are met; there is no requirement to make an election. The requirements for SSE relief for the investing company are as follows:

(a)   It must hold at least 10% of the investee company's ordinary share capital and be entitled to at least 10% of the profits and assets available for distribution to equity holders.

(b)   It must have held the shares for a continuous period of at least 12 months beginning not more than two years before the disposal (*TCGA 1992, Sch 7AC, para 7*).

Group member holdings can be aggregated in order to calculate whether the 10% holding condition is met (*TCGA 1992, Sch 7AC, para 9*). The capital gains tax group definition is used (see **9.33**) but a 51% relationship is required rather than a 75% relationship.

The period of ownership may be extended to take account of earlier no gain, no loss transfers and share reorganisations. There are provisions dealing with deemed disposals and reacquisitions, repurchase agreements, stock-lending arrangements, demergers and liquidations (*TCGA 1992, Sch 7AC, paras 10–16*).

The SSE relief applies to gains or losses made on all disposals of all types of shares in the investee company, not just the ordinary shares which are held to meet the 10% test. SSE relief does not apply where the disposal is deemed to be a no gain, no loss transfer for capital gains under *TCGA 1992, s 171* (see **9.34**).

Conditions affecting the investing company

9.49   The investing company must have been a sole trading company or a member of a trading group throughout the 12-month period (see **9.48**) and immediately after the disposal. The SSE relief also applies in a group situation where the company holding the shares does not qualify but, assuming an intra-group transfer under *TCGA 1992, s 171*, another company would qualify. Where completion takes place after the time of disposal (as provided by *TCGA 1992, s 28*), the investing company must qualify at the time of completion (*TCGA 1992, Sch 7AC, para 18*).

Conditions affecting the investee company

9.50   The investee company must have been a trading company or the holding company of a trading group during the 12-month period (see **9.48**), and it must also be a qualifying company immediately after the disposal of the shares. The responsibility for determining whether a company in which shares (or an interest in shares or assets related to shares) were held and since disposed of was a qualifying company lies with the investor company concerned (see CG53120). Where there is uncertainty over the trading status of the investee company the investing company can ask HMRC for an opinion on this point under their non-statutory business clearance service (see www.hmrc.gov.uk/manuals/nbcgmanual/index.htm).

Where completion takes place after the time of disposal (as provided by *TCGA 1992, s 28*), the investee company must qualify at the time of completion (*TCGA 1992, Sch 7AC, para 19*).

Trading company

9.51   The meanings of 'trading company', 'trading group' and 'holding company' are now common to all capital gains reliefs and are defined in *TCGA 1992, s 165A*. See **11.11–11.18** for a detailed discussion of these terms. Where a company has an interest in a joint venture (JV), or an organisation which does not have ordinary share capital, the trading activities of that JV or other organisation can be included when considering whether the group as a whole is a trading group (see Revenue & Customs Brief 29/11).

Example 9.8

Atlantic Ltd is a trading company, with two wholly owned subsidiary companies, India Ltd and China Ltd.

On 1 July 2008, Atlantic Ltd acquired 25% of the ordinary share capital of Pacific Ltd.

On 1 September 2008, Pacific Ltd is taken over by Adriatic Ltd.

Atlantic Ltd received an exchange of shares under the no gain, no loss treatment (*TCGA, 1992, s 127*). As a result, Atlantic Ltd now owns 20% of Adriatic Ltd.

On 1 March 2009, Atlantic Ltd transfers its holding in Adriatic Ltd (on a no gain, no loss basis so that *TCGA 1992, s 171* applies) to its 100% subsidiary India Ltd.

On 1 July 2013, India Ltd sells the holding to a third party.

The holding was bought on 1 July 2008 and sold on 1 July 2013. It is necessary to look back through the period of ownership to ascertain whether the substantial shareholdings exemption applies (*TCGA 1992, Sch 7AC, para 10*). The holding throughout has remained within the group. India Ltd is treated as owning the shares for an unbroken period of 12 months prior to disposal, and so the exemption applies.

Corporate venturing scheme

9.52   Relief under the corporate venturing scheme was available for investments in qualifying shares issued during the period from 1 April 2000 to 31 March 2010. The scheme is discussed in detail in Chapter 12 of *Corporation Tax 2009/10* (Bloomsbury Professional), and the legislation is found in *FA 2000, s 63* and *Sch 15*. HMRC guidance is available in the Venture Capital Schemes Manual at VCM90000–VCM93090.

Tax reliefs

9.53   Three types of relief are available:

- investment relief – relief against corporation tax of up 20% of the amount subscribed for the full-risk ordinary shares (CVS shares) held for at least three years;

- deferral relief – any gain on the sale of CVS shares can be rolled into the cost of new shares acquired under the scheme; and

- loss relief – any loss on the sale of the CVS shares can be relieved against income or chargeable gains.

The conditions for the reliefs to apply are not discussed here, as the schéme has closed for new investments. Only loss relief may be relevant to companies who held CVS shares on 1 April 2010.

Focus

If the qualifying conditions for SSE apply (see **9.48**), any gain arising on the disposal of the CVS shares is ignored for corporation tax purposes.

The deferral relief is unnecessary and the loss relief (see **9.54**) is overridden.

Relief for losses

9.54   A loss accruing on a disposal of shares that have attracted CVS investment relief may be set against a chargeable gain, or carried forward to set against future chargeable gains, in the normal way, provided the loss is not overridden by SSE relief (see **9.53**). Alternatively, the investing company may claim that the loss be set against its income for the accounting period in which the disposal was made, with any excess carried back to periods ending in the 12 months before that period. Several conditions are set out in *FA 2000, Sch 15, paras 67–72*.

Example 9.9

An investing company subscribes £100,000 for 100,000 shares (obtaining investment relief of £20,000).

It retains the shares for four years before disposing of them all for £55,000.

The allowable loss is calculated as follows:

Disposal proceeds: £55,000 − £80,000 (consideration given for shares less investment relief given and not withdrawn), giving an allowable loss of £25,000.

Any unutilised loss cannot be carried forward as a trading loss but may be carried forward as a capital loss.

DISINCORPORATION RELIEF

When it applies

9.55   This is a form of hold-over relief between a company and its shareholders, on the transfer of the business as a going concern to some or all of its shareholders (*FA 2013, ss 58–61* HMRC guidance on this new relief is found in their Capital Gains Manual at CG65800–CG65850.

Disincorporation relief only applies to defer gains arising on the transfer of qualifying assets where the total market value does not exceed £100,000. The qualifying assets are limited to goodwill and/or land and buildings which are not held as trading stock. The held-over gain is taxed in the hands of the shareholders, when they eventually dispose of the qualifying asset.

All the shareholders who receive the assets must be individuals who have held their shares in the company for at least one year to the date of business transfer. Those individuals are permitted to be members of an ordinary partnership, but they must not be members of an LLP. However, there is no requirement for all the shareholders of the company to receive a share of the assets.

The relief has a limited life. It can only apply to business transfers undertaken in the period from 1 April 2013 to 31 March 2018. Where the transfer is made by contract, the transfer date is determined by *TCGA 1992, s 28* (see **2.8**).

Procedure for claims

9.56   All the parties to the transfer of the business (ie the company and individual shareholders) must jointly elect under *FA 2013, s 58* within two years of the business transfer date. The election has the effect of transferring the qualifying assets at a value which produces no gain and no loss for the company (*TCGA 1992, s 162B*).

This is achieved by deeming the transfer value to be the lower of cost of the asset to the company and its market value. The cost of pre-April 2002 goodwill is likely to be nil. Where the goodwill transferred was acquired or created by the company after March 2002, it is included in the corporate intangible assets regime (see **14.27**). In this case, the value of the goodwill transferred is nil for the company, as determined by *CTA 2009, s 849A*.

Focus

Disincorporation relief only protects the company from the gain that would otherwise arise on the distribution of the assets to a connected party at market value. It does not protect the shareholders from the income tax or CGT charge due on the receipt of income distributions from the company or capital distributions as part of a winding up (see **2.23**).

Chapter 10

Tax planning versus tax avoidance

SIGNPOSTS

- **The boundaries** – Tax planning and tax avoidance (**10.1–10.2**).

- **Basic tax planning** – Residence and domicile, exemptions, the computation, losses, spouses and civil partners, connected persons, ownership of assets, 'bed and breakfast' transactions, hold-over reliefs, entrepreneurs' relief, main residence relief (see **10.3–10.15**).

- **Anti-avoidance rules** – GAAR, TAARs, HMRC guidance and clearance procedures, other anti-avoidance rules (see **10.16–10.22**).

- **Disclosure of tax avoidance schemes** – Outline, which tax arrangements, the hallmarks, how a disclosure is made, HMRC guidance (see **10.23–10.27**).

TAX PLANNING

10.1   This chapter provides an overview of some of the matters that should be considered by, or on behalf of, taxpayers who want to ensure that they pay no more CGT than the law requires.

The actions described here are recognised as mainstream tax planning, which makes use of prescribed reliefs and exemptions in the manner as intended by the law makers. This should be distinguished from the use of artificial or contrived schemes to avoid tax. HMRC regard the former as legitimate, but are determined to eliminate the latter.

When undertaking a capital transaction, there may well be a choice over how, when and where it is conducted, and how the proceeds are reinvested. Those choices can lead to different amounts of tax being due at different times. Understanding the outcomes of those choices is the basis of mainstream tax planning.

This is only a brief summary of the basic planning issues to be considered when dealing with capital gains. For a more detailed discussion of tax planning for capital transactions, see *Capital Gains Tax Planning* (Bloomsbury Professional).

TAX AVOIDANCE

10.2 The meaning of 'tax avoidance' has become twisted and confused in recent times, to make it seem to the ordinary taxpayer that any choices made over how transactions are undertaken must be wrong. That is nonsense: case law acknowledges that taxpayers can choose how to arrange their financial affairs, and there is no obligation to make those arrangements in a manner which yields the greatest amount of tax (see *Ayrshire Pullman Motor Services v CIR* (1929) 14 TC 754).

However, the law may be altered (occasionally with little warning) to discourage taxpayers from executing financial transactions in particular ways, and tax advisers need to react to those changes. For example, see the new ATED and CGTED charges described in **Chapter 4**.

Where the tax law is being abused to create outcomes favourable to the taxpayer, which were never intended by Parliament, anti-avoidance rules can come into play. This chapter includes a brief summary of the anti-avoidance structures now in place (see **10.16–10.27**).

BASIC TAX PLANNING

Residence and domicile

10.3 In most cases, it is the residence and domicile status of the taxpayer, rather than the location of the assets, that determines liability to CGT. Non-residents are generally not chargeable except in relation to gains on assets used in connection with a UK business, but CGT may be charged on ATED-related gains realised by UK-resident or non-resident property owners who are not natural persons (see **4.43**).

Certain UK-resident individuals who retain a non-UK domicile can use the remittance basis to shelter from UK tax gains accruing outside the UK, and in this respect they have a distinct advantage over UK-domiciled taxpayers. However, the use of the remittance basis for any tax year from 2008/09 onwards means that the annual exemption is lost for that particular tax year (see **Chapter 5**).

The scope for avoiding CGT by attaining non-resident status for a relatively short period and making disposals during the period of absence from the UK was significantly reduced by the special rules for temporary non-residents (see **5.33**).

Exemptions

10.4   The next question to consider is whether a gain is going to be exempt as a result of a specific provision or because it falls within the annual CGT exemption. Exemptions for specific persons, assets or gains are listed at **1.9**. An outright exemption is clearly better than a deferral of CGT.

Annual exemption

10.5   The annual CGT exemption is discussed at **1.17**. It is currently worth £10,900 (for 2013/14) to an individual and, in effect, £21,800 for a couple (£10,600 per person for 2011/12 and 2012/13).

Planning regarding the use of the exemption became more complicated in 2010/11, as for that tax year and later years the taxpayer has the freedom to deduct the annual exemption in the way that produces the lowest possible tax charge (*TCGA 1992, s 4B*). This flexibility is necessary due to the different rates of CGT that may apply to gains realised before and after 23 June 2010 (see **1.23**). However, the annual exemption cannot be carried forward from one tax year to the next. Any part of it that is unused in the current year is lost for good.

The benefit of the annual exemption may be maximised by careful timing of the disposal of assets, but as ever it is important to remember that personal and commercial considerations will often be more important than saving tax. The taxpayer should also bear in mind that HMRC may wish to examine the timing of disposals stated to fall shortly before or after the end of a tax year, or any change in the rate of CGT. The practice of 'bed and breakfasting' shares just before the tax year end was made largely ineffective by a change in the identification rules, but variations on the theme remain possible (see **10.12**).

A member of a married couple or civil partnership who has already used their annual exemption might consider transferring an asset to the other spouse or partner, leaving the transferee free to sell the asset and utilise their own annual exemption. Care is needed to safeguard against a possible HMRC challenge here. HMRC may seek to establish that the transferor has made a transfer of sale proceeds rather than the asset itself.

A deferral relief claim, made on the basis that a gain has been reinvested in enterprise investment scheme shares (see **Chapter 16**) operates by reducing the allowable expenditure on the shares. The claim may be limited in order to set the annual exemption against a part of the gain that would otherwise be deferred and subject to a potential CGT charge in the future.

For gains made in 2012/13 or 2013/14, a 100% or 50% exemption may be possible where the gain is invested in shares under the Seed Enterprise Investment Scheme (SEIS) within the same tax year (see **Chapter 16**).

The structure of hold-over relief for gifts, roll-over relief for replacement of business assets and incorporation relief (see **Chapters 13, 14** and **15**) is such that some gains may be left in charge to be covered by the annual exemption. These reliefs may also be combined in some cases with entrepreneurs' relief (see **Chapter 11**). However, the conditions required for entrepreneurs' relief to apply are, in most circumstances, more restrictive than other CGT reliefs.

Exemption on death

10.6   The general CGT exemption that applies to deemed disposals on a taxpayer's death should not be overlooked in any tax-planning exercise. Assets that the taxpayer was competent to dispose of are deemed to be acquired by the personal representatives or legatees at their market value (see **Chapter 7**). The absence of a CGT charge, on what may well be significant capital appreciation in many cases, means it may be worthwhile retaining an asset until death rather than, for example, making a lifetime gift.

The computation

10.7   In the absence of any exemption, it is useful to estimate a potential CGT liability in order to establish whether any claim or other action to reduce or defer the liability is appropriate or desirable. The increase in the rate of CGT to 28% for trustees, personal representatives, and those paying higher rate tax, from 23 June 2010 may stimulate further tax planning both before and after the gain is realised.

The disposal of businesses and business assets often generate very large gains, which may be subject to CGT at 10% if entrepreneurs' relief can be claimed in respect of the disposal (see **Chapter 11**).

It is important to check for any reduction in allowable expenditure that may be required as a result of a claim to roll-over or hold-over relief, increasing the chargeable gain on the disposal being considered.

From 6 April 2008, all assets held by non-corporate taxpayers on 31 March 1982 need to have the value at 31 March 1982 substituted for the actual cost of an asset (see **3.59**). The benefits of obtaining a professional valuation and ensuring that all items of allowable enhancement expenditure are identified can be substantial. The value at that date will determine the amount of the gain before any other CGT reliefs.

Where the disposal has already taken place and a valuation is required, it may well be useful to apply for a post-transaction valuation check from HMRC using form CG34 (see **1.35**) before the end of the tax year, to allow time for consideration of any other possible action as part of a pre-year end tax planning review.

Losses

10.8   Allowable losses must be set against chargeable gains arising in the same tax year. There is no facility to restrict the set-off of losses against chargeable gains for the same year (see **1.20**). However, in 2010/11 and in subsequent years where the taxpayer has gains that are chargeable to CGT at more than one rate, the taxpayer can choose which gains their losses are set against, such that the CGT liability for the year is reduced to the lowest possible charge (*TCGA 1992, s 4B*) (see **1.23**).

A taxpayer who is contemplating a disposal on which a loss will accrue might consider deferring the disposal until after 5 April if the gains would be covered in any event by the annual exemption. The delay would avoid wasting the exemption, and having the loss accruing in the following tax year might have the effect of reducing a potential CGT liability on other gains. Relief for allowable losses carried forward is more flexible. The set-off of losses may be restricted in order to preserve the benefit of the annual exemption for the tax year.

Spouses or civil partners may consider a transfer of assets under the no gain, no loss rule (see **3.62**) where one spouse or partner has an unrealised loss that he or she is unlikely to use. The transferee may be able to realise the loss on a later disposal to an unconnected third party and set it against chargeable gains in excess of the annual exemption. Care is needed to safeguard against a possible HMRC challenge under *TCGA 1992, s 16A*, as discussed in **10.18**.

Monitoring unrealised gains and losses, and planning to make the best use of the annual exemption, are key features of basic CGT planning. It is also important to identify any allowable losses that might be generated by means of, for example:

- realising a loss on quoted shares;
- making a negligible value claim (see **2.10**); or
- claiming relief on a loan to a trader, where the loan has become irrecoverable (see **17.9**).

The possibility of setting any unused trading losses against capital gains (see **3.52**) might also be considered, although care is needed in assessing the interaction of this relief with the annual exemption. A capital loss arising on shares subscribed for in an unlisted trading company may be relieved against income tax where certain conditions are met (see **17.14**).

Focus

Capital losses may only be carried back to an earlier tax year in rare circumstances:

- when the loss arises in the year the taxpayer dies (see **7.3**); and

- on disposal of unascertainable deferred consideration (see **3.29**).

Spouses and civil partners

10.9   Each member of a married couple or registered civil partnership is taxed independently of the other and is required to make a separate return of his or her own chargeable gains. There is no joint assessment, and losses borne by one spouse cannot be set against gains accruing to the other. However, chargeable assets transferred from one spouse or civil partner to the other, in a tax year in which they are living together, are treated as taking place on a no gain, no loss basis (see **3.62**).

Connected persons

10.10   The possible impact of the market value rule outlined in **3.6** should be considered where, for example, there are transactions within a family and the no gain, no loss rule mentioned in **10.9** does not apply.

Losses accruing on a disposal to a connected person cannot be set against gains other than those accruing on a disposal to the same connected person (see **3.21**). On the other hand, the gift of a chargeable asset showing a gain may be eligible for hold-over relief (see **Chapter 13**), so in some cases care in choosing which asset to give away can be worthwhile. Other provisions that may be relevant to transactions between connected persons include those applying to:

- assets disposed of in a series of transactions (see **3.12**);

- the disposal of chattels forming part of a 'set of articles' in order to secure the chattels exemption (**4.26**); and

- the value shifting provisions in *TCGA 1992, s 29* (see **2.6**).

Ownership of assets

10.11   There may be some flexibility as to who should be the beneficial owner of an asset, for example, where a family company is involved. Factors that might be considered, preferably before an asset is acquired, include:

- whether the value of the asset is likely to increase significantly in the future;

- the effect of any deferral relief on the new owner's allowable expenditure for CGT purposes;

- the potential 'double charge' to tax on gains accruing on a disposal of assets owned by a company, and then realised by the shareholder in the form of increased gains on sale of the shares or on a liquidation;

- the availability of main residence relief (this is not available to companies);

- whether the conditions for entrepreneurs' relief are likely to be met;

- the potential tax and other benefits of having business property owned by a pension scheme; and

- the merits of any trust arrangements (bearing in mind the reduced IHT advantages of many types of trust following *FA 2006*).

'Bed and breakfast' transactions

10.12 'Bed and breakfasting' is the practice of selling shares and repurchasing them the following day. This used to be a common year-end tax-planning technique, undertaken by taxpayers wishing to:

- utilise their annual CGT exemption;

- realise gains that could be covered by unused capital losses; or

- realise losses and set them against gains that would otherwise give rise to a tax liability.

The cost of the new acquisition would represent the allowable expenditure on its future disposal. The exercise would, therefore, achieve an uplift in the CGT base cost of the investment.

However, the effect of the 30-day rule introduced in April 1998 (see **4.2**) was to negate the effect of such transactions. The disposal on day 1 would now be matched with the acquisition on day 2, leaving a small loss in most cases where there was little movement in the share price.

'Bed and spousing' is the rather undignified term for a technique that is sometimes suggested as an alternative to a 'bed and breakfast' arrangement. One spouse or civil partner sells the shares and the other spouse or partner buys a similar holding shortly afterwards. This technique can now be attacked under *TCGA 1992, s 16A* where the sale of the original shares has generated a loss (see **10.18**). Alternatively, the taxpayer might:

- identify shares in the same industry sector that would make a suitable replacement for the initial investment; or

- sell the shares in one capacity and buy the new holding in another capacity – shares bought within an ISA or SIPP are free of CGT in the hands of the investor (see **1.9**).

Hold-over reliefs

10.13 Hold-over relief for gifts effectively transfers the potential CGT liability to the transferee (see **Chapter 13**). It is worth noting that this liability is based on the market value of the asset gifted at the time of the transfer – regardless of any later reduction in value.

As the time period for making a hold-over election is now four years from the end of the tax year of disposal, taxpayers have an opportunity to review transactions undertaken in the years from 2009/10 onwards, to see if a hold-over claim should be made before 6 April 2014.

Focus

Once a hold-over relief claim has been made, and accepted by HMRC without a valuation of the transferred assets considered, it cannot be withdrawn (see **13.47**).

Where an asset previously gifted has been sold, there may be an initial tax saving if the gain could be held over completely on the gift, rather than being subject to CGT at 18% or 28%. However, caution must be exercised in respect of hold-over claims for gains, since on a second disposal by the donee the CGT rate applicable may be higher, depending on the taxpayer's net taxable income for the year of disposal. There is no substitute for calculating the net assessable gain with and without the hold-over relief as may apply in the earlier tax year as opposed to the later year in which the gain falls back into charge to CGT.

The inheritance tax position may point towards lifetime giving, but in many cases the potential IHT bill can be substantially reduced or eliminated by business property relief or agricultural property relief available on death. For further discussion of those reliefs, refer to *Inheritance Tax 2013/14* (Bloomsbury Professional).

Entrepreneurs' relief

10.14 As indicated in **Chapter 11**, the conditions for entrepreneurs' relief to apply are complex, as different conditions attach to both the owner of the asset and the use to which it was put before disposal. In the case of shares, there may be uncertainty surrounding the company's status as a trading company, where it has significant non-trading activities. It is important to monitor the company's activities and examine the possible impact of non-trading activities such as the letting of surplus property.

Shares must be held in the individual's own personal company, the definition of which depends on the individual holding at least 5% of ordinary share capital and voting rights in their own name, not jointly with another person or trust. Although this condition is relaxed for shares acquired through EMI share options (see **4.6**). Any adjustment in the number of shares issued by the company should be monitored closely, to ensure that the 5% holding of ordinary share capital is not diluted for the key shareholders.

The definition of ordinary share capital includes all the company's issued share capital, with the exclusion of shares which carry a right to a dividend at a fixed rate (see Appendix 11 to the HMRC Capital Gains Manual).

Focus

The shareholder must be an office holder or employee of their personal company, or a company in the same group, for at least a 12-month period ending with the date of disposal of shares in the personal company.

Directors who resign their post, or employees who leave before selling their shares, may miss out on entrepreneurs' relief due to the timing of their departure from the company.

Non-working shareholders may be appointed as non-executive directors to achieve the office-holder status required.

The interaction of entrepreneurs' relief, and the deferral of gains using EIS, VCT or qualifying corporate bonds, can produce some unexpected results (see **11.39–11.44**).

Main residence relief

10.15 The CGT exemption for an individual's only or main residence can be very valuable. The relief is extended to cover certain periods of absence and periods during which a house is let. The opportunity to make an election to nominate one home as the main residence for tax purposes should always be investigated where more than one property is occupied as a home (see **12.19**). This relief is examined in detail in **Chapter 12**.

ANTI-AVOIDANCE RULES

The GAAR

10.16 The general anti-abuse rule (GAAR) is introduced by *FA 2013, Pt 5* to be used alongside the existing tools available to HMRC, so it is unlikely that any of the existing anti-avoidance legislation will be repealed in the near future. The GAAR applies to income tax, corporation tax, the bank levy, CGT, NIC, IHT, SDLT, ATED, petroleum revenue tax (PRT) and other oil supplementary charges, but not to VAT. Other taxes may be added later.

The GAAR has effect in relation to any tax arrangement which is 'abusive', entered into on or after 17 July 2013. Tax arrangements are 'abusive' if entering into them or carrying them out cannot reasonably be regarded as a reasonable course of action, taking into account all of the following:

- the principles on which the law is based;

- whether the arrangements are intended to exploit shortcomings in the law; and

- whether the means of achieving the results involve one or more contrived or abnormal steps.

If a party who benefits from the arrangement can show that it was entered into entirely for non-tax reasons, and it was not designed or carried out to receive a relevant tax advantage, the arrangement will not be brought within the GAAR. Also, if the arrangement accords with established practice, and HMRC at the time of the arrangement had indicated their acceptance of this practice, the arrangement is not likely to be abusive.

Application of the GAAR

10.17   There is no clearance mechanism to determine whether arrangements do or do not fall within the GAAR. Taxpayers are expected to self-assess the effect of the GAAR on their tax returns. HMRC have published guidance on the operation of the GAAR (www.hmrc.gov.uk/avoidance/gaar.htm). A self-declaration by a taxpayer that his tax arrangements fall within the GAAR is quite unlikely, but it could happen where the taxpayer has used an egregious tax avoidance scheme and then wishes to confess.

The GAAR will normally be applied by HMRC through a written notice sent to the taxpayer, which specifies the arrangements and the tax advantage in question. The HMRC officer must set out the reasons for applying the GAAR and the steps that the taxpayer can take to avoid counteraction (ie pay extra tax). The taxpayer has 45 days to submit written representations objecting to the use of the GAAR. The HMRC officer considers the representations and, if he still considers counteractions to be appropriate, he will refer the matter to the GAAR advisory panel.

The GAAR advisory panel is a safeguard for the taxpayer. The members are unpaid, but highly regarded tax practitioners who are independent of HMRC.

The panel's function is to consider the actions of the taxpayer in context, to ensure that the GAAR is only used against transactions which are abusive. Three members of the panel will consider whether the arrangements in question are 'reasonable', in the light of the relevant anti-avoidance provisions, and provide their opinion. The anonymised decisions of the GAAR panel will be published.

HMRC is not obliged to back down if the GAAR panel concludes that the tax arrangements were reasonable (ie not within the GAAR). However, the courts and tax tribunals are required to take into account the HMRC guidance and any opinion expressed by the GAAR advisory panel on the application of the GAAR to a particular tax scheme.

Three TAARs

10.18   Three targeted anti-avoidance rules (TAARs) were introduced with effect from 5 December 2005, which apply to the use of capital losses by companies (see **9.29**). From 6 December 2006, those anti-avoidance provisions were effectively replaced, but not removed, by *TCGA 1992, s 16A*, which also covers the use of capital losses by individuals, trustees and personal representatives of deceased persons.

Where *TCGA 1992, s 16A* applies to a capital loss, that loss is not an allowable loss for the purposes of CGT and cannot be offset against chargeable gains, or against income, to reduce income tax or corporation tax. It is irrelevant that there are no chargeable gains available at the time the loss arises, from which it may have been deductible.

Scope of the TAAR

10.19   *TCGA 1992, s 16A* (the TAAR) is effective for individuals, trustees and personal representatives from 6 December 2006, so it potentially catches transactions in the 2006/07 tax year, as well as subsequent periods. It is intended to apply where a person (which can be a company or an individual) deliberately and knowingly enters into an arrangement to gain a tax advantage. The terms 'arrangement' and 'tax advantage' are very widely drawn. As a result, the TAAR potentially catches a wide range of transactions, including those that have been previously ignored for CGT purposes, such as transfers between spouses.

HMRC guidance

10.20   In practice, the scope of *TCGA 1992, s 16A* is limited by the HMRC guidance set out in Appendix 9 to their Capital Gains Manual. Specifically, the

HMRC guidance seeks to limit the extent of the TAAR to artificially created losses. It states, under 'restriction on allowable losses':

> 'This legislation will not apply where there is a genuine economic transaction that gives rise to a real economic loss as a result of a real disposal. In these circumstances there will be no arrangements with a main purpose of securing a tax advantage. Conversely, where there is either no real disposal, or no real economic loss, or any combination of the foregoing, then there are likely to be arrangements in place with a main purpose of securing a tax advantage so the legislation will apply.'

In addition, the guidance appears further to limit the scope of the TAAR at para 3 of the introduction to Appendix 9:

> 'In particular it is unlikely that individuals with a normal portfolio of investments who make disposals in the ordinary course of managing their portfolio would be affected by these new rules because there is currently little evidence to suggest that such individuals undertake the type of arrangements that are targeted by this legislation.'

In spite of this comforting statement, many active investors do use capital losses arising on their investments to reduce the taxable gains from other holdings.

Focus

The HMRC guidance does not affect a taxpayer's right to argue for a different interpretation, if necessary in an appeal to the First-tier Tribunal.

The HMRC guidance does not have the force of law; it can be amended at any time, with retrospective effect, and it cannot be the subject of an appeal in the courts.

There is no HMRC guidance on the records that a taxpayer must keep in order to prove that the capital losses achieved are not blocked by the TAAR.

There is no guidance on the level of disclosure that a taxpayer should make on their tax return to provide HMRC with enough evidence to show that the TAAR does not apply.

Clearance procedure

10.21   There is no specific clearance procedure attached to the TAAR to provide taxpayers with certainty that a particular transaction will not fall within the rules. The 18 examples provided in Appendix 9 to the Capital Gains Manual are not templates for deciding whether a loss is or is not caught by the TAAR.

HMRC have said that they will give guidance on the TAAR under the clearance and approvals (CAP1) procedure for transactions undertaken by taxpayers who are not businesses (see www.hmrc.gov.uk/cap/cap1.htm).

Taxpayers who have a business transaction that may be caught by the TAAR can seek guidance under the non-statutory business clearance procedure, as set out in the HMRC Non-statutory Business Clearance Guidance Manual (NBCG). However, HMRC will only give guidance under the NBCG on direct tax matters where there is material uncertainty around a tax issue arising from tax legislation passed within the last four years. Where the query relates to older legislation, HMRC will only provide a clearance if the uncertainty relates to a commercially significant issue.

Other anti-avoidance legislation

10.22   A series of appeals heard by the courts during the 1980s established the principle that one or more steps in a pre-ordained tax avoidance scheme could be ignored, with the result that the scheme did not have the intended tax consequences. See, in particular, *W T Ramsay Ltd v CIR* [1981] 54 TC 101, HL and *Furniss v Dawson* (1984) 55 TC 324, HL. Subsequent cases have scaled back the impact of the *Ramsay* (or *Furniss v Dawson*) principle, but the possibility of an HMRC challenge on these grounds should always be borne in mind.

The ever-increasing length and complexity of recent *Finance Acts* is largely due to the addition of detailed legislation to counter artificial or contrived arrangements designed to obtain a tax advantage, and to close loopholes (ie flaws in the legislation which mean that it did not work as intended). They include the following anti-avoidance measures, which are discussed where appropriate in the relevant paragraphs of this book or in other books published by Bloomsbury Professional:

	TCGA 1992	*See para*
Temporary non-residents	*s 10A*	**5.33**
Attribution of gains to members of non-resident companies	*s 13*	**5.52**
Transactions between connected persons	*s 18*	**3.11**
Assets disposed of in a series of transactions	*ss 19–20*	**3.12**
Value shifting	*ss 29–34*	**2.6**
Shares in close company transferring assets at an undervalue	*s 125*	*Note 1*
Company reconstructions	*s 137*	**16.24**

Emigration of donee	*s 168*	**13.21**
Concessions that defer a charge	*s 284A*	**15.10**
For companies:	*CTA 2010*	
Transactions in securities	*Pt 15*	*Note 2*
Transactions in land	*Pt 18*	**1.7**
For individuals and trustees:	*ITA 2007*	
Transactions in securities	*Pt 13, Ch 1*	*Note 2*
Transfer of assets abroad	*Pt 13, Ch 2*	*Note 3*
Transactions in land	*Pt 13, Ch 3*	**3.5**

Notes:

1. See *Tax Indemnities and Warranties* (Bloomsbury Professional).

2. See *Tax Aspects of the Purchase and Sale of a Private Company's Shares* (Bloomsbury Professional).

3. See *Tax Advisers' Guide to Trusts* (Bloomsbury Professional).

DISCLOSURE OF TAX AVOIDANCE SCHEMES

Outline of DOTAS

10.23 The regime requiring disclosure of tax avoidance schemes (DOTAS) is designed to alert HMRC to certain schemes or arrangements that are intended to provide a tax advantage when compared to a different course of action. It is not intended to catch mainstream or 'legitimate' tax planning.

Which tax arrangements?

10.24 The DOTAS regime applies generally to income tax, National Insurance contributions, corporation tax, CGT, VAT, inheritance tax and stamp duty land tax. A tax arrangement must be disclosed when:

- it will, or might be expected to, enable any person to obtain a tax advantage;

- that tax advantage is, or might be expected to be, the main benefit or one of the main benefits of the arrangement; and

- it is a tax arrangement that falls within any prescribed hallmarks.

The hallmarks

10.25 The current hallmarks for income tax, CGT and corporation tax schemes are:

- confidentiality from competitors;
- confidentiality from HMRC;
- premium fee could reasonably be obtained;
- off-market terms;
- standardised tax products;
- loss schemes;
- certain leasing arrangements; and
- certain pension benefits.

The disclosure requirements for schemes involving the avoidance of NIC, VAT, IHT or SDLT are based on different hallmarks, and have varying *de minimis* levels below which a disclosure is not required.

How a disclosure is made

10.26 In most situations where a disclosure is required, it must be made by the scheme 'promoter' within five days of it being made available. However, the scheme user may need to make the disclosure where:

- the promoter is based outside the UK;
- the promoter is a lawyer and legal privilege applies; or
- there is no promoter.

On disclosure of the scheme, HMRC issue the promoter with an eight-digit scheme reference number (the DOTAS number), which each client who uses the scheme must include on their tax return or on form AAG4. A person who designs and implements their own scheme must disclose it within 30 days of it being implemented.

Focus

The DOTAS number does not indicate that the scheme has been approved by HMRC, as is claimed by some scheme promoters.

A person who uses a DOTAS-registered scheme must also make an adequate disclosure of the scheme on their tax return.

Scheme promoters must also provide HMRC with a quarterly list of clients to whom they have issued a DOTAS number.

HMRC guidance

10.27 Detailed guidance of the operation of DOTAS is available at www. hmrc.gov.uk/aiu/index.htm. These pages are also used by HMRC to announce 'spotlights', which are arrangements or schemes that HMRC have become aware of and are likely to challenge.

Chapter 11

Entrepreneurs' relief

SIGNPOSTS

- **Introduction** – Background, legislation and guidance (see **11.1–11.2**).

- **Operation of the relief** – Which disposals qualify, how the relief is calculated, the lifetime limit, aggregation of gains and losses, interaction with other losses (see **11.3–11.7**).

- **Claiming the relief** – See **11.8**.

- **Shareholders** – Personal company, employment requirement, trading company, HMRC rulings (see **11.9–11.19**).

- **Sole traders** – When the relief applies, disposal of a business, part of a business (see **11.20–11.22**).

- **Partners** – Special rules, post-cessation disposals (see **11.23–11.25**).

- **Trustees** – See **8.35**.

- **Post-cessation disposals** – Business assets, use after the business ceased, shares disposed of after the company has ceased trading (see **11.27–11.32**).

- **Associated disposals** – When a disposal is 'associated', when shares are also disposed of, when a partnership interest is reduced or disposed of, restrictions on the qualifying gain (see **11.33–11.38**).

- **Deferred gains** – By acquiring QCBs which are disposed of pre or post 6 April 2008 and pre or post 22 June 2010, share-for-share exchanges, acquisition and disposal of EIS and VCT shares (see **11.39–11.49**).

- **Interaction with other reliefs** – The order of set-off (see **11.50**).

INTRODUCTION

Background

11.1   Entrepreneurs' relief (ER) has effect for qualifying disposals made on and after 6 April 2008. The relief can be claimed in respect of gains made by individuals, by trustees of interest in possession trusts where there is a qualifying beneficiary (see **8.35**), but not for gains made by companies, or by personal representatives.

The relief was introduced in response to the abolition of business asset taper relief from 6 April 2008, which reduced the effective rate of CGT from 40% to 10% on the disposal of qualifying business assets held for two years or more. Entrepreneurs' relief also reduces the effective rate of CGT to 10% on gains arising from qualifying disposals of businesses and certain business assets. However, the mechanism that achieves the 10% rate changed with effect for disposals made on and after 23 June 2010 (see **11.4**).

The range of assets that qualify as business assets under entrepreneurs' relief is much more restrictive than those which qualified as business assets for taper relief (see **11.9** and **11.21**). The amount of gains that can be covered by entrepreneurs' relief is also limited by the taxpayer's lifetime limit (see **11.5**). Entrepreneurs' relief must be claimed (see **11.8**); it does not apply automatically like taper relief where the conditions were met. The taxpayer can choose not to claim the relief to preserve the lifetime limit so it can be used for another disposal, or to claim an alternative CGT relief.

Legislation and guidance

11.2   The legislation that governs entrepreneurs' relief is crammed into *TCGA 1992, ss 169H–169S* in such a fashion as to make its comprehension even more difficult than it has to be. There are transitional reliefs for gains that arose before 6 April 2008, which have been deferred using VCTs or EIS (*FA 2008, Sch 3, para 7*) (see **11.49**). Also where gains from the disposal of shares or securities have been rolled into qualifying corporate bonds on a company reorganisation before 6 April 2008, those gains can be subject to entrepreneurs' relief if they fall into charge on or after 6 April 2008 (*FA 2008, Sch 3, para 6*) (see **11.40**).

The HMRC guidance on the operation of entrepreneurs' relief is found in its Capital Gains Manual at CG63950–CG64171. This chapter refers to that guidance where necessary, but please note that the HMRC guidance does not have legal effect and there may be other valid interpretations of the law. In January 2012, the ICAEW Tax Faculty published a guidance note covering practical points concerning entrepreneurs' relief raised with HMRC by the professional bodies, including the HMRC answers. That guidance is referred to in this chapter as 'TAXGUIDE 01/12'.

OPERATION OF THE RELIEF

What disposals qualify

11.3   Entrepreneurs' relief is available on gains made by individuals arising from qualifying business disposals, which consist of:

(a)   all or part of a sole trader business (see **11.20**);

(b)   all or part of an interest in a partnership, including an interest in an LLP (see **11.23**);

(c)   shares or securities held in the shareholder's personal company (see **11.9**);

(d)   certain post-cessation disposals of former business assets (see **11.27**); and

(e)   associated disposals (see **11.33**) which are disposals of assets owned by the individual but used in the business of either:

  – a partnership of which he was a member; or

  – his personal company.

In addition, disposals of certain business assets by trustees can qualify for entrepreneurs' relief, but only where there is a qualifying beneficiary who also holds enough shares in their own right for the company to qualify as his personal company, or operates or has operated the business that used the assets (see **8.35**).

A disposal for entrepreneurs' relief can be:

• a sale;

• a gift or transfer at undervalue;

• where a capital distribution is received in respect of shares held in a company, for example on the liquidation of that company; or

• a capital sum derived from an asset (see **2.12**).

How the relief is calculated

11.4   Where gains were made between 6 April 2008 and 22 June 2010, entrepreneurs' relief is given by reducing the amount of the capital gain by

4/9ths, leaving the residue of 5/9ths to be charged to CGT at 18%, before deduction of unrelated losses and the annual exemption. As the rate of CGT increased to 28% for higher rate taxpayers on 23 June 2010 (see **1.23**), this fractional reduction would no longer produce a 10% rate for taxpayers subject to the higher rate. Gains that accrue on and after 23 June 2010 and are subject to entrepreneurs' relief are taxed at 10%, irrespective of the level of the taxpayers' other income for the year (see Example 11.1).

However, when calculating taxpayers' available basic rate band to determine the rate of CGT to apply to gains (18% or 28%), those gains subject to entrepreneurs' relief are deemed to take priority over the available basic rate band before other gains (*TCGA 1992, s 4(6)*; see Example 11.2).

Taxpayers can choose which gains should absorb their annual exemption or losses to achieve the lowest possible charge to CGT (*TCGA 1992, s 4B*).

Example 11.1

Milo gave 25% of the shares in his company M Ltd to his son on 10 May 2010, and sold the remaining shares in M Ltd on 12 July 2013 for £3 million. Milo formed M Ltd in 1980 and was a director until the sale in July 2013. The 31 March 1982 value of M Ltd was £400,000. The market value of the gift in May 2010 is judged to be £1 million. Milo claims entrepreneurs' relief on both disposals, and chooses to set his annual exemption against other unrelated gains in both tax years. His CGT liability on the gains made on the disposal of M Ltd is calculated as follows:

	May 2010 £	July 2013 £
Lifetime limit:	2,000,000	10,000,000
Market value/proceeds	1,000,000	3,000,000
31 March 1982 value	(100,000)	(300,000)
Gain	900,000	2,700,000
Entrepreneurs' relief reduction 4/9 × £900,000	(400,000)	–
Taxable gain:	500,000	2,700,000
CGT due at 18%/10%	90,000	270,000

The effective or actual rate of CGT on both gains is 10%.

11.5 *Entrepreneurs' relief*

Operation of the lifetime limit

11.5   It is important to identify the lifetime limit in force at the time the gain accrues:

Period:	Lifetime limit in force:
6 April 2008–5 April 2010	£1 million
6 April 2010–22 June 2010	£2 million
23 June 2010–5 April 2011	£5 million
6 April 2011 onwards	£10 million

All gains that the taxpayer includes in a claim for entrepreneurs' relief are deducted from the available lifetime limit. Any amount of gain that is not covered by the lifetime limit that existed at the time the gain arose is taxed at the relevant rate of CGT that applies in that period. It is the taxpayer's responsibility to keep a record of the total gains that have been subject to a claim for entrepreneurs' relief, but HMRC should also keep a record on the taxpayer's self-assessment permanent notes (CG63960).

The taxpayer can only take advantage of the increased lifetime limit where gains are made on or after the dates of increase in the lifetime limit (see Example 11.2).

Example 11.2

Fred is the director and sole shareholder of F Ltd, which is a trading company. He gives half his shares in F Ltd to his son on 5 March 2011, making a gain of £2.5 million. He chooses to claim entrepreneurs' relief rather than hold-over relief (see **Chapter 13**). Fred sells his remaining stake in F Ltd on 4 July 2013, making a gain of £9 million, which also qualifies for entrepreneurs' relief. Fred has not previously used any of his lifetime limit, and has net taxable income of £24,370 in 2013/14. His CGT liability on both sales is calculated as follows:

	March 2011 *gain*	*2010/11* *CGT* *payable*	*July 2013* *gain*	*2013/14* *CGT* *payable*
	£	£	£	£
Taxable income	N/A		24,370	
Basic rate threshold	N/A		32,010	
Available basic rate band			7,640	
Gross gains	2,500,000		9,000,000	
ER lifetime limit available	5,000,000		7,500,000	
Gain not subject to ER	–		1,500,000	
Less annual exemption	10,100		10,900	
Taxable at 28%			1,489,100	416,948
Gains subject to ER, *taxed at 10%*	2,489,900	248,990	7,500,000	750,000
Total CGT payable		248,990		1,166,948

Fred has used £2.5 million of his lifetime limit against his March 2011 gain; so, although the lifetime limit increased to £10 million on 6 April 2011, he has only £7.5 million of his lifetime limit available for his 2013/14 entrepreneurs' relief claim.

Although Fred has £7,640 of basic rate band available in 2013/14, the full July 2013 gain is taken into account when considering his total income and gains for 2013/14, even though part of that gain is automatically subject to CGT at 10% as it qualifies for entrepreneurs' relief. Thus, no part of the July 2013 gain is actually taxed at 18%. Fred's total CGT liability for 2013/14 is £1,166,948 which is payable by 31 January 2015.

Aggregation of gains and losses

11.6   When a business is sold some assets may crystallise gains and other disposals may create losses. Before calculating entrepreneurs' relief the gains and losses arising on the same business disposal must be aggregated (*TCGA 1992, s 169N(1)*). Note that separate disposals of shares and securities from one company should never be aggregated before the relief is applied (see **11.9**).

There is no requirement for the disposal of the business to be made in one contract to one purchaser to qualify for the relief. In practice, the business assets may be sold to a number of different purchasers over a period of time. The disposal of a single business could conceivably be spread over two tax years.

11.6 *Entrepreneurs' relief*

However, a distinction must be drawn between assets that are disposed of as part of the business, and assets that are disposed of after cessation of the business (see **11.27**). The taxpayer may claim entrepreneurs' relief on several qualifying disposals, as long as the lifetime limit is not breached. The difficulty in practice will be distinguishing between the disposal of parts of the business which each separately qualify for entrepreneurs' relief, and the disposal of qualifying assets after the business has ceased trading. The gains and losses realised by disposing of separate parts of the business should not be aggregated before the relief is applied; but, where assets comprising of a single business disposal accrue both gains and losses, those should be aggregated before the relief is applied. This is illustrated in Example 11.3.

Example 11.3

Nelson owned a grocery business for which he had two outlets: a freehold shop and a leasehold shop. He retired in April 2013 and sold the freehold premises and business on 2 April 2013 and the leasehold shop and business on 17 May 2013, each as a going concern. He made the following gains and losses on the property and goodwill in each case. After claiming entrepreneurs' relief, Nelson's assessable gains are calculated as follows:

2012/13	£	£
Freehold shop – sold 2 April 2013		
Freehold		520,000
Goodwill		200,000
Net gain		720,000
Lifetime limit available	10,000,000	
Gain subject to ER:		720,000
2013/14		
Leasehold shop – sold 17 May 2013		
Leasehold		(40,000)
Goodwill		400,000
Net gain		360,000
Lifetime limit for entrepreneurs' relief	10,000,000	
Gains used in an ER claim previously	(720,000)	
Available to use against 2013/14 gain	9,280,000	
Gain subject to ER:		360,000

The two grocery shops are parts of Nelson's whole business which could be operated as independent businesses, so they are each qualifying disposals of part of a business (see **11.22**). The gains from the two shops are thus

298

not aggregated before applying the relief. Nelson's claim for entrepreneurs' relief in 2013/14 is not restricted, as his total qualifying gains do not exceed the lifetime limit of £10 million that applies in that period.

Interaction with losses

11.7 Once the losses arising on the disposal of the assets of a single business have been aggregated with gains from that business (see **11.6**), any other allowable capital losses brought forward or arising in the same tax year may be offset against the gains in the year as the taxpayer chooses (*TCGA 1992, s 4B*).

If entrepreneurs' relief is claimed for a pre-23 June 2010 gain, any loss is deducted after the reduction of 4/9ths is applied to the gain, and thus achieves relief at 18%. For gains made on and after 23 June 2010, there is no reduction to achieve entrepreneurs' relief, as the full gain is taxable at 10% where the relief applies. Any loss is deducted from the full gain and receives relief at only 10%.

Focus

To achieve the lowest possible charge to CGT, the taxpayer should offset any available capital losses against the gains which bear the highest rate of CGT in the year.

Example 11.4

Oliver sold 25% of the shares in his personal company in September 2013, making a gain of £200,000. This gain qualifies for entrepreneurs' relief. Oliver also gave a property to his grand-daughter in December 2013, which realised a gain of £270,000. This gain did not qualify for entrepreneurs' relief. Oliver has a capital loss brought forward of £100,000 and net taxable income after allowances of £150,000 in 2013/14. He needs to decide how to offset the loss and his annual exemption for 2013/14.

2013/14	Gain subject to ER £	Gain not subject to ER £
Gain on sale/gift	200,000	270,000
Loss brought forward		(100,000)
Annual exemption		(10,900)
Taxable gain	200,000	159,100
Taxable at 10%/28%	20,000	44,548

The losses have been relieved at the higher rate of CGT of 28%.

CLAIMING THE RELIEF

11.8   Entrepreneurs' relief must be claimed by the individual who makes the gain; although, in the case of gains made by trustees, the claim must be signed by both the trustee and the qualifying beneficiary (*TCGA 1992, s 169M*) (see **8.35**). The claim will normally be attached to the tax return for the tax year in which the gain arose, and there is a template for the claim in HMRC helpsheet HS275 to assist with this. Where no tax return is issued, or the return has already been submitted, the claim may be made by letter to HMRC.

The claim must be made by the first anniversary of 31 January following the tax year in which the gain arose. The claim may be amended or withdrawn within the same period. If an assessment is made under *TMA 1970, s 36* to make good a loss of tax, the time limit for the claim may be extended (CG63970).

SHAREHOLDERS

11.9   In order for a shareholder to claim entrepreneurs' relief on the disposal of shares or securities (referred to in this section as 'shares'), all of the following conditions generally need to be met:

(a)   the company in which those shares are held must be the individual's personal company (see **11.10**);

(b)   the shareholder must be an employee or officer of the company, or of a company in the same trading group (see **11.11**); and

(c)   the company must be a trading company or a holding company of a trading group (see **11.12**).

All three of these conditions must be met for the whole of a 12-month period that ends with one of the following events:

●   the disposal of the shares;

●   the cessation of the trade; or

●   the company leaving the trading group and not becoming a member of another trading group.

There is a relaxation of condition (a) for shares acquired through the exercise of qualifying EMI options after 5 April 2013 (see **4.6**).

The relief may also be claimed if the business has ceased trading when the shares are disposed of, if the disposal date falls up to three years after the date the company ceased to be a trading company or to be a member of a trading group (see **11.18**). The relief can thus apply to distributions made where the company has been liquidated, or to distributions made in anticipation of an informal company dissolution, where the total distribution does not exceed £25,000 (see **11.32**).

Personal company

11.10   A company is the personal company of the individual at any time when both the following conditions apply (*TCGA 1992, s 169S(3)*):

- the individual holds at least 5% of the ordinary share capital of the company; and
- the individual controls at least 5% of the voting rights of the company which are associated with the above shareholding.

The shareholding must meet the 5% threshold without including shares held by associates or shares held in another capacity, for instance as a trustee of a settlement. Where shares are held in the joint names of a married couple or civil partners, each spouse is deemed to have a 50% beneficial interest in the whole shareholding. The 5% measure is taken of the nominal value of the ordinary share capital, not the number of ordinary shares in issue (see TAXGUIDE 1/12).

> **Example 11.5**
>
> Terry and June are married and jointly own 9.4% of the ordinary shares of Sweet Home Ltd. They are each treated as owning 4.7% of Sweet Home Ltd, so the company will not qualify as their personal company. If they each acquire a further 0.3% of the ordinary shares in their sole names Sweet Home Ltd will qualify as their personal company, but they both need to meet the employment requirement for their disposals of shares in Sweet Home Ltd to qualify for entrepreneurs' relief (see **11.11**).

Focus

'Ordinary share capital' is all of a company's issued share capital, except fixed dividend shares which have no other rights to share in the company's profits (*ITA 2007, s 989*).

Any shares issued by the individual's personal company can qualify for entrepreneurs' relief, even preference shares.

The shareholder who makes several disposals of shares in the same company may claim entrepreneurs' relief on all gains made, as long as the employment requirement is met for the required one-year period in respect of each disposal.

Employment requirement

11.11 The shareholder must be either an officer or employee of the company in which he disposed of shares (*TCGA 1992, s 169I(6)(b)*). However, if the company was a member of a trading group (see **11.18**), the employment requirement is satisfied where the shareholder was employed by another member company of that trading group.

Example 11.6

Pauline has worked for Laundrette Ltd for 20 years and owns 7% of the ordinary shares and voting rights. She also owns 5% of the ordinary shares in Handwash Ltd, but she does not work for Handwash Ltd. The remaining shares in Laundrette and Handwash are held by the holding company, East Ltd. When Laundrette and Handwash are sold, Pauline will qualify for entrepreneurs' relief in respect of her shareholdings in both companies, as she has satisfied the employment requirement by working for either the actual trading company or another trading company in the same trading group.

Whether an individual was an officer of the company (director or company secretary) should easily be confirmed by records held at Companies House. The position of company secretary became optional for private companies from 6 April 2008. Private family companies may consider retaining this post, so a member of the family can hold the office of company secretary and qualify for entrepreneurs' relief. Non-executive directors count as officers, but shadow directors do not (*ITEPA 2003, s 5(3)*).

An employee is defined in *ITEPA 2003, s 4*; but, for the purposes of entrepreneurs' relief, the employment does not need to be full time or cover any minimum hours. There is also no requirement for the shareholder/employee to be paid; although, without a contract of employment, it may be difficult to show that an individual who received no pay was actually employed. The requirements of the national minimum wage will normally mean the company has to make some payment to all of its employees (CG64110).

Trading company

11.12 The definitions of trading company, trading group and holding company are found in *TCGA 1992, s 165A*. Unfortunately, there is no decided tax case that examines the question of whether a company is a trading company for entrepreneurs' relief purposes, but it may be possible to obtain a ruling from HMRC on this point (see **11.19**).

Trading company means a company carrying on 'trading activities' whose activities do not include, to a substantial extent (see **11.16**), activities other than trading activities.

Trading activities

11.13 HMRC interpret 'activities' as meaning 'what a company does'. Activities would include 'engaging in trading operations, making and holding investments, planning, holding meetings and so forth'.

Trading activities are those carried on by the company in the course of, or for the purposes of, a trade that it is carrying on or is preparing to carry on. HMRC regard such activities as including certain activities that a company has to carry out before it can start trading, such as developing a business plan, acquiring premises, hiring staff, ordering materials and incurring pre-trading expenditure (CG64065).

Trading activities also include activities undertaken with a view to the company acquiring or starting to carry on a trade, or with a view to its acquiring a 'significant interest' (see **11.14**) in the share capital of another company that is a trading company or the holding company (see **11.17**) of a trading group (so long as, where the acquiring company is a member of a group of companies, it is not a member of the target company's group). These activities qualify as trading activities only if the acquisition is made, or (as the case may be) the company starts to carry on the trade, as soon as is reasonably practicable. HMRC accept that a company that has disposed of its trade and invested the proceeds and is 'actively seeking' to acquire a new trade or trading subsidiary might still be a trading company if it does not have substantial non-trading activities. What is 'reasonably practicable in the circumstances' will depend on the particular facts of the case (CG64070).

Where a company holds a significant cash balance generated from trading activities, it may not be clear whether the company has become an investment company, due to the ratio of investment activities to trading activities. The HMRC guidance is that short-term lodgement of surplus funds in a deposit account could count as a trading activity rather than an investment activity. Also funds retained to distribute as dividends would not be an investment activity. However, the long-term retention of surplus earnings would be considered an investment activity unless those funds had been earmarked for a particular trading purpose (CG64060).

See **11.16** regarding the letting of surplus business property.

Significant interest

11.14 An acquisition by a company (A) of a 'significant interest' in the share capital of another company (B) is defined as an acquisition of ordinary share capital in company B that would make company B a 51% subsidiary of company A, or would give company A a 'qualifying shareholding in a joint venture company' without making the two companies members of the same group of companies (*TCGA 1992, s 165A(6)*). Ordinary share capital takes the meaning given by *ITA 2007, s 989*. See **11.17** for the definition of a subsidiary.

Trade

11.15   'Trade' means anything which:

- is a trade profession or vocation within the meaning of the *Income Tax Acts*; and

- is conducted on a commercial basis with a view to the realisation of profits (*ITA 2007, s 989*).

For entrepreneurs' relief, a trade also includes the commercial letting of furnished holiday accommodation (*TCGA 1992, s 241(3A)*). For the purposes of this relief, the persons who carry on the furnished holiday lettings are generally treated as sole traders even where the property is jointly owned (see **4.24**). The conditions that must be met for commercial letting of furnished holiday accommodation are discussed in detail in Chapter 7 of *Income Tax 2013/14* (Bloomsbury Professional).

Substantial extent

11.16   Where a company carries on activities other than trading activities, the existence of those non-trading activities will not disturb the trading status of the company if they are not carried on to a substantial extent. HMRC regard 'substantial extent' in this context as meaning more than 20% (CG64090). There is no hard and fast rule about what must be considered in ascertaining a company's trading status, but HMRC indicate the following may be indicators:

- income from non-trading activities;

- the company's asset base;

- expenses incurred, or time spent, by officers and employees of the company in undertaking its activities; and

- the company's history.

These measures should not be regarded as individual tests which all need to be passed; they are just factors which may point one way or the other. The HMRC officer is instructed to weigh up the relevance of each measure in the context of the individual case and judge the matter 'in the round', as demonstrated by the approach of the Special Commissioner in *Farmer (Farmer's Executors) v IRC* [1999] STC (SCD) 321.

Where a company lets property surplus to its current requirements, HMRC do not consider that the following necessarily consist of non-trading activities (CG64085):

- letting part of the trading premises;

- letting properties that are no longer required for the purpose of the trade, where the company's or group's objective is to sell them;

- subletting property where it would be impractical or uneconomic in terms of the trade to assign or surrender the lease; or

- the acquisition of property (whether vacant or already let) where it can be shown that the intention is that it will be brought into use for trading activities.

Holding company

11.17   A holding company is a company that has one or more 51% subsidiaries (*TCGA 1992, s 165A(2)*).

A 51% subsidiary takes its meaning from *CTA 2010, s 1154* so that, for entrepreneurs' relief purposes, a company (B) is a 51% subsidiary of another company (A) if company A owns directly or indirectly more than 50% of company B's ordinary share capital. Thus, a company where 50.1% of its ordinary shares were held by another company would count as a 51% subsidiary.

Trading group

11.18   A group of companies means a company that has one or more 51% subsidiaries.

Focus

The company where the shareholder is employed must be identified as a member of the trading group based on the 51% subsidiary definition, and not just as an associated company.

When looking at whether the group is trading, all the activities of the members of the group are taken together as one business (*TCGA 1992, s 165A(13)*). This allows the group to contain one or more companies that are not trading and still qualify as a trading group. The intra-group transactions are ignored.

However, where a minority individual shareholder disposes of shares in a subsidiary company, that particular subsidiary company must be a trading company in order to qualify for entrepreneurs' relief. The only circumstances in which shares in a non-trading company will qualify for the relief is if the company is a holding company of a trading group or the shares are disposed of within three years after the company has ceased to be a trading company and left the trading group (see **11.32**).

HMRC ruling

11.19   Where a taxpayer has disposed of, or plans to dispose of shares, and is unsure as to whether the company would qualify as a trading company during the relevant period, he should in the first instance apply to the company for confirmation. HMRC suggest that where the company cannot confirm its trading status the taxpayer should record this fact on the additional information area of their tax return, and take a view themselves on the trading status in order to complete their claim for relief (CG64100). This seems a particularly unsatisfactory solution for the taxpayer, as it provides him with no certainty that his claim for entrepreneurs' relief is valid, and hence whether he has self-assessed the right amount of CGT.

An alternative approach is for the individual to apply to HMRC for a ruling under CAP1 for non-business transactions. This procedure is limited to guidance on tax legislation passed in the last four years. However, HMRC will provide views on circumstances which are not covered in the published HMRC guidance, and there is uncertainty about the right tax treatment.

Where a company wishes to clarify its trading status, it may ask HMRC for an opinion in accordance with the non-statutory clearance service, as described in the HMRC Non-statutory Business Clearance Guidance Manual (NBCG). HMRC have confirmed that clearance will be given under the NBCG procedure, if a company wishes to confirm its trading status for entrepreneurs' relief to be claimed by its shareholders, or for SSE to be claimed by the company (see TAXGUIDE 1/12).

SOLE TRADERS

When the relief applies

11.20   A sole trader may qualify for entrepreneurs' relief on gains arising in three specific sets of circumstances:

- on the disposal of his whole business;

- on the disposal of part of his business (see **11.22**); or

- on the disposal of qualifying business assets up to three years after the cessation of his business (see **11.28**).

Disposal of a business

11.21   The disposal of a business will qualify for entrepreneurs' relief if the following conditions are met at the date of disposal:

(a)   the business has been owned by the individual who is making the claim for relief for at least 12 months ending with the date of disposal; and

(b)   the disposal includes at least one relevant business asset (see **11.29**).

The disposal of the business does not need to be made as a going concern, and all of the assets do not have to be sold to the same purchaser. Where several purchasers are involved, careful timing of the disposals of the main assets will be required.

Focus

Where some assets are sold well before the main part of the business and the trade continues after those disposals, the gains on those early disposals may not qualify for entrepreneurs' relief.

This applies where those early disposals do not comprise 'part of a business' (see **11.22**) and the assets were not in use in the business at the time the business ceases to trade (see **11.27**).

HMRC are prepared to accept that the disposal of a business may be spread over several weeks, in which case the delay between disposals should not prevent the relief from applying to all the assets (see Example 11.7).

Example 11.7

Ross ran a retail shop for many years from his freehold property, but wished to retire. He found a company willing to buy the freehold property, but that company did not want to take on the retail business. Ross exchanged contracts to sell the property on 6 June 2013, but did not complete the contract until 31 July 2013 when he sold the retail business, including the goodwill, to a different purchaser. Ross ceased trading on 31 July 2013.

The disposal of the retail business on 31 July 2013 will qualify for entrepreneurs' relief, as Ross has disposed of the whole of his business. Although the disposal date of the property for CGT purposes is 6 June 2013 (see **2.8**), that disposal is treated as being part of the disposal of the whole business on 31 July 2013, so will also qualify for entrepreneurs' relief (see TAXGUIDE 1/12).

Disposal of part of a business

11.22   It is often difficult to distinguish between the disposal of a collection of business assets and the disposal of 'part of a business'. The disposal of one or more business assets will not attract the relief if those assets were either not in use when business ceased, or the business has not ceased (see **11.28** for post-cessation disposals), whilst the disposal of 'part of a business' will attract entrepreneurs' relief. There is no clear definition of 'part of a business' and, as this term has been imported from the retirement relief provisions, the tax cases on this issue heard for retirement relief are now considered to be relevant to entrepreneurs' relief (see CG64010).

In particular, the case of *McGregor (HMIT) v Adcock* (1977) 51 TC 692 established the 'interference test', where the HMRC officer would look at the impact of the sale on the business and establish what had changed. If the sale made a significant difference to the way the business operated, there had been a sale of part of the business; if not, the sale was probably one of assets out of the business, which would not qualify for relief.

There were many cases of farmland disposals under retirement relief, and an unofficial practice emerged of treating disposals of 50% or more of the farmland occupied by the farm as a disposal of part of the business, although the facts would have to be established in each case. In *WSG Russell v HMRC* [2012] UKFTT 623 (TC), just 35% of the farmland was disposed of, but the owner claimed entrepreneurs' relief. The claim was rejected on the basis that the disposal was not part of a business, but merely an asset used in the business.

A key case concerning entrepreneurs' relief on the disposal of part of a business is *M Gilbert (T/A United Foods) v HMRC* [2011] UKFTT 705 (TC). Mr Gilbert acted as an independent sales representative for nine different wholesale food suppliers, and had about 120 customers. He sold the business that related to one of these suppliers as a going concern. This included customer lists, goodwill and trademarks, and the benefit and burden of unperformed contracts. The tribunal judge rejected the interference test presented by HMRC (as per *McGregor v Adcock*) as being only relevant to the disposal of farmland. Instead, the judge looked for a 'viable section' test to see whether the part of the business disposed of could operate as a separate business. The fact that the assets disposed of were treated as a going concern for VAT purposes appeared to influence his decision to agree the taxpayer's claim for entrepreneurs' relief.

PARTNERS

11.23   The taxation of gains made by partners and members of LLPs are dealt with in **Chapter 6**. Disposals by the partnership of the whole or part of the business attract entrepreneurs' relief as if the whole partnership was one sole trader (see **11.20**). However, there are three special rules in *TCGA 1992, s 169I(8)* which ensure that certain disposals made by an individual partner attract entrepreneurs' relief as if he had been a sole trader.

Special rules for partnerships

11.24 The three circumstances that attract entrepreneurs' relief for established or new partners are as follows:

(a) where an individual transfers assets to a partnership, on the occasion of him joining that partnership and the partnership takes over his business (*TCGA 1992, s 169I(8)(a)*);

(b) where a partner disposes of the whole of part of his interest in the assets of the partnership (*TCGA 1992, s 169I(8)(b)*); and

(c) where any partner disposes of a business asset, he is treated as if he had owned the whole of the partnership business (*TCGA 1992, s 169I(8)(c)*).

The situation in (a) would provide relief for the capital gains that arise when a new partner introduces an asset to the partnership as the whole or part of his capital contribution (see **6.18**). Prior to 21 January 2008, it was thought that a gain would not arise in this situation, using the well-established practice in Statement of Practice D12 (SP D12). However, Revenue & Customs Brief 03/08 announced a new practice in this area, which has yet to be challenged in the courts (see **6.19**).

Where a sole trader merges his business with an established partnership, the provisions in (a) and (b) above will ensure that any gains arising on the transfer of assets between those partners, either the new partner transferring his assets into the partnership or the existing partners transferring an interest in the partnership assets (such as goodwill) to the new partner, will be covered by entrepreneurs' relief.

Example 11.8

Brian and Tony have been trading in partnership for some years sharing profits 60:40 (Brian: Tony). Charles joins the partnership and the profits are to be shared from that point on as 40:30:30 (Brian: Tony: Charles). Under SP D12, Brian has disposed of one-third of his interest in the partnership, and Tony has disposed of one-quarter of his interest in the partnership to Charles. The gains arising to Brian and Tony may be reduced by entrepreneurs' relief.

The rule described in (c) above is required to ensure that every partner in the partnership qualifies for the relief where there is a disposal of all or part of the partnership business, but the following conditions must also apply:

(a) the partnership business has been carried on for at least a year at the date of disposal; and

(b) the disposal consists of one or more relevant assets (see **11.29**).

Example 11.9

Rachel and Martyn established a nursery business as a partnership on 1 October 2012. Helen joins the partnership on 1 May 2013, paying £30,000 for her share of the goodwill of the business. Entrepreneurs' relief is not available on the gains realised by Rachel and Martyn, as the business has not been established for at least one year. If Rachel had run the nursery business as a sole trader for some years before Martyn joined as a partner on 1 October 2012, the gains realised by Rachel on 1 May 2013 would qualify for entrepreneurs' relief, but the gain made by Martyn on that date would not qualify.

Post-cessation disposals

11.25   Where a partnership business ceases and, within three years after that cessation, the partnership disposes of some assets which were in use at the time the business ceased, entrepreneurs' relief should be available to the gains realised by all the partners. The rules follow those that apply for sole traders (see **11.27**).

TRUSTEES

11.26   This chapter discusses entrepreneurs' relief as it applies to disposals made by individuals disposing of assets as a sole trader, a partner or a shareholder. It does not deal with individuals' disposals of assets as a beneficiary of a trust or as a trustee. These aspects of entrepreneurs' relief are discussed in **8.35**.

POST-CESSATION DISPOSALS

Business assets

11.27   Where the owners of an unincorporated business cease trading, they may retain certain business assets to be disposed of at a later date. Entrepreneurs' relief can still apply to these later disposals if they occur within three years after the date the business ceased (*TCGA 1992, s 169I(4)*) and the other conditions listed in **11.28** apply.

Focus

It is vital to accurately identify the business cessation date.

Any disposals outside the three-year period will not qualify for entrepreneurs' relief, even if the asset can be clearly linked to the disposal of the main business.

HMRC have no discretion to extend the three-year period for post-cessation disposals.

The date the business ceased is a question of fact, according to HMRC (CG64045), but there will be cases where the cessation date is not clear cut. Further guidance on this issue is given in the HMRC Business Income Manual at BIM70565–BIM70585. The cessation of the business does not have to fall after the commencement of entrepreneurs' relief, as long as the disposal of the asset does.

Example 11.10

Stephen ran a hairdressing salon from his freehold property until 20 May 2010 when he stopped trading due to ill-health. He managed to sub-let the property from 1 September 2010 until the date of disposal on 1 May 2013. Stephen's gain on the sale of the property should qualify for entrepreneurs' relief, as it was used in Stephen's business at the date the trade ceased on 20 May 2010, which is less than three years before the date of disposal. The letting of the property after cessation of the business does not affect his claim to entrepreneurs' relief (see **11.31**).

11.28   The other conditions that must apply for the gain on the disposal of the asset to qualify for entrepreneurs' relief are:

(a)   the asset must have been a relevant business asset for the business;

(b)   the asset must have been in use at the time the business ceased; and

(c)   the owner of the asset must have owned the business for at least 12 months ending with the date the business ceased.

Relevant business asset

11.29   Relevant business assets are any assets, including goodwill, used for the purposes of the business carried on by the sole trader or partnership, but not 'excluded assets' which are:

•   shares and securities; and

- other assets held as investments (*TCGA 1992, s 169L(4)*).

Shares and securities held by a sole trader or partnership will never be relevant business assets, even if there is some business-related reason for holding the shares. For example, a farmer may hold shares in a milk marketing co-operative.

Used in the business

11.30   For the asset to qualify under (b) in **11.28**, it does not have to be used for any particular length of time before the business ceased; it just needs to be in use at the date the business ceased (*TCGA 1992, s 169I(2)(b)*).

Focus

If the business was operated through a company, the disposal of the asset used by the company is covered by the rules for associated disposals (see **11.33**), and not by these provisions.

Assets that have a mixed business and non-business use can qualify as relevant business assets. There is no requirement for the asset to be used *wholly* for the purposes of the business at the date of cessation.

Use after the business ceased

11.31   There is no restriction on the use of the asset between the date the business ceased and the disposal of that asset. This period can be up to three years, so the owner is free to let the asset at a commercial rent for that three-year period and still claim entrepreneurs' relief on the disposal of the asset. The asset could even be used in a different business operated and owned by the asset owner and then, when it is sold, relief is claimed in respect of the use of the asset in the ceased business. This contrasts with the restrictions on the use of assets sold as an associated disposal, where the gain that qualifies for entrepreneurs' relief may be reduced (see **11.38**).

Shares

11.32   Shares or securities in a company may be disposed of after the company has ceased trading on the occasion of the liquidation or winding up of the company. The shareholder is treated as if he had disposed of his interest in the shares when he receives a capital distribution (*TCGA 1992, s 122*), which will apply where a formal liquidation is undertaken. On an informal winding up, the distributions made to shareholders can only be treated as capital for tax purposes where the total of all the distributions from the company in anticipation of the winding up do not exceed £25,000. Otherwise, all the distributions made in anticipation of the winding up are subject to income tax (*CTA 2010, ss 1030A, 1030B*). Prior to 1 March 2012, where clearance was granted by HMRC under ESC C16, capital treatment could apply to all distributions made by the company as part of the winding up, with no limits.

Where the distribution is treated as a capital payment, it can qualify for entrepreneurs' relief under *TCGA 1992, s 169S(2)* if the conditions listed below apply:

(a) the company must have been the individual's personal company (see **11.10**);

(b) the shareholder must have been an employee or officer of the company, or of a company in the same group (see **11.11**); and

(c) the company must have been a trading company or a holding company of a trading group (see **11.12**).

All of these three conditions must apply for the whole of the 12-month period that ends with either the cessation of the trade of the company, or the date the company left the trading group and did not continue to trade outside that group. This date must also fall not more than three years before the date the shares are treated as being disposed of, which will normally be the date the shareholder receives the capital distribution.

However, where the shares disposed of were acquired through EMI qualifying options, condition (a) above is not required (see **4.6**). In such a case, the EMI shares will qualify for entrepreneurs' relief if the option grant date fell at least one year before the cessation date, and the other conditions are met (*TCGA 1992, s 169I(7B)*).

ASSOCIATED DISPOSALS

11.33 This is a tricky concept to grasp. It is not well explained in the legislation, so it may catch out taxpayers and their advisers. The concept of an associated disposal has been imported from the retirement relief legislation, so cases concerning the determination of an associated disposal under those provisions are considered to be relevant to entrepreneurs' relief (CG63995).

An associated disposal of business assets can only occur in connection with:

- the disposal of shares or securities in a company (see **11.9**); or

- the disposal of a partnership interest (see **11.23**).

The relief cannot apply on the disposal of assets following the disposal of a sole trader business, as such a disposal would fall into the more flexible post-cessation rules (see **11.27**).

Disposal of shares

11.34   If a shareholder who is also an employee or officer of his personal company disposes of shares or securities in that company, the gain arising will be eligible for entrepreneurs' relief if the other conditions apply (see **11.9**). Where that individual disposes of an asset which was used by the company, at around the same time as the share disposal (see **11.36**), the gain on that asset will qualify for the relief as an associated disposal, if both of the following conditions also apply:

(a)   the asset is disposed of as part of the shareholder's withdrawal from participation in the business carried on by his personal company or the business carried on by the trading group (*TCGA 1992, s 169K(3), (5)*); and

(b)   the asset was used for the purpose of the business for at least one year to the date of disposal of the shares, or to the date of cessation of the company's business if earlier (*TCGA 1992, s 169K(4)*).

To summarise:

•   the first disposal of shares must qualify for entrepreneurs' relief, or would qualify if a gain had been made on that disposal but a claim for entrepreneurs' relief does not have to be made for this gain; and

•   the second disposal of the asset must meet conditions (a) and (b) above.

Withdrawal from participation in the business

11.35   This condition is imposed to prevent a shareholder from disposing of a single asset and claiming it was an associated disposal because he also disposed of a small number of shares at the same time. The two disposals must be clearly linked and in total comprise a withdrawal from participation in the business. This was established in *Clarke v Mayo* (1994) 66 TC 728 (see TAXGUIDE 1/12).

However, this withdrawal need not be a complete divorce from the business, and there is no *de minimis* amount of shares which must be disposed of for the two disposals to constitute a withdrawal from the business. The HMRC guidance (at CG63995) says it is not necessary for the individual actually to reduce the amount of work they do for the business for this condition to be met.

Example 11.11

Lewpyn has owned the intellectual property used by his internet games company Level 6 Ltd (his personal company) since it was created on 6 April 2009. He sold Level 6 Ltd on 6 August 2013, and on the same date he sold the intellectual property used by the company. Lewpyn remains the technical director for the company under the terms of the sale. Lewpyn has withdrawn from the business of the company because he has disposed of all his shares and, in connection with that disposal, also sold his interest in the intellectual property used by the company. The disposal of the intellectual property therefore qualifies as an associated disposal.

Time limit

11.36   The legislation does not specify a time period during which the associated disposal must be made, but the HMRC guidance (at CG63995) stipulates that both the disposal of the shares and the associated disposal of the asset must be caused by the same event and there should be no significant time interval between the disposals. It is also implied in the HMRC guidance that the event causing both disposals should be the withdrawal from participation in the business, although the legislation only says the asset disposal must be connected with the withdrawal from the business.

HMRC realise that there will often be a delay between the disposal of the shares, perhaps on the cessation of the business, and the disposal of the asset which potentially qualifies as the associated disposal. They have therefore laid down some guidelines as to when a later disposal of an asset can be accepted as an associated disposal.

The disposal may be an associated disposal if the disposal occurs:

- within one year of the cessation of business;

- within three years of the cessation of business and the asset has not been leased or used for any other purpose at any time after business ceased; or

- where the business has not ceased, within three years of the material disposal, provided the asset has not been used for any purpose other than that of the business.

These extra-statutory conditions are not as flexible as the legally imposed conditions relating to the post-cessation disposals for a sole trader business (see **11.28**). HMRC guidance (at CG63995) indicates that any significant use of the asset, other than for the business of the company, between the first disposal of shares and the disposal of the asset will disqualify that asset from being an associated disposal. This is in addition to the statutory restrictions imposed by *TCGA 1992, s 169P* (see **11.38**).

Disposal of partnership interest

11.37 Where a partner disposes of his interest or part of that interest in the partnership, so the disposal would qualify for entrepreneurs' relief where a gain arises (see **11.23**), a disposal of an asset held personally may qualify as an associated disposal for the relief if the following conditions apply:

(a) the asset is disposed of as part of the partner's withdrawal from participation in the business carried on by the partnership (*TCGA 1992, s 169K(3), (5)*); and

(b) the asset was used for the purpose of the partnership business for at least one year to the date of disposal of the partnership interest, or to the date or cessation of the partnership business if earlier (*TCGA 1992, s 169K(4)*).

The definition of withdrawal from the business of the partnership is similar to that discussed with reference to a company (see **11.35**). The HMRC guidance (at CG63995) indicates that the partner does not have to step down as a partner completely. There is no *de minimis* amount by which the withdrawing partner must reduce his interest in the partnership for the combined disposals to constitute a withdrawal from the business.

Example 11.12

Graham is in partnership with his son Tristan, sharing all profits: 7/8ths to Graham, 1/8th to Tristan. Graham owns the office that the partnership trades from. On his sixtieth birthday, Graham gives the office to his son, and the profit-sharing ratios are changed to 1/4 to Graham and 3/4 to Tristan, but Graham continues to work full-time for the partnership. The reduction by Graham of his interest in the partnership is a material disposal, and the disposal of the office to Tristan qualifies as an associated disposal. Both these disposals are caused by the same event: Graham withdrawing from participation in the partnership business.

The time period in which the associated disposal by the partner must take place is subject to the same restrictions as apply to disposals associated with the withdrawal from the business of a trading company (see **11.36**).

Restrictions

11.38   Where there is a material disposal of shares or of a partnership interest, there are four additional restrictions on the use of any asset that is the subject of the associated disposal (*TCGA 1992, s 169P(4)*). If any of the following apply, the amount of the gain arising on the associated disposal of the asset, which would be subject to entrepreneurs' relief, is reduced on a just and reasonable basis:

(a)   The asset has only been used by the business for part of the period of ownership by the individual, in which case the gain taken into account will reflect the period of business use.

(b)   Where only part of the asset has been used for the purposes of the business, the gain taken into account for the relief must reflect the proportion of the asset used for business purposes.

(c)   The individual concerned has only been involved in the business as a partner of the partnership or employee/officer of the company for part of the time during which the asset was used by the business. This is less likely than situation (a) or (b), but is possible where an individual was a salaried partner before becoming a full partner.

(d)   Any payment of rent was made for the use of the asset by the personal company or partnership for a period after 5 April 2008.

The payment of 'rent' in restriction (d) means any form of consideration paid for the use of the asset, including licence fees for the use of intellectual property (see Example 11.13). Where the rent paid is less than a full market rent for the use of the asset, the gain is restricted proportionately. However, 'rent' does not include a higher profit share paid to a partner as a result of letting the partnership use his personally held property (see TAXGUIDE 1/12).

The restriction in (d) is likely to cause the most aggravation as, prior to 6 April 2008, it was good tax-planning practice to hold business property outside the company, and to charge the company a commercial rent for its use. Full business asset taper relief would apply on any gain made on the disposal of the let property, and the rent paid was a useful way to extract funds free of NIC from the company. Now that situation is turned on its head, so property owners must calculate whether the long-term possibility of entrepreneurs' relief is worth more than the short-term benefit of NIC-free rent. There may be strong commercial reasons for keeping the property in personal hands. Even if it is desirable to hold the property within the company, the transfer into the company may well involve high transactional costs such as stamp duty land tax, mortgage and valuation fees. The transfer may also create a personal capital gain that will not qualify for entrepreneurs' relief.

Example 11.13

In Example 11.11, Lewpyn sold the intellectual property, created on 6 April 2009 and used by Level 6 Ltd, on 6 August 2013, making a gain of £280,000. However, Level 6 Ltd had paid Lewpyn a commercial rate licence fee for the use of that intellectual property from 6 April 2009 until 6 July 2009, when his tax advisers realised such a payment could cause a problem on a future sale. The gain to be brought into account for entrepreneurs' relief must be reduced by 3/52 months. The total CGT payable on the associated disposal is calculated as:

2013/14	£	Tax £
Total gain	312,000	
Reduction for rent received: £312,000 × 3/52	(18,000)	
Net gain charged to CGT at entrepreneurs' relief rate:	294,000	29,400
Gain not subject to ER	18,000	
Annual exemption	(10,900)	
Gain subject to CGT payable at 28%	7,100	1,988
Total CGT payable:		31,388

DEFERRED GAINS

11.39   Where a gain is rolled over or deferred on the acquisition of new shares or corporate bonds, that deferred gain will fall into charge for CGT on the disposal of the new security. That later disposal may not meet all the qualifying conditions for entrepreneurs' relief. In these cases, special provisions may apply to grant entrepreneurs' relief in respect of gains deferred by acquiring the following shares or securities:

- qualifying corporate bonds (QCBs) (see **11.40**);

- share-for-share exchanges (see **11.46**); and

- Enterprise Investment Scheme (EIS) or Venture Capital Trust (VCT) shares (see **11.49**).

Qualifying corporate bonds

11.40   When a shareholder sells his personal company, he may receive qualifying corporate bonds (QCBs) in exchange for some or all of his shares. The gain that arises on the disposal of the personal company shares is rolled into the QCBs and becomes taxable at the point the QCBs are disposed of, normally on the maturity of the bonds. Under the taper relief rules, the gain on the disposal of the shares was frozen and taper relief would apply when the gain became chargeable, but only in relation to the period the original shares were held and not the period for which the QCBs were held. QCBs exchanged for shares prior to 6 April 2008 thus present a problem, as the gain is frozen but taper relief no longer applies.

This problem is eased by a special relief for QCBs that were exchanged for shares before 6 April 2008 (*FA 2008, Sch 3, para 7*) (see **11.41**). There is also a separate relief for QCBs exchanged for shares on or after 6 April 2008 (*TCGA 1992, s 169R*) (see **11.42**).

Focus

HMRC have produced two tables that summarise the CGT position where a deferred gain comes into charge following a disposal of QCBs or EIS or VCT shares (see TAXGUIDE 1/12).

Pre-6 April 2008 QCBs

11.41   Where an individual disposes of QCBs that were acquired in exchange for shares or securities in his personal company before 6 April 2008, any chargeable gain that was rolled into the QCB on the exchange for the shares becomes chargeable to tax on disposal of the QCBs. However, the individual may not hold 5% of the ordinary shares of the company that issued the QCBs, or meet the employment condition (see **11.11**). Unless both these conditions are met, the individual will not qualify for entrepreneurs' relief on the gain realised on the disposal of the QCBs.

In this situation, the gain deferred by acquiring the QCBs can qualify for entrepreneurs' relief if, at the time the QCBs were acquired, the gain would have qualified for that relief, assuming for this purpose that the relief had been in place at that date. The tests discussed in **11.9** must effectively be backdated to the point that the original gain arose. However, to benefit from the relief on the chargeable gain, the taxpayer must make a claim under *FA 2008, Sch 3, para 7* no later than the first anniversary of 31 January following the end of the tax year in which the first disposal of his QCBs occurs, where this is on or after 6 April 2008. The QCBs must be held by the same person who acquired them before 6 April 2008, in order for the gain that becomes chargeable after 5 April 2008 to qualify for the relief. See HMRC examples at CG64166.

There is a quirk to watch out for with this transitional relief. The claim for entrepreneurs' relief on the deferred gain applies to the whole of the gain rolled into the QCBs, and has the effect of reducing the whole gain by 4/9ths. The reduced gain falls into charge when the QCBs are disposed of. If, at that time, the reduced gain is charged to CGT at 18%, there is an effective rate of CGT of 10% on the full deferred gain. However, where some of those QCBs are disposed of on or after 23 June 2010, the rate of CGT may be 28%, in which case the effective rate of CGT with entrepreneurs' relief is not 10% but 15.5% (see Example 11.14). Where the first disposal of the QCBs is made on or after 23 June 2010, the full deferred gain is chargeable to CGT at 10%.

Post-6 April 2008 QCBs

11.42   Where an individual acquires QCBs in exchange for shares in his personal company on or after 6 April 2008, the gain inherent in those personal company shares is rolled into the QCBs and falls into charge to CGT when the QCBs are disposed of (*TCGA 1992, s 116(10)*). On the disposal of those QCBs, the tests for entrepreneurs' relief to apply to the deferred gain would normally look at the individual's shareholding and employment conditions in the company that issued the QCBs, not the original personal company. The individual must meet both shareholding and employment tests (see **11.9** and **11.11**), for the company that issued the QCBs, to claim entrepreneurs' relief on the gain realised on disposal of the QCBs.

The taxpayer can elect under *TCGA 1992, s 169R* for the gain that arose on the disposal of the personal company shares to qualify for entrepreneurs' relief, if that disposal would have qualified for entrepreneurs' relief using the tests outlined in **11.9** and **11.11**. However, the effect of the election under *s 169R* is quite different when the exchange of the personal company shares for QCBs occurs before 23 June 2010 (see **11.43**) or after 22 June 2010 (see **11.44**).

Pre-23 June 2010 exchanges

11.43   The gain on the disposal of the personal company shares is reduced by 4/9ths. When that gain comes into charge on the disposal of the QCBs, the reduced amount of gain may be subject to CGT at 18%, giving an effective rate of 10% on the full gain. If the gain comes into charge on or after 23 June 2010, the rate of CGT applying may be 28%, giving an effective rate of CGT on the full gain of 15.5% (see Example 11.14).

Post-22 June 2010 exchanges

11.44   If the taxpayer so elects under *TCGA 1992, s 169R*, the gain arising on the disposal of the personal company shares is not deferred at all. That gain is subject to entrepreneurs' relief at the time of the share for QCB exchange, and bears CGT at the entrepreneurs' relief rate of 10% (within the lifetime limit).

> **Focus**
>
> If the taxpayer makes the election under *s 169R*, CGT at 10% is paid on the gain realised on the disposal of the shares.
>
> As the consideration for the shares is QCBs and not cash, the taxpayer may not have the cash to pay the tax due on that part of the deal.

The alternative is not to elect under *s 169R*, and to accept the automatic deferral of the gain under *TCGA 1992, s 116(10)*. The deferred gain can then fall into charge as the QCBs are gradually cashed, but that gain will be subject to CGT at 18% or 28%, depending on the taxpayer's level of income and gains for the tax year of encashment.

Timing of election

11.45   In both cases, the election under *TCGA 1992, s 169R* must be made by the first anniversary of 31 January following the end of the tax year in which the shares in the personal company were disposed of.

> **Focus**
>
> The deadline for making the election under *s 169R* is based on the acquisition date of the QCBs, and not the disposal date of the QCBs.

Tax advisers need to watch this election deadline, as the deferred gain may not come into charge for some years, by which time it will be too late to elect under *TCGA 1992, s 169R* for entrepreneurs' relief to apply.

> **Example 11.14**
>
> On 20 June 2008, Alice exchanged all her shares in her personal company, Wonderland Ltd, for QCBs issued by Red Queen Plc. Alice had formed Wonderland Ltd and had been its sole director and shareholder for ten years. The gain accruing on the disposal of her shares was £990,000, which was just within the lifetime cap at the time of the disposal. This gain was fully deferred by the acceptance of QCBs, and Alice elected under *TCGA 1992, s 169R* for the gain to be subject to entrepreneurs' relief. This had the effect of reducing the deferred gain to £550,000 (5/9ths × £990,000).
>
> On 20 June 2010, Alice received a cash payment for half of her QCBs, so half the reduced deferred gain (ie £275,000) came into charge. Alice pays CGT of £49,500 (18% × £275,000) on this gain.

On 20 June 2013, Alice received a cash payment for her remaining QCBs, which brings into charge the balance of the deferred gain (ie £275,000). Alice's net taxable income for 2013/14 is £40,000, which exceeds her basic rate band, so the full gain of £275,000 is taxed at 28%. Alice's CGT liability on the second encashment of the QCBs is £77,000 (£275,000 × 28%), but she paid CGT of £49,500 on the first half of her gain.

Share exchanges

11.46   Another situation where gains may be deferred is on a share-for-share exchange, which often occurs on the takeover of a company. A shareholder may exchange shares in his personal company (the old shares) for a small holding of shares (new shares) issued by the acquiring company. No capital gain arises at the time of the share exchange as the new shares are considered to stand in the shoes of the old shares (*TCGA 1992, s 127*). However, on disposal of the new shares, entrepreneurs' relief may not apply if the minority shareholder does not hold 5% of the ordinary shares of the acquiring company (see **11.10**).

In this situation, the shareholder can choose whether to defer the gain using *s 127* or to disapply *s 127* (using the election under *TCGA 1992, s 169Q*) and claim entrepreneurs' relief on the gain as it arises on the disposal of the old shares. This will make the effective rate of CGT on that gain 10%, whether the share exchange occurs before or after 23 June 2010.

Focus

If the shareholder elects under s 169Q to disapply the deferral of the gain under *s 127*, he will have to pay CGT on the residue of the gain at 10%.

The shareholder may have difficulty in funding the CGT due, as he has not received cash proceeds for those old shares.

Making the election

11.47   The election under *TCGA 1992, s 169Q* can only apply where the share exchange occurs on or after 6 April 2008. It must be made by the first anniversary of 31 January following the tax year in which the old shares were exchanged. Where the old shares were held by a trust, the election must be made jointly by the trustee and the qualifying beneficiary. It is not possible to make a partial election to apply to only some of the shares involved in the reorganisation (CG64155).

As with the election under *TCGA 1992, s 169R*, the timing of this election is likely to trip up taxpayers and tax advisers alike. The gain on the old shares is rolled over into the new shares, and likely to be forgotten until the new shares are disposed of. However, by that date it may be too late to elect under *TCGA 1992, s 169Q*.

Swift sale of new shares

11.48   Another problem that can arise is when the new shares are disposed of very shortly after acquisition. Where the taxpayer would qualify for entrepreneurs' relief on the basis of his holding of ordinary shares and employment in the acquiring company (see **11.10**), he still needs to satisfy those conditions for 12 months to the date of disposal of the new shares. HMRC have confirmed that, where *s 127* applies, such that the new shares are treated as the same asset as the old shares, the exchange can be looked through to ascertain the 12-month holding period for the ordinary shares and the employment condition. This look-through can only apply if the election under *TCGA 1992, s 169Q* has not been made, and the old shares also qualified for entrepreneurs' relief (CG64155).

Enterprise investment scheme or venture capital trust shares

11.49   Deferral of gains by acquiring enterprise investment scheme (EIS) shares is discussed in **Chapter 16**, and the similar deferral of gains that applied on the acquisition of venture capital trust (VCT) shares before 6 April 2004 is discussed in **16.51**.

Where such gains were deferred before 6 April 2008 and fall into charge after that date for any reason, the shareholder may claim entrepreneurs' relief in respect of that deferred gain if the conditions applied at the time of the original gain (*FA 2008, Sch 3, para 8*). Those conditions are broadly that the original gain, which was rolled into the EIS or VCT shares, would have qualified for entrepreneurs' relief if it had accrued on or after 6 April 2008. So a fiction is invented to apply the tests set out in **11.9** or **11.20**, as appropriate, to the original gain, looking at the ownership circumstances that related to the original asset which was disposed of.

This claim for entrepreneurs' relief must apply to the whole of the deferred gain that attaches to the EIS or VCT shares, which were acquired to defer the original gain, even if some of those shares continue to be held, such that part of the deferred gain has not yet fallen into charge to CGT (CG64170).

If the first chargeable event for the shares occurs before 23 June 2010, but after 5 April 2008, and a claim for entrepreneurs' relief is made, the whole of the deferred gain is reduced by 4/9ths at that time. This is not the point at which all the gain comes back into charge for CGT. This means that the same problem created by the change of the rate of CGT applies to this deferred gain as it does to gains deferred using QCBs (see **11.44**).

Where the first chargeable event for the EIS or VCT shares occurs on or after 23 June 2010, and entrepreneurs' relief is claimed, the deferred gain is charged at the entrepreneurs' relief rate of 10%.

The taxpayer must claim this relief by the first anniversary of 31 January following the end of the tax year in which he first disposed of the EIS or VCT shares after 5 April 2008.

There may also be a separate gain that has arisen through the growth in value of the EIS shares themselves. This EIS company-generated gain will be exempt from CGT if the EIS shares have been held for at least three years and income tax relief has been given and not been withdrawn (see **16.3**). Where these conditions are not met, the EIS company gain will be subject to CGT. However, entrepreneurs' relief may be available on that EIS company gain where the conditions in **11.9** apply in respect of those EIS shares.

INTERACTION WITH OTHER RELIEFS

11.50   When the legislation for entrepreneurs' relief was drafted, little thought was given to the interaction between this relief and the existing CGT reliefs. HMRC do not consider that entrepreneurs' relief takes the same place in the order of reliefs as was previously defined by retirement relief (see CG60120). The HMRC view on the interaction of entrepreneurs' relief and certain other CGT reliefs is as follows:

- Roll-over relief (*TCGA 1992, s 152*) applies before entrepreneurs' relief (CG64136).

- EIS deferral relief (*TCGA 1992, Sch 5B*) applies after entrepreneurs' relief (CG64135).

- Incorporation relief (*TCGA 1992, s 162*) applies before entrepreneurs' relief (see **15.20**).

- Hold-over relief (*TCGA 1992, s 165*) applies before entrepreneurs' relief (CG64137).

Chapter 12

Main residence relief

SIGNPOSTS

- **Scope of the relief** – The legislation, how the relief is given (see **12.1–12.2**).

- **What constitutes residence** – A dwelling house, occupation, relief may be denied when the property is purchased to make a profit or as part of a trade (see **12.3–12.7**).

- **Other uses of a residence** – Business purposes, accommodation for an adult in care, letting relief, for a dependent relative, purchased by employer (see **12.8–12.12**).

- **The extent of the property** – Curtilage, 'permitted area', surplus land, sale of building plot (see **12.13–12.16**).

- **Periods of residence** – Delay in taking up occupation, deemed occupation for last 36 months, periods of absence due to work, job-related occupation (see **12.17–12.23**).

- **Two or more residences** – Nomination of a property as main residence, varying the notice, licences and tenancies, marriage and civil partnership (see **12.24–12.29**).

- **Trustees and personal representatives** – Discretionary trusts, nil rate band trusts, IHT or CGT burden, valuation of property on death, quick sale after death, relief of residence of major beneficiary, property as asset of beneficiary (see **12.30–12.37**).

- **Hold-over of gain under** *s 260* – For transactions after 9 December 2003, it is not possible to claim main residence relief and hold-over relief under *s 260* (see **12.38–12.42**).

- **Divorce and separation** – No gain, no loss transfers in the tax year of separation, *Mesher* orders (see **12.43–12.44**).

SCOPE OF THE RELIEF

12.1   The relief from CGT on disposal of the taxpayer's main private residence, also known as principal private residence relief, is possibly the best known CGT relief, but it is also the relief which is most challenged in the tax tribunals and higher courts. The primary relief for individuals is set out in *TCGA 1992, ss 222–224*. Variations of the relief are given in *TCGA 1992, ss 225–226* for:

- homes occupied under the terms of a trust (see **12.30**);

- home occupied by a dependent relative (see **12.11**);

- part of the home occupied by an adult in the placement care scheme (see **12.9**);

- disposal by PRs to occupier who was major beneficiary of the will (see **12.36**);

- disposal connected with a divorce or civil partnership dissolution (see **12.44**); and

- disposal under a home purchase agreement with the taxpayer's employer (see **12.12**).

There are also anti-avoidance rules in *TCGA 1992, s 226A–226B* where hold-over relief under *TCGA 1992, s 260* has been claimed in respect of the same property.

HMRC guidance is found in their Capital Gains Manual at CG64200–CG65681. This guidance is extensive, and is frequently updated, so be sure to refer to the latest version if you need to rely on HMRC's opinion.

How the relief takes effect

12.2   The CGT relief under *TCGA 1992, s 222* is automatic; it does not have to be claimed by an individual. However, where the taxpayer holds an interest in more than one residence, nomination of one residence as the main residence may be required (see **12.22**). Subject to the many qualifications discussed in this chapter in relation to the extent of the property, and periods of absence, most disposals of residential property that has been occupied by the taxpayer as a residence will escape CGT. No entry is required on a tax return in such cases (CG64206).

WHAT CONSTITUTES A RESIDENCE?

A dwelling-house

12.3   Main residence relief applies to a gain accruing to an individual on the disposal of, or of an interest in, 'a dwelling house or part of a dwelling house which is, or has at any time in his period of ownership been his only or main residence' *(TCGA 1992, s 222(1)(a))*. That legislation does not define 'dwelling house' or 'residence', so guidance must be taken from decided cases. The annual tax on enveloped dwellings (ATED) includes a meaning of 'dwelling' for the purpose of that charge in *FA 2013, s 112*. However, the definition is quite circular, as it says:

> 'A building or part of building counts as a dwelling at any time when it is:
>
> (a)   used or suitable for use as a single dwelling, or
>
> (b)   in the process of being constructed or adapted for such use.'

For further discussion of the ATED, see **Chapter 4**.

The HMRC opinion, which sometimes takes a selective view of decided cases, is given for:

- 'dwelling house' at CG64230–CG64328; and

- 'only or main residence' at CG64420–CG64555.

A mobile caravan does not qualify for relief, but a static one may do. A 'live aboard' yacht in a marina does not qualify, even if on 'shore power', as many cruising yachts are; but a houseboat permanently located, and connected to all mains services, may do. It seems that the claim in such cases usually relates to the site, rather than the caravan or vessel.

Quality of occupation

12.4   Lord Widgery described a residence in *Fox v Stirk, Ricketts v Registration Officer for the City of Cambridge* [1970] 3 All ER 7 as 'the place where he sleeps and shelters and has his house'.

Occupation of the dwelling house is a key factor which turns a house into a home, and thus a 'residence' for relief purposes. There are many cases which concern the redevelopment of a property, or the temporary occupation of a property. For example, *Goodwin v Curtis (Inspector of Taxes)* [1996] STC 1146 concerned the redevelopment of a farmhouse and its outbuildings by a company set up for that purpose. One of the two directors of the company (Mr Goodwin) purchased the farmhouse from the company for his own use on 1 April 1985. He took up occupation and had the services and telephone connected. After only a matter of days, the property was offered for sale. On 3 May 1985, contracts were exchanged to sell the property at a very substantial profit. The property was placed on the market for sale before Goodwin even took up 'residence', and there was little evidence that he intended to make the property his permanent home. He was denied relief on the gain.

However, that case is not decisive: there is actually no minimum period for occupation – what matters is the quality of the occupation: see *Moore v Thompson (Inspector of Taxes)* [1986] STC 170.

Usually, a careful examination of the facts will support or deny a claim to occupy a house as a residence. Where a taxpayer has more than one residence available to him, and he has not filed a notice under *TCGA 1992, s 222(5)(a)* (see **12.22**), he will be forced to show where he is resident. In such cases, the following facts will be relevant to indicate where the taxpayer claims to live:

- where he is registered to vote;
- where the children of the family go to school;
- where the family spends most of its time;
- the correspondence address for bank and building society accounts, credit cards and investments;
- where his main place of work is;
- where he is registered with a doctor or dentist;
- where the individual's car is registered and insured; and
- which property is the main address for council tax.

Evidence will be examined including the way that a property is furnished and, in extreme cases, the level of electricity used in each property as an indication of which was occupied for the greater time (CG64545).

The quality of the occupation was examined in *Harte v HMRC* [2012] UKFTT 258 (TC). The Hartes inherited the property which was close to their own home. They elected for the property to be treated as their main residence for a short period before sale, but this claim was rejected on the basis that the taxpayers did not:

- take any personal possessions to the property;
- acquire a TV licence at the property;
- have a computer or internet connection at the property;
- entertain there or have anyone to stay; or
- change the name on the bills from 'occupier'.

Where the taxpayer occupies the property on a temporary basis while it is being renovated, that occupation may not have sufficient quality to make it a residence (see *Jason Terrence Moore v HMRC* [2010] UKFTT 445 and *Malcolm Springthorpe v HMRC* [2010] UKFTT 582 (TC)). In *Benford v HMRC* [2011] UKFTT 457 (TC), the taxpayer was a builder who claimed to be separated from his wife while he renovated a property in Naseby. However, his correspondence was sent to his former family home, where he also took showers and some meals during his apparent occupation of the Naseby property. Also, the Naseby property had no heating, cooking facilities, place to hang clothes, carpet, rugs or furniture, other than an inflatable bed.

Profit or loss motive

12.5   One way to deny the relief under *s 222* is to assert that the property was acquired wholly or partly for the purpose of making a gain from the disposal *(TCGA 1992, s 224(3))*. HMRC use this section to challenge cases where renovation of the property is followed by a quick sale. For example, in *Lowrie v HMRC* [2011] UKFTT 309 (TC), the taxpayer bought a property on 16 May 2003, moved in on 2 June 2003, and gutted the property for renovation in July 2003. In the meantime, his sister died, and he lost heart in the renovation project, put the property on the market in December 2003 and sold it in January 2004. The Tribunal accepted that the property had not been bought with an intention to sell, but there was not the degree of permanence to the occupation to make it a residence.

Where the relief under *TCGA 1992, s 222* for gain arising on the main residence applies, any loss made on the disposal of the same property is not an allowable loss for CGT purposes. However, the taxpayer in *Jones v Wilcox (Inspector of Taxes)* [1996] STI 1349 attempted to use *s 224(3)* to create an allowable loss from disposal of his own home, in order to set that loss against a separate and unconnected gain. The taxpayer's case fell down on the evidence. He and his family had lived in the property for a number of years. Children had been born and brought up there. The taxpayer and his wife had considered a number of properties. The only reasonable inference was that this particular house had been chosen, not to make a profit, but because they wanted to live there. Whilst making a gain from the eventual disposal of the house might have been a hope or even an expectation, everyone has to live somewhere, and the main purpose of the purchase had been as a residence. There was no evidence that profit was the main motive for the purchase. As a result, in the same way that a gain would not have been chargeable, the loss was not relievable.

Trading

12.6   HMRC will seek to impose an income tax charge under the trading income provisions, in priority to a CGT assessment, on the gain that falls out of the main residence exemption by way of *TCGA 1992, s 224(3)* (CG65320).

This is illustrated in *John & Sylvia Regan v HMRC* [2012] UKFTT 569 (TC), where HMRC raised income tax assessments on the taxpayers, on the basis that profit made on the sale of 93 Rowan Avenue was a trading transaction. The taxpayers lived in the property for only 10 months, although they owned it for 41 months. During the periods both before and after occupation, the property was renovated and an extension was added. The Tribunal concluded that the badges of trade were not proven, so the purchase and sale of the property did not constitute a trade, and the taxpayers were entitled to CGT relief on the sale as their main residence.

Lynch v Edmondson (Inspector of Taxes) [1998] STI 968 illustrates some of the principles of a trading transaction. A bricklayer purchased two plots of land. He developed them into two flats. One of them was immediately let at a premium for a term of 99 years. Evidence put before the Special Commissioner of the way in which the property had been financed, and transactions between the bricklayer and the woman with whom he was living, all tended to support the conclusion that the taxpayer was trading.

Helpfully, the Special Commissioner summarised the various tests that led to the final decision. Thus:

- this was a single transaction that could nevertheless amount to trading;

- it was a transaction in land, which was certainly a commodity in which it was possible to trade;

- the way that the taxpayer went about developing the land pointed towards trading, in that he realised substantial money from one of the units by letting it as soon as it was built;

- the way that the project was financed was consistent with trading, in that much of the cost of the development was repaid from the premium that was taken on the grant of the lease of the first unit to be finished;

- the fact that the bricklayer himself carried out the work was consistent with trading;

- the fact that the original purchase of the land was divided up into units for sale was consistent with trading; and

- it was relevant to consider the motive of the taxpayer. He had told the bank that had lent him the money that he would sell one of the flats. That was consistent with trading.

On the other hand, there were factors that tended to point the other way, such as the fact that one of the units was not immediately disposed of on a long lease but was instead let in a manner that was more consistent with investment than with trade. Also, the way that the asset was used in the overall circumstances was ambiguous. Nevertheless, on balance, the taxpayer was held to be trading.

12.7 Where a clear pattern of dealing can be discerned, for example where a person buys properties, renovates them and resells them on a regular basis, HMRC may well regard this as trading. As a rule of thumb, to renovate one run down property or perhaps two is no more than 'nest building' for a young couple; but, by the time a taxpayer embarks on a third renovation project, it becomes easier to infer that he is engaged in a trade. The speed with which a taxpayer moves from one property to another is relevant, as was clear from the decision in *Goodwin v Curtis*. The statute stipulates nothing about a period of occupation required to establish a residence. Residence in a property for a full year is probably long enough to establish relief, but evidence of the quality of occupation will also be required (see **12.3**).

OTHER USES OF A RESIDENCE

For business purposes

12.8   Relief under *s 222* is available in respect of the entirety of a dwelling house or of a part only. As will be seen at **12.13**, the main apportionment of a residence required, where it does not all qualify for relief, is between the part that is within the 'permitted area' and the part that is not. A separate apportionment is recognised by *s 224(1)* for dwelling houses or part of dwelling houses which are exclusively used for a trade, business, profession or vocation. This will be the case where a person works from home and either has an annex or outbuilding designated as an office or has a room within his property which is exclusively used for office work.

The emphasis is on exclusive use: any area which is used partly for business and partly for residential purposes will qualify in full for the relief. Thus full relief for CGT purposes applies, even if the taxpayer has claimed a deduction from trading profits for a proportion of the expenses of the building in which the business is carried on. However, where a room has been used exclusively for business, such as a doctor's surgery, HMRC say that minor and occasional residential use should be disregarded (CG64663).

Example 12.1—Soft furnishings business

Alice lives in a small house. She also owns a small row of lock-up garages adjoining her home. Alice uses one garage for her domestic car, one for her delivery van, one for the stock of finished goods and she lets the remainder. She continues to run the business itself from the house. She uses the dining room to make curtains, but there is just enough room to have family meals in there as well.

On disposal of the house and the garages at a gain, Alice must apportion the gain between the different parts of the property. The garages that were let are a simple investment and taxable as such. The garages used respectively for the storage of stock and to house the delivery van have been used exclusively for the business and not for any domestic purpose, and are therefore outside the scope of *s 222*.

The remainder of the property qualifies for main residence relief, even though Alice may have claimed a proportion of the costs of services etc against her business profits. There is only one dining room and the family spend considerable time in there; it is not used exclusively for the business. The garage for the family car is not used for business. Any reasonable apportionment of the gain should be accepted by HMRC: see CG64670.

To care for adults

12.9   The 'exclusive business use' rule discussed in **12.8** could adversely affect individuals who use a part of their home to care exclusively for adults. Under the adult placement scheme, a carer provides accommodation for the adult who needs care in the carer's home, and the carer is regarded as carrying on a caring business from that property. The adult who needs care will normally require exclusive use of part of the property.

Where these circumstances apply, the exclusive use of the property for the caring business is disregarded for the purposes of the relief (*TCGA 1992, s 225D*). This provision applies for disposals made on or after 9 December 2009 (CG64695).

Lettings relief

12.10   'Buy to let' properties do not qualify for main residence relief, as a property which is fully let cannot also be the taxpayer's main residence at the same time. However, there is a specific relief in *TGCA 1992, s 223(4)* which can apply where a person lets all or part of his own home, either while he also occupies the property (see Example 12.2) or during another period of the ownership, when the property is fully let (see Example 12.3).

For the relief to apply, the dwelling house, or the part on which the gain arises, must at some time in the ownership of the taxpayer have been a residence within the general terms of *s 222*, ie his only or main residence or a property that he owned whilst in job-related employment (see **12.19**). The let area must be let as residential accommodation, not as office space or as a trade. The tax relief is limited to the lowest of the following amounts:

- the part of the gain exempt because it was used as the taxpayer's main home;
- the gain attributed to the let period; and
- £40,000 per owner.

Example 12.2—Money in the cellar

Henry bought an urban terraced property for £480,000 of which 25% is represented by the value of accommodation in the basement that could be occupied separately; the remainder relates to the ground floor and upper floor. He lives there, allowing a lodger to occupy the basement, and later sells the entire property for £660,000. There is valuation evidence that the basement flat is still worth 25% of the whole. The gain from the upper 75% of the property (75% × 180,000) = £135,000 is exempt under *s 222*.

The gain on the basement is £45,000, of which £40,000 is exempt under *s 223(4)(b)*. Note that, if the basement had always been self-contained, it might have been regarded as a separate dwelling house and thus not part of Henry's property, and not subject to the lettings relief.

Example 12.3—Letting the second home

Jane bought a holiday cottage in Dorset and owned it for 13 years. She occupied it as her sole residence for the first three months, let it for eight years, and used it as a second home for the remainder of the period. The gain is £130,000 or £10,000 per year of ownership. The taxable gain is calculated as follows:

	£
Capital gain before tax relief:	130,000
Exemption for main home for 3 months, plus last 3 years of ownership:	32,500
Relief for letting restricted to lowest of:	
Gain exempt as main residence period: £32,500;	
Actual letting period: 8 years × £10,000; and	
£40,000	32,500
Net gain chargeable:	65,000

Dependent relative relief

12.11   This relief is now seldom encountered in practice, although it is very valuable where it applies. The requirements are that, on or before 5 April 1988, an interest in a dwelling house or part of a dwelling house owned by the taxpayer was the sole residence of a dependent relative of that taxpayer and was provided rent free and without any other consideration (*TCGA 1992, s 226*). For this purpose, 'dependent relative' means:

- any relative of the taxpayer or of his spouse or civil partner who is incapacitated by old age or infirmity from maintaining himself; or

- the mother of the taxpayer or spouse or civil partner who, whether or not incapacitated, is widowed or living apart from her husband, or who is a single woman in consequence of dissolution or annulment of marriage.

Relief is available only if claimed. If allowed, the property occupied by the relative is treated as if it had been the only or main residence of the taxpayer for as long as the dependent relative lived there and regardless of the fact that the taxpayer may have had another residence qualifying for relief. There is further apportionment, so that a period of ownership after the property ceases to be the sole residence of the dependent relative is disregarded and qualifies for no relief. The taxpayer may claim relief in respect of only one such occupied property at a time.

The chief difficulty in making a claim to this relief is likely to be proof of occupation. Arrangements between family members may have been informal. It may be difficult to show that the residence was 'provided' by the taxpayer, particularly where part of the funding of the residence arose on the sale of the relative's home and the whole scheme was intended to save the relative's estate from IHT or care fees.

Employer buys the home

12.12   When an employee is required to relocate to work in a new area, the employer may provide assistance by reimbursing the employee's relocation costs. The benefit provided in this way is free of income tax and National Insurance for up to £8,000 of costs incurred per move (*ITEPA 2003, s 217*). For further details, see *Income Tax 2013/14* (Bloomsbury Professional).

As part of the relocation, the employer may agree to buy the employee's home, so the employee has the capital available to purchase a new home in the new area. In some cases, the employer (or a company acting on behalf of the employer) and employee enter a 'home purchase agreement', under which they agree to share any profit made on the disposal of the old home when it is eventually sold to a third party. In this situation, CGT relief is given to the employee on his share of the profit under that agreement, as long as the following conditions are met (*TCGA 1992, s 225C*):

- the old home must have been the individual's main residence;

- the disposal of that property (the initial disposal) occurs in consequence of the individual's (or his or her co-owner's) relocation, as required by that person's employer;

- the initial disposal is under a home purchase agreement;

- the individual receives profit under the home purchase agreement within three years of the initial disposal; and

- that profit would be taxable under *TCGA 1992, s 22* (see **2.12**).

Under *TCGA 1992, s 225C*, the gain is treated as being part of the gain accruing on the initial disposal of the individual's home but accruing at the time the capital sum under the home purchase agreement is received. As a result, the profit share under the home purchase agreement will generally be exempt from CGT to the extent that the gain on the initial disposal was itself exempt (CG64611).

EXTENT OF THE PROPERTY

The 'curtilage' of the dwelling house

12.13   The 'curtilage' is a legal concept which helps define the extent of the dwelling house, whether it includes outbuildings etc. In layman's terms, the sundry buildings that obviously 'go with' the house, the part that, if the layman had to describe the extent of the property, he would not treat such parts as extra or needing specific mention. The curtilage is the house, not the grounds.

HMRC are clear that, to be part of an entity making up the dwelling house, the other buildings must have a residential purpose and not be stables or barns (CG64245–CG64260).

The 'permitted area'

12.14   The CGT relief for the gain on a taxpayer's main residence extends to 'land which he has for his own occupation and enjoyment with that residence as its garden or grounds, up to the permitted area' *(TCGA 1992, s 222(1)(b))*. On the disposal of urban properties, there is usually little difficulty in claiming that the whole of the gain realised on a residence should qualify for relief, but larger country properties can create difficulties.

The permitted area is defined as being an area, which includes the house, of up to 0.5 of a hectare (about 1.25 acres; see CG64815 for an explanation for this limit) being, in case of dispute, the part of the grounds that is 'the most suitable for occupation and enjoyment with the residence'.

Section 222(3) recognises that the size and character of a dwelling house may make some larger area than 0.5 of a hectare appropriate as 'required for the reasonable enjoyment of the dwelling house' or of the part of the dwelling house with which the transaction is concerned. There are many cases on the subject. It is possible that, over time, our perception of how much of this planet we should each occupy may have changed. Some of the earlier cases on 'permitted area' are redolent of a more leisured and spacious age. The phrase 'garden or grounds' in *s 222(1)(b)* carries its normal meaning: it is a question of fact.

Lewis v Lady Rook [1992] STC 171 is a good starting point, being of high authority. A woman had purchased an eight-bedroomed house. The land extended to over ten acres. There were two cottages, one of which she sold many years later. It had been occupied by a gardener and it stood 190 yards from the main house. When assessed on the gain, she appealed, claiming main residence relief.

The Court of Appeal held that the true test was whether the cottage was within the 'curtilage' of, and appurtenant to, the main property. For relief to be allowed, the cottage must be part of the entity which, together with the main house, constituted the dwelling house for the purposes of *s 222* as being occupied by the taxpayer as her main residence. The cottage was too far away from the main building. It was separated by a large garden. It was not part of the main residence.

Another example of the principle is *Longson v Baker* [2001] STC 6. The Longsons were keen on riding, so they purchased a property amounting to over 7.5 hectares which included a farmhouse, some stables and an outhouse. A building was added for use as a riding school. As part of a settlement between husband and wife, the interest in the property was transferred to the wife. It became necessary to decide the extent of the 'permitted area'. The husband argued that 'required' in *s 222(3)* meant 'called for', whereas the Inspector argued that it meant no more than 'necessary'. Thus, whilst it was certainly convenient for a family interested in riding to enjoy the whole of the land that was available, that was not actually necessary for the enjoyment of the property. The judge agreed with the Revenue, allowing relief only in respect of a much smaller area, observing that to hold otherwise might tend to encourage widespread interest in riding to shelter gains on properties with substantial amenities.

Land which is separated from a house may not be its garden or grounds, although HMRC recognise that cottage gardens may lie across the village street (CG64367).

Surplus land

12.15 If the taxpayer sells land which forms part of the grounds of his home, he will expect any gain to be covered by the exemption in *s 222*. This is the case if the land disposed of is within the permitted area. Then the relief in *s 222* automatically extends to all of the accompanying land, whether sold as one with the house or with a plot sold off separately. In such a case, the issue of 'surplus' land does not apply (CG64815), but the rule in *Varty v Lynes* [1976] STC 508 (see **12.16**) is still relevant.

Problems arise where the land associated with the house is larger than the permitted area, and it has been assumed that the larger area of land is required for the reasonable enjoyment of the house. If, in that case, a plot of surplus land is sold, HMRC may argue that the part sold was not needed for the enjoyment of the property, so the gain is not covered by the exemption in *s 222* (CG64832).

Example 12.4—Stable block conversion

Belinda lives in the Old Coach House, built in 1850 as part of a much more extensive property. The Old Coach House has 1 hectare of garden which includes a former stable block and access to a side road. Belinda secures planning permission to convert the stable block into a mews residence, which she sells with 0.25 of a hectare of land.

It is difficult for Belinda to resist the HMRC argument that, if she is now selling the stable block and a parcel of land, that land is not 'required for the reasonable enjoyment of the (retained) dwelling house'. Clearly, if Belinda goes on living at the Old Coach House, the land is not now so required. An argument may perhaps be advanced that times have changed. Originally, the Coach House itself was part of a much larger property. For most of the time that Belinda has owned it, properties in that area have enjoyed large gardens and she has actually with her family occupied the whole property as a single unit. It is only recently, with changes in the locality, that it has been possible for her to obtain planning permission and, therefore, for most of her period of ownership of the stables, the requirements of *s 222* have been met.

Care should be taken where land exceeding the permitted area is owned before a residence is built on it. In *Henke and another v HMRC* [2006] STC (SCD) 561, the taxpayers bought 2.66 acres of land in 1982. In 1993, they built their main residence on part of the land. They later sold some of the land, on which houses were built. The taxpayers appealed against HMRC's refusal to allow main residence relief on the whole gain arising from the disposal of the land. The Special Commissioner considered that the permitted area should extend to 2.03 acres, based on the circumstances at the time of disposal. It was also held that, because the land was owned for a period before the house was built, main residence relief should be apportioned (under *s 223(2)*), as the 'throughout the period of ownership' requirement in *s 223(1)* was not satisfied (see **12.17**).

The problem of the residual building plot

12.16   A common pitfall is illustrated by the case of *Varty v Lynes* [1976] STC 508. In that case, Mr Lynes sold his home and retained part of the garden which he sold at a later date. The High Court found that the relief in *s 222* could not apply to the later sale of the garden, as at the date of the sale it was no longer part of the residence occupied by Mr Lynes. The wording in *TCGA 1992, s 222(1)(b)* is precise in distinguishing the house from its grounds on this point (CG64377).

Example 12.5—Sale of land delayed

Charles owned and occupied a large property with a five hectare plot. He obtained planning permission for a single dwelling on the plot. He then put both his home and the plot with planning permission on the market. In the end, the contracts for sale of his former house were exchanged before the sale of the adjoining plot. Any gain on the sale of the house itself, after apportionment, is covered by main residence relief.

Unfortunately for Charles, in general there can be no CGT relief on the eventual sale of the plot. It would have been better for Charles to have sold the house and the plot together but with the benefit of the planning permission.

HMRC are prepared to relax the strict rule in CG64377 where all the land was formerly occupied as garden, and the land is disposed of between the date the contracts are exchanged on the house and the contracts are completed with conveyance of the house to the new owner. In that situation, the relief under *s 222* is given in respect of the land sold separately, but not if the land is sold after conveyance of the former home (CG64385).

PERIODS OF RESIDENCE

12.17   To benefit from the relief in *s 222*, the dwelling house must be the taxpayer's only or main residence throughout the period of ownership, or except for any or all of the last 36 months (*TCGA 1992, s 223(1)*). If the property is not occupied as the residence, or deemed to be occupied, for the entire period of ownership, some apportionment of the gain is required between parts that are exempt and parts that are not.

There are also a number of concessions and reliefs relating to the period of ownership and occupation, which are discussed below.

Delay in taking up occupation

12.18 HMRC will, under concession ESC D49, ignore a short delay in taking up occupation, when considering whether *s 222* relief applies to the full gain on disposal of the property. There are three circumstances in which ESC D49 may apply:

(a) the taxpayer has acquired land and is having a house built on the land;

(b) the taxpayer has acquired a property, but alterations and decorations are being carried out before the taxpayer occupies that property; or

(c) the taxpayer has acquired a property, but has remained in occupation of his former home until that can be sold or disposed of.

Provided that the delay is no more than one year, this period of non-residence is treated as if it were a period of residence. If a taxpayer needs more than one year, he may have a second year if there are good reasons for delay which are outside the control of the taxpayer. If, however, the individual fails to move into the property within the period of one year (or two if extended), no relief will be given at all for that period of non-occupation. In all cases, the new property must become the taxpayer's only or main residence. If effective occupation of the new property is never achieved, the relief will not be due (CG65003). There may be overlap between the period of deemed occupation under this concession and relief on another property in respect of the same period.

> **Example 12.6—Relocation plans undermined**
>
> David lives in Warwick. He buys a scruffy house in Markfield, Leicestershire, with a view to renovating it and living there because it will be near his work. In fact, the property suffers from mining subsidence that was not revealed before the purchase and the renovation takes 18 months.
>
> Meanwhile, David has been promoted by his employers, so Markfield will no longer be convenient for him. The house in Warwick has increased in value, as has that in Markfield. If David had moved into the renovated house, the delay would not prejudice relief because it was not his fault.
>
> If he decides simply to sell the house in Markfield without taking up occupation, the whole of the gain will be taxable. It might have been better for him to consider the possibilities that are discussed below in connection with owning two or more residences. As will be seen below, an election in relation to residences need not be permanent. Even a short period of residence at Markfield may serve to bring David within ESC D49.

Last 36 months

12.19   Homeowners may experience significant delays in finding purchasers, whilst personal circumstances compel them to move and to acquire a new residence before disposing of the old. Recognising this, *TCGA 1992, s 223(2) (a)* has the effect that, provided the taxpayer has been resident in the dwelling house at some point in his period of ownership, the last 36 months of ownership will qualify to be treated as a period of ownership 'in any event'. Apart from that, the basic rule is that main residence relief is calculated on a time-apportionment basis and is allowed in respect of periods of ownership but not of periods of absence.

Example 12.7—Last 36 months

Evan bought a property 'ripe for renovation' on 1 January 2009. He undertook the renovation work himself, which took until 31 March 2011. He occupied the property as his main residence from 1 April 2011 to 31 December 2012. He sold it on 31 March 2013 at a good profit, even after deducting the cost of the improvements.

Evan does not benefit from ESC D49 because the improvements took more than two years. He qualifies for main residence relief from 1 April 2011 to 31 March 2013 under general principles, giving him relief in respect of ownership of 24 months out of 51. However, by virtue of *s 223(2)(a)*, main residence relief will be allowed in respect of 36 months out of 51.

'Sandwich' reliefs

12.20   A person may be unable to continue to live at a property throughout his period of ownership, but such periods of absence can be deemed to be periods of occupation under *TCGA 1992, s 223(3)*. For *s 223(3)* to apply, the dwelling house must have been the only or main residence of the taxpayer both before and after the period of absence, ie sandwiched between periods of genuine occupation. If that condition is satisfied, the following periods of absence will be treated as if they were periods of occupation:

- Any length of time during all of which the taxpayer worked outside the UK (*TCGA 1992, s 223(3)(b)*).

- A period, up to four years, or periods together not exceeding four years, during which the taxpayer could not live at the residence because of where he was working or as a result of any condition imposed by his employer that required him to live elsewhere. The condition must have been reasonable to secure the effective performance of his duties by the employee *(TCGA 1992, s 223(3)(c))*. Also, where the taxpayer did not occupy the property as he or she was living with their spouse or civil partner who was working away and met the conditions of *s 223(3)(c)*.

- Any other period of absence up to three years, or periods together not exceeding three years *(TCGA 1992, s 223(3)(a))*.

Focus

A period of absence can only be deemed to be a period of occupation if the taxpayer had no other residence or main residence eligible for relief under *s 222* for that period *(TCGA 1992, s 223(7))*.

Example 12.8—Home from abroad

Frances worked in the gas industry and, on 1 January 2005, purchased a property in Bacton, Norfolk where she lived until 31 December 2005. She was then seconded to Aberdeen, working there until 31 December 2007; then she was seconded to Norway, where she worked until 31 December 2008. Tiring of life on gas rigs, Frances took an extended holiday from 1 January 2009 to 31 December 2011, returning to Bacton and living there from 1 January 2012 to 30 June 2013, when she sold the property at a profit.

The whole of the gain qualifies for relief. There are periods of residence to satisfy the 'sandwich' requirement. The period in Scotland is two years, less than the maximum stipulated by *s 223(3)(c)*. Frances worked for the whole of the year she lived in Norway, so the absence therefore complied with *s 223(3)(b)*. The extended holiday of two years is less than the maximum stipulated by *s 223(3)(a)*.

Job-related accommodation

12.21 Apart from the provisions of *s 223* treating a period of absence as if it were a period of residence, there is a separate rule under *s 222(8)* which can help the taxpayer. If a property or part of it has been purchased with the intention that it should eventually be a residence, but the owner for the time being lives in job-related accommodation, the owner is deemed to occupy the property. It does not matter that the house is never, in fact, occupied, provided that the intention to occupy can be proved (CG64555).

Example 12.9—Getting away from work

Gemma is a prison officer on a low salary. She purchases at auction a terraced property in poor condition which is occupied by a tenant who is entitled to remain at the property for the rest of his life. Gemma meanwhile is required by the terms of her employment to live onsite, though not always at the same secure establishment.

The tenant dies. Gemma is still employed as a prison officer but uses her holidays to renovate the property. That takes time and it is seven years from the date of the purchase before Gemma is actually able to start to use the property as her home when she is on leave. Although she has always intended to use the property as her home, a change in her circumstances involves a move to a completely different part of the country and she sells the property.

She can show that she always intended, once the property was available and fit for her use, to occupy it as her only or main residence. She can also show, in compliance with s 222(8A) and following, that her accommodation with the prison service is job related (see **12.22**).

Accommodation is job-related where a person or his spouse or civil partner has some kind of work, whether employed or self-employed, that meets the conditions set out in **12.22** or **12.23**.

Employee

12.22   If accommodation is provided by reasons of the taxpayer's employment, or the taxpayer's spouse's or civil partner's employment, there are three sets of circumstances in which the accommodation is job related (*TCGA 1992, s 222(8A)(a)*):

- it is necessary for the proper performance of the work to live in specific accommodation;

- it is provided by the employer for the better performance by the employee of his duties and it is customary in that trade or employment to provide living accommodation for employees; or

- it is provided as part of special security arrangements, as there is a special threat to the security of the employee.

Anti-avoidance rules apply where a company provides the accommodation to an employee, and that employee is a director of that company or of an associated company. In this situation, a person might artificially create job-related accommodation for his own benefit, so the provisions as to job-related accommodation for employees described at **12.21** will not apply, unless two further conditions are satisfied (*TCGA 1992, s 222(8B)*):

(1)   the employee/director has no material interest in the company, and

(2)   one of the following sub-conditions is satisfied:

– the taxpayer is a full-time working director;

– the company is non-profit making, meaning that it does not carry on a trade or hold investments; or

– the company is a charitable company.

Self-employed

12.23   Where the taxpayer, his spouse or civil partner is self-employed, the self-employed worker's contract must be at arm's length. Two conditions must be satisfied (*TCGA 1992, s 222(8A)(b)*):

• the worker is required as part of the contract to carry on the work on premises that are provided by another person (who may, but need not, be the other party to the contract); and

• it is a term of the contract that the contractor should live on those premises or on some other premises provided by the other party to the contract.

To avoid abuse, relief in respect of job-related accommodation for a self-employed person described at **12.21** is not available where the living accommodation is wholly or partly provided by certain entities that have a link to the taxpayer. In *TCGA 1992 s 222(8C)*, the person who would otherwise claim relief is described as 'the borrower'. The relief will not apply where the accommodation has been provided either by a company in which the borrower or his spouse or civil partner has a material interest; or by anyone who, together with the borrower or his spouse or civil partner, carries on any trade or business in partnership.

These provisions as to job-related accommodation were tightened up by *FA 1999*. The references to matters such as 'employment', 'director', 'full-time working director' and 'material interest' are taken from *ITEPA 2003*. The changes relate to residence on or after 6 April 1983.

TWO OR MORE RESIDENCES

12.24   This is probably the area of main residence relief that gives the most difficulties and perhaps spawns more negligence claims against tax advisers than the rest of the main residence relief code. An individual living with his spouse or civil partner can have only one main residence for both of them as long as they are living together (*TCGA 1992, s 222(6)*).

Where the taxpayer has two or more residences, the taxpayer may nominate, by notice to HMRC, which of those residences is to be treated as his main residence for the purposes of *TCGA 1992, s 222*. A couple must nominate a residence jointly. If no action is taken by the taxpayer to nominate a residence as the main residence, the question of which property is the main residence is one of fact (CG64485).

In *Fox v Stirk, Ricketts v Registration Officer for the City of Cambridge* [1970] 3 All ER 7, Lord Denning observed that a man may have 'a flat in London and a house in the country. He is resident in both'.

Example 12.10—Home for the weekend

Ian, a VAT consultant, has a home at Empingham, overlooking Rutland Water, but the main demand for his services is from construction companies based in North London. He buys a studio flat in Hendon for use during the week. He and his family spend as much time as possible in Empingham and the minimum time in Hendon. On the balance of the facts, the property in Rutland is his main residence.

Nomination of a property as the main residence

12.25   Where a taxpayer has two or more properties that he could call home, *TCGA 1992, s 222(5)(a)* provides that, within two years of the date on which the second or subsequent residence was available to him, he may give notice to HMRC identifying which property is his main residence. Note that it is not the date of acquisition of a second or subsequent property which triggers the need for this notice, but the date the second property is first used as a residence (CG64495).

The taxpayer does not have to nominate the property which has the greatest use as a residence, ie the one which is factually his main residence. The nomination can apply to any property which is actually a residence (CG64485).

HMRC suggest that a dwelling may not be nominated under *TCGA 1992, s 222(5)(a)* unless it is a 'residence' (see **12.3–12.7**) or deemed to be a residence (see **12.17–12.21**), since otherwise it is outside *s 222(1)* (CG64477).

Where the taxpayer is married or in a civil partnership, and living with that partner/spouse, the notice binds them both. The taxpayer has an opportunity to make or vary a notice each time another property becomes a residence, or from the date of a marriage/civil partnership, when the partner to the marriage already owns a residence (see **12.27**). This was established by the case of *Griffin v Craig-Harvey* [1994] STC 54.

The first notice applies from the date the individual had a particular combination of residences which created the need to make the notice. However, this date must not be more than two years before the date of the notice. There is no precise form of the notice, but it must be signed by the taxpayer and not by his agent (CG64520).

Focus

HMRC collect information from many sources concerning the ownership of properties, such as the Land Registry and estate agents.

HMRC may be aware that the taxpayer has more than one residence, even where nomination has not been made under *s 222(5)* for a property to be treated as the main residence (CG64208).

Example 12.11—Timeous notice

Jessica buys her first home, a city-centre flat near where she works, on 10 January 2008. On 1 July 2011 her aunt dies, leaving Jessica a cottage in the country. Jessica starts to use this cottage as a holiday home from 1 September 2011. Jessica has from 1 September 2011 to 31 August 2013 in which she may serve notice under *TCGA 1992, s 222(5)(a)* as to whether the flat or the cottage is to be treated as her main residence. If she does serve notice, the property notified is treated as Jessica's main residence, whether in fact she lives there for any appreciable time or not.

Difficulties for the taxpayer arise because it is not always possible to predict which of two properties will appreciate in value the most, and which the taxpayer will want to retain long term. Particular problems arise where, in fact, both properties will be sold.

Example 12.12—Overlap and sandwich reliefs

Returning to the example of Jessica, she gives notice to treat the cottage as her main residence from 1 September 2011 onwards. She serves the notice within the two-year period, and sells the flat on 31 December 2013.

The flat has not been treated as her main residence for over two years, but there is no reduction in relief because that period of absence falls within the last 36 months (discussed at **12.19**). In the event of a later sale of the cottage at a profit, the gain apportioned for the period from 1 September 2011 is relieved as well. The gain accruing for the two-month period before Jessica occupied the cottage is likely to be covered by her annual exemption.

Varying the notice

12.26   The taxpayer may vary a notice given under *TCGA 1992, s 222(5) (a)* by giving further notice. The statute does not require any minimum period during which a person must reside at a property in order to claim relief. However, the quality of occupation in the nominated property must be such as to constitute 'residence' (see **12.4**). The nomination may be varied to apply to a second home for very short period, even a few days, which will give that second home a CGT exemption for gain arising in respect of the last 36 months of ownership (CG64510). This is the process known as flipping, which has been reportedly used by a number MPs, who may be obliged to have homes in both central London and their constituency.

Example 12.13—Well-sheltered gains

Kylie bought Flat A on 1 January 2002. She bought a second property (Flat B) on 1 July 2003, which she let until 31 December 2007. On 1 January 2008, Kylie moved into Flat B, as it was bigger and in a better area. She kept Flat A and sometimes stayed there during the week, as it was closer to work. Kylie was thus occupying both flats as her residence from 1 January 2008. Both properties were appreciating in value, and Kylie gave notice to treat Flat B as her main residence with effect from 1 January 2008.

Financial difficulties forced Kylie to move back into Flat A and to let Flat B from 1 January 2009. She later varied the notice so as to treat Flat A as her residence again, with effect from 1 January 2009. Flat B was then let until its sale on 30 June 2013, realising a gain which is treated as accruing evenly over time (monthly, in this example).

Flat B has, both in fact and by virtue of the notice, been (for a time) Kylie's main residence. She has owned it for 120 months in all. During the first 54 months, the property was no more than an investment. For the whole of 2009, it was Kylie's main residence under the terms of the notice. For the last 36 months, the property is treated as her main residence under *s 223(1)*. The periods of letting may qualify for some relief under *s 223(4)*, because the property has been Kylie's main residence and it was let as residential accommodation.

As a result, 72/120ths of the gain on Flat B does not qualify for main residence relief, but the remaining 48/120ths of the gain is covered.

On the eventual sale of Flat A, main residence relief is available from 1 January 2002 to 31 December 2007 and from 1 January 2009 until sale. The period of non-residence (year of 2008) is sandwiched between two periods of residence and does not exceed three years. However, that year does not qualify as a period of absence under *s 223(3)(a)*, as Kylie had another property (Flat B) which was her main residence during that period (see **12.18**).

12.27 It is essential to file the notice under *TCGA 1992, s 222(5)* within the set two-year period and to submit any variation of that notice timeously.

Example 12.14—Filing the notices

Lucy and Greg are artists. They met whilst working in Cornwall where Lucy had bought a small studio on 5 January 2002, and Greg bought a cottage on 10 January 2003. Both their careers and their relationship flourished and, on 1 January 2008, they jointly bought a flat in Highgate, London and occupied it immediately. Thereafter they spent the summer months in Cornwall and the winter in London. They married on 31 March 2009, and at that date they each owned a property in Cornwall and an interest in the Highgate property.

Hurriedly completing tax returns for 2008/09, they each included a notice to treat Highgate as their main residence from the date they moved in. In April 2009, they wished to sell one of the Cornwall properties to reduce the mortgage on the Highgate property.

The notices were sent with the tax returns. Greg submitted his on 31 December 2009, so his notice is effective, as it is just within two years of acquiring an interest in a second residence. But Lucy submitted her tax return on 30 January 2010, so her notice for the Highgate property is, strictly speaking, out of time. Highgate has been Lucy's residence since 1 January 2008, so she should have lodged her notice at least one month earlier.

Due to their marriage on 31 March 2009, Lucy and Greg have another opportunity to nominate one of the three properties they own between them as their main residence. However, that nomination can only apply from the date of their marriage, not from the date they moved into the Highgate property (see **12.29**).

Licence or tenancy

12.28 It was originally thought that any residence, including one's club in London, could trigger the need for an election under *TCGA 1992, s 222(5)* but, since October 1994, HMRC advice has been to interpret *s 222(5)* purposively, within the context of that section as a whole. Since the relief relates to gains on property in which the taxpayer has a legal or equitable interest, it is not appropriate to consider notice of election where the second residence is merely occupied under licence and the taxpayer has neither a legal nor an equitable interest in it (CG64536).

Thus, in Example 12.14, the fact that Lucy might spend time at Greg's cottage would not of itself be reason to serve notice because, absent any agreement to the contrary, Lucy would have neither a legal nor an equitable interest in the cottage. HMRC's Capital Gains Manual (at CG64536) specifically confirms that no notice of election under *s 222(5)*, which relies on a residence occupied only under licence and which is made after 16 October 1994, will be regarded as valid. Clearly, therefore, Lucy in Example 12.14 cannot use Greg's cottage as a peg on which to hang a late election in respect of her studio.

ESC D21 addresses the issue of late claims in the very reasonable situation where a taxpayer becomes entitled to an interest in a second property without realising that, by so doing, time will begin to run against him or her under *TCGA 1992, s 222(5)(a)*. This could occur, for example, where a property is rented under a tenancy which has the legal effect of passing an interest in the property from the landlord to the tenant. A tenancy would thus be a residence under *TCGA 1992, s 222*.

There is an extension of the two-year time limit where:

- the interest in the second property – or in each property if there is more than one – has a negligible capital value on the open market; and

- the individual is unaware that a nomination could be made.

In each case, the nomination to treat the other property, being the one in which the taxpayer does have a substantial interest, as the main residence may be made within a reasonable time of when the taxpayer first became aware of a possibility of making an election, and it will be effectively backdated as far as is necessary.

Focus

Most residential accommodation is let under a short term licence rather than a tenancy.

A licence creates no interest in the land or building.

Marriage or civil partnership

12.29   Where each party to a relationship has a residence, each may claim main residence relief unless and until they begin to be treated as living together within the context of marriage or a civil partnership. There can be only one main residence for both parties to a marriage or a civil partnership by virtue of *TCGA 1992, s 222(6)(a)*. The married couple must therefore do the sums and decide which property is to be their main home. If they give notice in time, they can make the decision; otherwise, it will be based on the facts.

In Example 12.14, Lucy and Greg married on 31 March 2009, so they have two years from that date in which to decide whether their home together is to be Highgate, Lucy's Cornwall studio or Greg's Cornwall cottage (CG64525). Applying the rules relating to the last 36 months of ownership, they may decide to make sure that any property that is to be sold has been their main residence for a period so that, at the very least, the last 36 months of ownership qualify for relief.

When a property or an interest in a property is transferred between spouses (or civil partners) who are living together, the transfer is treated as taking place on a no gain, no loss basis (*TCGA 1992, s 58*). However, where an interest in the sole or main residence is transferred, the recipient spouse's period of ownership is deemed to commence at the date of the original acquisition by the transferor spouse, and not at the date of transfer of the interest between the spouses. Also, any period during which the property was the main residence of the transferor spouse is deemed to be that of the recipient spouse (*TCGA 1992, s 222(7)*).

In effect the transaction is completely backdated, so the spouse who receives the property effectively stands in the shoes of the transferor spouse, provided the following conditions are met at the date of transfer:

- the individuals are married to each other (or civil partners);
- they are living together; and
- the property in which the interest is transferred is the couple's sole or main residence.

Example 12.15—Transfer of interest

Continuing the example of Greg and Lucy above in Example 12.14, they nominate Greg's cottage to be their main residence from the date of their marriage on 31 March 2009. Greg gives Lucy a half share in that cottage on 10 April 2009, and they vary the notice under *s 222(5)* so that the Highgate property is once again their main residence from 5 July 2010. The cottage is sold on 5 July 2013.

When calculating the taxable gain on the disposal of the cottage, Lucy is regarded as owning the cottage from 10 January 2003, when Greg acquired it. The cottage is treated for tax purposes as the main residence of both Lucy and Greg from 10 January 2003 to 31 December 2007, and from 31 March 2009 to 4 July 2010. The last 36 months of ownership will also be free of CGT.

RESIDENCES HELD BY TRUSTEES OR PERSONAL REPRESENTATIVES

12.30   The general rule is that, where trustees hold residential property and a beneficiary is 'entitled to occupy it under the terms of the settlement', main residence relief will be available. Specifically, *TCGA 1992, s 225* operates by substituting a reference to the trustees for a reference to the individual in *ss 222–224* and by providing that a notice under *s 222(5)(a)*, where there is more than one residence, is to be a joint notice by the trustees and the beneficiary.

The enactment of *FA 2006* will, over time, limit the number of life interest settlements. However, the amendments introduced in *FA 2006, Sch 20* do not specifically refer to main residence relief. As will be seen at **12.32**, this change may affect a situation, which has given difficulty in the past, where IHT and CGT interact. In a straightforward case, the relief is valuable.

Example 12.16—Council house sold at a profit

In 1992, Norma was encouraged by her daughter Olive to buy the council house in which Norma had lived for many years. The open market value was £60,000 but Norma could buy it for £30,000. Olive agreed to help with the cost. Norma was advised that, if she entered into a deed of trust at the same time as buying the property, that would not contravene the restrictions on resale of council houses.

She therefore signed a declaration of trust, the first essential term of which was that she was entitled to live in the house and to any rents and profits of the house until sale or until her death, whichever should first occur. Subject to that prior interest, she declared herself trustee of the property for her only daughter Olive absolutely. The house was sold, many years later, for £180,000.

The gain was entirely sheltered by relief under *TCGA 1992, s 225* because Norma was entitled to occupy the residence under the terms of the settlement. Had the property been retained until Norma's death, relief would have been available not only under the provisions of main residence relief but, this being a pre-2006 situation, by virtue of the tax-free uplift on death allowed by *TCGA 1992, s 73(1)(a)*.

Discretionary trusts

12.31   Where a trust instrument gives the trustees a complete discretion over what benefit may be enjoyed by any of the objects of the trust, the effect is that, until the trustees take action, none of the beneficiaries actually has a right to any of the trust assets. This principle is seen in the rather specialist circumstances of *Judge and another (personal representatives of Walden, dec'd) v HMRC* (2005) SpC 506, which concerned the wording of a poorly drawn will where it was held, on the particular facts, that the widow of the testator did not have an interest in possession in the former matrimonial home. The result was that the house was not treated as part of her estate for IHT, which was the main point at issue; but the collateral consequence was that, if there had been any increase in the value of the property during her period of occupation since her husband's death, no relief was available under *TCGA 1992, s 225*, because she did not have a right to occupy as required by that section.

The correct treatment of gains arising to trustees of discretionary trusts on properties occupied as residences by beneficiaries was decided in *Sansom v Peay* [1976] STC 494. It had previously been thought that no beneficiary was entitled to occupy a dwelling house under the terms of the settlement, so as to benefit from *s 225*, unless the trust instrument specifically gave a right of occupation to that beneficiary.

The trust in *Sansom v Peay* was a discretionary one, allowing the trustees 'to permit any beneficiary to reside in any dwelling house or occupy any property or building ... for the time being subject to the trust hereof upon such conditions ... as the trustees ... think fit'. Beneficiaries occupied a trust property and it was held that the occupations resulted from the exercise by the trustees of their powers under the deed. When the beneficiaries moved into the house, they were entitled to stay there unless and until permission was withdrawn by the trustees. As at the date of the disposal of the house, the beneficiaries were still entitled to occupy it and were occupying it under the terms of the trust deed. The gain was therefore sheltered by main residence relief.

Nil rate band discretionary will trusts

12.32   The issue will commonly arise in the context of will trusts. For a full discussion of the IHT implications, please refer to *Inheritance Tax 2013/14* (Bloomsbury Professional). The issue has been relieved to a considerable extent by the introduction of the transferable nil rate band, but many situations still exist under the old rules that cannot be disturbed without significant IHT cost.

In outline, there are many families whose main wealth is the family home, the value of which exceeds the nil rate band for IHT (frozen at £325,000 until 2017/18). Under the law as it was before *FA 2008, s 10* and *Sch 4*, any transfer between husband and wife was exempt, which it still is; but, on the death of the survivor of them, any value in excess of the nil rate band attracted a charge to IHT at 40%. That has now changed, as the nil rate band for the first deceased can be transferred to the survivor. Formerly, with a view to using the nil rate band on the first death, wills used to be drawn which left value up to the nil rate band on discretionary trusts to beneficiaries including the surviving spouse, commonly with residue to that surviving spouse absolutely. The hope was that using the nil rate band on each death would combine to exempt the family property from IHT.

The argument ran that, where the house was occupied as tenants in common, each joint owner could occupy the entirety of it for the rest of their life, regardless of the fact that the other half of the property may have been given away. This argument was not always accepted by HMRC from the point of view of IHT. Circumstances might suggest that, even though the trustees were under no obligation to do so, they had actually so exercised their powers under the trust instrument that they had, in effect, created the situation that arose in *Sansom v Peay* and had therefore given the surviving spouse an interest in possession in the half of the property that that spouse did not own, with the result that, on the second death, the whole of the house becomes subject to IHT and the tax planning was thrown away.

Where the trustees could satisfy HMRC, from the standpoint of IHT, that in fact they had not exercised their powers in such a way as to grant the surviving spouse an interest in possession, the interest in the property that is held within the discretionary trust might escape IHT but, on any disposal of the property at a gain, CGT will become due because main residence relief is not available. Under the new rules, trustees will want to use their powers to create an immediate post-death interest in favour of the surviving spouse; but, if more than two years have elapsed since the death, that will be outside *IHTA 1984, s 144*, so the trustees must 'stick with' the original terms of the will.

Example 12.17—Hit for CGT but not for IHT

Percy was married to Prudence. Their house was worth £360,000 and held by them as tenants in common in equal shares. Percy died on 5 April 2001, having by his will left the nil rate band on discretionary trusts for the benefit of his children and Prudence. At the time of his death, the nil rate band was £234,000. His estate comprised the house and cash of £50,000, all of which passed to the trustees. There was no residue and no IHT was payable.

The trustees then held the half of the house on discretionary trusts, but took no steps to grant Prudence any right of occupation of it. On 17 May 2011, the house was sold and realised a gain of £140,000. On her share of the property, Prudence was able to take her gain tax free. The gain of £70,000 on half of the house within the discretionary trust is subject to CGT (after allowance for the reduced annual exemption available to the trustees).

On the death of Prudence shortly after the sale, the matter is reopened for IHT purposes, but it appears that the trustees have not handed over to her any part of the proceeds of sale that they received nor have they given Prudence benefit out of the trust fund. They insisted that she pay all outgoings, to save any burden on the small liquid trust fund. It also appears that they have met from time to time to consider their powers, so the trust has not just been 'in limbo'. The result for IHT purposes is that the estate of Prudence will be limited to her own share of the proceeds of sale of the house and to any other assets that she has, and will not be deemed to include the half share in the house that sits within the discretionary trust.

Example 12.18—Hit for IHT but not for CGT

Contrast the result in Example 12.17, where the trustees have either taken no steps at all since Percy's death or can be seen positively to have exercised their powers in favour of Prudence with regard to the house as, for example, taking unequivocal steps to show that they are unwilling to sell the house whilst Prudence is still alive, even though other beneficiaries are in urgent need of money.

In such a case, the argument by HMRC that Prudence effectively has an interest in possession in the half of the house that sits within the trust is very likely to succeed. The tax consequence is that, on the sale for a gain of £140,000, there will be no CGT. However, the trust fund, being the part that is represented by the share in the house rather than the cash, will be treated as aggregated with the estate of Prudence on her death. This may not create an IHT charge, as Prudence is likely to have the benefit of Percy's transferable nil rate band.

Disregarding expenses and the like, in the event of the death of Prudence at any time in the seven years after the time when her interest ceased, which will probably be the date of sale of the house, the value of the half of the house in the trust will be added to her free estate to establish the chargeable transfer on death.

The IHT charge, after taking account of the nil rate band (including any nil rate band from Percy) is at 40% of the capital value. The CGT charge would have been at 28%, but only on the gain and would have been subject to reliefs. It may be better to structure similar transactions so that the tax paid is CGT rather than IHT. The downside is, of course, that CGT becomes payable as soon as there is a disposal of the property, which is likely to reduce the money then available for alternative accommodation. The transfer rules for IHT will remove much of the difficulty, though many lawyers advise retaining the nil rate trust for other reasons, including defence of the estate from care-home fees.

Estates in administration

12.33 Sometimes there will be a substantial increase in the value of a dwelling house from the date of the death of its owner to the date on which the property can be sold. Delays can arise where there is a dispute about the terms of a will or where a claim is made under the *Inheritance (Provision for Family and Dependants) Act 1975* or where, quite simply, everything takes rather longer than it should.

Valuation issues

12.34 In the simple situation of a property that becomes vacant on death and is not thereafter occupied until sale, the normal rules will apply, as set out in **3.6**. Executors sometimes try to obtain valuations of a property at an artificially low level and hope that it can later be sold for much more and tax free.

That idea exhibits not only a cavalier attitude to the payment of tax, but some fundamental errors of tax law. First, there is no such thing as 'probate value', meaning some artificially low value approximating to the lowest price that anyone could accept in the open market further discounted by the costs of sale. The correct value for IHT purposes, as is explained in *Inheritance Tax 2013/14* (Bloomsbury Professional), is 'the price which the property might reasonably be expected to fetch if sold in the open market': see *IHTA 1984, s 160*. That value is, as a general rule, imported into the CGT code by *TCGA 1992, s 274*, which provides that, where the value at the date of death has been 'ascertained' for the purposes of IHT, that value is the market value of the asset at the date of death for CGT purposes, with the knock-on effect that, under *TCGA 1992, s 62*, it is the value at which the personal representatives are deemed to acquire the property as at the date of death of the deceased. From 6 April 2008, *TCGA 1992, s 274* only applies for the purpose of the application of IHT to the chargeable estate, not to the estate which, by virtue of the transferable nil rate band, escapes IHT.

Quick sale

12.35 If sale on the open market takes place quite soon after death, this is a strong guide as to market value at the earlier date. However, if the value is established as at the date of death on a proper basis and with full disclosure, and a substantial time elapses until sale, it will not be necessary to substitute the eventual sale price for the probate value at date of death.

In this context, some 'hope' value should be included in the value at date of death if there is, say, a potential building plot. The case of *Prosser v IRC* (DET/1/2000) suggests that hope value is no more than 25% of the full development value.

Example 12.19—IHT followed by CGT

Quentin died on 4 April 2013. His estate comprised his home and other assets that were exactly matched by liabilities. The fair open market value of the house at date of death was £335,000. The nil rate band at that date was £325,000, so IHT was payable of £4,000, being 40% of the excess. Probate is obtained quickly, and the property is sold on 3 August 2013 for £362,000 less expenses (inclusive of VAT) of 3%.

CGT is calculated as follows:

	£
Proceeds of sale less 3% expenses	351,140
Less probate value	(335,000)
Less allowance available under SP 2/04 (band C) at 1%	(3,350)
Gain after allowance	12,790
Deduct annual allowance*	(10,900)
Taxable gain	1,890
Tax at 28%	592

* This being a disposal within the tax year in which death occurred or one of the two years following, the executors may claim the full allowance of £10,900.

Ongoing residence by major beneficiary

12.36   On a death, the main asset of an estate may be a house that is given to an individual who was living with the property owner prior to death. The CGT arising on the disposal of such a property during the administration of the estate can be sheltered by *TCGA 1992, s 225A* if these two conditions are met:

(1)   Both before and after the death of the deceased, the property in question 'was the only or main residence of one or more individuals'.

(2)   The individual (or group of individuals) living in the property before and after the relevant death is entitled to at least three-quarters of the proceeds of sale of the property in question.

The entitlement to the property may thus be shared among several beneficiaries if they can all show that they were resident before and after the death and that they have a 'relevant entitlement', meaning an entitlement as a legatee of the person who has died or an entitlement to an interest in possession in the whole or some part of the net proceeds of the disposal of the house.

The 'net proceeds of disposal' are defined as the proceeds realised by the personal representatives less incidental costs as are allowable on computing the gain that would otherwise arise to the personal representatives (*TCGA 1992, s 225A(4)*). This assumes that no part of the proceeds of sale is needed to meet liabilities of the estate (including liability to IHT). Relief is available only if the personal representatives claim it.

Example 12.20—*Section 225A* not satisfied

Babette died on 9 July 2012, leaving a house worth £300,000 and net cash of £100,000 after all liabilities. Her niece Linda and her husband Jim moved in with Babette to look after her two years before she died. They continued to live in Babette's house after her death. Babette's will leaves her estate equally between Linda, who lives with her, and Linda's brother Victor.

Relief under *TCGA 1992, s 225* is not available. The estate benefits from the nil rate band of £325,000, but the excess (ie £75,000) attracts IHT of £30,000. The net estate to divide between Linda and Victor is £370,000, ie £185,000 each. Even though Linda and Jim might like to take the house, if necessary providing money by way of equalisation, they are outside the requirements of *TCGA 1992, s 225A(3)(b)* because their entitlement under the will is less than 75% of the proceeds of the disposal, if it were now to take place, of the house.

Example 12.21—A better solution

The facts are as in Example 12.20 except that Babette, in recognition of the care provided by her niece, had given Linda and her husband each a third of the residue, with her brother Victor taking the other third. On Babette's death, Victor would be entitled, net of IHT, to £123,333, whereas Linda and Jim between them would be entitled to £246,667. That is more than 75% of the value of the house, unless (somewhat unusually in the present market) it has risen substantially in value since the death. Relief may therefore be available.

Property as asset of beneficiary

12.37   Relief under *TCGA 1992, s 225A* is not very common because, in many circumstances, there will be a simpler solution. If the value of the estate is sufficient, and liquidity is available for a property in the estate to be transferred to a beneficiary outright, there will be no need for *s 225A* relief. The beneficiary will acquire the property as 'legatee' within the meaning of *TCGA 1992, s 64(3)* and will, on acquiring the property, step into the shoes of the personal representatives and be deemed to have acquired it at probate value. If that beneficiary then occupies the property, giving notice as appropriate if already the owner of another property, main residence relief will be available under general principles and there will be no need for *s 225A* relief.

However, the payment of IHT may be a problem. For an asset to be dealt with, and any gain realised, by the beneficiary in this way, the asset must first be placed unreservedly at the disposal of the beneficiary. Appropriation 'in book form', as sometimes suggested by exempt beneficiaries, is not in truth appropriation at all. The desire to avoid the trouble and fees involved in 'doing the job properly' can threaten the relief. In theory at least, the house could be assented to the beneficiary subject to a lien or charge in favour of the personal representatives for unpaid IHT, but that situation is far from ideal, especially in the light of the principles seen in *Howarth's Executors v IRC* [1997] STC (SCD) 162 relating to accountability of executors for tax after parting with estate assets. A compromise might be to assent to the vesting in the beneficiary of a share only in the house equal to the proportion that can be released free of any lien for tax. The rest of the gain would then sit (and be taxed) in the estate, but that might be better than tax on the whole gain and, in any case, the total exemption would increase.

HOLD-OVER OF GAIN UNDER SECTION 260

Washing the gain through a trust

12.38   Advisers need to be aware of the anti-avoidance provision in *TCGA 1992, s 226A*, which applies to transactions on or after 9 December 2003. The background to this legislation was the perceived abuse of 'washing the holiday cottage gain'. HMRC guidance on this anti-avoidance rule is found in CG65440–CG65447.

How it worked

12.39   A family owns a main residence and a country cottage which had been acquired cheaply many years earlier. The cottage has to be sold.

Commonly, the parents would settle the cottage on discretionary trusts, holding over the accrued gain under *TCGA 1992, s 260*. The tax planning required one of the children to be over the age of 18, and to be able to live in the cottage for a time.

Under one version of the scheme, the property would then be appointed out entirely to that child and the gain held over under *TCGA 1992, s 260*. The child would occupy the property as his or her main residence and soon afterwards sell it, claiming main residence relief on the gain that then arose. This gain would include the gain that had been held over on the transfer of the property into the trust and any further gain that had arisen since that event and was likewise held over, with the previous held-over gain, on removal of the property from the trust. Thus, within the space of a few months, the gain arising on the holiday cottage could be 'washed out'. The only disadvantage with this plan was that the entire proceeds of sale ended legally, if not actually, in the hands of the child.

A variant of the scheme involved the appointment by the trustees of an interest in possession in the cottage to the beneficiary child. Some time later, the trustees would sell the property and, because it had been the residence of a beneficiary entitled to occupy it under the terms of the settlement, part of the gain would be exempt under *s 225*. It did not matter too much that the trustees had not owned the property for very long; the period of ownership before the appointment of the life interest to the child would not qualify for main residence relief but, where the gain held over was substantial, the ability to shelter most of it by main residence relief made the exercise very worthwhile. Under this version, the money ended up in the 'right' place.

The statutory change

12.40   The 'gain washing' scheme was nullified by *TCGA 1992, s 226A*, which applies where:

- main residence relief would otherwise apply to a gain or part gain accruing to an individual or trustees on the eventual disposal of a property;

- on the later disposal, the amount of the gain would be reduced but for the effect of *TCGA 1992, s 223*; and

- the reduction would result, directly or indirectly, from a hold-over claim under *TCGA 1992, s 260* at an earlier stage in the arrangement.

Where a claim to hold over a gain under *s 260* was made on the earlier transaction (or any of them, if more than one), main residence relief is not available on the later disposal of the property. Where a hold-over claim is made under *s 260* after the later disposal of the property and the provision just described does not apply, it is to be assumed for the purposes of CGT that main residence relief was never available in relation to the gain or part gain arising on the later disposal. The relief, if claimed, is withdrawn and adjustments are made that give effect to the anti-avoidance legislation.

It is possible for the taxpayer to be wise after the event. Where a gain was held over under *TCGA 1992, s 260* and it now appears that it would have been better to have relied on main residence relief and to have paid the tax on the earlier gain, the earlier claim for hold-over relief can be revoked and, if revoked, it is as if the claim had never been made.

There are exceptions from *s 226A* in connection with maintenance funds for heritage property (*TCGA 1992, s 226B*).

Transitional relief

12.41   At the time of its introduction, *TCGA 1992, s 226A* was widely seen to be retrospective. The scheme described at **12.39** had been in quite common use, and it is fair to say that taxation advisers were taken by surprise. Their indignation, righteous or otherwise, was not really defused by the transitional provisions of *FA 2004, Sch 22, para 8*, inserting extra provisions into *s 226A*. The effect was to confer limited transitional relief where the held-over disposal occurred before 10 December 2003.

The residence in question was deemed not to have been the only or main residence of the individual from 10 December 2003, and any gain was apportioned between the time before that date and the time after. The gain that was time-apportioned included both the held-over gain and any later gain, even though all the held-over gain had accrued before 10 December 2003. The effect was that, unless action was taken very quickly after 10 December 2003 to ameliorate the situation, an increasing proportion of the gain fell into the tax net.

Effect of FA 2006

Trusts of houses

12.42   The subject of the *FA 2006* changes affecting settlements is discussed in **Chapter 8**. As the creation of a lifetime trust is generally a chargeable transfer for IHT, there are more opportunities to hold over gains under *TCGA 1992, s 260*. However, the ability to hold over a gain into a new trust is of limited value in the context of residences, as *TCGA 1992, s 226A* will undermine any useful planning, as discussed in **12.38–12.41**.

Other changes introduced by *FA 2006* may be relevant to trusts of houses, not because of main residence relief but because of those occasions where, on death, there is effectively a tax-free uplift. Thus, *TCGA 1992, s 72(1A)–(1C)* cuts down the availability of uplift on death so that it applies only to an immediate post-death interest (IPDI), a transitional serial interest (TSI), a bereaved minor's trust (BMT) or a disabled trust.

DIVORCE AND SEPARATION

No gain, no loss transfer

12.43 A common feature of the breakdown of marriage or of civil partnership is the disposal, by one party, of an interest in the residence that was formerly shared. Timing is everything, because a disposal between the parties that takes place within the tax year of separation is treated by *TCGA 1992, s 58* as if made on a no gain, no loss basis; whilst the more usual situation, where negotiations drag into the following or even a later year, triggers a disposal that may attract CGT.

Example 12.22—Swift divorce

Selena and Richard decide to divorce. They bought their flat for £500,000 on marriage, 75% with Selena's money, Richard taking a mortgage for the balance. It had been worth much more, but thanks to the recession is worth only £800,000 on 31 December 2012.

Richard leaves the flat. Selena pays him £200,000 to go, completing the arrangement on 31 March 2013. This is treated as the disposal by Richard of his share to Selena for £125,000 and his true gains of £75,000 are sheltered, not by main residence relief but by *TCGA 1992, s 58*. Selena is treated as acquiring Richard's share at an undervalue, but that does not worry her: even if she later sells that share of the flat for more than the deemed acquisition value of £125,000, that gain will be sheltered by main residence relief.

Example 12.23—Usual situation on divorce

Jenny and Paul bought their house for £175,000 in July 2009. They drifted apart and finally separated in October 2012. Negotiations became bitter, and finance for any settlement from any commercial lender became impossible by March 2013.

With help from her parents, Jenny bought Paul's half share in May 2013 for £100,000, after allowing for the mortgage. The transaction is at market value anyway, but would be treated as taking place at that value by *TCGA 1992, ss 17* and *18* because Jenny and Paul are connected persons. Paul has made a gain of £12,500. However, after apportioning this over his period of ownership and claiming exemptions, Paul's gain escapes tax.

Mesher orders

12.44 *Section 225B* (formerly Extra-statutory Concession D6) recognises that money may well be tight and that divorce may result in a *Mesher* order, so-called from the 1980 case of that name, under which the house remains in the ownership of both parties and is not sold until the children are grown up. However, this will apply only to shelter a 'solo' gain; so, if the 'dispossessed' party later acquires another residence, the relief is curtailed (CG65365).

Example 12.24—Life moves on

Ginny and Peter were in a similar situation to Jenny and Paul (in Example 12.23), except that Ginny's parents could not help finance the arrangement and, in any case, there was a daughter, Emily, aged seven. They therefore agreed that the house would continue to be owned by them jointly as a home for Ginny and Emily until Emily turns 18.

At around the time that Emily is 18, Ginny's friend, Gordon, moves in. Emily soon moves out and, after some difficulty, Gordon buys Peter's share of the house for much more than Peter paid for it. Peter has been in rented accommodation so has had no alternative residence. *TCGA 1992*, s *225B* gives Peter main residence relief on the whole of his gain, even though for several years he has not been living at the house.

The situation is more complicated where the non-resident spouse has in fact acquired another residence and has elected to treat it as his main residence. Relief under *TCGA 1992, s 225B* does not, under its terms, then apply. *Section 225B* does not refer to any form of apportionment.

Strictly, HMRC regard the *Mesher* arrangement as creating a settlement of the entire house and therefore a disposal to the trustees, which is an occasion of charge under *TCGA 1992, s 70*. Thus the interest of the trustees is exempt, not under *TCGA 1992, s 222* but under *TCGA 1992, s 225*. When the deemed trust expires, as at Emily's eighteenth birthday in the previous example, there is a deemed disposal by the trustees. The share of each spouse attracts a charge under *TCGA 1992, s 71* because each now becomes absolutely entitled to a share as against the (deemed) trustees, but the entire gain qualifies for main residence relief under *TCGA 1992, s 225*. However, if there had, in a situation such as the example quoted above, been no Gordon but there had been a delay in selling after Emily was 18, any gain that might arise could attract tax.

For houses of moderate value, the *Mesher* order often works well, but it is a settlement for IHT purposes; so, where the values are high, the parties may seek other structures, such as charges over the property in favour of the non-resident party.

Chapter 13

Hold-over relief for gifts

SIGNPOSTS

- **Forms of hold-over relief** (see **13.1**).

- *Section 165* **relief** – Conditions, exceptions, qualifying assets (see **13.2–13.5**).

- **Operation of** *s 165* **relief** – How it is deducted, consideration received, partial relief and definitions (see **13.6–13.14**).

- **Special situations** – When IHT has been paid, on separation or divorce, for trust disposals, when the asset is agricultural property, and on incorporation of a business (see **13.15–13.19**).

- **Where relief is denied or clawed back** – For gifts to non-residents, settlor-interested trusts, dual-resident trusts, foreign-controlled companies, shares to companies, on disposal of QCBs and when the donee emigrates (see **13.20–13.34**).

- *Section 260* **relief** – Conditions, operation, consideration received, partial relief, where IHT is paid (see **13.35–13.40**).

- **Where relief is denied or clawed back** – On gifts to non-residents, or on emigration (see **13.41–13.42**).

- **Claims and valuation issues** – How to claim for either relief, interaction with other reliefs, valuations and Statement of Practice 8/92 (see **13.43–13.47**).

FORMS OF HOLD-OVER RELIEF

13.1   The gift of a chargeable asset, or the sale of a chargeable asset 'otherwise than at arm's length' (see **13.2**), is treated for CGT purposes as a disposal at market value. See **3.6** regarding the market value rule (but note the special rules explained at **3.63** for transfers between spouses and civil partners). The person acquiring the asset is treated as acquiring it at its market value.

Two forms of hold-over relief are available to defer the CGT liability until there is a disposal by the transferee:

(a)   hold-over relief for gifts of business assets under *TCGA 1992, s 165* (see **13.2–13.34**); and

(b)   hold-over relief under *TCGA 1992, s 260* for gifts on which inheritance tax is either immediately chargeable, or not chargeable because of a particular exemption (see **13.35–13.40**).

The relief in (b) takes precedence over the relief in (a). A more detailed discussion of both of these reliefs can be found in *Capital Gains Tax: Roll-over, Hold-over and Deferral Reliefs 2013/14* (Bloomsbury Professional). Guidance on CGT and gifts which includes hold-over relief is given in HMRC's Capital Gains Manual at CG66450–CG67360.

Certain gifts are exempt from CGT (see **1.8**), so that hold-over relief is not necessary. Where neither an exemption nor any form of hold-over relief applies, it may be possible for the CGT due on the gift to be paid in instalments (see **3.34**). If the transferor does not pay the tax, it may be recovered from the transferee under *TCGA 1992, ss 281, 282* (see **1.4**).

GIFTS OF BUSINESS ASSETS (SECTION 165)

13.2   Where an individual (or a trustee in some cases, see **13.17**) disposes of an asset otherwise than under a bargain at arm's length, any gain accruing may be deferred where the conditions in *TCGA 1992, s 165* are met. The amount held over reduces the transferee's acquisition (or base) cost used in calculating the gain on the subsequent disposal of the same asset. The capital gain is, in effect, transferred to the person who receives the asset.

'Otherwise than under a bargain at arm's length' encompasses outright gifts, and sales which include some gratuitous intention on behalf of one of the parties, so will generally be at less than market value. HMRC regard a bargain as made at arm's length if it is a normal commercial transaction and all the parties involved try to obtain the best deal for themselves in their particular circumstances (CG14541).

The date of an outright gift is the date on which it becomes effective. The date of a sale at a price below market value is, broadly, the date of the contract – see **2.8** regarding the time of a disposal.

Conditions

13.3   Hold-over relief is generally available where:

(a)   an individual ('the transferor') makes a disposal otherwise than under a bargain at arm's length of an asset mentioned in **13.5**;

(b)   both the transferor and the person acquiring the asset ('the transferee') make a claim to relief (see **13.43**); and

(c)   the transferee is UK resident (see **13.20**).

There is no requirement for the transferee to join in the claim if the transferee is the trustee (or a body of trustees) of settled property (*TCGA 1992, s 165(1)*).

Exceptions

13.4   Relief is not available:

- where relief would be available under *TCGA 1992, s 260* (see **13.35**);
- on a transfer of shares or securities to a company (see **13.26**);
- where the transfer is to a foreign-controlled company (see **13.24**);
- where the transfer is to a dual-resident trust (see **13.25**);
- where the transfer is into a settlor-interested trust (see **13.28**); or
- where a gain is deemed to accrue on the disposal of qualifying corporate bonds which were acquired in exchange for shares (see **13.27**).

Qualifying assets

13.5   An asset may be the subject of a hold-over relief claim if it falls within one of (a)–(d) below:

(a)   an asset, or an interest in an asset, used for the purposes of a trade, profession or vocation (henceforth referred to as a 'trade'), carried on by:

- the transferor (either alone or in partnership): or
- his personal company;
- a member of a trading group whose holding company is his personal company (*TCGA 1992, s 165(2)*);

(b)   shares or securities of a trading company, or of the holding company of a trading group, where either:

- the trading company or holding company is the transferor's personal company: or
- the shares or securities are not listed on a recognised stock exchange (shares listed on the alternative investment market (AIM) being regarded as not listed) (*TCGA 1992, s 165(2)*);

(c)   farmland and buildings that would be eligible for inheritance tax agricultural property relief (see **13.18**); or

(d)   certain settled property disposed of by the trustees of a settlement (see **13.17**).

HMRC regard the condition in (a) as meaning that the asset has to have been in use for the trade etc just before it was gifted (CG66950). See **13.8** regarding partial relief where an asset other than shares has not been used wholly for the purposes of the trade during the entire period of ownership.

OPERATION OF TCGA 1992, S 165 RELIEF

How it is deducted

13.6   The effect of this relief, which must be claimed (see **13.43**), is that the 'held-over gain' (see below) is deducted from both:

● the chargeable gain (if any) that would otherwise accrue to the transferor; and

● the consideration which the transferee would otherwise be regarded as having given for the acquisition of the asset (or the shares or securities) (*TCGA 1992, s 165(4)*).

The 'held-over gain' on a disposal, where this relief is not restricted by reference to actual consideration received for the disposal, is the chargeable gain that would have accrued in the absence of hold-over relief (*TCGA 1992, s 165(6)*). The relief may be restricted where consideration is received (see **13.7**) or as described in **13.8**. See **13.45** regarding the interaction between hold-over relief and other CGT reliefs including entrepreneurs' relief and taper relief.

Example 13.1

Anthony has carried on a business as a sole trader since June 2001. His only chargeable asset is goodwill, which is now worth £150,000, although he paid only £10,000 for it.

He gives the business to Ziva in August 2013, and they jointly claim hold-over relief under *TCGA 1992, s 165*. There is no actual consideration, so the whole of the gain accruing is held over. Anthony's gain of £140,000 is therefore reduced to nil, and Ziva's allowable expenditure on any future disposal is reduced from £150,000 to £10,000.

Example 13.2

Barnaby purchased shares in Beach Plc, a company quoted on AIM, in May 1999 for £50,000. In September 2009, when they are worth £160,000, he settles the shares in a discretionary trust which is not settlor-interested (see **13.28**). Barnaby claims hold-over relief.

The held-over gain is £110,000 and the trustees' allowable expenditure is reduced from £160,000 to £50,000. The trustees sell the shares for £180,000 in April 2013. The gain accruing on this disposal by the trustees is £180,000 – £50,000 = £130,000.

Consideration received

13.7   It may be difficult to ascertain whether consideration has been received where the transaction has involved an exchange of assets. Where land subject to a mortgage is transferred, and the transferee takes on responsibility for the mortgage, the amount of debt outstanding at the date of the transfer is treated as the actual consideration.

Where there is actual consideration for the disposal the calculation of the held-over gain becomes:

- the 'unrelieved gain' on the disposal (ie the chargeable gain that would have accrued in the absence of hold-over relief), *less*

- the excess of the actual consideration for the disposal over the allowable deductions (under *TCGA 1992, s 38*) in computing the gain (*TCGA 1992, s 165(7)*).

Where the value of the actual consideration does not exceed the allowable deductions, no adjustment is necessary.

Example 13.3

The facts are as in Example 13.1, but Ziva pays Anthony £40,000 for the goodwill. The held-over gain becomes £110,000:

Anthony's gain	£	*Gain* £
Unrelieved gain		140,000
less		
consideration received	40,000	
less allowable expenditure on the goodwill	(10,000)	
		(30,000)
Held-over gain		110,000

Anthony's gain is reduced from £140,000 to £30,000 (being the consideration received less his allowable expenditure), and Ziva's allowable expenditure on any future disposal is £150,000 – £110,000 = £40,000.

Partial relief

13.8   Hold-over relief is restricted if the asset transferred has not been used wholly for the purposes of the trade during the entire period of ownership. This restriction also applies if a building is transferred and part was used for the trade and part was not (see **13.10**).

The rules are different where the asset transferred is shares or securities in a trading company or holding company of a trading group. In this case, the gain eligible for hold-over relief may be restricted if the company's chargeable assets include non-business assets (see **13.11**).

Asset not used for trade throughout period of ownership

13.9   If the asset was not used for the purposes of the trade throughout the transferor's period of ownership, the held-over gain is reduced by multiplying it by the fraction A/B, where:

* A is the number of days in that period of ownership during which the asset was used for the trade; and

* B is the number of days in the entire period of ownership.

There is no restriction under this rule where the asset would qualify for inheritance tax agricultural property relief (see **13.18**).

Focus

HMRC have confirmed that:

* Period A can include periods where the asset was used by different entities, such as a sole trader and a company; and

* Period B should ignore any part of the ownership that falls before 31 March 1982.

Partial use for the trade of a building or structure

13.10   If the asset disposed of is a building or structure, and during the transferor's period of ownership (or any 'substantial part' of that period) only a part of the building or structure was used for the purposes of the trade, the gain is apportioned on a just and reasonable basis and only the fraction of the gain apportioned to the part of the building so used is held over. Again, there is no restriction where the asset would qualify for inheritance tax agricultural property relief.

Where both this restriction and the time restriction in **13.9** are appropriate, HMRC consider that the time restriction should be applied first (*TCGA 1992, Sch 7, paras 4, 6*; CG66952).

Example 13.4

Julian bought a shop, with a flat above, for £180,000. He gave the property to his son James five years later, having used the shop for the purpose of his trade throughout the last three years of ownership. Market values at the time of the gift are agreed at £660,000 for the whole property and £220,000 for the shop. The proportion of Julian's gain which is available for hold-over relief is calculated as follows:

		£	£	£
Gain on whole property	660,000 – 180,000			480,000
Time restriction for allowable gain	3/5 years × 480,000		288,000	
Partial business use restriction (value of shop to value of whole building):	220/660 × 288,000		96,000	
Total held-over gain				(96,000)
Chargeable gain:				384,000

If the period of non-business use had occurred at the end of Julian's ownership period, HMRC would challenge Julian's right to make the hold-over claim, on the basis that the asset was not in use in the trade just before it was transferred (CG66950).

This business use requirement is not interpreted so strictly for roll-over relief claims, where business use of the asset can cease before the transfer date (see **14.30**).

Shares: restriction for chargeable non-business assets

13.11   Where the disposal consists of shares or securities in the transferor's personal company (see **13.12**), you may have to look through the company veil to the chargeable assets held by the company at the time of the disposal. This restriction can also apply where the transferor was able to exercise at least 25% of the voting rights of that company, both at any time within 12 months of the disposal date (*TCGA 1992, Sch 7, para 7*).

The held-over gain on the disposal of the shares is reduced by multiplying it by the fraction A/B, where:

- A is the market value of the company's (or group's) 'chargeable assets' that are 'business assets' (see definitions below); and

- B is the market value of all the company's (or group's) chargeable assets including non-business assets.

In both cases, the market value is taken at the date of the disposal. For the purpose of this restriction, an asset is a business asset if it is used for the purposes of a trade, profession or vocation carried on by the company (or member of the group). An asset is a chargeable asset if, on a disposal of it, a gain accruing to the company (or member of the group) would be a chargeable gain.

In the case of a disposal of shares in the holding company of a trading group, a holding by one member of the group of the ordinary share capital of another member is not counted as a chargeable asset. If the holding company (X) does not own, directly or indirectly, all of the ordinary share capital of a 51% subsidiary (Y), the value of company Y's chargeable assets is reduced by multiplying it by the fraction A/B, where:

- A is the amount of company Y's ordinary share capital owned directly or indirectly by company X; and

- B is the whole of company Y's share capital.

Definitions

Personal company

13.12   A company is an individual's 'personal company' if he is able to exercise at least 5% of the voting rights in the company (*TCGA 1992, s 165(8)*). This is not the same definition of 'personal company' which is used for entrepreneurs' relief (*TCGA 1992, s 169S(3)*; see **11.10**).

Trading company

13.13   Broadly, a company is a trading company if its business does not include non-trading activities 'to a substantial extent'. 'Holding company', 'trading company' and 'trading group' take the definitions given for entrepreneurs' relief purposes (see **11.12**). All three definitions are now brought together in *TCGA 1992, s 165A*.

Trade

13.14   'Trade', 'profession' and 'vocation' have the same meaning as in the *Income Tax Acts*. 'Trade' is taken to include the occupation of woodlands managed by the occupier on a commercial basis and with a view to the realisation of profits, both for the general purposes of hold-over relief and in determining whether a company is a trading company (*TCGA 1992, s 165(8), (9)*). 'Trade' for this purpose also includes the commercial letting of furnished holiday accommodation (*TCGA 1992, s 241(3)*).

SPECIAL SITUATIONS

Relief for inheritance tax

13.15   Where the transfer of an asset is subject to both IHT and a claim to hold-over relief under *TCGA 1992, s 165*, the transferee may receive relief for the IHT paid when calculating the gain arising on later disposal of the same asset. However, the deduction for the IHT paid cannot exceed the amount of the chargeable gain before the deduction.

The deduction is adjusted if the IHT liability is varied after it has been taken into account in this way, and in the event that a disposal which is a potentially exempt transfer for inheritance tax purposes becomes a chargeable transfer (*TCGA 1992, s 165(10), (11)*).

Example 13.5

In July 2013, Barbara sold a plot of land for £500,000. Her father gave her the land in March 1993 when it was valued at £150,000. He died shortly after the gift, and inheritance tax of £60,000 was payable. He had purchased the land in May 1982 for £40,000. The held-over gain and Barbara's chargeable gain on the 2013/14 disposal are computed as follows:

Held-over gain on gift in March 1993:	£	£
Market value in March 1993		150,000
Cost in May 1982		(40,000)
Unindexed gain		110,000
Indexation to March 1993 £40,000 × 0.707		(28,280)
Held-over gain		81,720
2013/14		
Gain on Barbara's disposal:		
Sale proceeds, July 2013		500,000
Market value in March 1993	150,000	
Less gain held over	(81,720)	
		(68,280)
		431,720
Deduction for inheritance tax		(60,000)
Chargeable gain		371,720

Separation, divorce or dissolution of civil partnership

13.16 A transfer between spouses or civil partners is generally made at no gain, no loss (see **3.63**), but not if it takes place after the end of the tax year in which the parties separate. Hold-over relief may be available to relieve the gain, in either of the following circumstances:

- a disposal from one spouse or civil partner to the other after the end of the tax year in which they separate but prior to the divorce decree absolute (or prior to the final dissolution order); or

- a transfer made under a court order, whether or not by consent, after divorce or dissolution.

HMRC consider that such a disposal or transfer is, where there is no recourse to the courts, usually made in exchange for a surrender by the transferee of rights to obtain alternative financial provision. The value of the rights surrendered would represent actual consideration, reducing the potential hold-over relief claim to nil. However, hold-over relief may be available if the parties can demonstrate a 'substantial gratuitous element' in the transfer.

The position where certain court orders are made is viewed differently. A court order may reflect 'the exercise by the court of its independent statutory jurisdiction' rather than being the consequence of a party to the proceedings surrendering alternative rights in return for assets. In such a case, HMRC consider that the spouse or civil partner to whom the assets are transferred does not give actual consideration for the transfer (CG67190–CG67192).

Trust disposals

13.17 Hold-over relief under *TCGA 1992, s 165* is available where the trustees of a settlement make a disposal of an asset mentioned in (a) or (b) below otherwise than under a bargain at arm's length:

(a) an asset, or an interest in an asset, used for the purposes of a trade, profession or vocation carried on by the trustees making the disposal, or by a beneficiary who had an interest in possession in the settled property immediately before the disposal;

(b) shares or securities of a trading company, or of the holding company of a trading group, where either the shares/securities are not listed on a recognised stock exchange, or the trustees are able to exercise at least 25% of the voting rights.

Such a disposal may occur where a person becomes absolutely entitled to the trust property as against the trustees and a deemed charge to CGT arises (see **Chapter 8**). Claims to hold-over relief in respect of disposals by trustees are made by trustees and the transferee (or by the trustees alone if the trustees of a settlement are also the transferee) (*TCGA 1992, Sch 7, para 2*).

The relief is extended to a disposal of agricultural property by trustees, as described in **13.18** in relation to non-settled property (*TCGA 1992, Sch 7, para 3*).

Hold-over relief under *TCGA 1992, s 260* is also available for transfers from certain trusts where an inheritance tax charge would arise but for their 'tax-favoured' status (see **13.36**).

Agricultural property

13.18   Hold-over relief under *TCGA 1992, s 165* is available where the asset disposed of is, or is an interest in, agricultural property (as defined in *IHTA 1984, s 115*) if:

(a)   the disposal does not qualify for hold-over relief under the normal rules only because the agricultural property is not used for the purposes of a trade carried on as set out in **13.5**; and

(b)   agricultural property relief (APR) is obtained in respect of the transfer of value for inheritance tax purposes, or it would be obtained if the transfer was a chargeable transfer, or it would be obtained but for certain rules relating to transfers within seven years before the transferor's death (*TCGA 1992, s 165, Sch 7, para 1*).

'Agricultural property' is defined as including all agricultural land situated in any EEA state, plus land in the Channel Islands and the Isle of Man (*IHTA 1984, s 115*). Hold-over relief claims under *TCGA 1992, s 165* for disposals made in the tax year 2009/10 need to be made by 5 April 2014; claims for earlier years are now out of time.

APR is available in respect of the agricultural value of the property only, ie it is not available for any 'hope or development value' inherent in the property. However, HMRC consider that CGT hold-over relief can be allowed on the whole of the gain (not just the part reflecting agricultural value) because hold-over relief is given by reference to the nature of the asset transferred rather than its value (CG66962).

Incorporation of a business

13.19   Hold-over relief under *TCGA 1992, s 165* may be available where a business carried on by an individual or a partnership is transferred to a company. Incorporation relief under *TCGA 1992, s 162* applies automatically where the business, together with all of its assets (or all of its assets other than cash), is transferred to the company as a going concern in exchange for shares in the company, but the taxpayer can choose to disapply *TCGA 1992, s 162* by electing under *TCGA 1992, s 162A*. Incorporation relief is examined further in **Chapter 15**.

Where the taxpayer elects out of the automatic incorporation relief, or the conditions for that relief do not apply, hold-over relief under *TCGA 1992, s 165* may be used to defer gains on some or all of the assets transferred. Hold-over relief under *TCGA 1992, s 165* is a very flexible tool, as it can be used where only some of the assets of the business are transferred to the company.

The taxpayer must claim *s 165* relief on an asset-by-asset basis, so can choose which assets *s 165* is to apply to. However, hold-over relief can only apply where the disposal is made otherwise than by way of a bargain at arm's length. In most cases, the transaction will be deemed to be made otherwise than by way of a bargain at arm's length because it will be made between connected persons – the individual and the company he now controls (see **3.20**).

Where a claim to hold-over relief under *TCGA 1992, s 165* is made in relation to the incorporation of a business and there is actual consideration for the disposal, the held-over gain is reduced as explained at **13.7**.

Focus

Where the consideration for goodwill takes the form of shares issued by the acquiring company, the amount of that consideration is determined by reference to the market value of the shares.

However, hold-over relief should be available without restriction on the transfer of goodwill if:

- the shares are subscribed for separately;

- goodwill is transferred to the company for a nominal cash sum;

- other assets are transferred at their book value; and

- the total consideration is credited to the transferor's loan account with the company.

HMRC guidance indicates that each asset will be considered separately, provided there is no reason to suppose that the sale price of any of the assets is 'excessive'. HMRC may ask to see the sale agreement and compare it with the company's opening statement of affairs in order to determine precisely what consideration has been given for the various assets (CG66978, CG66979).

Example 13.6

Susan has carried on her antique dealing business for ten years. She let out the shop premises for one year before she commenced trading. In October 2013, Susan transferred the business as a going concern to a limited company that she formed with share capital of £1,000, and elects not to use incorporation relief. The transfer consideration is £1.

The gain arising in respect of the freehold premises is £220,000 and on goodwill it is £30,000. Susan and the company must jointly elect to hold over the gain on the gift of business assets to the company. Susan's net taxable income for 2013/14 is £38,000, which exceeds her basic rate band, so the gain that is not held over is subject to CGT at 28%.

2013/14	Freehold	Goodwill	Total
	£	£	£
Total gains	220,000	30,000	250,000
Reduction for non-trade use 1/11 yrs	(20,000)		(20,000)
Held-over gains	200,000	30,000	230,000
Chargeable gain			20,000
Less annual exemption			(10,900)
Taxable gain			9,100
CGT due at 28%			2,548

Susan could claim entrepreneurs' relief instead of hold-over relief on the entire gain generated by the disposal of the business (see **13.46**), but the tax due under entrepreneurs' relief would be £23,910.

WHEN RELIEF IS DENIED

Gifts to non-residents

13.20   Hold-over relief under *TCGA 1992, s 165* is denied where the transferee is:

(a)   non-resident in the UK (see **5.20**); or

(b)   the individual is resident in the UK, but under a double taxation agreement he is regarded as resident for tax purposes in another territory and he would not be liable in the UK to tax on a gain arising on a disposal of the asset (*TCGA 1992, s 166*).

Emigration of transferee

13.21 Where hold-over relief has been given under *TCGA 1992, s 165* or *s 260* on a disposal of an asset to an individual, and that individual becomes non-resident for tax purposes in the UK at a time when he still holds the asset (see **13.22**), a chargeable gain equal to the held-over gain is deemed to accrue to the transferee immediately before he becomes non-resident.

The CGT annual exemption and any allowable losses available to the transferee at that time may be set against the deemed gain. However, the gain would not be eligible, for example, for roll-over relief on replacement of business assets (see **Chapter 14**) or SEIS reinvestment relief (see **16.43**), because it would not accrue on the actual disposal of an asset. Once the held-over gain has been clawed back in this way, the transferee's chargeable gain on a subsequent disposal of the asset is computed without any reduction in respect of the held-over gain.

No deemed gain arises where the transferee's change of residence status occurs more than six years after the end of the tax year in which the relevant disposal was made (*TCGA 1992, s 168(1), (4), (10)*).

Transferee's disposal of the asset

13.22 It may not be clear whether the transferee has disposed of all or only part of the asset he received, for which he has jointly claimed hold-over relief, before he emigrated. All disposals of similar assets made by the transferee before emigration should be reviewed to check whether all of the held-over gain has been taken into account in the computations of the gains/losses on those disposals. If only part of the held-over gain has been taken into account in gains/losses arising on pre-emigration disposals, the balance of the held-over gain is deemed to accrue on the change of residence (*TCGA 1992, s 168(2)*).

The transferee's disposal of an asset to his spouse or civil partner under a no gain, no loss transfer (under *TCGA 1992, s 58*) does not count as a disposal for this purpose, but a subsequent disposal by the spouse or civil partner is taken into account as if the original transferee (not the spouse or civil partner) made that disposal (*TCGA 1992, s 168(3)*).

Example 13.7

Sidney gave a property to his brother Harry in May 1998, when they were both UK resident and they claimed hold-over relief. Harry gave the property to his wife Madeleine in 2010, and Harry and Madeleine emigrated in August 2013. A deemed gain does not arise at that time as the date of emigration is more than six years after the end of the tax year in which Harry acquired the property.

A temporary change of residence status will not trigger a deemed chargeable gain where the transferee:

- becomes non-resident in the UK because he works in an employment or office and all the duties are performed outside the UK;

- becomes resident in the UK once again within three years of losing that status; and

- has not disposed of the asset in the meantime.

With regard to this last condition, the transferee is taken to have disposed of an asset only if he has made a disposal on which the allowable expenditure, deducted in computing his gain, would have been reduced by the held-over gain on the relevant disposal if he had been UK resident (*TCGA 1992, s 168(5), (6)*).

Payment of tax

13.23   The tax on the chargeable gain deemed to accrue to the transferee on emigration may be assessed and charged on the transferor, in the name of the transferee, if it has been assessed on the transferee but not paid within 12 months of the due date. The transferor is entitled to recover the tax from the transferee. No such assessment may be made more than six years after the end of the tax year in which the transferor made the relevant disposal (*TCGA 1992, s 168(7), (8), (9)*).

Gifts to foreign-controlled companies

13.24   In the past, the following trick has been used to avoid UK CGT. Assets were transferred to a UK company that was controlled by non-residents, and a claim for hold-over relief was submitted in respect of the gain. The non-resident owners would then sell the UK company, avoiding UK tax on the underlying assets.

Hold-over relief under *TCGA 1992, s 165* is thus denied where the transferee is a company that is controlled by one or more persons who are non-resident in the UK, and who are connected with the person making the disposal. The connection between the transferor and the company owners may be purely a commercial relationship, as shown in *Foulser and anor v MacDougall* [2007] STC 973.

A person who is resident in the UK is regarded as non-resident in the UK for this purpose if:

- he controls a company – alone or with others – by virtue of holding assets relating to that company or another company; and

- double taxation relief arrangements have the effect that he is regarded as resident in another territory and would not be liable in the UK to tax on a gain arising on a disposal of the assets (*TCGA 1992, s 167*).

Gifts to dual-resident trusts

13.25   This is a similar anti-avoidance provision which denies hold-over relief available under *TCGA 1992, s 165* or *s 260* where the held-over gain could slip out of the UK tax net, as the transfer is made into a dual-resident trust (*TCGA 1992, s 169(3)*). A dual-resident trust is one whose trustees are resident in the UK, but who are treated as being resident in another territory and therefore exempt from UK CGT under the terms of a double taxation agreement.

Transfer of shares to a company

13.26   Hold-over relief under *TCGA 1992, s 165* is not available where shares or securities are transferred to a company. This is to counter the type of tax avoidance arrangement which commonly involved the 'gift' of shares to a company followed by the disposal of shares by that company in circumstances attracting no tax liability. It might involve a series of arrangements whereby shares in the transferee company were taken outside the UK tax net. This exclusion does not deny hold-over relief where a disposal is made to a trust with a corporate trustee.

Disposal of QCBs

13.27   Where qualifying corporate bonds (QCBs) have been received in exchange for shares or other securities, the gain arising on the disposal of those shares or securities will normally be rolled into the corporate bond. This defers the CGT due on the disposal of the shares until those QCBs are in turn disposed of. The gift of the QCBs, which would be a disposal bringing the deferred gain into charge, cannot support a claim to hold-over relief (*TCGA 1992, s 165(3)(c)*; CG66943).

Focus

Where an individual shareholder receives QCBs in return for shares, he must choose between claiming entrepreneurs' relief on the gain arising on disposal of the shares and deferring that gain through the mechanism of QCBs (see **11.40–11.48**).

377

Gifts to settlor-interested settlements

13.28   Hold-over relief under *TCGA 1992, s 165* or *s 260* is generally not available on a disposal to the trustees of a settlement in which the settlor has an interest (*TCGA 1992, ss 169B, 169C, 169D*). The settlor here can be someone other than the person making the disposal. The anti-avoidance provisions in *TCGA 1992, ss 169B–169G* were introduced with effect from 9 December 2003 to block schemes designed to wash out gains through trusts (see **12.32**). This type of tax scheme was mostly used to eliminate a gain on a second home.

Relief may also be denied where there is an 'arrangement' for the settlor to acquire an interest in the settlement, and relief may be clawed back or blocked if the settlement becomes settlor-interested in the period ending six years following the tax year in which the disposal was made (see **13.29**).

Hold-over relief is excluded where the disposal (the 'relevant disposal') is made by a person ('the transferor') to the trustees of a settlement and either of the following two conditions is satisfied in relation to the disposal:

- Condition 1 is that, immediately after the relevant disposal, there is a 'settlor' who has an 'interest in the settlement', or an 'arrangement' exists under which the settlor will (or may) acquire such an interest. The various terms are defined in **13.30–13.34**.

- Condition 2 is that:

  (a)   a chargeable gain would (in the absence of hold-over relief under either *TCGA 1992, s 165* or *s 260*) accrue to the transferor on the disposal to the trustees;

  (b)   in computing the transferor's gain on that disposal, his allowable expenditure would be reduced directly or indirectly because of a hold-over relief claim made on an earlier disposal made by an individual; and

  (c)   immediately after the relevant disposal, that individual has an interest in the settlement, or an arrangement exists under which that individual will or may acquire such an interest.

Relief is not available where either condition 1 or condition 2 is met. There are exceptions for maintenance funds for historic buildings and certain settlements for people with disabilities (*TCGA 1992, ss 169B, 169D*).

Clawback of relief: settlement becoming settlor-interested

13.29   Once obtained, hold-over relief may be clawed back where either condition 1 or condition 2 in **13.28** is met at any time during the 'clawback period'. This is the period beginning with the relevant disposal and ending six years after the end of the tax year in which the disposal took place.

> **Example 13.8**
>
> Mervyn transfers to trustees an asset used for the purposes of a trade carried on by his personal company. The transfer takes place on 10 May 2007 and he claims hold-over relief. He is the only settlor and does not have an interest in the settlement (see the definitions below). The relief may be clawed back if he acquires an interest in the settlement before 6 April 2014.

Where the clawback is triggered, a chargeable gain of an amount equal to the held-over gain is treated as accruing to the transferor at the 'material time', ie the time when either condition 1 or condition 2 is first met, not at the time of the relevant disposal. If no claim to hold-over relief is made before the material time, the relief may not be claimed in relation to that disposal.

Once again, there are exceptions for maintenance funds for historic buildings and certain settlements for people with disabilities (*TCGA 1992, ss 169C, 169D*).

Definitions

13.30   The following definitions are provided for the purpose of the rules governing gifts to settlor-interested settlements.

'Settlor'

13.31   A person is a settlor in relation to a settlement if he is an individual and the settled property consists of, or includes, property originating from him. Property is deemed to originate from him if he has provided it directly or indirectly, or it represents such property (or any part of it, or accumulated income from it). Property provided directly or indirectly by another person under reciprocal arrangements with the settlor is treated as provided directly or indirectly by the settlor (*TCGA 1992, s 169E*).

'Interest in a settlement'

13.32   An individual is regarded as having an interest in a settlement if either (a) or (b) below applies:

(a)   any property that is or may at any time be comprised in the settlement, or any 'derived property' (see **13.34**), is, or will or may become, in any circumstances, either payable to the individual or his spouse or civil partner, or a dependent child of the individual or applicable for their benefit; or

(b)   the individual or his spouse or civil partner or dependent child enjoys a benefit deriving directly or indirectly from property comprised in the settlement, or from 'derived property'.

A separated spouse or civil partner, and a widow (or widower or surviving civil partner), are ignored in determining whether an individual has an interest in a settlement. 'Dependent child' means a child who is under the age of 18, is unmarried, and does not have a civil partner. 'Child' includes a stepchild (*TCGA 1992, s 169F(4), (4A)*).

A future interest is ignored for this purpose if it could only arise:

•   in the case of a marriage settlement or civil partnership settlement, on the death of both parties to the marriage or civil partnership and of all or any of their children; or

•   on the death of a child of the individual where the child had become beneficially entitled to the property (or any derived property) by age 25 (*TCGA 1992, s 169F(5)*).

Arrangement

13.33   An arrangement includes any scheme, agreement or understanding, whether or not legally enforceable (*TCGA 1992, s 169G*).

Derived property

13.34   Property is 'derived property', in relation to any other property, if it is:

(a)   income from that other property;

(b)   property directly or indirectly representing either proceeds of that other property or proceeds of income from that other property; or

(c)   income from property that is derived property because it is within (b) above (*TCGA 1992, s 169F(6)*).

GIFTS SUBJECT TO IHT (SECTION 260)

13.35   Hold-over relief under *TCGA 1992, s 260* is available for gifts on which inheritance tax is immediately chargeable, or would be chargeable but for an exemption or the availability of the inheritance tax nil rate band. Such gifts include transfers to and from discretionary trusts.

Where such a hold-over claim is made (or could have been made), a deduction is available, in computing the gain on the subsequent disposal, for any IHT charged on the gift (see **13.40**).

Conditions

13.36   Both the transferor and the transferee must be either an individual or trustees of a settlement. Where the conditions set out below are met, the relief remains subject to various restrictions including:

- the restrictions set out in **13.8** in relation to *TCGA 1992, s 165* relief; and

- the exclusion mentioned at **13.41** for gifts to non-residents (*TCGA 1992, s 260(1)*).

The relief applies to a disposal that is made otherwise than under a bargain at arm's length, where the disposal meets any of the following inheritance tax provisions concerning:

(a)   chargeable transfers (see *IHTA 1984, ss 2, 3A* and *19*);

(b)   exempt transfers (*IHTA 1984, ss 24, 27, 30*);

(c)   property entering a maintenance fund (*IHTA 1984, s 57A*);

(d)   transfer by trustees of favoured trusts (*IHTA 1984, ss 71(4), 71B(2), 71E(2)*);

(e)   works of art etc qualifying for the conditional exemption (*IHTA 1984, s 78(1)*); or

(f)   transfers to maintenance funds for historic buildings (*IHTA 1984, Sch 4, paras 9, 16* and *17*).

Operation of TCGA 1992, s 260 relief

13.37   The effect of this relief, which must be claimed (see **13.43**), is that the 'held-over gain' (see below) is deducted from both:

- the chargeable gain (if any) that would otherwise accrue to the transferor; and

- the consideration which the transferee would otherwise be regarded as having given for the acquisition of the asset (*TCGA 1992, s 260(3)*).

The 'held-over gain' on a disposal, where this relief is not restricted by reference to actual consideration received for the disposal, is the chargeable gain that would have accrued in the absence of hold-over relief (*TCGA 1992, s 260(4)*).

The relief may be restricted where consideration is received (see **13.38**), or as described in **13.39**.

Consideration received

13.38   Where a claim to hold-over relief is made and there is actual consideration for the disposal, and that consideration exceeds the allowable expenditure deductible in computing the gain, the held-over gain is reduced by that excess. This restriction does not apply, however, to certain disposals deemed to occur in relation to accumulation and maintenance trusts, employee trusts or newspaper trusts (within *IHTA 1984, s 71(1)* or *s 72(1)*) (*TCGA 1992, s 260(5), (9)*).

Partial relief

13.39   If the disposal only partly meets the conditions in **13.36**, or the condition in **13.36**(f) is met and the inheritance tax charge is reduced but not eliminated, hold-over relief applies only to an 'appropriate part' of the disposal (*TCGA 1992, s 260(10)*).

Relief for inheritance tax

13.40   Where there is a chargeable transfer for inheritance tax purposes as mentioned in **13.36**(a), CGT relief is available to the transferee as follows, whether or not hold-over relief is obtained under *TCGA 1992, s 260*.

The transferee is entitled to a deduction in computing for CGT purposes the chargeable gain accruing on his disposal of the asset. The deduction is equal to the inheritance tax attributable to the value of the asset, but it cannot exceed the amount of the chargeable gain before the deduction. The deduction is adjusted in the event that the inheritance tax is varied after it has been taken into account in this way (*TCGA 1992, s 260(7), (8)*).

WHERE RELIEF IS DENIED OR CLAWED BACK

Gifts to non-residents

13.41   Hold-over relief under *TCGA 1992, s 260* is denied where the transferee is:

(a)   non-resident in the UK; or

(b) an individual who is resident in the UK, but under a double taxation relief agreement he is regarded as resident in another territory and he would not be liable in the UK to tax on a gain arising on a disposal of the asset (*TCGA 1992, s 261*).

Emigration of transferee

13.42 Where hold-over relief has been given under either *TCGA 1992, s 165* or *s 260* on a disposal ('the relevant disposal') to an individual, and the transferee becomes non-resident for tax purposes in the UK at a time when he still holds the asset (see **13.22**), a chargeable gain equal to the held-over gain is deemed to accrue to the transferee immediately before the date he becomes non-resident.

CLAIMS AND VALUATIONS

Claim under s 165 or s 260

13.43 Claims for hold-over relief under *TCGA 1992, s 165* or *s 260* must be made jointly by both the transferor and the transferee. However, if the gift is made into a trust, the relief claim is made by the transferor alone.

HMRC require claimants to use the form in the HMRC helpsheet HS295, or a copy of that form. Their guidance refers to 'serious problems' having arisen in some cases from a lack of information held by the transferee at the time of the eventual disposal of the asset. A claim must be made by the taxpayer personally, or by his personal representatives (CG66914).

The claim will usually be made when submitting the tax return, but otherwise it must be made within four years of the end of the tax year in which the disposal was made (*TMA 1970, s 43*). This time limit may effectively be extended where an assessment is made to recover tax lost through fraudulent or negligent conduct (under *TMA 1970, s 36*).

HMRC will accept claims to hold-over relief under *TCGA 1992, s 165* or *s 260*, in certain circumstances, without agreeing the market value of the asset transferred (see **13.47**).

Partial claims

13.44 It is not possible to limit the scope of a claim to hold-over relief under *TCGA 1992, s 165* in order to utilise the donor's annual exemption, or to make use of losses. However, where several assets are transferred, the parties may choose to claim hold-over relief on some assets and not on others.

Interaction with other reliefs

13.45 Where the conditions exist to allow hold-over relief for gifts of business assets to be claimed under *TCGA 1992, s 165*, those conditions may also permit certain other CGT reliefs to apply, either automatically or by way of a claim. Where several CGT reliefs potentially apply to the same disposal hold-over relief is given:

- after indexation allowance, for disposals made before 6 April 2008;

- before taper relief, for transfers made before 6 April 2008;

- before entrepreneurs' relief, for disposals made after 5 April 2008 (see **13.46**).

Where hold-over relief is obtained without restriction for disposal before 6 April 2008, any taper relief relating to the transferor's period of ownership is lost. The interaction of various CGT reliefs is examined further in **14.48–14.50**.

Entrepreneurs' relief

13.46 Hold-over relief takes precedence over entrepreneurs' relief (see **11.50**) where hold-over relief covers the full gain accruing on the disposal of the business, or part of the business. However, where hold-over relief is only claimed in respect of certain assets leaving a chargeable gain accruing on other assets which form part of a business disposal, entrepreneurs' relief may be claimed to cover that residual gain that remains in charge (CG64137).

Valuations

13.47 HMRC will accept claims to hold-over relief under either *TCGA 1992, s 165* or *s 260*, in certain circumstances, without formal agreement of the market value of the asset transferred. The conditions and procedures are set out in HMRC Statement of Practice 8/92 and are summarised below.

The gift is deemed to be made at market value (see **13.1**), and the transferor needs to establish the market value of the asset at the date of the transfer in order to compute the chargeable gain accruing and the held-over gain where a claim is made. However, where hold-over relief is available without restriction, agreement of the asset's market value at the date of transfer has no bearing on the transferor's CGT liability.

HMRC will admit a claim to hold-over relief without requiring a computation of the held-over gain where both the transferor and transferee complete the 'request for valuations to be deferred', found on page ten of HMRC's helpsheet HS295 (and forming the second page of the hold-over relief claim). The form requires:

- a joint application by the transferor and the transferee;

- details of the asset, its history and an informal estimate of the asset's market value at the date of transfer – such an estimate is not binding on either the claimants or HMRC; and

- a statement that both parties are satisfied that the value of the asset at the date of transfer was such that there would be a chargeable gain but for the claim.

HMRC's guidance indicates that taxpayers will not be asked for a computation of the held-over gain so long as the asset is properly identified and the formalities of the hold-over relief claim are satisfied. The requirement for both parties to sign the application for deferral of the valuation applies where the transferee is a body of trustees, even though the trustees are not required to sign the actual hold-over claim. HMRC regard it as essential that anyone whose liability may be affected by the valuation has agreed to the postponement (CG67131, CG67132).

Focus

Once HMRC have accepted a hold-over relief claim made under Statement of Practice 8/92, the claim may not be withdrawn.

The relevant statutory provisions will be applied, and tax assessments made as necessary, if it emerges that any information provided by either the transferor or transferee was incorrect or incomplete.

HMRC will not apply Statement of Practice 8/92 in a case where the held-over gain is restricted as shown in **13.8** (as provided in *TCGA 1992, Sch 7, paras 5, 6* and *7*), because the amount of chargeable gain accruing to the transferor depends in such a case on a valuation being made.

In some other cases, it will be necessary to establish market value before a later disposal of the asset by the transferee. Statement of Practice 8/92 outlines some of those circumstances in relation to:

- assets held at 31 March 1982;

- retirement relief;

- relief in respect of deferred charges on gains before 31 March 1982; and

- time apportionment for assets held on 6 April 1965.

Chapter 14

Roll-over relief for business assets

SIGNPOSTS

- **Overview of roll-over relief** (see **14.1**).

- **Conditions** – When the relief is available, effect of roll-over relief tracing the disposal proceeds, allocating consideration, consideration reimbursed, deemed consideration, deemed disposals, location of assets and residence of taxpayers (see **14.2–14.10**).

- **Period for reinvestment** – The four-year period, extension of period, where compulsory purchase applies (see **14.11–14.13**).

- **Qualifying activities** – Two or more trades, activities other than trades, trade carried on by company or partnership, LLPs, groups of companies (see **14.14–14.21**).

- **Asset classes** – Land and buildings, fixed plant, ships and aircraft, goodwill, intangibles, repurchase of the same asset (see **14.22–14.28**).

- **Use of assets** – New assets used on acquisition, assets only partly used for business purposes, period of ownership (see **14.29–14.33**).

- **Operation of roll-over relief** – Full relief, partial relief, assets held at 31 March 1982 (see **14.34–14.36**).

- **Depreciating assets** – Special rules, postponing the held-over gain, acquisition of third asset, assets transferred to European Company (see **14.37–14.40**).

- **Claims** – Time limits for individuals and companies, how to claim, claiming provisional relief, declarations, interest and penalties (see **14.41–14.47**).

- **Interaction with other reliefs** – Incorporation relief, entrepreneurs' relief (see **14.48–14.49**).

OVERVIEW OF ROLL-OVER RELIEF

14.1   The effect of roll-over relief for business assets is to defer a chargeable gain where the proceeds of disposal of business assets (the 'old assets') are used to invest in new business assets. The old and the new assets must both be used in the business. Spouses and civil partners are separate persons for roll-over relief. The rules specific to groups of companies are examined at **9.33–9.45**. This chapter is of general application to corporates and non-corporates, except where stated otherwise.

Roll-over relief is applied by deducting the gain from the acquisition cost of the new assets. The gain deferred – or rolled over – in this way may give rise to a CGT liability on a disposal of the replacement assets, but roll-over relief may be claimed on that subsequent disposal if the conditions are met. A chargeable gain may arise on the disposal of the old assets if the relief claimed on that disposal is restricted (see **14.35**). The rules for business asset roll-over relief are found in *TCGA 1992, ss 152–159*, and HMRC guidance is found in their Capital Gains Manual at CG60250–CG61560.

A rolled-over gain escapes CGT in the event of the taxpayer's death. In some cases, however, the gain on the old asset is 'postponed' instead of being 'rolled over' or deducted from the cost of the new asset (see **14.37**).

There are separate time limits for reinvestment of the consideration for the disposal (see **14.11**) and claims (see **14.41**).

CONDITIONS

When relief is available

14.2   Roll-over relief must be claimed by the person carrying on the business in which the asset is used. It is available if the taxpayer:

- carries on a trade or another qualifying activity (see **14.14**);
- disposes of assets (or his interest in assets) used only for the purposes of that trade throughout the period of ownership (the 'old assets') (see **14.30**);
- applies the consideration obtained for the disposal in acquiring other assets within the specified classes (see **14.22**) (the 'new assets');
- acquires those new assets within the permitted period (see **14.11**); and
- takes the new assets into use on acquisition, to be used solely for the purposes of the trade (see **14.28**).

'Trade' has the same meaning for roll-over relief as it has in the *Income Tax Acts*, and *ITA 2007, s 989* provides that 'trade' includes any venture in the nature of trade. However, relief is extended to other activities (see **14.16**) (*TCGA 1992, s 158(2)*).

Effect of roll-over relief

14.3   The effect of the relief is that:

(a)   the consideration for the disposal of the old assets is reduced to the amount that would give rise to neither a gain nor a loss accruing on the disposal; and

(b)   the amount (or value) of the consideration that the taxpayer gives for the acquisition of the new assets is reduced by the amount of the reduction in (a).

Focus

It is the consideration (or deemed disposal) from the disposal of the old asset that must be reinvested, not the gain from the disposal as applies for EIS deferral relief (see **Chapter 16**).

The CGT treatment of the other parties to the transactions is not affected. Both the old assets and new assets must be within the classes of assets listed in *TCGA 1992, s 155*, although they do not need to be in the same class as each other (see **14.22**) (*TCGA 1992, s 152(1)*).

Tracing the disposal proceeds

14.4   It is not normally necessary to trace the actual proceeds and match them to the funds invested in the new assets. The new assets can, for example, be funded by borrowings. HMRC recognise that seeking to trace the disposal proceeds through to the acquisition of the new assets would result in relief being denied in most cases. The permitted period for reinvestment starts one year before the old asset is disposed of (see **14.11**), so the new asset may be acquired with borrowed funds before the old one is disposed of (CG60760).

There is an exception, however, where the taxpayer is seeking an extension to the reinvestment period. In this case he may need to be able to demonstrate a continuing intention to reinvest the disposal consideration within the extended time limit (see **14.12**).

Example 14.1

Giles used a mortgage to fund the purchase of farmland on 1 September 2012 for £140,000, which was immediately incorporated into his farming business. He sold a barn for £100,000 less expenses of £5,000 on 3 May 2013. For his roll-over relief claim, Giles matches his sale of the barn with the purchase of the land eight months previously. The net disposal consideration of £95,000 is fully applied in acquiring the new asset comprising the farmland, so full roll-over relief is given.

Allocating the consideration

14.5 Where there is more than one acquisition, HMRC will accept the taxpayer's allocation of the gain to be rolled over against the new assets. HMRC consider that there must be a specific allocation before the claim can be allowed (CG60770).

Consideration reimbursed

14.6 *Wardhaugh v Penrith Rugby Union Football Club* (2002) 74 TC 499 established that, for roll-over relief purposes, the amount or value of the consideration taken to be applied in the acquisition of the new asset is the amount before any reduction under *TCGA 1992, s 50*. That section provides that a CGT computation excludes any expenditure met directly or indirectly by the Crown or by any government, public or local authority. HMRC argued that *TCGA 1992, s 152(10)* (see **14.7**) applied, but the court disagreed on the basis that *TCGA 1992, s 50* related to the non-deductibility of acquisition expenditure. It was not a provision that fixed the amount of the consideration deemed to be given for the acquisition of an asset.

Deemed consideration

14.7 Any provision of *TCGA 1992* fixing the amount of consideration deemed to be given for the acquisition or disposal of an asset – for example, where a transaction between connected persons is treated as having a consideration equal to the market value of the asset – is applied before roll-over relief. This means that, in some cases, the amount that the taxpayer needs to 'reinvest' to secure full relief will be greater than the proceeds actually received (*TCGA 1992, s 152(10)*).

Deemed disposals

14.8 HMRC do not consider that roll-over relief is available where there is a deemed disposal and reacquisition of the same asset, because the deemed consideration for the deemed disposal is not available to be applied in acquiring 'other assets' (CG60780). However, relief may be available where a qualifying asset is deemed to be disposed of or deemed to be acquired. For example, gains arising when a capital sum is derived from an asset (see **2.12**), or when an asset is appropriated to trading stock (see **4.36**), may be the subject of a claim. A deemed acquisition of a qualifying asset, for example, acquisition of an asset as legatee, may also give rise to roll-over relief.

Residence

14.9   HMRC accept that relief may be claimed even if the replacement assets are outside the UK. Relief will not be denied where all the conditions are met and at the time the new assets are acquired, the taxpayer has ceased to be resident in the UK (CG60270).

However, there is a potential charge for 'temporary non-residents' (see **5.33**) where a gain has been the subject of a roll-over relief claim, either under the normal rules or under the special rules for new assets that are depreciating assets (see **14.37**), and there is a disposal of the new asset during a period of temporary non-residence. The gain may be treated as accruing to the temporary non-resident on his return to the UK (see **5.35**) (*TCGA 1992, s 10A(3), (4)*).

Non-residents with UK presence

14.10   If a gain arising on the old assets would be chargeable under *TCGA 1992, s 10(1)* (non-resident with a UK branch or agency) or *s 10B* (non-resident company with a UK permanent establishment), roll-over relief is not available unless the new assets, immediately after they are acquired, would also fall within *s 10(1)* or *s 10B* on a disposal (*TCGA 1992, s 159(1)*).

This condition does not apply if:

(a)   the relevant acquisition takes place after the disposal and the taxpayer is resident for tax purposes in the UK immediately after the acquisition; or

(b)   immediately after the time the new assets are acquired:

- the taxpayer is a 'dual resident', ie a person who is both resident in the UK and regarded for double tax relief purposes as resident elsewhere; and

- the assets are 'prescribed assets', ie assets specified in a double tax agreement with the effect that the dual resident is regarded as not liable in the UK to tax on gains accruing to him on a disposal (*TCGA 1992, s 159(2), (3), (5)*).

PERIOD FOR REINVESTMENT

14.11   The general rule is that the new asset must be acquired in the period beginning one year before and ending three years after the disposal of the old asset, but this period may be extended either forwards or backwards (see **14.12**) as HMRC allow (*TCGA 1992, s 152(3)*).

An unconditional contract for the acquisition, made within the time limit, will be sufficient. The relief may be applied on a provisional basis where an unconditional contract for the acquisition is entered into, without waiting to see whether the contract is completed. Adjustments are to be made as necessary when the outcome is known. This rule is separate from the facility for the taxpayer to claim provisional relief before he has entered into any contract for acquisition of a replacement asset (see **14.45**) (*TCGA 1992, s 152(4)*).

Where the replacement asset is newly constructed, or represented by improvement to an existing asset, HMRC consider that the date of acquisition may be taken as the date on which the asset or the works are completed and ready for use (CG60620).

Extension of time limits for reinvestment

14.12   HMRC guidance indicates that extension of the time limits is permitted where the claimant can demonstrate that he:

- firmly intended to acquire replacement assets within the time limit; but

- was prevented from acquiring the replacement assets or any assets by some fact or circumstance beyond his control; and

- acted 'as soon as he reasonably could' after ceasing to be so prevented.

Each case is considered on its merits. Circumstances outside the claimant's control might include the death or serious illness of a vital party at a crucial time, unsettled disputes, difficulty in establishing good title or finding suitable replacement assets, or delay in receipt of disposal proceeds. They would not normally include a change of intention at a late stage, or a shortage of funds that arose because the taxpayer spent the proceeds on something other than new, qualifying assets.

The HMRC Business Unit Head or grade 6 Compliance Team Leader can agree to extend the time limit for reinvestment to up to three years before, or six years after the disposal of the old asset, if there are acceptable reasons for the delay. However, HMRC will not make a decision about the extension of the time limit until after the facts have been established, when the new asset has been acquired and the old asset disposed of (CG60640). The discretion to extend the time limit is vested solely in the HMRC officers. The taxpayer cannot appeal against a decision of an HMRC officer not to use this discretion (*R (on application of Barnett) v IRC* [2004] STC 763).

Compulsory purchase

14.13   The Board of HMRC may allow an extension to the time limit in the case of the disposal of land:

- where there is a compulsory purchase order, or there is a threat of such an order, so long as the conditions set out in Statement of Practice D6 (see below) are satisfied; or

- where the new asset was acquired more than three years before or six years after the disposal of the old asset and there are acceptable reasons for the delay.

HMRC give the following examples of acceptable reasons for delay:

- the threat of compulsory acquisition of the old asset;

- difficulty in disposing of the old asset;

- the acquisition of land with the intention of erecting a building on it;

- the need to have new premises functioning before the old premises can be vacated.

In the case of delayed compensation from compulsory purchase, HMRC may allow the time limit to apply as if the date when the first tranche of compensation was received was the date of disposal of the asset (CG60660).

Statement of Practice D6 covers situations where land is acquired by a local authority or new town corporation for development and leased back to the taxpayer for a period before it is developed, and reads:

'Where new town corporations and similar authorities acquire by compulsory purchase land for development and then immediately grant a previous owner a lease of the land until they are ready to commence building, Commissioners for HMRC will be prepared to extend the time limit for rollover relief under *TCGA 1992, ss 152 to 158* to three years after the land ceases to be used by the previous owner for his trade, provided that there is a clear continuing intention that the sale proceeds will be used to acquire qualifying assets; assurances will be given in appropriate cases subject to the need to raise a protective assessment if the lease extends beyond the statutory six-year time limit for making assessments.'

In any application of Statement of Practice D6, HMRC will look for evidence of the taxpayer's continuing intention to reinvest the disposal proceeds within the extended time limit, including:

- an annual affirmation from the taxpayer or agent that such is the intention; and

- an assurance that the disposal proceeds remain available (although not necessarily in a completely liquid form) for the purchase. HMRC say that temporary investment of the funds in equities or real property 'should not of itself be taken as making the proceeds unavailable'.

It appears from the HMRC guidance (CG60660) that the land need not be purchased by compulsory purchase order to qualify for this concession.

Focus

There is a similar roll-over relief available specifically for compulsory purchase of land, where the proceeds are reinvested in other land (*TCGA 1992, s 247*).

The land must be purchased by an authority which has compulsory purchase powers, but those powers need not be exercised in the transaction concerned (see **4.20**).

QUALIFYING ACTIVITIES

14.14   Roll-over relief is available where a person carrying on a trade reinvests the proceeds from the disposal of assets used for the purposes of the trade in the acquisition of new assets to be used for the purposes of the same trade, profession or vocation. However, two or more trades may be regarded as a single trade (**14.15**); for other qualifying activities, see **14.16**.

No relief is due if the new assets are acquired with a view to realising a profit from their disposal (*TCGA 1992, s 152(5)*). HMRC accept that this rule is not intended to deny relief merely because it is expected that the asset will be sold at a profit at some stage. However, they will look at the intention of the taxpayer at the time of acquisition; for example, if a large farm is acquired, and part of the land is sold quickly as it is not required for the trade, roll-over relief will be denied on the acquisition cost of the surplus land (CG60390).

Two or more trades

14.15   A person who carries on two or more trades, either at the same time or in succession, is regarded as carrying on a single trade (*TCGA 1992, s 152(8)*).

HMRC are prepared to regard trades as being carried on 'successively' if the interval does not exceed three years, but the time limits for reinvestment must still be met (see **14.11**). Relief will be available, but may be restricted by reference to non-trade use, if the old assets are disposed of during the interval. New assets acquired during the interval may qualify as replacement assets provided they are not used or leased for any purpose before the new trade begins, and are taken into use for the purpose of the trade on commencement (HMRC Statement of Practice 8/81; CG60500).

Activities other than trades

14.16 The main roll-over relief provisions in *TCGA 1992, ss 152–157* refer only to trades. The relief is extended to replacement of assets used for the purpose of a profession, vocation, office or employment (*TCGA 1992, s 158*).

Where relief is claimed in respect of assets used for the purposes of the claimant's office or employment it will not be denied because the asset is also used by the employer for the purposes of the employer's trade. HMRC regard the 'sole use' condition as satisfied unless the asset is used for some purpose 'alien to' the office or employment (CG60530).

So far as land and buildings are concerned, the employee must occupy the asset as owner and not merely as a licensee of the employer. HMRC Statement of Practice 5/86 says:

> 'If land or buildings are owned by an employee etc, but made available to the employer for general use in his trade, the employee etc may nonetheless satisfy the occupation test of *TCGA 1992, s 155* provided the employer does not make any payment (or give other consideration) for his use of the property nor otherwise occupy it under a lease or tenancy.
>
> The qualifying use of assets by an employee etc for the purposes of *TCGA 1992, ss 152* and *153* will include any use or occupation of those assets by him, in the course of performing the duties of his employment or office, as directed by the employer.'

A taxpayer who is an officer or employee of his personal company (see **14.17**) may meet the conditions of *TCGA 1992, s 152* by reference to his office or employment and simultaneously meet the conditions of *TCGA 1992, s 157*. He can then choose to make a claim for roll-over relief under either section (CG60510).

The taxpayer may carry on two different activities, for example a trade and an employment, at the same time or successively. The fact that the two activities are different does not prevent relief applying so long as the various conditions including, where appropriate, the terms of HMRC Statement of Practice 8/81 (see **14.14**) are met.

'Trade', 'profession', 'vocation', 'office' and 'employment' have the same meaning for roll-over relief as they have in the *Income Tax Acts*, so that farming, and the commercial letting of furnished holiday accommodation that falls within *TCGA 1992, s 241*, may qualify (*TCGA 1992, ss 158(2), 241(3), (3A)*).

The relief also applies to the replacement of assets used for the purposes of the following activities, as it applies in relation to trades:

(a) the discharge of the functions of a public authority;

(b) the occupation of woodlands managed by the occupier on a commercial basis;

(c) the activities of a non-profit making body that are wholly or mainly directed to the protection or promotion of its members' trade or professional interests; and

(d) the activities of an unincorporated association or other body chargeable to corporation tax, but not established for profit, whose activities are wholly or mainly carried on otherwise than for profit, or a company owned by such a body.

Category (d) may include trade unions, sports clubs and local constituency associations of political parties and companies owned at least 90% by such bodies (*TCGA 1992, s 158(1A)*). The parent body must use the assets for the purpose of its activities. In the case of land and buildings within Head A of Class 1 (see **14.22**), the parent body must both occupy and use them for those activities, rather than letting them (*TCGA 1992, s 158(1)(f)*).

Trade carried on by the taxpayer's personal company

14.17   Roll-over relief is extended to the situation where the owner of the asset is an individual but the trade is carried on by a company. The individual is deemed to be carrying on the trade(s), for the purpose of the conditions in *TCGA 1992, ss 152–156*, where:

(a) the person disposing of the old assets (or an interest in them) and acquiring the new assets (or an interest in them) is an individual; and

(b) the trade or trades in question are carried on by a company which is his 'personal company' (*TCGA 1992, s 157*).

The condition in (b) must be met both at the time of the disposal and at the time of the acquisition referred to in (a). A company is the taxpayer's 'personal company' if he can exercise at least 5% of the voting rights. Note this is not the same definition of 'personal company' as applies for entrepreneurs' relief (see **11.10**).

HMRC consider that both the old and new assets must be used for qualifying activities of the same personal company, on the basis that *TCGA 1992, s 157* directs that *TCGA 1992, s 152* should be read as if it said:

'If the consideration which an individual obtains for the disposal of ... the old assets used and used only for the purposes of the trade carried on by his ... personal company ... is applied by him in acquiring ... the new assets which on the acquisition are taken into use, and used only, for the purposes of the trade carried on by that personal company ...' (CG60510)

Trade carried on by a partnership

14.18   The CGT treatment of partnerships is examined in detail in **Chapter 6**. Roll-over relief extends to a business partner's interest in the chargeable assets of a partnership (*TCGA 1992, s 157*).

Where the partnership disposes of an asset qualifying for roll-over relief, or there is a reduction in the partner's share of the partnership's capital assets following a change in the asset-sharing ratio, the partner may obtain roll-over relief by means of either:

- the partnership's acquisition of qualifying assets in which the partner has an interest; or

- the partner's acquisition in qualifying assets, either used by the partnership (see below) or unrelated to the partnership's business.

Relief is also available for assets used in the partnership's trade but owned by an individual partner rather than the partnership. This applies even if the partner receives rent for the use of the asset (Statement of Practice D11).

Where land used for the purposes of a partnership's trade is 'partitioned' by the partners on a dissolution of the partnership, strictly speaking no roll-over relief is due because an exchange of interests in a single asset does not involve the acquisition of 'other assets'. Under ESC D23, HMRC will treat the land acquired as a new asset providing that the partnership is dissolved immediately after the exchange. The guidance at CG61170 adds two further conditions to this concession:

- the purpose of the exchange is to enable the partnership to be dissolved; and

- the former partners retain an interest only in land used by them in a new trading enterprise and do not retain any interest in that part of the land no longer used by them for trade purposes.

Example 14.2

A family partnership made up of Peggy, Philip and David jointly and equally own land which they farm as one business. David wishes to leave the partnership and farm one-third of the land on his own. David's interest in two-thirds of the land is exchanged for Peggy and Philip's interest in one-third of the land. David leaves the partnership, and Peggy and Philip continue to farm the remaining two-thirds of the land now jointly owned by them as a new partnership. Roll-over relief is available to David, Peggy and Philip, based on the value of the land at the date the interests were exchanged.

Spouse and civil partners

14.19 In *Tod v Mudd* (1986) 60 TC 237, Ch D, it was established that spouses are separate persons for the purpose of roll-over relief so that the conditions for relief apply separately to each person's interest in an asset used by a husband and wife partnership. The same principle would extend to registered civil partners who are also partners in business.

Mr Mudd disposed of his accountancy practice, making a gain. He and his wife acquired a property as tenants in common as the new asset, and claimed roll-over relief for the gain from the practice disposal. The Mudds lived in 25% of the property and used 75% as a guest house. A trust deed recorded that the property would be held by them upon trust as to 75% for Mr Mudd and as to 25% for his wife. Mr Mudd claimed that 75% of the cost of acquisition of the premises qualified for roll-over relief.

It was held that he was entitled to relief only in respect of 56.25% of the premises, being 75% × 75% of his undivided share of the premises. This also illustrates the principle of restricting the relief where only part of the building is used for business purposes (see **14.31**).

Limited liability partnerships

14.20 A limited liability partnership (LLP) is treated for CGT purposes in the same way as any other partnership while it is trading, despite being a body corporate (see **6.24**). The LLP itself is regarded as transparent for CGT purposes, with each member being charged to tax on his share of any gains accruing to the LLP (*TCGA 1992, s 59A*).

However, when an LLP ceases to trade, it loses its tax 'transparency' and reverts to its corporate status. This applies unless there is merely a temporary break in trading where, for example, the LLP has ceased to carry on one trade and disposed of its assets in order to raise funds to start another trade (*TCGA 1992, s 59A(2), (3)*).

Any gains rolled over or postponed by a member of the LLP might escape as a result of the reversion to corporate status, but for a special rule that deems the member to have realised a chargeable gain immediately before the LLP ceased to be transparent. This rule operates as set out below:

● Where, immediately before 'the time of cessation of trade' (see below), an LLP member holds an asset (or an interest in an asset) that he acquired for a consideration treated as reduced by virtue of a roll-over relief claim under *s 152* or *s 153*, he is treated as if a chargeable gain equal to the amount of the reduction accrued to him immediately before that time.

14.21 *Roll-over relief for business assets*

- Where a gain postponed by virtue of a *s 154(2)* claim (see **14.38**) made by an LLP member has not accrued before the time of cessation of trade, he is treated as if that gain accrued immediately before that time.

- The 'time of cessation of trade' is the time when *s 59A(1)* ceases to apply to the LLP, ie when it loses its tax transparency (*TCGA 1992, s 156A*).

Groups of companies

14.21 The trades carried on by members of a group of companies (as defined) are treated as a single trade for roll-over relief purposes. The definition of a 'group of companies' is examined in **9.33**.

ASSET CLASSES

14.22 Both the old assets and the new assets must fall within one of the classes listed in *TCGA 1992, s 155*, but they do not have to fall within the same class as each other. These classes are summarised in Table 14.1, and are explained further in the following paragraphs.

Table 14.1

Class	
Class 1, Head A	1. Any building or part of a building, and any permanent or semi-permanent structure in the nature of a building, occupied (as well as used) only for the purposes of the trade. 2. Any land occupied (as well as used) only for the purposes of the trade.
Class 1, Head B	Fixed plant or machinery that does not form part of a building or of a permanent or semi-permanent structure in the nature of a building.
Class 2	Ships, aircraft and hovercraft
Class 3	Satellites, space stations and spacecraft (including launch vehicles)
Class 4	Goodwill
Class 5	Milk quotas (and formerly potato quotas)
Class 6	Ewe and suckler cow premium quotas
Class 7	Fish quotas
Class 7A	Payment entitlements under the single payment scheme for farmers
Class 8A	Lloyd's underwriters syndicate capacity
Class 8B	Lloyd's members' agent pooling arrangements

Land and buildings

14.23   Head A of Class 1 is excluded where the trade is a trade of dealing in or developing land. However, Head A can apply where a profit on the sale of any land held for the purposes of the trade would not form part of the trading profits.

Head A does not apply where the trade is a trade of providing services for the occupier of land in which the trader has an estate or interest. A lessor of tied premises is treated as both occupying and using the premises for the purposes of the trade (*TCGA 1992, s 156*).

Fixed plant or machinery

14.24   It was established in *Williams v Evans* (1982) 59 TC 509 that, in Head B of Class 1, the word 'fixed' applies to both plant and machinery. Motor vehicles, for example, would normally be excluded. HMRC apply four tests in determining whether an item of plant or plant or machinery is fixed:

(a)   In the context of the particular trade, is the object plant or machinery as opposed to, for example, trading stock or part of a building?

(b)   Does the taxpayer intend to hold the object in a particular location indefinitely for use in his trade?

(c)   Is the location of the object in a particular site essential to its function in the trade?

(d)   What means of permanent fixing are available, or necessary, without rendering the object part of the land or buildings, and without damaging or destroying the object? (CG60960).

HMRC will not include in this category items of plant and machinery that have become part of a building, such as lifts or escalators. Those items may well qualify for roll-over relief, but under Class 1, Head A rather than Head B (CG60960).

Ships, aircraft and hovercraft

14.25   For the purposes of Class 3 in Table 14.1, hovercraft are as defined in *Hovercraft Act 1968, s 4*. The definition of 'ships' is taken from *Merchant Shipping Act 1995, s 742* as 'every description of vessel used in navigation not propelled by oars'. HMRC accept that 'ships' for this purpose includes fishing boats, motorised cruisers and yachts, and that 'aircraft' includes aeroplanes, helicopters, airships and hot air balloons (CG61020).

Goodwill

14.26   Goodwill is not defined in *TCGA 1992*, possibly because it means different things for different businesses. HMRC's current guidance, at CG68000–CG68330, acknowledges that goodwill comprises a variety of elements within a business (CG68010). However, the key roll-over relief case involving goodwill, *Balloon Promotions Ltd v HMRC* [2006] SpC 524, is mentioned only briefly, and the bulk of the HMRC guidance appears to ignore entirely the view of the Special Commissioner in that case.

In *Balloon Promotions Ltd*, a franchisee operating a restaurant business sold the business to the franchisor and allocated part of the consideration to goodwill not inherent in the property. HMRC contended that there was no saleable goodwill and that the consideration represented compensation for early termination of the franchise agreements. The Special Commissioner held that goodwill was attached to the franchisee's business, and that the consideration obtained for it qualified for roll-over relief.

In relation to the disposal and acquisition of business assets, the point of contention is whether the goodwill is inseparable from the business, or is inseparable from a particular asset used by the business, such as a building (see **15.9**). It is fair to say that the issue of goodwill as it attaches to a business property, or not as the case may be, is a controversial one.

HMRC's view is that only goodwill which is not personal goodwill or inherent goodwill can be freely transferred, although inherent goodwill may be sold where the associated building is also transferred to the purchaser.

Goodwill is classified as a type of intangible asset for the corporate intangible asset regime (see **14.27**), but other intangible assets, such as copyrights, are not classified as 'goodwill' for the purposes of roll-over relief. For a detailed discussion of the taxation of intangible assets such as copyrights, trademarks and patents, see *Taxation of Intellectual Property* (Bloomsbury Professional), 3rd edition.

Intangible assets

14.27   Classes 4–7A in Table 14.1 do not apply to companies, except where transitional rules apply for acquisitions before 1 April 2002, because those assets listed are included in the corporation tax regime for intangible assets (*CTA 2009, Pt 8*). Chapter 10 of *Corporation Tax 2013/14* (Bloomsbury Professional) contains detailed coverage of the intangible assets regime.

Class 7A refers to rights under the Single Payment Scheme (SPS) for farmers, which is governed by EC regulations: *Council Regulation (EC) 73/2009*.

Acquisition of the same asset

14.28   The legislation refers to investment in 'other assets'; but, by concession, where a person disposes of a trade (or a trade asset) and repurchases the same asset later for purely commercial reasons, HMRC will regard that asset as a 'new asset' unless the disposal and reacquisition 'appears to have been carried out for avoidance purposes'. This concession may be applied to partnership changes resulting in reacquisition of fractional shares in partnership assets (ESC D16).

However, it was held in *Watton v Tippett* (1997) 69 TC 491 that a gain arising on a part disposal of land and buildings cannot be rolled over against the acquisition of the part retained after the part disposal.

By concession, capital expenditure to enhance the value of other assets is treated as incurred in acquiring other assets provided that:

● the other assets are used only for the purposes of the trade; or

● on completion of the work, the assets are immediately taken into use and used only for the purposes of the trade (ESC D22).

Another concession applies where a person carrying on a trade uses the proceeds from the disposal of an old asset to acquire a further interest in another asset that is already in use for the purposes of the trade. That further interest is treated as a new asset taken into use for the purposes of the trade (ESC D25).

A right to unascertainable future consideration may be received as part of the consideration for disposal of the old asset. Roll-over relief is not available on a later disposal of that right, because the right is not among the classes of asset listed in *TCGA 1992, s 155* (CG14970).

USE OF ASSETS

New assets to be used 'on acquisition'

14.29   A new asset must be taken into use for the purpose of the business 'on the acquisition' of the asset if it is to form part of a roll-over relief claim (*TCGA 1992, s 152(1)*).

HMRC interpret this as meaning that the asset must be taken into use at the time any contracts are completed – by conveyance or delivery – and possession has been obtained. See also **14.32** regarding the period of ownership, in relation to the restriction of relief where there is non-business use.

However, allowance is made for necessary alterations, adaptations or other steps required before the asset can be taken into use. HMRC guidance indicates that relief should not be denied solely on the grounds that the asset was not brought into use as soon as it was acquired, provided that it was brought into use as soon as practicable after the acquisition and without unnecessary delay. HMRC would expect the interval to be short in most cases (CG60800).

In *Milton v Chivers (HMIT)* [1995] SpC 57, the Special Commissioner held that the phrase 'on the acquisition' did not mean 'immediately on the acquisition', but it did mean that the taking into use and the acquisition must be 'reasonably proximate' to one another.

By concession (ESC D24), HMRC will allow relief where a new asset is not taken into use for the purposes of a trade immediately on acquisition but:

- the owner proposes to incur capital expenditure on enhancing its value;

- any work arising from such expenditure begins as soon as possible after acquisition and is completed within a reasonable time;

- the asset is taken into use – and, in the case of land and buildings, occupied – for the purpose of the trade (and for no other purpose) on completion of the work; and

- the asset is neither let nor used for any non-trading purpose in the period between acquisition and the time it is taken into use for the purpose of the trade.

HMRC regard this approach as an interpretation of *TCGA 1992, s 152(1)* that gained judicial approval in *Steibelt (Inspector of Taxes) v Paling* (1999) 71 TC 376, Ch D, rather than as a concession, but have indicated that they will continue to draw on that interpretation where appropriate (CG60810).

Asset not fully used for business

14.30   There are two situations in which the taxpayer needs to calculate the acquisition or disposal consideration relating to a deemed 'separate asset' qualifying for roll-over relief.

Whole of building not used for business

14.31   Where, during the period of ownership (or any substantial part of it), part of a building or structure is used for the purposes of a trade and part is not so used, then the part used only for trade purposes – together with any land occupied for purposes ancillary to it – is treated as a separate asset. HMRC regard this rule, together with the reference in Head A of Class 1 of the list of qualifying assets to 'any building or part of a building', as applying to the new assets as well as the old assets. The rule applies only to buildings. Assets in other classes must be used for the purpose of the business and for no other purpose (*TCGA 1992, s 152(6)*; CG60520).

The availability of roll-over relief for a domestic property partly used for business is illustrated in *PEMS Butler Ltd and others v HMRC* [2012] UKFTT 73 (TC). The company owned a small farm. The farmhouse was occupied as a home by the company directors, and also used in part for the company's trade (making toy model kits), as were a number of the outbuildings. The tribunal found that only the areas of the property entirely used for the trade (storage and office areas) could be brought into a roll-over relief claim; the residential areas could not be included.

Asset not used for full ownership period

14.32   If the old asset was not used for the purposes of the trade throughout the period of ownership (see **14.33**), a part of the asset representing its use for the purposes of the trade is treated as a separate asset used wholly for the purposes of the trade. This part is to be calculated having regard to the time and extent to which it was, and was not, used for the purposes of the trade (*TCGA 1992, s 152(7)*). This rule can apply to assets other than buildings.

Any period of ownership before 31 March 1982 is ignored for these purposes. Any apportionment of consideration for the above purposes is to be made in a just and reasonable manner and where appropriate (*TCGA 1992, s 152(11)*).

Example 14.3

Khaled bought a freehold property on 1 September 2004 and let it to a tenant for three years before occupying and using it for the purpose of his trade from 1 September 2007. He used the whole of the property for the purpose of the trade until he sold it six years later for £150,000.

A chargeable gain of £90,000 accrued for the nine-year ownership period. Two-thirds of the gain arising is deemed to relate to the business use of the asset, ie £60,000. This part of the gain may be rolled over if Khaled reinvests the proceeds of £150,000 in qualifying assets.

The period of ownership

14.33   HMRC consider that the period of ownership of an asset for roll-over relief purposes is the period of beneficial ownership and possession. This period may not be the same as the period from the time of the acquisition and the time of disposal, as defined for the general purposes of CGT. For example, *TCGA 1992, s 28* provides that, where an asset is acquired under an unconditional contract, the date on which the acquisition is made is the date the contract is made (and not, if different, the date on which the asset is conveyed or transferred). However, beneficial ownership may not be obtained until completion and the period of ownership for roll-over relief begins when beneficial ownership is obtained, but HMRC have indicated that they will not pursue 'trivial adjustments' (CG60520).

OPERATION OF THE RELIEF

Full relief

14.34   Roll-over relief is given without restriction if an amount equal to the net consideration for the disposal (after deducting allowable costs of disposal) of the old asset is reinvested in a new, qualifying asset. For this purpose the net consideration for the old asset is compared with the cost of acquisition, including allowable incidental costs, of the replacement asset (CG60770).

First, the actual consideration for the disposal is reduced and treated as if it were of such an amount as would give rise to neither a gain nor a loss. Where indexation allowance is available on the disposal (see **9.14**), this means that the disposal proceeds are deemed to be equal to the sum of the original cost plus the indexation allowance. Then the amount of this reduction is deducted from the amount (or value used for CGT purposes) of the consideration for the acquisition of the new asset.

Where the taxpayer is a company, the application of indexation allowance can result in a greater gain accruing on the disposal of the second asset than would accrue in total on the disposal of both assets without roll-over relief. This is because the roll-over relief claim reduces the base cost of the second asset and thus reduces the effect of indexation allowance. The advantage is that the tax due on the disposal of the first asset is postponed for some years.

For the interaction of roll-over relief with other CGT reliefs, see **14.48–14.50**.

Example 14.4

On 30 May 2005, Art Ltd sold a warehouse for £300,000, which cost £100,000 on 1 July 1996. The incidental costs of disposal were £6,000. Art Ltd acquired a freehold property on 1 November 2005 also for £300,000 and incurred incidental costs of acquisition amounting to £5,000. The total cost of acquisition is £305,000, and full roll-over relief is due because this exceeds the net proceeds of £294,000. The freehold building was sold on 23 April 2013 for £500,000.

The taxable gain on the disposal of the freehold property is calculated as follows:		
Warehouse	£	£
Disposal proceeds May 2005		300,000
Less incidental costs of disposal		(6,000)
Less cost in 1996	100,000	
Indexation allowance: 0.260 × £100,000	26,000	(126,000)
Chargeable gain rolled over:		168,000
Freehold		
Disposal proceeds in April 2013		500,000
Costs of acquisition in Nov 2005	305,000	
Less rolled-over gain	(168,000)	
	137,000	
Indexation allowance 0.253 × 137,000	39,593	(176,593)
Chargeable gain:		323,407

Partial relief

14.35 Some relief may be available if only a part of the consideration for the disposal of the old assets is reinvested in new assets. The part not reinvested must be less than the amount of the gain if any relief is to be obtained. In this situation:

(a)   the chargeable gain is reduced to the amount not reinvested; and

(b)   the amount of this reduction is deducted from the consideration for the acquisition of the new asset.

The reduction in (a) and (b) does not affect the tax treatment of the other parties to the transactions (*TCGA 1992, s 153(1)*).

Example 14.5

Bernard sold a hovercraft in October 2010 for £150,000, realising a chargeable gain of £50,000. He acquired a new passenger ferry (a ship) in June 2012 for £120,000. Bernard is treated in effect as having reinvested the cost of the hovercraft, ie £100,000, first.

The remaining £20,000 invested is treated as derived from the gain, so that £30,000 of the gain was not reinvested. The chargeable gain accruing on disposal of the old hovercraft is reduced by £20,000 to £30,000, and the acquisition cost of the new ship is also reduced by £20,000.

Assets held on 31 March 1982

14.36   Assets held by non-corporate taxpayers on 6 April 2008, which were also held by the same taxpayer in the same capacity on 31 March 1982, are automatically rebased to their market value at 31 March 1982. Before 6 April 2008, all taxpayers could elect for all their assets held on 31 March 1982 to be rebased to that date. This rebasing election still applies for companies (see **9.10**). Rebasing excludes from tax any gains arising before 31 March 1982.

Halving relief applies to the 'deferred charge' arising where roll-over relief was obtained on a disposal before 6 April 1988 of an asset held on 31 March 1982. If no adjustment were made on the occasion of a post-1988 disposal of the new asset, the pre-1982 element of the deferred gain would be taxed. In broad terms and subject to certain exceptions, where the deferred gain accrues after 5 April 1988, it is halved (see **9.12**) (*TCGA 1992, Sch 4*). Halving relief only applies to taxpayers subject to corporation tax from 6 April 2008.

DEPRECIATING ASSETS

14.37   Special rules apply where the new assets are 'depreciating assets'. The provisions of *TCGA 1992, ss 152* and *153* (roll-over relief for business assets) and *s 229* (roll-over relief on disposals to employee share ownership trusts) are modified and the following definitions are applied for the purpose of the special rules described below:

- the 'held-over gain' is the amount by which, under the normal rules, the chargeable gain on the first asset ('asset A') is reduced, with a corresponding reduction of the allowable expenditure on another asset ('asset B'); and

- where a gain of any amount is described as being 'carried forward to any asset', this refers to a reduction of that amount in a chargeable gain, coupled with a reduction of the same amount in expenditure allowable in respect of the asset (*TCGA 1992, s 154(1)*).

An asset is a 'depreciating asset' at a particular time if it is a wasting asset (as defined in *TCGA 1992, s 44*) or will become a wasting asset within ten years. *TCGA 1992, s 44* provides that, subject to certain exceptions, an asset is a wasting asset if it has a predictable life not exceeding 50 years. An asset is a depreciating asset, therefore, if it has a predictable life of no more than 60 years (*TCGA 1992, s 154(7)*).

Postponing the held-over gain

14.38   Where asset B is a depreciating asset, the gain accruing on asset A is not carried forward as described above. Instead, the taxpayer is treated as if the held-over gain did not accrue until the first of the following events occurs:

- he disposes of asset B;

- he ceases to use asset B for the purposes of a trade carried on by him; or

- on the expiration of a period of ten years beginning with the acquisition of asset B (*TCGA 1992, s 154(2)*).

By concession, no gain is deemed to accrue under this rule where the asset ceases to be used for the purpose of the trade because of the taxpayer's death (ESC D45).

Acquisition of a third asset

14.39   The taxpayer might acquire asset C, a non-depreciating asset, before the postponed gain is deemed to accrue as set out in **14.38**. In such a case, he could make a claim to roll over the gain on the disposal of asset A against the acquisition cost of asset C. The time limits for reinvestment (see **14.11**) would be regarded as met, and the initial claim, relating to the acquisition of asset B, would be treated as withdrawn. The claim to roll-over relief against the cost of asset C would be limited to the amount of the gain that was held over on the acquisition of asset B (*TCGA 1992, s 154(4), (5)*).

The amount invested in asset C may be less than the net proceeds of asset A. In that event, the above rule might give rise to a CGT liability because only partial relief would be available. However, the taxpayer may ask for the postponed gain to be treated as derived from two separate assets. The effect would be to split the gain on disposal of asset A into two parts:

- the first part being rolled over against the acquisition of asset C (as in **14.34**); and

- the second part being postponed (as in **14.38**) (*TCGA 1992, s 154(4), (6)*).

Example 14.6

On 25 May 2010, Farmer Gooney sold a barn making a gain of £84,000. On 28 September 2012, he acquired a leasehold interest in a vineyard at a cost of £105,000, which had 35 years to run at that time. Gooney immediately started to cultivate the vineyard as part of his farm, and submitted a roll-over relief claim.

If the new asset had not been a depreciating asset, the gain of £84,000 would be reduced to nil and the cost of acquiring the leasehold reduced to £21,000 (£105,000 less £84,000). However, the cost of acquiring the leasehold vineyard is not reduced. The held-over gain of £84,000 is treated as accruing on the earliest of:

(a)   the date of disposal of the leasehold interest;

(b)   Gooney ceasing to use the leasehold for the purposes of a trade; and

(c)   28 September 2022, being ten years following the date of acquisition of the leasehold.

On 31 March 2013, Gooney purchased additional agricultural land at a cost of £100,000, and immediately used it in his farming business. Gooney made a claim for roll-over relief in respect of this new land, but continued to use the leasehold vineyard for the purposes of his business. None of the events (a)–(c) above had yet occurred.

The result of this latest roll-over claim is as follows:

		£
Asset A – barn		
Disposal proceeds		84,000
Less roll-over relief to asset C – agricultural land		(84,000)
Revised gain		Nil
Asset B – leasehold vineyard		
Previous claim withdrawn – no liability on postponed charge		
Asset C – agricultural land		
Cost of acquisition		100,000
Less roll-over relief		(84,000)
Revised cost		16,000

Transfer to a European Company or Societas Europaea ('SE')

14.40   The treatment of the postponed gain is modified where the taxpayer transfers asset B, or shares in a company that holds asset B, to an 'SE' in circumstances in which *TCGA 1992, s 140E* (merger leaving assets within UK tax charge) applies. The postponed gain is not brought into charge. Instead, the SE is treated as though it claimed the roll-over relief (*TCGA 1992, s 154(2A)*).

CLAIMS

Time limits

14.41 The time limits set out in **14.42** and **14.43** begin with the end of the tax year or accounting period in which the disposal takes place, or the one in which the new assets are acquired, whichever is the later. See **14.45** regarding provisional relief. The time limits may be extended in the event of an assessment being made to recover tax lost through fraud or neglect (*TMA 1970, ss 36(3), 43(2), 43A–43C*). A claim may be made after a CGT assessment has become final (CG60600).

Individuals, trustees and personal representatives

14.42 A taxpayer within self-assessment has to submit the claim within four years after the end of the tax year in which the old asset is disposed of, or that in which the new asset is acquired, whichever is the later (CG60600; *TMA 1970, s 43*). HMRC can exercise their discretion to accept a late claim, if the claim is made in writing with all the necessary details (see **14.44**). The HMRC view on when late claims can be accepted is set out in their Self Assessment Claims Manual at SACM10035.

Companies

14.43 A company must claim within four years from the end of the accounting period to which the claim relates, which (as above) will be the later of the period in which the old asset is disposed of and the new asset is acquired (CG60600; *FA 1998, Sch 18, para 55*).

How to claim

14.44 A claim must be in writing and must specify:

- the claimant;
- the assets disposed of;
- the date of disposal of each of those assets;
- the consideration received for the disposal of each of those assets;
- the assets acquired;
- the dates of acquisition of each of those assets (or the dates on which unconditional contracts for acquisition were entered into);
- the consideration given for each of those assets; and

- the amount of the consideration received for the disposal of each of the specified assets that has been applied in the acquisition of each replacement asset (CG60605).

HMRC provide a claim form for individuals, PRs and trustees to use in helpsheet HS290.

Provisional relief

14.45   In some cases the CGT payable on the gain arising on the disposal may become due before a claim to roll-over relief can be established. Provisional relief is available to ensure that the funds available for reinvestment are not depleted by a payment of tax that would be recovered later. The taxpayer is required to make a declaration, in his tax return for the tax year (or accounting period) in which the disposal took place, that:

(a)   the whole (or a specified part) of the consideration will be applied in the acquisition of, or of an interest in, other assets ('the new assets') which on the acquisition will be taken into use, and used only, for the purposes of the trade;

(b)   the acquisition will take place as mentioned within the time limits for reinvestment set out in *TCGA 1992, s 152(3)* (see **14.11**); and

(c)   the new assets will be within the classes listed in *TCGA 1992, s 155* (see **14.22**).

The declaration may be made on the form provided in HMRC's helpsheet HS290, or in any other form, provided it is attached to the tax return and it contains sufficient information as detailed in helpsheet HS290. Until the declaration ceases to have effect (see **14.46**), relief will be available as if the taxpayer had acquired the new assets and made a claim for relief. The rules set out in *s 152* regarding partial business use, successive trades, deemed consideration and apportionments are applied accordingly (*TCGA 1992, s 153A*).

Declaration ceasing to have effect

14.46   The declaration ceases to have effect:

- if it is withdrawn before the 'relevant day', on the day on which it is withdrawn;

- if it is superseded by a valid claim to roll-over relief, on the day on which it is superseded;

- in other cases, on the 'relevant day' (*TCGA 1992, s 153A(3)*).

The 'relevant day' for CGT is the third anniversary of 31 January following the tax year in which the disposal of the old assets took place. For corporation tax, it is the fourth anniversary of the last day of the accounting period in which the disposal took place (*TCGA 1992, s 153A(5)*).

Once a declaration has ceased to have effect, all necessary adjustments are to be made, including the making or amending of assessments, irrespective of any time limits that would otherwise apply. If the taxpayer who has obtained provisional relief dies before the relevant day and before having made a valid claim to roll-over relief, HMRC will ask his personal representatives to withdraw the declaration (*TCGA 1992, s 153A(4)*; CG60700).

Interest and penalties

14.47   Interest may be charged on any tax ultimately found to be payable in the event that the taxpayer does not proceed with reinvestment, or partial relief only is obtained. HMRC guidance says:

'The deterrent of frivolous declarations lies in the taxpayer's liability to pay interest from the time the tax should have been paid if the declared intention does not lead to an acquisition. Only if, exceptionally, the declaration is clearly found to have been made fraudulently or negligently should you consider the possibility of penalties.' (CG60700)

INTERACTION WITH OTHER RELIEFS

Incorporation relief

14.48   Roll-over relief under *TCGA 1992, s 152* takes precedence over relief on the transfer of a business to a company under *TCGA 1992, s 162* (see **15.18**).

Roll-over relief on the transfer of a business to a company in exchange for shares is given automatically under *TCGA 1992, s 162*, although the taxpayer may elect to disapply the relief on such a transfer. If a *TCGA 1992, s 152* roll-over relief claim is made later, the computation of any *TCGA 1992, s 162* relief given may be reopened and revised.

However, HMRC consider that this is not possible once there has been a disposal of any of the shares and an assessment of a chargeable gain on that disposal has become final and conclusive (CG61560).

Entrepreneurs' relief

14.49   The HMRC view is that roll-over relief under *TCGA 1992, s 152* takes priority over entrepreneurs' relief (CG64136). Any part of the gain not rolled over may be eligible for entrepreneurs' relief.

Chapter 15

Incorporation of a business

OVERVIEW

15.1   Where a sole trader or partners in a partnership transfer their business into a company, this will normally involve the transfer of all the assets of the business into the ownership of the company. In some cases, the business owners may wish to retain certain assets such as property in their own hands, in order to avoid an SDLT charge on the transfer and potentially enable funds to be extracted from the company in the form of rent. However, where business assets are retained, this can restrict the CGT relief available on incorporation (see **15.8**).

The transfer of the assets to the new company is a disposal for CGT purposes. Normally the new company and the individuals who become the shareholders in that company are then connected persons, as those shareholders will control the company (*TCGA 1992, s 286(6)*). In this case, the value of consideration must be taken as the open market value of the assets that are transferred (see **3.6**).

The assets of the business may include stock, plant and machinery, land, buildings, investments and goodwill. The goodwill may not have been included on the balance sheet of the original business, but it will have a value. However, some forms of goodwill are not separable from the proprietors, so cannot be transferred to the company (see **15.9**).

Taxable capital gains are likely to arise on the land, buildings, investments and goodwill, but these gains can be deferred with a form of roll-over relief known as incorporation relief (*TCGA 1992, s 162*). Guidance on this form of roll-over relief is found in the HMRC Capital Gains Manual at CG65700–CG65780.

Incorporation relief is automatic, if the conditions apply, but it may be disapplied by election (see **15.11**). Where incorporation relief does not apply, hold-over relief for gifts of business assets may be available, as discussed in **15.21** and **Chapter 13** (*TCGA 1992, s 165*). Entrepreneurs' relief (see **Chapter 11**) may also be used, independently or in conjunction with hold-over relief, to reduce any residue of gains not covered by hold-over relief (see **Chapter 13**).

Focus

Incorporation relief does not require a claim and has no time limit (see **15.5**).

Disincorporation relief must be jointly claimed by company and shareholders, and is restricted to disincorporations occurring before 1 April 2018 (see **Chapter 9**).

EFFECT OF THE RELIEF

Full relief

15.2   The effect of incorporation relief is that the total of the chargeable gains less allowable losses accruing on the transfer of assets (the 'old assets') to the company is deducted from the acquisition cost of the shares received in exchange for those assets.

The gains are therefore deferred until a subsequent disposal of those shares. Where the shares are not all of the same class, the relief is apportioned by reference to the market value of the shares (*TCGA 1992, s 162(2), (3)*).

Full relief is available only where the business assets are exchanged wholly for shares in the company. However, full CGT relief may not always be desirable, as other exemptions or reliefs may be preferred.

Partial relief

15.3   If the transfer is made partly for cash, the gains are apportioned by reference to the value of the shares and the other proceeds received. The amount of relief available is found by applying the fraction A/B to the gain on the old assets, where:

- A is the 'cost of the new assets', ie the shares; and

- B is the value of the whole of the consideration received in exchange for the business.

The cost of the shares (A) is found by adding together the items of expenditure that would be allowable as a deduction (under *TCGA 1992, s 38(1)(a)*) in the event of a chargeable gain arising on a disposal of the shares. This will normally be the market value of the assets transferred to the company (see **15.15**). The relief cannot exceed the cost of the shares. The gains attributed to the shares are rolled over, while the remaining gains are immediately chargeable to CGT (*TCGA 1992, s 162(4), (5)*).

See **15.17** regarding the consideration received for the transfer and how relief is restricted where part of the consideration is not in the form of shares.

Incorporation of a partnership

15.4   Where the business transferred to the company was carried on in partnership, incorporation relief is computed separately for each individual partner based on the consideration he receives. Relief is not denied to the individuals where one of the partners is a company, so long as the whole of the business is transferred to a company; but, as indicated in **15.5**, the corporate partner is not eligible for relief.

This means that it is possible to obtain incorporation relief for a partner who transfers his interest in the business in exchange for shares, while his fellow partner who receives only cash for his interest is unable to roll over any capital gain arising. This provides considerable flexibility when arranging the transfer of a business previously carried on by a partnership.

THE CONDITIONS

15.5   The gains arising on the transfer of assets to the company are automatically deferred if the conditions are met. No claim is required, but the relief can be disapplied by election (see **15.11**). The key conditions are set out below:

(a)   the transfer must be made by a person other than a company (see below);

(b)   the business must be transferred as a going concern (see **15.7**);

(c)   the transfer must include the whole assets of the business, or the whole of those assets other than cash (see **15.8**); and

(d)   the transfer must be made wholly or partly in exchange for shares issued by the company to the transferor – these shares are known as the 'new assets' (*TCGA 1992, s 162(1)*).

Incorporation relief is available for transfers of a business (see **15.6**) by an individual, trustee or personal representative. 'Company' includes any unincorporated association (but not a partnership), so that condition (a) means that relief is not available where an unincorporated association transfers a business to a company (*TCGA 1992, s 288(1)*; CG65710).

Focus

The company that receives the assets need not be specially formed for the purpose. It can be an existing company.

The company does not to have to be resident in the UK, or liable to UK tax.

Incorporation relief is not available where a business conducted by a sole trader or ordinary partnership is transferred to an LLP. This is because, for CGT purposes, the LLP is treated exactly like an ordinary partnership (see **6.24**). Where the business of an LLP is transferred entirely to a company, incorporation relief may apply. However, where the new company is invited to join the LLP as a member and the LLP continues trading as a going concern, the business remains owned by the LLP, and incorporation relief cannot apply.

'Business'

15.6   The relief applies to the transfer of a 'business', which is not defined in the legislation (*TCGA 1992, s 162(1)*). HMRC regard 'business' as taking its normal meaning, which is 'wider than trade' (and would probably include a profession or vocation). HMRC guidance recognises that it is not always easy to draw the line between a business and other activities, but a claim that the passive holding of investments or an investment property amounted to a business is likely to be resisted (CG65715). Having said that, the commercial letting of furnished holiday accommodation may well be accepted by HMRC as a 'business', as it is treated as being a trade for various CGT reliefs (*TCGA 1992, s 241(3), (3A)*).

15.6 *Incorporation of a business*

The definition of 'business' for incorporation relief was explored in *Elizabeth Ramsay v HMRC* [2013] UKUT 226 (TCC). Mrs Ramsay owned a large property that was divided into ten let flats. On incorporation of this business in 2004, she claimed relief under *TCGA 1992, s 162*. Mr and Mrs Ramsay spent about 20 hours a week on tasks connected with the let properties, and it had always been understood that the active management of property would qualify for incorporation relief. However, the First-tier Tribunal denied the relief, on the basis that the activities were more akin to those carried out by a passive owner of an investment property than those of a business owner.

The Upper Tribunal disagreed, saying that the concept of business in the context of this relief is very broad; it does not have to amount to a trade, and there is no exclusion for an investment business. The Upper Tribunal indicated that activities will amount to a business for incorporation relief where they:

- are a serious undertaking or occupation earnestly pursued;

- are something that is actively pursued with reasonable or recognisable continuity;

- have a certain amount of substance in terms of turnover;

- are conducted in a regular manner and on sound business principles; and

- are of a kind which, subject to differences of detail, are commonly made by those who seek to profit from them.

It seems that the degree and regularity of the activities are crucial to qualification as a 'business'.

HMRC will provide businesses with written confirmation of the application of tax law to specific transactions, where there is material uncertainty, or the issue is commercially significant, under the non-statutory business clearance service (see the HMRC Non-statutory Business Clearance Guidance Manual). This service applies to all tax law as it affects UK businesses. Where the question to be addressed is whether the activities of the taxpayer are considered to be a 'business' or a 'trade' for a particular provision, the taxpayer can use the CAP1 clearance service for non-business transactions (see www.hmrc.gov.uk/cap/cap1.htm).

Focus

Under the clearance services described above, HMRC will generally only provide a full answer if the query relates to tax legislation passed within the last four *Finance Acts* or to recent tax cases relating to older legislation.

Going concern

15.7 The business must be transferred as a 'going concern' together with all of the assets of the business (*TCGA 1992, s 162(1)*). HMRC take this to mean that the transfer must comprise 'something more than a collection of assets' (CG65710).

HMRC guidance refers to an Australian case, *Reference under the Electricity Commission (Balmain Electric Light Co Purchase) Act 1950* [1957] 57 SR (NSW) 100, cited in *CIR v Gordon* (see below), where Sugerman J said:

> 'To describe an undertaking as a "going concern" imports no more than that, at the point of time to which the description applies, its doors are open for business; that it is then active and operating, and perhaps also that it has all the plant etc which is necessary to keep it in operation, as distinct from its being only an inert aggregation of plant.'

In *Gordon v CIR* (1991) 64 TC 173, Lord Hope said the Special Commissioner had considered the ability of the business to continue as a going concern for some time in the future after the transfer to the company, but the question whether the activities could be carried on without interruption should be directed to the date of the transfer, and not to some later date. Lord Hope referred to *Kenmir Ltd v Frizzell* [1968] 1 WLR 329, in which Widgery J said that the vital consideration was 'whether the effect of the transaction was to put the transferee in possession of a going concern, the activities of which he could carry on without interruption'.

Whole of the assets of the business

15.8 The transfer must include the whole assets of the business, or the whole of those assets other than cash. HMRC regard cash as including sums held in a bank deposit or current account (*TCGA 1992, s 162(1)*; CG65710).

If an asset is a business asset, it must be transferred to the company. Whether an asset is on the balance sheet is not conclusive, and an asset may remain a business asset after it has been taken off the balance sheet. See **15.9** regarding goodwill.

The requirement that all assets (except cash) must be transferred to the company may be unattractive to the business proprietor. For example, transfers of land and buildings may result in substantial stamp duty land tax liabilities.

As an alternative to securing incorporation relief under *TCGA 1992, s 162*, the proprietor may consider retaining assets outside the company and transferring the remaining chargeable assets to the company for a consideration less than market value. In those circumstances, hold-over relief for gifts, under *TCGA 1992, s 165* (see **15.21**), may be available.

Goodwill

15.9   The goodwill of the business may not appear on the balance sheet, but goodwill can be the most valuable asset to be transferred to the company.

The latest HMRC approach to defining and valuing goodwill is set out at CG68000–CG68330. The definition of goodwill is based on the reputation of the business as it is built up over its lifetime, so a young business has very little goodwill and a more established business should expect to carry a significant value of goodwill. The HMRC view is that goodwill generated within a business cannot be separated from that business when the business is transferred as a going concern, and thus the goodwill is transferred to the company on incorporation of the business (CG68050).

However, this overarching definition is qualified by the following conditions which will restrict the value of goodwill that can be transferred to the company:

- Personal goodwill. This derives from the technical skills, and personal attributes of the business proprietor, such as the personal skills of an author or chef. This form of goodwill cannot be separated from the individual to be transferred into the company (CG68010).

- Inherent goodwill. This is connected to the location where the business is carried out. The HMRC view is that this type of goodwill can be transferred, but generally only when the premises in which the business is run is also transferred to the company. The attachment of this type of goodwill to the property value has implications for stamp duty land tax, as at present HMRC are insisting that SDLT be paid on the value of the goodwill attached to the property which is transferred to the company on incorporation of a business.

Once the personal and inherent aspects of the goodwill are isolated, the balance should be free goodwill that can be transferred to the company, without the need also to transfer the business property. It should be noted that the allocation of goodwill in the sale or transfer agreement does not dictate the tax treatment of the goodwill. However, any apportionment of the total transfer value by HMRC should be done on a just and reasonable basis.

Focus

Where the goodwill to be transferred is likely to have a significant value, you should use the post-transaction valuation procedure (form CG34) to agree the value with HMRC (see **1.35**).

It is important to achieve a realistic valuation of the transferable goodwill, as HMRC frequently challenge valuations that appear over-optimistic.

When submitting the CG34 to check a goodwill valuation, the following should be attached:

- a full summary of all relevant facts, including a full description of the business;

- accounts for the three years before the valuation date; and

- copies of the sale agreement.

The share and assets valuation (SAV) division of HMRC handles all queries relating to the valuation of goodwill, but the CG34 form should be sent to the HMRC office indicated on the form. The CG34 procedure takes at least two months, so a full answer may not be received in time for the tax return filing date.

Example 15.1

In November 2013, Herman transferred his art gallery business, including all the assets and liabilities, to Artware Limited in consideration for 1,000 shares in Artware Limited. Herman started the business in June 2002 and ran it from that date as a sole trader. He did not elect under *TCGA 1992, s 162A* to disapply incorporation relief. The only chargeable asset of the business is goodwill, which is judged to be free goodwill based on the future value of art sales. The value of the business transferred is agreed as follows:

	Value £
Free goodwill (based on the value of the music sales)	250,000
Non-chargeable assets	100,000
Cash	25,000
	375,000
Creditors	(255,000)
Net value of the business	120,000

The gain arising on the transfer is £250,000, ie the value of the free goodwill which has no base cost. The consideration for the business is wholly in the form of shares, so the shares are worth £120,000. The amount of the gain to be rolled over cannot exceed the cost of the shares, which is £120,000.

Thus, £120,000 of the gain is rolled over and the balance of £130,000 is chargeable to CGT in 2013/14, subject to further reliefs and the annual exemption. Artware Limited can claim a corporation tax deduction for the cost of the goodwill it has purchased from Herman under the intangibles regime. Although Herman is connected with Artware Limited, as he controls all the shares, the intangibles regime applies as the goodwill was wholly created after 31 March 2002 (*CTA 2009, s 882*).

Liabilities

15.10   The company may well assume some or all of the liabilities of the business, although there is no requirement for liabilities as well as assets to be transferred to the company for incorporation relief to apply. The company's assumption of liabilities represents additional consideration for the business but, by concession (ESC D32), HMRC do not take this point because they recognise that the transferor does not receive cash to meet the tax liability that would arise by reference to that consideration (CG65745).

HMRC also recognise that the transfer of liabilities reduces the value of the shares issued to the transferor (see Example 15.3). ESC D32 reads:

> 'Where liabilities are taken over by a company on the transfer of a business to the company, HMRC are prepared for the purposes of the "rollover" provision in *TCGA 1992, s 162* not to treat such liabilities as consideration. If therefore the other conditions of *s 162* are satisfied, no capital gain arises on the transfer. Relief under *s 162* is not precluded by the fact that some or all of the liabilities of the business are not taken over by the company.'

Any personal liabilities of the transferor assumed by the company, including his capital account and any tax liability relating to the transfer of the business, are outside the terms of this concession and are treated as part of the consideration. The concession does not affect the calculation of the net cost of the shares (see **15.16**).

Where incorporation relief is obtained by concession, the taxpayer is required by statute to account for the deferred gain becoming chargeable (*TCGA 1992, ss 284A, 284B*).

Example 15.2

Walter carries on an antiquarian bookselling business. He decides to form a company, Bookend Limited, to carry on the business. In August 2013, he transfers the whole of the business undertaking, assets and liabilities to Bookend Limited in exchange for shares. The business assets and liabilities transferred are valued as follows:

		Value	Chargeable gain
Assets	£	£	£
Freehold shop premises		180,000	100,000
Goodwill		36,000	36,000
Fixtures and fittings		4,000	0
Trading stock		52,000	0
Debtors		28,000	0
		300,000	
Liabilities			
Mortgage on shop	50,000		
Trade creditors	20,000	(70,000)	
		230,000	136,000

Bookend Ltd issues 230,000 £1 ordinary shares, valued at par, to Walter. The amount of chargeable gain rolled over on transfer of the business to Bookend Ltd is:

£136,000 × (£230,000 / £230,000) = £136,000.

See **15.13** regarding the formula to calculate the relief due.

ELECTION TO FORGO INCORPORATION RELIEF

Why this is desirable

15.11   Incorporation relief under *TCGA 1992, s 162* does not have to be claimed, but the taxpayer may elect to disapply the relief (*TCGA 1992, s 162A*).

For transfers occurring before 6 April 2008, the disapplication of incorporation relief would crystallise a gain for taper relief. This would be desirable when the shares of the new company were sold within two years of incorporation, which would not allow enough time for full business asset taper relief to build up, or indeed because taper relief was about to be abolished. The available business asset taper relief plus the application of the CGT annual exemption to the balance could reduce the taxable gain to an acceptable level.

The uncertainty surrounding future rates of CGT may encourage the taxpayer to pay tax on the gain in the current period at a known rate, such as at 10% under entrepreneurs' relief, rather than to defer the gain to a future date where the rate of CGT may well be higher.

Once an election under *TCGA 1992, s 162A* is made, all necessary adjustments – eg by means of discharge or repayment of tax – are made to give effect to it (*TCGA 1992, s 162A(1), (6)*).

If two or more individuals owned the business transferred to the company – including ownership by a partnership of which they are partners – then each of them is entitled to elect to disclaim incorporation relief as he or she sees fit, in relation to their own share of the gain accruing on the old assets and their share of the new assets (*TCGA 1992, s 162A(7), (8)*).

Time limit for election

15.12   The election must be made by a notice given to HMRC no later than:

- the first anniversary of 31 January following the tax year in which the transfer took place, where the transferor has disposed of all the new assets by the end of the tax year following the one in which the transfer took place; or

- the second anniversary of 31 January following the tax year in which the transfer took place in any other case.

HMRC advise taxpayers to write to them if they do not want *s 162* to apply to their gains (Helpsheet HS276). The election could also be made by an amendment to the tax return.

For the purpose of this time limit, a disposal of new assets by the transferor is ignored if it is a disposal to a spouse or civil partner falling within the no gain, no loss provisions of *TCGA 1992, s 58* (see **3.63**). A later disposal by the transferee spouse or civil partner is treated as a disposal by the transferor, unless it is a disposal to the transferor (*TCGA 1992, s 162A(2)–(5)*).

Example 15.3

James and Jill ran a computer software business in partnership, sharing all profits equally, until they transferred the business to JJ Limited on 1 June 2012 in exchange for shares in the company. The asset of goodwill was not shown in the partnership balance sheet. On 27 May 2013, they sold their shares for £2 million more than the net asset value of the partnership business prior to incorporation, producing a gain of £1 million each. This excess represented the goodwill that was owned by the partnership but had no acquisition cost for CGT.

In the absence of an election to forgo incorporation relief, the gain of £2 million would be rolled over against the cost of the shares, and a gain of the same amount would arise on the sale of the shares. James and Jill cannot

---

claim entrepreneurs' relief on the disposal of the shares, because they had not owned the ordinary shares in JJ Limited for the minimum 12 months to qualify for that relief.

If an election under *TCGA 1992, s 162A* is made, incorporation relief does not apply and the gain of £2 million on the goodwill is eligible for entrepreneurs' relief as it accrues on 1 June 2012. Entrepreneurs' relief applies to tax the gain at 10% (see **11.4**). The gains accruing on other assets would also have to be considered. The election under *TCGA 1992, 162A* must be made by 31 January 2015 (the first anniversary of 31 January following the tax year in which the transfer took place), because the shares were sold by the end of the 2013/14 tax year following the tax year (2012/13) in which the incorporation took place. The claim for entrepreneurs' relief must also be made by 31 January 2015.

COMPUTING THE RELIEF

The components

15.13   The chargeable gains and allowable losses accruing on the transfer of chargeable assets to the company are computed and the net gains are aggregated. Calculating the incorporation relief can be confusing, as there are two figures arising from the disposal of the old assets:

(A)   the net gain realised on those assets; and

(B)   the net value of the assets transferred to the company.

In addition, the consideration given by the company may involve two amounts:

(C)   the cost of the new shares issued by the company; and

(D)   the value of any other consideration.

The consideration for the transfer needs to be identified and quantified (see **15.14**). Some of the consideration for the assets must be shares issued by the company, but there may be other consideration, such as cash or a loan account (see **15.17**). Where no other consideration is given for the old assets, the value of (D) will be nil, and the value of (B) will equal (C).

The amount of incorporation relief is found using this formula using the values for the list above:

$$(C / (C + D)) \times A.$$

Where there is consideration other than shares, the amount of the gain that can be relieved using incorporation relief is restricted, leaving the balance of the gain immediately chargeable to CGT (see **15.17**). This is best explained by a number of examples. In each case, John transfers his trading business to JDMS Ltd, and the figures of gain and consideration are labelled as per the above list.

Example 15.4

(A): the net gain on the assets transferred to JDMS Ltd was £100,000.

(B): the net value of the assets transferred was £210,000.

The only consideration given by JDMS Ltd was an issue of 210,000 ordinary shares of £1 each.

(C): The cost of the shares is £210,000. The amount of incorporation relief is calculated as:

$$\frac{C}{(C + D)} \times £100,000$$

ie $\dfrac{210,000}{210,000} \times £100,000 = £100,000$

The gain arising on the transfer to the company will be:

	£
Amount of the gain on the old assets	100,000
Less incorporation relief	(100,000)
Gain or loss remaining	Nil
Base cost of the new shares:	
Actual cost	210,000
Less incorporation relief	(100,000)
Revised base cost of new shares	110,000

Example 15.5

(A): the net gain on the assets transferred to JDMS Ltd was £100,000.

(B): the net value of the assets transferred was £75,000.

The only consideration is 75,000 shares issued at £1 per share.

(C): the cost of the shares is £75,000.

The total gain is £100,000, but the incorporation relief is restricted to the cost of the shares, ie £75,000.

The taxable gain arising on the transfer to the company is:

	£
Amount of the gain on the old assets	100,000
Less incorporation relief	(75,000)
Net gain subject to CGT immediately	25,000

The base cost of the new shares becomes:

	£
Actual cost	75,000
Less incorporation relief	(75,000)
Revised base cost	Nil

Example 15.6

(A): the net gain on the assets transferred to JDMS Ltd was £100,000.

(B): the net value of the assets transferred was £180,000.

In exchange, JDMS Ltd supplied the following consideration:

	£
110,000 shares of £1 each with no premium	110,000
Balance left outstanding on loan account	70,000
Total consideration	180,000

(C): the cost of the new shares is £110,000.

(D): the value of other consideration is £70,000.

The amount of incorporation relief becomes:

$$\frac{C}{(C + D)} \times £100,000$$

ie $$\frac{110,000}{180,000} \times £100,000 = £61,111$$

The gain arising on the transfer to JDMS Ltd is:

	£
Amount of the gain on the old assets	100,000
Less incorporation relief	(61,111)
Net gain chargeable to CGT	38,889

CGT will be payable on the gain of £38,889, but this could be subject to a claim for entrepreneurs' relief (see **Chapter 11**).

The base cost of the new shares in JDMS Ltd is:

	£
Actual cost	110,000
Less incorporation relief	(61,111)
Revised cost	48,889

Consideration for the transfer

15.14   The transfer must be made wholly or partly in exchange for shares actually issued by the company to the transferor – these shares are known as the 'new assets' (*TCGA 1992, s 162(1)*).

Focus

The necessary documentation (eg company board minutes, sale agreement) must be prepared, to demonstrate what has been transferred to the company and precisely what the company has given in return.

HMRC accept that there may be a delay in issuing the shares, where, for example, the authorised capital of the company has to be increased. Relief is not denied so long as the issue of shares takes place 'fairly promptly' after the reason for the delay has gone. The task should not be left until the company's first accounts are prepared (CG65720).

Incorporation relief is not available if the shares are issued:

- in consideration for something other than the transfer of the business; or

- to settle a loan account representing cash consideration.

Consideration in the form of shares

15.15   The individual who transfers the assets (the transferor) is not required to acquire any specific level of shareholding in the company. The number of shares may be decided in advance of the transfer, leaving the share premium to be calculated later by reference to the value of the business assets transferred to the company. The transferor is not required to work for the company.

As indicated in **15.2**, where the shares are not all of the same class, the relief is apportioned by reference to their relative market values.

The shares issued do not have to be ordinary shares, but if, for example, redeemable preference shares are issued, the relief may be denied by virtue of the anti-avoidance provisions in *ITA 2007, s 684*. In such a case, the taxpayer should consider requesting an advance clearance under *ITA 2007, s 701*.

The cost of the shares

15.16   As indicated in **15.13**, the effect of incorporation relief is that the net gain accruing on the transfer of assets (the 'old assets') to the company is reduced. That reduction is then apportioned among the shares and goes to reduce the allowable expenditure otherwise deductible on a future disposal of each new share (*TCGA 1992, s 162(2)*), as shown in Examples 15.4–15.6 above.

The cost of the new shares is found by adding together the items of expenditure that would be allowable as a deduction in computing the chargeable gain arising on a disposal of the new assets. The reduction is apportioned between shares of different classes on the basis of their relative market values.

The date of disposal of the old business is taken to be the date of acquisition of the shares.

The transferor and transferee company will normally be connected persons (see **3.20**), so that the chargeable assets will pass to the company at market value. The transferor's cost of acquiring the shares is, therefore, normally the market value of what he gives for those shares, ie the value of the business.

HMRC regard the value of the business as, broadly, the difference between its assets and liabilities – concession ESC D32 relating to liabilities (see **15.10**) is not in point. This may mean that incorporation relief is restricted because the amount of the relief set against the cost of the shares cannot exceed that cost (see Example 15.1). That cost may be very small in the case where the business has significant liabilities.

Consideration other than shares

15.17 Where part of the consideration for the transfer is in a form other than shares, a proportion of the gains accruing on the transfer will become chargeable to CGT. Such consideration would include a credit balance on the transferor's loan or current account with the company, except where the balance represents consideration which is to be satisfied in the form of shares and there is a delay in issuing the shares (see **15.14**). HMRC do not accept that cash consideration or other consideration can be regarded as being given for one or more specified assets (CG65720).

Focus

It may well be beneficial to arrange for part of the consideration to be in the form of a loan account balance, given that:

- any gain accruing on that part of the consideration may be covered by the CGT annual exemption; and

- the transferor may not wish to 'lock in' all of the consideration in the form of shares in the company.

INTERACTION WITH OTHER RELIEFS

15.18 The interaction of the reliefs available on the disposal of business assets is summarised below.

(a) Roll-over relief for replacement of business assets (*TCGA 1992, s 152*) takes precedence over the other CGT reliefs, because it reduces the consideration to be taken into account in computing the gain on disposal.

(b) Incorporation relief on the transfer of a business to a company (*TCGA 1992, s 162*) follows, because it reduces the net chargeable gains accruing on the assets transferred to the company.

(c) Hold-over relief for gifts of business assets (*TCGA 1992, s 165*) also reduces the chargeable gains; but, since incorporation relief under *TCGA 1992, s 162* is automatic (unless an election is made to forgo it), it must take precedence over *TCGA 1992, s 165* relief.

(d) Entrepreneurs' relief (*TCGA 1992, ss 169H–169S*) can apply to gains not relieved by incorporation relief or hold-over relief (see **15.19**).

Entrepreneurs' relief

15.19 The HMRC view is that roll-over relief under *TCGA 1992, s 152* takes precedence over entrepreneurs' relief and, where part of the gain is not rolled over, entrepreneurs' relief can apply to that part (CG64136). As incorporation relief is a form of roll-over relief, it must be presumed that HMRC believe incorporation relief takes precedence over entrepreneurs' relief.

An alternative view is that entrepreneurs' relief takes priority over incorporation relief for the following reasons:

- Incorporation relief operates by deducting a sum from the gain that would be taxed, but for the incorporation relief given, so the gain must be calculated first. The sum deducted from the gain is also used to reduce the base cost of the shares acquired.

- The taxpayer needs to claim entrepreneurs' relief, whereas incorporation relief under *TCGA 1992, s 162* is applied automatically if the conditions are met, subject to the election to disapply the relief (*TCGA 1992, s 162A*).

The cautious approach would be to disapply incorporation relief using the election (see **15.12**) and claim entrepreneurs' relief (see **Chapter 11**). The alternative is to structure the incorporation so that incorporation relief does not apply (see **15.20**).

Incorporation: using hold-over relief

15.20 A hold-over relief claim may be made on the transfer of a business to a company where *s 162* relief is either not available or is restricted. Hold-over relief may be useful if the sole trader or partners wish to retain assets outside the company, but the relief is restricted where there is actual consideration, either in the form of shares or a credit balance on a director's loan account with the company.

In order to qualify for hold-over relief, the transfer to the company must be a disposal otherwise than by way of a bargain at arm's length, including a transaction deemed to be such because it is between connected persons.

Table 15.1 sets out some of the key features of incorporation relief (*TCGA 1992, s 162*) and hold-over relief (*TCGA 1992, s 165*) to be considered by a taxpayer contemplating the incorporation of a business.

Table 15.1

Incorporation relief	*Hold-over relief for gifts of business assets*
Relief is automatic unless an election is made to disapply it	Relief must be claimed
Relief need not apply to all partners	Relief need not be claimed by all partners

Incorporation relief	Hold-over relief for gifts of business assets
Relief is given in full or in part on all chargeable assets transferred, depending on the extent of consideration other than shares	Relief may be claimed either on all assets or on specified assets only
Relief is available only if all the assets (or all the assets except cash) are transferred	Relief may be claimed even if some non-cash assets are not transferred
Gain is rolled over against the cost of the shares issued to the transferor(s) as consideration	Gain is held over against the cost of the chargeable asset(s) acquired by the company
Business must be transferred as a going concern	The transfer of one or more assets used for the purpose of the trade etc will suffice

Further reading

15.21   This chapter covers only the capital gains considerations for the incorporation of a business; for a full discussion of all the tax and practical issues involved with incorporation, see *Incorporating a Business* (Bloomsbury Professional), 4th edition.

Chapter 16

Venture capital reliefs

SIGNPOSTS

- **Three venture capital reliefs** – Key conditions and tax reliefs (see **16.1**).

- **EIS disposal relief** – When it applies, conditions, what happens if a loss results, when disposal relief may be restricted, why income tax relief may be reduced (see **16.2–16.6**).

- **Identification of shares** – Generally on FIFO basis, on company reorganisations, after rights issues, on exchange of shares (see **16.7–16.9**).

- **EIS deferral relief** – When it is available, investor must be an individual or trustee resident in the UK (see **16.10–16.12**).

- **How to claim EIS deferral relief** – Limiting the amount of relief, what is a qualifying investment, which shares are eligible, time limits for investment, how to submit a claim (see **16.13–16.17**).

- **What happens if the conditions are broken** – Chargeable events, death does not trigger a chargeable event, tax effect of chargeable event, who bears the tax, identifying the shares (see **16.18–16.23**).

- **Interaction with other reliefs** – Share-for-share exchange, taper relief, entrepreneurs' relief (see **16.24–16.26**).

- **When EIS deferral relief is blocked or clawed back** – Reinvesting in the same company, pre-arranged exit for investor, use of put and call options, value received by the investor, value received by another person, replacement of value received, use of investment-linked loans (see **16.27–16.36**).

- **Seed Enterprise Investment Scheme (SEIS)** – Limited reinvestment relief, disposal relief, conditions for the company, shares and the investor (see **16.37–16.44**).

- **Venture capital trusts** – Disposal relief and deferral relief for investments in venture capital trusts (see **16.45–16.53**).

THREE VENTURE CAPITAL RELIEFS

16.1 There are currently three venture capital schemes under which investors can achieve income tax relief, and certain capital gains tax reliefs, in return for directing investment into small and medium-sized unquoted trading companies:

- Enterprise Investment Scheme (EIS);

- Seed Enterprise Investment Scheme (SEIS); and

- Venture capital trusts (VCTs).

HMRC guidance on these schemes is available in their Venture Capital Schemes Manual.

These schemes contain similar conditions for the company that receives the investment (the investee company), and for the relationship between the company and the individual investor. Some key conditions are:

- *Qualifying trade* – The company must exist wholly for the purpose of carrying on one or more qualifying trades. For SEIS, the trade must be less than two years old at the time of the share issue. A qualifying trade is one conducted on a commercial basis which does not consist wholly, or as to a substantial part, of excluded activities *(ITA 2007, s 189)*.

- *Money raised* – The funds raised under an EIS issue must be used within two years of that issue for the qualifying trade; for SEIS issues, the funds raised must be used within three years, and 70% of those funds must be used before the EIS or VCT schemes can be used to raise additional funds.

- *Substantial interest* – For income tax relief to apply, the investor must not have a substantial interest in the company. This means that the investor must not directly or indirectly possess or be entitled to acquire more than 30% of the ordinary share capital, issued share capital, voting power or assets on a winding up. Loan capital is not included in the definition of 'substantial interest' (VCM11080).

- *Employee numbers* – for EIS and VCT, the company must employ no more than 250 full-time equivalents. For SEIS, the company must employ no more than 25 full-time equivalents.

- *Gross asset value* – For EIS and VCT, the cap on gross asset value before investment is £15 million, and £16 million after investment. For SEIS, the gross asset value is limited to £200,000 before the investment.

- *Maximum amount raised* – Under EIS and/ or VCT, the total raised in any 12-month period is limited to £5 million. Under SEIS, the maximum which can be raised per company is £150,000.

Various other conditions apply to both the investor and the EIS company, as discussed in Chapter 3 of *Income Tax 2013/14* (Bloomsbury Professional).

The tax reliefs available under these venture capital schemes are summarised in the following table:

Relief	Income tax relief in each tax year	CGT deferral	CGT disposal
EIS	30% on up to £1 million	On unlimited investment	After three years, if income tax relief not withdrawn.
SEIS	50% on up to £100,000	No	After three years, if income tax relief not withdrawn.
VCT	30% on up to £200,000	Withdrawn from 6 April 2004	If company was VCT at time of acquisition and disposal.

Investments that qualify for income tax relief under SEIS can also qualify for CGT reinvestment relief, which provides an absolute exemption on 100% or 50% of the gain reinvested (see **16.43**). The income tax relief is restricted by the taxpayer's income tax liability for the year, as the relief is given as a reduction of the taxpayer's income tax liability for the year, rather than as an income tax allowance.

EIS DISPOSAL RELIEF

When it applies

16.2   A gain accruing on an individual's disposal of EIS shares is not a chargeable gain, provided certain conditions are met. EIS shares are shares that have attracted income tax relief under the EIS scheme as set out in *ITA 2007, Pt 5*. There are detailed conditions in relation to the individual, the company and its activities.

Disposal relief is not available to trustees. For HMRC guidance regarding this exemption, see HMRC's Venture Capital Schemes Manual at VCM20000–VCM20200 and the HMRC Tax Return Helpsheet HS297.

Conditions

16.3   A gain arising on a disposal of EIS shares is not a chargeable gain if:

(a)   the disposal is made after the end of the 'relevant period' (see below) defined by reference to *ITA 2007, s 159* – this is normally three years;

(b)   the shares have qualified for EIS income tax relief;

(c)   that income tax relief has not been withdrawn; and

(d)   there would be a chargeable gain but for this relief (*TCGA 1992, s 150A*).

The income tax relief condition in (b) means that disposal relief is limited by reference to the maximum annual subscription for which income tax relief is available and the actual tax relief given (see **16.5**). From 6 April 2012, income tax relief can be given on up to £1 million invested in a tax year. Previously, the limit for income tax relief was £500,000 of shares issued in a tax year (*ITA 2007, s 158*). Where the shareholder dies within the qualifying period, the EIS relief is not withdrawn (*ITA 2007, s 209(6)*).

A gain accruing on a disposal within the relevant period (see below) is a chargeable gain, and any loss accruing is an allowable loss. However, a loss accruing on disposal of the shares after the end of the relevant period is also allowable (see **16.4**).

A gain that does not qualify for disposal relief is a chargeable gain. For gains realised before 6 April 2008, business asset taper relief should be available (see **1.15**). However, later gains will only qualify for entrepreneurs' relief if the shareholder held at least 5% of the ordinary shares and voting rights of the EIS company, and was either an employee or officer of the company, or of a company in the same group for 12 months to the date of disposal (see **11.9**).

The term 'relevant period' is defined in *TCGA 1992, Sch 5B, para 19(1)* and *ITA 2007, s 159*, where the relevant period is further split into periods A, B and C. These periods all end immediately before the 'termination date' relating to those shares. The termination date is the later of:

•   the third anniversary of the issue date of the shares; and

•   the third anniversary of the commencement of the trade (*ITA 2007, s 256*).

Losses

16.4   Disposal relief is excluded where a loss accrues on the disposal, with the result that a loss is an allowable capital loss. If disposal relief was not excluded, a loss would not be an allowable loss because *TCGA 1992, s 16(2)* provides that a loss is not an allowable loss if a gain accruing on the same disposal would not be a chargeable gain.

The loss is an allowable loss whether or not EIS income tax relief is withdrawn. However, in calculating the loss, the taxpayer's allowable expenditure is reduced by the amount of the income tax relief obtained and not withdrawn.

Relief for the loss may be claimed against income rather than set off against future capital gains; see **17.16** (*TCGA 1992, s 150A(1), (2), (2A); ITA 2007, s 131*). This restriction of loss relief also applies for the disposal of BES shares acquired before 1 January 1994 where the income tax relief has not been withdrawn (*TCGA 1992, s 150*).

Example 16.1

On 6 April 2008, Christina subscribed £100,000 for new ordinary shares in an EIS company and obtained income tax relief of £20,000. She sold the shares on 20 May 2013, after the termination date, for £90,000 and none of the income tax relief had been withdrawn. The restriction of allowable expenditure turns her loss into a gain, but that gain is not a chargeable gain.

2013/14	£	£
Sale proceeds		90,000
Allowable expenditure	100,000	
Less income tax relief not withdrawn	(20,000)	
		(80,000)
Gain not chargeable to tax:		10,000

Example 16.2

Isobel subscribed £200,000 for EIS shares on 1 July 2011 and obtained 30% income tax relief of £60,000. She sold the shares on 20 June 2013, before the termination date, for £150,000. The income tax relief withdrawn is 30% × £150,000 = £45,000 (*ITA 2007, s 209*). Her allowable loss is:

2013/14	£	£
Consideration		150,000
Allowable expenditure	200,000	
Less income tax relief not withdrawn	(15,000)	
		(185,000)
Allowable loss		35,000

Restriction of disposal relief

16.5
Disposal relief is restricted where the taxpayer did not obtain income tax relief on the whole of the amount subscribed for the shares, unless that restriction

was due solely to the fact that income tax relief is limited to the amount of the taxpayer's income tax liability.

This restriction applies to gains but not losses. It is normally a consequence of the subscription limit (see **16.3**) for income tax relief purposes. The fraction of the gain that is exempt in such a case is found by applying the fraction A/B to the gain, where:

- A is the amount of the income tax relief obtained; and

- B is an amount equal to tax at the rate at which tax relief was given (currently 30%) for that year on the amount subscribed for the shares (*TCGA 1992, s 150A(3); ITA 2007, ss 6, 989*).

Example 16.3

Richard subscribed £250,000 for shares in an EIS company in the tax year 2002/03, when the maximum amount on which income tax relief could be obtained was £150,000. He obtained income tax relief of £30,000 (20% × £150,000) for that year, although 20% tax relief on the full subscription would have been £50,000. He sells the shares in 2013/14 for £400,000. His chargeable gain is:

2013/14	£
Consideration	400,000
Allowable expenditure	(250,000)
Gain	150,000
Exemption:	
£150,000 × (30,000/50,000)	(90,000)
Chargeable gain	60,000

Reduction of income tax relief

16.6   Disposal relief is restricted if the EIS income tax relief was reduced because either or both of (a) or (b) below applied before the disposal (but after 28 November 1994):

(a)   value is received from the company in circumstances where income tax relief is reduced under *ITA 2007, s 213*;

(b)   there is a repayment, redemption, repurchase or payment in circumstances where income tax relief is reduced under *ITA 2007, s 224*.

In these circumstances, the gain is computed in the normal way (applying any restriction required by *TCGA 1992, s 150A(3)* as mentioned in **16.5** above), and the exemption is reduced by an amount found by applying the fraction A/B to the gain, where:

- A is the amount of the reduction in income tax relief; and

- B is the amount of income tax relief before the deduction.

Where the *TCGA 1992, s 150A(3)* restriction applies, the above fraction is applied to the exempt part of the gain, and the deduction is made from that part (*TCGA 1992, s 150B*; VCM20070–VCM20090).

Example 16.4

In May 2006, Sidney subscribed £80,000 for shares in an EIS company. This would normally provide him with income tax relief of £16,000 (20% × £80,000) but his income tax liability for the 2006/07 tax year was only £15,000, so his income tax relief was restricted to £15,000. This restriction of income tax relief does not reduce the exempt gain. However, Sidney received £5,000 of value from the EIS company in 2008. He sells the shares in 2013/14 for £200,000. His chargeable gain is:

2013/14		£	Gain £
Consideration		200,000	
Allowable expenditure		80,000	
Gain, potentially exempt		120,000	120,000
Exemption reduced by value received:	120,000 × (5,000/15,000)	(40,000)	
Exempt gain			(80,000)
Chargeable gain subject to CGT:			40,000

EIS SHARE IDENTIFICATION RULES

FIFO generally

16.7   Where it is necessary to identify shares disposed of with acquisitions made at different times, or to establish whether the shares disposed of were shares that attracted income tax relief, the EIS identification rules in *ITA 2007, s 246* are applied instead of the rules in *TCGA 1992*.

Broadly speaking, identification is made on a first in, first out (FIFO) basis. There are detailed rules for identification of shares acquired on the same day (*ITA 2007, s 246(3)*).

Reorganisations and rights

16.8   For disposal relief, the rules in *TCGA 1992, s 127* (where the new shares step into the shoes of the old shares) are to be applied, on a reorganisation of share capital within *TCGA 1992, s 126*, separately to each of the following kinds of shares:

- shares that have attracted income tax relief, where the investment has formed the basis of a deferral relief claim (see **16.10**) and there has been no chargeable event affecting the deferral relief;

- other shares that have attracted income tax relief; and

- shares that have not attracted income tax relief (*TCGA 1992, s 150A(6), (6A)*).

The effect of this rule is that shares of each kind are treated as a separate holding of original shares and identified with a separate new holding following the reorganisation. See **16.24** for the interaction of deferral relief on EIS shares and share reorganisations.

Where there is a rights issue in respect of an existing holding of ordinary shares, and either the existing shares or the new shares attract income tax relief and the other shares do not, the provisions of *TCGA 1992, ss 127–130* (which broadly treat the old and new shares as a single holding) are disapplied, and the taxpayer is treated as acquiring new shares at the date of the rights issue for the amount paid for those new shares (*TCGA 1992, s 150A(7)*).

Exchange of shares

16.9   Where the rules in *TCGA 1992, ss 135* and *136* apply to exchanges of shares and securities in a company (A) for those in another company (B), the effect for the capital gains position of shareholders is normally that there is no disposal of the original holding in company A (see **4.4**). Companies A and B are treated as if they were the same company, and the exchange is treated as a reorganisation of its share capital.

These rules are disapplied for EIS shares held in company A, unless:

- company B has issued shares eligible for EIS income tax relief and has issued certificates to investors in respect of those shares (as required by *ITA 2007, ss 204–205*);

- the shares in company B are new ordinary shares carrying no present or future preferential rights to dividends, or to assets in a winding up, and no present or future right to be redeemed; and

- the shares in company B are issued after the termination date for company A's issue of EIS shares.

The rules in *TCGA 1992, ss 135* and *136* may also apply where a new company (C), meeting the conditions in *ITA 2007, s 247*, acquires EIS shares in exchange for new shares in company C (*TCGA 1992, s 150A(8), (8A)–(8D)*).

EIS DEFERRAL RELIEF

When it is available

16.10 Deferral of CGT is available where a chargeable gain accrues to an individual ('the investor') on the disposal of an asset and the investor makes a 'qualifying investment' (see **16.14**). Deferral relief is discussed in detail in *Capital Gains Tax: Roll-over, Hold-over and Deferral Reliefs 2013/14* (Bloomsbury Professional).

The relief is also available where the gain accrues on a deemed disposal under the rules for EIS deferral relief, VCT deferral relief (abolished for shares issued after 5 April 2004), or reinvestment relief under *TCGA 1992, s 164A* (abolished for investments made after 5 April 1998). The time of the actual or deemed disposal giving rise to the gain is the 'accrual time'.

The asset disposed of – or deemed to be disposed of – may be any chargeable asset. The investment must be made generally within a period beginning one year before and ending three years after the accrual time (*TCGA 1992, Sch 5B, para 1(3)*).

There is no limit to the amount of the gain that can be deferred, but an individual cannot claim income tax relief for any amount subscribed for eligible EIS shares that exceeds £1 million, (from 6 April 2012, see **16.3**) (*ITA 2007, s 158*).

For HMRC guidance regarding CGT deferral relief, see VCM23000–VCM23540.

Residence condition

16.11 The investor must be an individual, or trustee of a qualifying settlement (see **16.12**), who is resident in the UK:

- at the time when the gain accrues; and

- at the time the EIS shares are issued.

There are two further conditions to be satisfied in relation to residence status:

- the investor must not be regarded as resident in a territory outside the UK by virtue of any double taxation relief arrangements; and

- relief is not available if the effect of those arrangements is that he would not be liable to CGT in the UK on a disposal of the EIS shares (disregarding for this purpose the exemption for a disposal of EIS shares in *TCGA 1992, s 150A*, see **16.2**) (*TCGA 1992, Sch 5B, para 1(1), (4)*).

Trustees

16.12   Trustees cannot claim EIS income tax relief or disposal relief. However, deferral relief is available to the trustees of a settlement where the asset on the disposal of which the chargeable gain accrued is settled property (a 'trust asset') (*TCGA 1992, Sch 5B, para 17(1)*).

Deferral relief applies to:

(a)   settled property in which there is no interest in possession (an interest in possession is, broadly, an immediate right to income of the settlement) so long as *all* the beneficiaries are individuals;

(b)   settled property in which the interests of the beneficiaries are interests in possession, if *any* of the beneficiaries are individuals (*TCGA 1992, Sch 5B, para 17(2)*).

Discretionary trusts and accumulation and maintenance trusts will fall within (a).

Where (b) applies but, at the time of the disposal of the trust asset, not all the beneficiaries are individuals, only a proportion of the gain that would accrue to the trustees on the disposal qualifies for deferral relief (*TCGA 1992, Sch 5B, para 17(3)*).

Deferral relief may be denied if the interests of the beneficiaries change between the time of the disposal and the time of the acquisition of the EIS shares. Where either (a) or (b) above applies, relief is available only if it applies both at the time of the disposal of the trust asset, and at the time of acquisition of the EIS shares (*TCGA 1992, Sch 5B, para 17(4), (5)*).

There is a further condition where (b) applies. If not all the beneficiaries are individuals, the 'relevant proportion' (see below) at the time of acquisition of the EIS shares must not be less than the relevant proportion at the time of the disposal of the trust asset (*TCGA 1992, Sch 5B, para 17(5)*).

If both individuals and others have interests in possession, 'the relevant proportion' is the proportion that A bears to B, where:

- A is the total amount of the income of the settled property representing interests held by beneficiaries who are individuals; and

- B is the total amount of all the income of the settled property (*TCGA 1992, Sch 5B, para 17(6)*).

There are complex anti-avoidance provisions relating to settled property (*TCGA 1992, Sch 5B, para 18*; see also VCM23510–VCM23540).

HOW TO CLAIM EIS DEFERRAL RELIEF

Limiting the amount of relief

16.13   Deferral relief must be claimed (see **16.17**). The investor specifies the amount of the qualifying expenditure (ie the amount subscribed for the EIS shares) that is to be set against a corresponding amount of the gain.

The investor may well wish to limit the amount of his claim in order to utilise:

- any unused part of his CGT annual exemption (see **1.17**);

- taper relief (for disposals before 6 April 2008 – see **16.25**);

- entrepreneurs' relief (for disposals made on or after 6 April 2008 – see **16.26**); or

- capital losses carried forward from earlier tax years.

Any part of the gain that has been matched with qualifying expenditure is treated as not having accrued at the accrual time (see **16.10**), but it is treated as accruing if there is a 'chargeable event' (see **16.19**) in relation to any of the shares (*TCGA 1992, Sch 5B, para 2(2)*).

Any amount of the original gain that has not had expenditure set against it in this way is 'unmatched', and qualifying expenditure is 'unused' to the extent that it has not already been set against a chargeable gain (*TCGA 1992, Sch 5B, para 2(1), (3), (4)*).

The actual proceeds of the disposal on which the gain accrued do not have to be applied directly in subscribing for the new shares (VCM23080).

Example 16.5

Kylie sold a commercial property in June 2013 and made a chargeable gain of £350,000. She subscribed for eligible shares in an EIS company of £140,000 in November 2013, and a further £200,000 for EIS shares in May 2014. Kylie's CGT position for 2013/14 is:

2013/14	£
Gain	350,000
Less deferred under EIS provisions:	(339,100)
Gain	10,900
Less annual exemption	(10,900)
Taxable gain for 2013/14	Nil

Kylie could claim deferral relief on up to £340,000 of chargeable gains, but she has chosen to limit the claim, to avoid wasting her 2013/14 annual exemption which cannot be carried forward.

Qualifying investment

16.14   The investor makes a qualifying investment if:

(a)   he subscribes for 'eligible shares' (EIS shares) in a company and the shares are issued to him at a 'qualifying time'. If the accrual time (see **16.10**) is later than the qualifying time, the investor must still hold the EIS shares at the accrual time;

(b)   he subscribes for the shares (other than any bonus shares) wholly in cash;

(c)   the company is a 'qualifying company' in relation to the shares. For instance, it must be an unquoted trading company and comply with the detailed conditions in *ITA 2007, ss 181–199*;

(d)   the shares (other than any bonus shares) are fully paid up when they are issued. Shares are not fully paid up for this purpose if there is any undertaking to pay cash to any person in the future in relation to the acquisition;

(e)   the shares are issued for bona fide commercial purposes, not in connection with any disqualifying arrangements and not as part of a tax avoidance scheme (see below);

(f)   the issuing company or a qualifying 90% subsidiary must carry on the qualifying activities, so where the relevant trade is carried on in partnership or by an LLP of which the EIS company is a member, the conditions in *ITA 2007, s 183* are not met (see Revenue & Customs Brief 77/2009);

(g)   the shares (other than any bonus shares) are issued in order to raise money for the purpose of a qualifying business activity;

(h)   all of the money raised by the issue of the shares (other than bonus shares), is employed wholly for the purpose of that qualifying business activity no later than the end of the period of two years beginning with either the issue of the eligible shares or, if later, the commencement of the qualifying trade; and

(i)   the total amount of investment the company has raised under EIS and VCT in the 12-month period ending with the issue of the EIS shares does not exceed £5 million (cap was £2 million from 19 July 2007 to 6 April 2012).

Focus

The condition in (h) above is still satisfied if an amount of money is employed for another purpose, so long as that amount is not significant (*TCGA 1992, Sch 5B, para 1(2), (5)*).

The time restriction on the use of funds in condition (h) has tripped up a number of EIS companies (see *Richards & Skye Inns Ltd v HMRC* [2011] UKUT 440 (TCC) and *Benson Partnership Ltd v Revenue & Customs* [2012] UKFTT 63 (TC)). Investors in these companies failed to convince the tribunal that the funds were employed for the purpose of the trade, where those funds were not specifically kept aside for that purpose. HMRC will accept that funds have been employed for the trade if the earmarking of those funds is quite clear. Board minutes and accounting entries may be required to support the commitment to spend.

HMRC consider that the condition in (e) above excludes a subscription that is motivated by benevolence. HMRC also consider that deathbed investments are 'unlikely to be made for genuine commercial reasons' (VCM11140).

Eligible shares

16.15   Shares are eligible shares for deferral relief purposes if they are new ordinary shares which, throughout the following period, carry no preferential right to a company's assets on its winding up, and the rights to dividends are not cumulative. That period:

(a)   begins with the issue of the shares; and

(b)   ends immediately before the 'termination date' relating to those shares (*TCGA 1992, Sch 5B, para 19(1); ITA 2007, s 173(2)*).

The termination date is the later of:

- the third anniversary of the issue of the shares; and

- the third anniversary of the commencement of the trade (*TCGA 1992, Sch 5B, para 19(1)*; *ITA 2007, s 256*).

Example 16.6

Play-time Ltd issued eligible shares on 1 January 2010 and used the funds for the purposes of a trade that commenced on 30 November 2009. The termination date is 1 January 2013. If Play-time's trade had commenced on 1 April 2010, the termination date would be 1 April 2013.

Time limits for reinvestment

16.16   The qualifying time in **16.14**(a) is any time in the period beginning one year before and ending three years after the accrual time, or any other such time as HMRC may allow (*TCGA 1992, Sch 5B, para 1(3)*).

HMRC have statutory power to extend the standard time limits, and the HMRC guidance (VCM23030) indicates this power will be exercised where the claimant can show that he:

- had a firm intention to comply with them, but

- was prevented from complying by some fact or circumstance beyond his control, and

- acted as soon as he reasonably could after ceasing to be so prevented.

Each case is considered on its own merits, but examples of circumstances outside the claimant's control might include death or serious illness of a vital party at a crucial time, unsettled disputes or litigation, or unexpected delay in receipt of disposal consideration.

HMRC say that a mere change of intention at a late stage, or a lack of funds due to the claimant having spent or invested the disposal consideration elsewhere, will not normally be regarded as circumstances beyond his control. If the claimant chooses to defer applying for the EIS shares until late in the standard reinvestment period, a subsequent issue of shares outside that period will not normally be regarded as a circumstance beyond his control.

Claims

16.17   The procedures and time limits for claims to deferral relief are set out by reference to the provisions for claims to income tax relief for an investment in EIS shares. *ITA 2007, s 202* is applied with some modifications, so that:

(a)   a claim may not be made earlier than the time when the requirement in *ITA 2007, s 176* is first satisfied – broadly when the trade (or research and development) concerned has been carried on for four months;

(b)   a claim may not be made later than five years after 31 January following the tax year in which the shares were issued (not amended by *FA 2008, Sch 39*); and

(c)   no claim may be made unless the claimant has received a compliance certificate (form EIS3) from the company, certifying that the conditions for EIS relief (other than those relating to the investor) are satisfied in relation to the shares.

The company is required, before issuing the EIS3 certificate, to declare to HMRC that certain conditions have been, and remain, satisfied. Further details of the company's obligations in this regard, and penalties for non-compliance, are set out in *ITA 2007, s 205 (TCGA 1992, Sch 5B, para 6)*.

There can be no provisional claim for relief. The investor is required to submit to HMRC part 2 of form EIS3 completed by the company, which includes a claim form, either with their tax return or separately.

There can be quite a delay between the investor making the EIS investment and receiving the EIS3 certificate. Without the EIS3 certificate, the taxpayer has no valid claim and is required to pay the full tax liability by the due date. However, HMRC are prepared to suspend payment of the tax which will be the subject of EIS relief, for a short period, to allow time for the EIS3 certificate to arrive. Any such arrangement to suspend or postpone tax must be agreed before the tax due date.

Focus

HMRC will give advance assurance as to whether a company will meet the EIS requirements, if the company's officers (or a person authorised by them) apply on form EIS/SEIS(AA).

This assurance procedure is voluntary, but recommended.

Investors who ask HMRC about the qualifying status of a company for EIS are referred to an officer of the EIS company.

WHAT HAPPENS WHEN THE CONDITIONS ARE BROKEN

16.18   The shares forming the investment are treated as never having been eligible for relief if the condition in **16.14**(g), relating to the purpose of the share issue, is not met (*TCGA 1992, Sch 5B, para 1A(3)*).

The shares cease to be eligible shares on the date of an event occurring after they have been issued if, as a result of that event, any of the following conditions is not satisfied:

- the qualifying company condition in **16.14**(c);

- the condition in **16.14**(f) relating to who carries on the qualifying activities (*TCGA 1992, Sch 5B, para 1A(1), (2)*); or

- the investment condition in **16.14**(i).

If the condition in **16.14**(h) above relating to the company's use of the money subscribed is not met, the shares are treated as:

- never having been eligible shares, if the claim is made after the time limit mentioned in **16.14**(h) has expired; or

- ceasing to be eligible shares on the expiration of that time limit in any other case (*TCGA 1992, Sch 5B, para 1A(4), (4A)*).

A notice, given by either the company or HMRC as appropriate, is required before any of these provisions can take effect (*TCGA 1992, Sch 5B, para 1A(5), (6), (7)*).

Chargeable events

16.19 The tax effect of a chargeable event is explained at **16.21**. There is a chargeable event in relation to the shares if, after the qualifying investment has been made:

(a) the investor disposes of the shares otherwise than as a no gain, no loss transfer between spouses or civil partners;

(b) the shares are disposed of (but not to the investor) by a person who acquired them on a disposal that the investor made within marriage or civil partnership;

(c) the investor becomes non-resident in the UK, while holding the shares and before the termination date – but see below regarding a temporary change of residence status;

(d) a person who acquired the shares on a disposal within marriage or civil partnership becomes a non-resident while holding them and before the termination date; or

(e) the shares cease (or are treated as ceasing) to be eligible shares, for example, where the company carries on non-qualifying activities (*TCGA 1992, Sch 5B, para 3(1)*).

A temporary change of residence status does not give rise to a chargeable event as described in (c) or (d) above where the investor or the transferee, leaves the

UK to take up an employment or office where all of the duties are performed outside the UK and he returns to take up residence in the UK within three years. The individual must not have disposed of the shares in the meantime (*TCGA 1992, Sch 5B, para 3(3), (4)*).

The investor or the company is required to notify HMRC of the chargeable event within 60 days or, in specified cases, within 60 days of coming to know of the event. *TCGA 1992, Sch 5B, para 16* sets out the detailed notification requirements and HMRC information powers (VCM23480).

Death of investor or transferee

16.20   An event within **16.19**(a)–(e) above is not a chargeable event, in relation to shares held by the deceased immediately before his death, where the event occurs at or after the time of the death of either the investor, or a person who acquired any of the relevant shares on a disposal within marriage or civil partnership (*TCGA 1992, Sch 5B, para 3(5)*).

Effect of chargeable event

16.21   Broadly, the 'deferred gain' (see below) becomes chargeable if a chargeable event (see **16.19**) occurs. A chargeable gain accrues on the occasion of a chargeable event in relation to any of the shares. The amount of the chargeable gain is equal to the part of the deferred gain that is attributable (see below) to the shares involved in the chargeable event (*TCGA 1992, Sch 5B, para 4(1)*).

The 'deferred gain' is the amount of the original gain that has been matched against qualifying expenditure, less the amount of any gain treated as accruing as a result of an earlier chargeable event (*TCGA 1992, Sch 5B, para 4(7)*).

The deferred gain attributable to any shares is found by attributing a proportionate part of the gain to each of the relevant shares held immediately before the chargeable event occurs (*TCGA 1992, Sch 5B, para 4(6)*; VCM23150).

Example 16.7

Monique subscribes £40,000 for eligible EIS shares on 4 July 2011 and makes a claim to defer a chargeable gain of £30,000 accruing on the disposal of an investment property on 15 July 2010. She sells the shares on 26 June 2013, before the termination date. The whole of the deferred gain of £30,000 becomes chargeable on 26 June 2013 and will be subject to CGT at 18% or 28% depending on the level of her taxable income for 2013/14, subject to deduction of her annual exemption and any available losses.

> **Example 16.8**
>
> Finbar subscribes £70,000 for eligible EIS shares on 17 August 2010 and makes a claim to defer a chargeable gain of £50,000 accruing on the disposal of land on 3 April 2008. He sells 50% of the shares on 13 July 2013 before the termination date. The same proportion of the deferred gain, ie £25,000, becomes chargeable on 13 July 2013, and will be subject to CGT at 18% or 28% depending on the level of Finbar's taxable income for 2013/14 and other gains he makes in 2013/14.

See **16.26** for the interaction with entrepreneurs' relief.

Identification rules

16.22   It may be necessary to determine whether deferral relief is attributable to the shares disposed of (including disposal by means of a no gain, no loss disposal within marriage or civil partnership).

Identification is generally made on a first in, first out basis, and the normal identification rules in *TCGA 1992, Pt IV, Ch I* are modified accordingly. There are detailed rules for identification of shares acquired on the same day and to cater for reorganisations (*TCGA 1992, Sch 5B, para 4(2)–(5)*; VCM23160).

Chargeable person

16.23   The chargeable gain accruing on the occurrence of a chargeable event is treated as accruing, as the case may be, to:

(a)   the person who makes the disposal;

(b)   the person who becomes a non-resident; or

(c)   the person who holds the shares when they cease (or are treated as ceasing) to be eligible shares.

With regard to (c), if the investor has transferred some of his shares on a no gain, no loss disposal within marriage or civil partnership, and the transferee retains those shares at the time of the chargeable event, the gains accruing to the investor and the transferee are computed separately (*TCGA 1992, Sch 5B, para 5*).

INTERACTION WITH OTHER RELIEFS

Share-for-share exchange

16.24   The rules for share exchanges in *TCGA 1992, s 127* (where the old shares stand in the shoes of the new shares) are to be applied, on a reorganisation of share capital within *TCGA 1992, s 126*, separately to each of the following kinds of shares. The effect of this rule is that shares of each kind are treated as a separate holding of original shares and identified with a separate new holding following the reorganisation:

(a)   shares which attract neither EIS income tax relief nor deferral relief;

(b)   shares to which only CGT deferral relief is attributable;

(c)   shares to which deferral relief is not attributable, but income tax relief does apply; and

(d)   shares to which both CGT deferral relief and income tax relief (and thus disposal relief) are attributable (*TCGA 1992, Sch 5B, para 7(1)*).

Where there is a rights issue in respect of an existing holding of ordinary shares, and either the existing shares or the new shares fall into the categories (b), (c) or (d) above, the provisions of *TCGA 1992, ss 127–130* (treating the old and new shares as a single holding) do not apply to the existing holding (*TCGA 1992, Sch 5B, para 7(2)*). The taxpayer is treated as having acquired the new shares at the date of the rights issue and for the amount paid for the new shares. Any shares acquired on a rights issue may qualify for deferral relief, but a separate claim will need to be made.

If a company (B) that has only subscriber shares acquires all the shares in an EIS company (A) in exchange for shares of a 'corresponding description' (see below) in company B, and the conditions in *TCGA 1992, s 135* are met so that *TCGA 1992, s 127* applies, the share exchange is not treated as involving a disposal of the shares in company A. The shares in company B attract deferral relief in place of the shares in company A, and there are detailed rules setting out the effect of this treatment.

Shares in company B are of a 'corresponding description' where, if they were shares in company A, they would be of the same class and carry the same rights as the original shares. Shares are of the same class where they would be so treated if dealt with on the Stock Exchange (*TCGA 1992, Sch 5B, para 8*).

From 22 April 2009, deferral relief may be lost where the EIS company is taken over and the acquiring company issues its own shares in exchange for the original EIS shares. If the original EIS shares attracted both income tax relief and deferral relief, neither of which has been withdrawn at the time of the share exchange, *TCGA 1992, ss 135–137* is disapplied, and the EIS shares are treated as being disposed of for the purposes of *TCGA 1992, Sch 5B, paras 3, 4*. The result is that the deferred gain comes into charge; but, for other provisions of *TCGA 1992*, the EIS shares are *not* treated as being disposed of, thus no other gain or loss attached to the EIS shares comes into charge at the time of the share exchange (*TCGA 1992, Sch 5B, para 9*).

Taper relief

16.25 Taper relief was withdrawn for disposals made on or after 6 April 2008. The relief applied at higher rates to gains arising from business assets and lower rates for gains from non-business assets. Where EIS deferral was claimed, it was the whole gain before taper relief that was deferred. A taxpayer would thus normally choose to defer a gain arising from a non-business asset, when allocating the expenditure from investing in EIS shares. This would have the effect of deferring the gain which would otherwise be subject to the smaller amount of taper relief.

Where an asset had both business and non-business use, either concurrently or in subsequent periods, the gain would be notionally divided into two gains, deemed to arise from separate business and non-business assets, in order to calculate the taper relief due on the different business and non-business parts of the gain. The question arose in *Stolkin v HMRC* [2011] UKFTT 831 (TC) as to whether the EIS investment could be set entirely against the notional non-business part of the gain, allowing the business part of the gain to attract full taper relief. The judge felt the case was finely balanced, but decided the taxpayer had the better argument, such that the division of a gain from a mixed-use asset into two deemed gains could apply for the purposes for EIS deferral as well as for taper relief.

Example 16.9

Edward sold a property on 5 April 2007 for a gain of £80,000. Throughout the four-year period of ownership, three quarters of the property was used for Edward's business and the remaining part let to private tenants (non-business use).The gain must be split into two parts, one deemed to accrue on disposal of a non-business asset and the other deemed to accrue on disposal of a business asset.

Edward subscribed £20,000 for EIS shares on 31 March 2009, and wished to set the whole of this investment against the non-business part of the gain from the sale of his property in 2007.

Non-business asset	£
Gain £80,000 × ¼ non-business use	20,000
EIS deferral relief:	(20,000)
Assessable gain	Nil
Business asset	
Gain £80,000 × ¾ business use	60,000
4-year holding period: 75% taper	(45,000)
Assessable gain:	15,000
Total chargeable gain:	15,000

Where a gain deferred using EIS became chargeable before 6 April 2008, taper relief could apply. In that case, taper relief on the deferred gain was calculated by reference to the date of the original disposal. No further taper relief was available for the period from the date of deferral (acquisition of the EIS shares) to the date of the chargeable event.

The calculation of the holding period of EIS shares for taper relief was adjusted where a taxpayer was a serial investor in EIS shares. In this limited case, the holding periods of EIS shares issued by different companies could be combined (*TCGA 1992, s 150D, Sch 5BA*).

Entrepreneurs' relief

16.26 The HMRC view is that entrepreneurs' relief takes precedence over EIS deferral relief under *TCGA 1992, Sch 5B*, as deferral relief merely postpones a gain and does not reduce it (CG64135). However, the position is changed for gains on or after 23 June 2010.

Before 23 June 2010

Any chargeable gain remaining, after the application of entrepreneurs' relief to a gain incurred, may be deferred by investing in EIS shares and electing for the defined amount of the gain to be deferred.

After 22 June 2010

The taxpayer has to choose between EIS deferral relief and entrepreneurs' relief. If the gain is subject to entrepreneurs' relief, the full gain, within the taxpayer's lifetime limit (see **11.5**), is subject to CGT at 10%. Only any excess gain above the lifetime limit, or which has otherwise been excluded from a claim for entrepreneurs' relief, can be deferred using EIS.

Transitional arrangements

Where a gain, which arose before 6 April 2008, has been deferred by way of a claim under EIS deferral relief, and becomes chargeable after 5 April 2008 due to a relevant chargeable event (see **16.21**), entrepreneurs' relief would not normally apply. However, where the deferred gain originally accrued before 6 April 2008, it can be reduced by entrepreneurs' relief under *FA 2008, Sch 3, para 8*, if the conditions for that relief apply (see **11.49**).

If the first chargeable event in respect of those EIS shares occurs on or after 23 June 2010, the whole of the gain becomes chargeable to CGT at the entrepreneurs' relief rate of 10%, when the specific parts of the gain fall into charge (see Example 16.10). If the first chargeable event occurs before 23 June 2010, but on or after 6 April 2008, the whole of the deferred gain is reduced by 4/9ths and is then charged to CGT at the taxpayer's marginal rate (18% or 28%) when it falls into charge.

The gain that accrues on the disposal of the EIS shares themselves may be eligible for entrepreneurs' relief if the EIS company is the shareholder's personal company at the time of the disposal, and the employment condition applies (see **11.10–11.11**).

Example 16.10

Peter sold his software company in June 2000, making a gain of £900,000. This gain would have qualified for entrepreneurs' relief if it had been in force at that time. On 10 April 2003, Peter invested the gain in EIS shares issued by MRC Ltd, and successfully claimed EIS deferral relief. This claim removed any possibility to reduce the gain by taper relief, as the full gain was covered by EIS deferral relief. Peter could have restricted his claim to EIS relief to leave an amount in charge subject to taper relief and the annual exemption, but that claim had to be submitted to HMRC by 31 January 2010.

Peter sold his entire holding of the EIS shares issued by MRC Ltd in July 2013. If Peter makes a claim for entrepreneurs' relief to apply to the disposal of the software company shares, the full gain of £900,000 is subject to CGT at 10%. Peter must make his claim for entrepreneurs' relief by 31 January 2015.

WHEN EIS RELIEF IS WITHDRAWN OR CLAWED BACK

Reinvesting in the same company or a group company

16.27   The taxpayer is not entitled to deferral relief if the gain he wishes to defer arose on the disposal of holding shares in a company (A) and:

- the company that issues the EIS shares (see **16.14**) is company A itself; or

- the EIS company is either a member of the same group of companies (see below) as company A at the time of the disposal of the company A shares, or a member of such a group when the EIS shares are issued (*TCGA 1992, Sch 5B, para 10(1)*).

EIS shares in a 'relevant company' (see below) are not regarded as a qualifying investment where the shares are issued after the taxpayer has already made a qualifying investment in a company (B) (the 'acquired holding') and obtained deferral relief on the disposal of either an asset or shares in a company (A). A company is a 'relevant company' for this purpose if:

- where the taxpayer has disposed of any of the acquired holding in company B, it is either company B itself or a company that was a member of the same group of companies as company B at any time since the acquisition of the 'acquired holding' of shares in company B;

- it is company A, ie it is the company the disposal of whose shares gave rise to the deferral relief claim by virtue of the acquisition of the holding in company B; or

- it is a company which was a member of the same group of companies as company A at the time of the disposal of shares in company A or at the time of the acquisition of the holding in company B (*TCGA 1992, Sch 5B, para 10(2), (3)*).

A group of companies for this purpose comprises a company that has one or more 51% subsidiaries, together with those subsidiaries (*TCGA 1992, Sch 5B, para 10(4)*).

Pre-arranged exits and disqualification arrangements

16.28   Where an individual subscribes for EIS shares in a company, no deferral relief is available if there are 'relevant arrangements' in place (see below) that include any of the following:

(a)   arrangements with a view to the repurchase, exchange or other disposal of the EIS shares (or of other shares in or securities of the same company) – subject to an exception for certain exchanges of shares etc;

(b)   arrangements for the cessation of a trade carried on, or to be carried on, by the company or a person connected with it, except where the arrangements apply only on a winding up for bona fide commercial reasons that does not feature in the relevant arrangements;

(c)   arrangements for the disposal of the company's assets (or of the assets of a person connected with the company), or of a substantial amount of those assets, subject to the exception mentioned in (b) for a winding up; and

(d)   arrangements the main purpose of which (or one of the main purposes of which) is to provide protection for people investing in shares in the company against the risks attached to the investment, regardless of how that protection is provided, but excluding protection that a company would reasonably be expected to provide for itself (or, in the case of the parent company of a trading group, for its subsidiaries).

(e)   disqualifying arrangements the main purpose of which (or one of the main purposes of which) is to ensure that the money raised under the EIS is paid to or on behalf of a party to the arrangements or, in the absence of such arrangements, it would be reasonable to expect that the activities of the EIS company would be carried on as part of another business by a person who is party to the arrangements.

'Relevant arrangements' are the arrangements under which the shares are issued and any other arrangements, made before that share issue, in relation to it or in connection with it. 'Arrangements' include any scheme, agreement or understanding, whether or not legally enforceable (*TCGA 1992, Sch 5B, paras 11, 11A, 19(1)*).

Put and call options

16.29   Special rules apply to put and call options granted during period A (see **16.32**). These do not affect the above rules relating to pre-arranged exits (*TCGA 1992, Sch 5B, para 12(4)*).

Options granted after shares are issued

16.30   Shares issued to the investor cease to be eligible shares on the date of the grant, during the 'relevant period' (see **16.32**), of:

(a)   a put option granted to the investor, where the exercise of the option would bind the grantor to buy the shares from the investor; or

(b)   a call option granted by the investor, where the exercise of the option would bind the investor to sell the shares to the grantee.

The shares affected by this rule are those to which the option relates, ie the shares that would be treated as disposed of in pursuance of the option if the option were exercised immediately after the grant, and there was an immediate disposal of the shares acquired on exercise of the option (*TCGA 1992, Sch 5B, para 12*).

Options granted before shares are issued

16.31   If an option within **16.30**(a) or (b) is granted before the date on which the shares are issued, the shares are treated as never having been eligible shares (*TCGA 1992, Sch 5B, para 12(2)(a)*).

Period A

16.32   Period A is the period beginning with the incorporation of the company or, if the company was incorporated more than two years before the date on which the shares were issued, two years before that date. It ends immediately before the termination date (see **16.15**) (*TCGA 1992, Sch 5B, para 19(1); ITA 2007, s 159*).

Value received by the investor

16.33 A chargeable event may arise if the investor receives value other than 'insignificant' value from the company at any time in the 'period of restriction'. The whole of the deferred gain becomes chargeable – there is no apportionment, even if the value received represents only a part of the investment (*TCGA 1992, Sch 5B, para 13A*).

The 'period of restriction' is the period beginning one year before the shares are issued and ending immediately before the termination date (see **16.15**) relating to the shares (*TCGA 1992, Sch 5B, para 19(1)*).

An amount is of 'insignificant value' if it is no more than £1,000, or it is greater than £1,000 but is insignificant in relation to the investment set against gains in a deferral relief claim.

HMRC guidance says that 'insignificant' should be given its dictionary meaning of 'trifling or completely unimportant'. HMRC also consider that, if a receipt of value falls within periods of restriction relating to more than one share issue, there is no apportionment and the receipt must be taken into account in regard to each issue (VCM23380, VCM23390).

However, no amount of value received is treated as a receipt of insignificant value if arrangements existed, in the period of 12 months prior to the share issue, which provided for the investor (or an 'associate' of his) to receive value from the issuing company (or a person connected with it) in the period of restriction. 'Associate' takes its meaning from *ITA 2007, s 253*, except that brothers and sisters are excluded (*TCGA 1992, Sch 5B, paras 13A(2)–(5), 19(1)*).

This was illustrated in the case of *Segesta Limited v HMRC* [2012] UKUT 176 (TCC). Mr Oyston subscribed for EIS shares issued by Segesta Ltd in 1999. However, a subsidiary of Segesta – the Blackpool Football Club Ltd (BFC) – already owed money to Mr Oyston. Funds borrowed from Mr Oyston by Segesta travelled in a circular fashion back through BFC to Mr Oyston, who used some of this money to subscribe for the EIS shares in Segesta. The First-tier and Upper Tribunals found that this amounted to an arrangement under *TCGA 1992, Sch 5B, para 13*, so the EIS shares were never eligible shares.

The shares are treated as never having been eligible shares if the investor receives value before the date of issue of the shares. If he receives value after that date, the shares cease to be eligible shares on the date when the value is received. There is no receipt of value by virtue of a disposal of shares that gives rise to a chargeable event (see **16.19**) (*TCGA 1992, Sch 5B, para 13(1), (6)*).

Receipts of insignificant value during the period of restriction are aggregated for this purpose, and a chargeable event arises if the total value of the receipts is not an amount of insignificant value (*TCGA 1992, Sch 5B, para 13(1B)*).

The investor receives value from the company if the company does anything that is mentioned in the first column of Table 16.1 below, and the value received by the investor in each case is as set out in the second column (*TCGA 1992, Sch 5B, paras 13(2), (8), 13A(1)*).

Table 16.1

The company	*The value received is*
repays, redeems or repurchases any of its share capital or securities belonging to the investor or pays him to give up his right to any of the share capital or any security on its cancellation or extinguishment;	the amount received by the investor or, if greater, the market value of the share capital, securities or debt
repays, under arrangements connected with the acquisition of the shares, any debt owed to him other than a debt incurred by the company (i) on or after the date of issue of the shares, and (ii) otherwise than in consideration of extinguishment of a debt incurred before that date; or	
pays him to give up his right to any debt on its extinguishment;	
releases or waives his liability to the company or discharges, or undertakes to discharge, his liability to someone else (a liability that is not discharged within 12 months of the time when it ought to have been discharged is treated as released or waived for this purpose);	the amount of the liability
makes a loan or advance to him that is not repaid in full before the shares are issued (see below);	the amount of the loan or advance less the amount of any repayment made before the issue of the shares
provides a benefit or facility for him;	the cost to the company of providing the benefit or facility less any consideration given for it by the investor

The company	The value received is
disposes of an asset to him for no consideration, or for a consideration less than (or worth less than) the asset's market value; or	the difference between the market value of the asset and the consideration (if any) given for it
acquires an asset from him for a consideration more than (or worth more than) the asset's market value;	
makes any payment to him other than a 'qualifying payment' (see below)	the amount of the payment

The investor also receives value from the company if a person connected with the company (as defined in *ITA 2007, s 166*) either buys any of its share capital or securities belonging to the individual, or pays him for giving up a right in relation to any share capital or securities of the company. In this case the value received is the amount received by the investor or, if greater, the market value of the share capital or securities (*TCGA 1992, Sch 5B, paras 13(5), 13A(1)*).

A loan is regarded as being made by the company to the investor where he incurs a debt to the company (other than an 'ordinary trade debt'), or a debt due from the investor to a third party is assigned to the company. An 'ordinary trade debt' is a debt for goods or services supplied in the ordinary course of a trade or business, so long as the credit period is no longer than six months and no longer than that normally given to customers of the business (*TCGA 1992, Sch 5B, para 13(3), (11)*).

A debt or a liability is disregarded if a qualifying payment (see below) would discharge it, and a benefit or facility is disregarded if payment of equal value would be a qualifying payment (*TCGA 1992, Sch 5B, para 13(9)*).

A 'qualifying payment' includes:

- a payment (by any company) of reasonable remuneration for service as an officer or employee, having regard to the duties of that position;

- a payment or reimbursement (by any company) of travelling or other expenses wholly, exclusively and necessarily incurred by the payee in the performance of duties as an officer or employee of that company;

- the payment (by any company) of any interest representing no more than a reasonable commercial return on money lent to that company;

- the payment (by any company) of a dividend or other distribution not exceeding a normal return on any investment in that company's shares or securities;

- a payment for the supply of goods that does not exceed their market value;

- a payment for the acquisition of an asset that does not exceed its market value;

- the payment (by any company), of a reasonable and commercial rent for property occupied by the company;

- reasonable and necessary remuneration paid (by any company) for services rendered to that company in the course of a UK trade or profession where the payment is included in the profits of that trade or profession for tax purposes; and

- a payment in discharge of an ordinary trade debt (*TCGA 1992, Sch 5B, para 13(7)*).

The scope of these provisions is widened so that:

- a payment or disposal to the investor includes a payment or disposal made to him indirectly, or to his order, or for his benefit;

- anything received by an associate of the investor is treated as received by the investor; and

- a reference to a company includes a reference to a person who is connected with the company at any time in the 'relevant period' (see below) (*TCGA 1992, Sch 5B, para 13(10)*).

The 'relevant period' for shares issued after 5 April 2000 is the period beginning with the incorporation of the company or, if the company was incorporated more than two years before the date on which the shares were issued, two years before that date. It ends immediately before the termination date (*TCGA 1992, Sch 5B, para 19(1)*; *ITA 2007, s 159*).

Value received by another person

16.34   Value received by persons other than the investor may give rise to a chargeable event; see **16.19**. Detailed rules are set out in *TCGA 1992, Sch 5B, paras 14, 14AA and 14A*.

Example 16.11

In November 2008, Reggie realised a gain of £1,500,000 when he disposed of his personal company, Scream Ltd, of which he owned all the ordinary shares and was a director. On 7 October 2010, he reinvested all of this gain by subscribing for eligible EIS shares in Perrin Ltd. In May 2013, Reggie's

---

wife received £5,000 from CJ Ltd, an associated company of Perrin Ltd. That amounts to a return of value, which creates a chargeable event for the Perrin Ltd shares. Reggie claims entrepreneurs' relief (ER) in respect of the gain arising on the disposal of Scream Ltd, but his capital gains tax position for 2013/14 becomes:

2013/14	£
Deferred gain now chargeable, subject to ER	1,500,000
Less annual exemption for 2013/14	(10,900)
Taxable gain	1,489,100
CGT due at ER rate of 10%	148,910

Reggie's CGT liability for 2013/14 will be £148,910, which is payable by 31 January 2015, although most of his money is still invested in Perrin Ltd.

Replacement value

16.35 Value received by the investor (the 'original value') may be disregarded where, broadly:

- the shares were issued after 6 March 2001 or the original value was received after that date;

- the original value was received in any of the circumstances set out in Table 16.1 (see **16.33**), except for value received in connection with the repayment of a debt;

- the person from whom the original value was received (the 'original supplier') receives replacement value in the form of a 'qualifying receipt', from the person who received the original value (the 'original recipient');

- the replacement value is not less than the original value; and

- the receipt of replacement value is not disregarded.

In broad terms, a 'qualifying receipt' may arise by means of a payment by the original recipient or the transfer of an asset between him and the original supplier for a consideration greater or less than market value. The detailed rules are set out in *TCGA 1992, Sch 5B, paras 13B, 13C*.

Investment-linked loans

16.36 If an 'investment-linked loan' (see below) is made by any person, at any time in the relevant period, to an individual who subscribes for eligible shares (or to his associate), the shares are treated as:

- never having been eligible shares, if the loan is made on or before the date of the issue of the shares; and

- ceasing to be eligible shares when the loan is made, if it is made after that date.

A loan is 'investment-linked' if it would not have been made – or would not have been made on the same terms – if the individual had not subscribed for, or had not been proposing to subscribe for, the shares.

A loan is regarded as made by a person to an individual if the person gives him any credit, or a debt due from the individual to someone else is assigned to that person (*TCGA 1992, Sch 5B, para 16*).

HMRC have said that their primary concern is why the lender made the loan rather than why the borrower applied for it, and relief is not necessarily denied just because a loan is used to finance the investment. HMRC said in Statement of Practice 6/98 (VCM11030):

> 'The test is whether the lender makes the loan on terms which are influenced by the fact that the borrower, or an associate of the borrower, has acquired, or is proposing to acquire, the shares.

> The rules would not have effect to deny or withdraw relief where a person proposing to acquire shares receives a loan from a bank, if the bank would have made a loan on the same terms to a similar borrower who was intending to use it for a different purpose. But if, for example, a loan is made on a specified security which consists of, or includes, the shares in question, it would be one which would not otherwise have been made on the same terms.

> In such a case, the loan would be linked with the shares, and the investor would not qualify for relief in respect of them. This would apply only where the shares, or any rights associated with them, are specified as all or part of the security. It would not apply, for example, in any case where the lender had recourse against the borrower's assets generally.

> In considering the terms of any particular loan, HMRC will have regard to such features as the qualifying conditions which must be satisfied by the borrower, the existence of incentives or benefits offered to the borrower, the time allowed for repayment, the amount of repayment and interest charged, the timing of interest payments, and the nature of the security pledged.'

SEED ENTERPRISE INVESTMENT SCHEME

Overview

16.37 The Seed Enterprise Investment Scheme (SEIS) is designed to attract equity investment into much smaller companies than those which are the target of the EIS and VCT schemes. An investment under the SEIS is likely to carry a much higher commercial risk (due to the smaller size of the enterprise and the lack of trading history) than an EIS investment. To compensate for this high risk, the investor receives income tax relief at 50% of the value of his investment, rather than 30% for EIS investments.

The SEIS investor can benefit from reinvestment relief to reduce the effect of CGT on any gains arising from disposals made in 2012/13 or 2013/14, where that gain is reinvested in SEIS shares in the same tax year (see **16.43**).

Where the SEIS shares are retained for at least three years, any gain arising on their disposal will be free of CGT, but losses on a similar disposal will be allowable (see **16.44**).

The legislation for SEIS is found in *ITA 2007, Pt 5A* and *TCGA 1992, ss 150E–150G, Sch 5BB*. HMRC guidance is given at www.hmrc.gov.uk/ seedeis/index.htm and at VCM30000. The SEIS currently applies to shares issued in the period from 6 April 2012 to 5 April 2017. However, this period may be extended by Treasury order.

Scope of SEIS relief

16.38   An investor can subscribe for up to £100,000 of SEIS shares in one tax year. From 2013/14, the investor can carry back part or all of their SEIS investment to the previous tax year, if the maximum annual SEIS investment was not made in that earlier period. However, the conditions that the SEIS investor has to meet regarding connections with the company will disqualify many potential investors from achieving the tax relief (see **16.39**).

Focus

The conditions affecting the investor and the company apply for two key periods:

● from incorporation of the company to three years after the SEIS shares are subscribed for ('period A'); and

● the period of three years starting from the day the shares are subscribed for ('period B').

The taxpayer must make a claim for income tax relief on the SEIS investment and a separate claim for SEIS reinvestment relief. If the income tax relief on the SEIS shares is withdrawn or reduced, the reinvestment relief will also be proportionately reduced (see **16.43**).

Investor conditions

16.39   The investor (or any of his associates) must not be an employee of the SEIS company, at any time during period B. Thus, former employees can apply for SEIS relief, but current employees cannot. However, directors of the company, both current and former, are permitted to claim SEIS relief, as those directors are not considered to be employees of the company as well.

The investor must not control or be able to acquire (directly or indirectly) more than 30% of the company's votes, share capital or assets on a winding up, throughout period A. Holding initial subscriber shares does not break this 30% rule if the company has not started trade preparations.

The investor must not receive a loan linked to the SEIS investment from the company, or be party to arrangements whereby a reciprocal investment is made in another associated company.

The 'receipt of value' rules prevent an investor from taking any value from the company in period A, although reimbursement of reasonable expenses incurred as a director, interest on loans, and rent for business premises are permitted. These rules are much the same as apply for EIS (see **16.33–16.34**) but are set out in new legislation (*ITA 2007, ss 257FE–257FO*).

Finally, the investor must not subscribe for the SEIS shares as part of a tax avoidance scheme.

Company conditions

16.40   The SEIS company must be unquoted and must have been trading for less than two years before the date when the SEIS shares are issued, which is the start of period B. It also must not be in financial difficulty at this date.

The gross assets of the company, or those of the group if it is a holding company, must be no more than £200,000 immediately before the issue of the SEIS shares. The company (or group if a parent company) must have no more than 25 full-time equivalent employees at the time when the SEIS shares are issued.

The company, or its 90% subsidiaries, must be undertaking, or planning to undertake, a new qualifying trade as a permanent establishment in the UK. Non-qualifying trades are the same as apply for EIS (see *ITA 2007, ss 189, 192–200*). A 'new' trade means no-one has started it within two years before the share issue. The SEIS company and its subsidiaries must not have traded at all before the SEIS trading. Anti-avoidance clauses prevent the company from acquiring the trade, trading assets or share capital of a business that the SEIS investor has controlled.

In period A, the company must not be:

- a member of a partnership;
- a subsidiary; or
- controlled by a company or by a connected person.

The requirement of 'no company control' is amended, for shares issued on and after 6 April 2013, to ignore periods in which the company was held by corporate formation agents (*ITA 2007, s 257DG(2)*). This prevents off-the-shelf companies from being disqualified from using the SEIS. The company may have subsidiaries, provided those subsidiaries are qualifying companies. 'Control' is defined in *CTA 2010, ss 450, 451*.

The company can only accept up to £150,000 of funds under the SEIS, which must be used for the purpose of the qualifying trade within three years (see **16.42**). This is an overall limit, and not an annual amount.

The SEIS company can go on to raise money under EIS or the VCT scheme once at least 70% of the SEIS money is utilised.

Focus

It is essential to use the SEIS, EIS and VCT scheme in the right order.

To qualify for SEIS, the company must not already have a compliance certificate accepted by HMRC for EIS or VCT funding.

The shares

16.41   The shares issued under the SEIS must be ordinary, non-redeemable shares, with no preferential rights to assets on winding up. However, they can carry preferential dividend rights, provided neither the company, nor another person, can vary the dividend's fixed percentage entitlement or manipulate the payment date.

The investor must subscribe for the shares in cash and pay the full amount due at the time of subscription. There must be no pre-arranged exit arrangements for the investor, such that he can sell or dispose of the shares or other securities in the company, or dispose of some or all of the assets of the company. There must also be no arrangements that might lead to the cessation of the company's trade. This does not prevent the directors of this company from indicating, in advance, how they envisage that the shares of the company may be disposed of at a later date (VCM33060). All put and call options are treated as disposals.

The purpose of making the SEIS share issue is to raise money for the qualifying trade, which is a genuine commercial activity. There must be no tax avoidance motive behind the share issue.

Use of funds

16.42   The funds raised by the SEIS share issue must be spent for the purposes of the qualifying trade (excepting an incidental amount) within period B.

In addition, the investment must meet the wide-ranging 'no disqualifying arrangements' requirements which have been imposed to counter perceived risk limitation strategies (*ITA 2007, s 257CF*). Similar provisions are being introduced for EIS and VCT. There are two key conditions that trigger the disqualification:

(1)   where an amount representing the sum invested finds its way back to anyone who is a party to the transactions; and

(2)   where the relevant business activities would probably have been part of another business carried on by associated persons, were it not for SEIS tax advantages. Thus, it should eliminate artificial business splitting.

SEIS reinvestment relief

16.43   Reinvestment relief is given for gains arising from disposals in 2012/13 and/or 2013/14, and reinvested in SEIS shares in the same year that the gain arose. However, where the investment is treated as being made in an earlier tax year as a result of the carry-back election (see **16.38**), the reinvestment relief is given for that earlier year (VCM45010).

The reinvestment relief is given at 100% of the gain for investments in 2012/13, and at 50% of the gain for investments in 2013/14. The maximum tax relief for SEIS investments made in 2012/13 is 78% of the amount invested. For investments made in 2013/14, the maximum tax relief is 64% of the amount invested.

The reinvested gain can arise on the disposal of any type of asset. It is only the gain from the disposal that needs to be reinvested in SEIS shares, and not the full proceeds. Not all of the investment in SEIS shares need be claimed for reinvestment relief.

As the conditions for SEIS income tax relief must be met for the SEIS shares, for the CGT reinvestment relief to apply, the maximum reinvestment relief is limited to £100,000 per tax year.

Focus

If more than £100,000 is subscribed for SEIS shares during the tax year, the income tax relief is limited to £100,000, and the extra SEIS shares acquired are ignored.

For reinvestment relief, the amount of investment available to set against the gain is reduced proportionately with regard to the 'excess' shares, making the reinvestment relief less than £100,000.

Do not subscribe for more than £100,000 shares in the SEIS company to be given tax relief in 2012/13 or 2013/14, if reinvestment relief is also required.

The investor must be eligible for SEIS income tax relief for the SEIS shares acquired, and a successful claim must be made for it. The claims period runs until five years after the normal self-assessment filing date for the tax return (31 January); this is unusual, as most claims periods are now four years from the end of the relevant tax year (see **1.39**). Thus, claims for SEIS investments made in 2013/14 can be made at any time up to 31 January 2020.

The taxpayer cannot make a claim for SEIS income tax relief until the company has met the requirements for the SEIS scheme and has:

• been trading for at least four months; or

• spent at least 70% of the money raised by the SEIS share issue.

When one of these stages has been reached, the company must apply for a compliance certificate, by submitting form SEIS1 to the HMRC Small Company Enterprise Centre. If HMRC accept that all conditions of the SEIS have been met, they will supply claim forms to the company to provide to the investors, which those investors must use to apply for their income tax relief. This process could take some time, hence the five-year claims period.

Disposal relief

16.44   In a similar manner to EIS disposal relief (see **16.3**), gains on the disposal of SEIS shares after the end of period B are free from CGT. However, any capital loss sustained qualifies to provide relief against capital gains, or income tax relief under *ITA 2007, s 131* (see **17.14**[). However, the amount of the allowable loss is reduced by the income tax relief previously obtained (see EIS examples at **16.5**).

465

VENTURE CAPITAL TRUSTS

Overview

16.45   Venture capital trusts (VCTs) are quoted companies, similar to investment trusts, which specialise in investing in small unquoted trading companies. An approved VCT is exempt from corporation tax on chargeable gains.

The main conditions for approval include the requirement that at least 70% of the company's investments are in qualifying unquoted trading companies (including companies listed on the alternative investment market or AIM), with at least 70% of the investments being in eligible shares (for shares issued from 6 April 2011). No single holding in one company must represent more than 15% of the VCT investments.

There are also limits on the value of the company's (or group's) gross assets, and on the size of company that the VCT can invest in. The investee company must employ no more than 250 full-time equivalent employees at the time that the shares are issued to the VCT (*ITA 2007, s 297A*). The investee company cannot raise more than £5 million using any of the venture capital schemes (CVS, EIS and VCT) within a 12-month period (*ITA 2007, s 292A*).

The reliefs available for VCT investors are similar to those available for investments in EIS shares:

- income tax relief (including an exemption for dividends – see Chapter 3 of *Income Tax 2013/14* (Bloomsbury Professional));

- capital gains tax disposal relief; and

- capital gains tax deferral relief (only for VCT shares issued before 6 April 2004).

VCT disposal relief

16.46   A gain is not a chargeable gain if it accrues to an individual on a 'qualifying disposal' (see below) of ordinary shares in a company which:

- was a VCT when the shares were acquired; and

- is still a VCT at the time of the disposal.

Any loss accruing where these conditions are met is not an allowable loss. Shares are ordinary shares if they form part of the company's ordinary share capital (*TCGA 1992, s 151A(7)*; *ITA 2007, s 989*).

A 'qualifying disposal' is a disposal of shares, made by an individual, which meets the following conditions:

(a)   the individual has attained the age of 18 at the time of the disposal;

(b)   the shares were not acquired in excess of the 'permitted maximum' (see below) for any tax year; and

(c)   the taxpayer acquired the shares for bona fide commercial purposes and not as part of a scheme or arrangement the main purpose of which, or one of the main purposes of which, is the avoidance of tax (*TCGA 1992, s 151A(2)*).

Disposal relief is available regardless of whether the taxpayer subscribed for the shares or acquired them from someone else. The 'permitted maximum' in (b) above requires, broadly speaking, that in any tax year the market value of all VCT shares acquired by an individual (or his nominees) must not exceed £200,000 at the time of acquisition (*TCGA 1992, s 151A(6)*; *ITA 2007, s 263*).

HMRC guidance indicates that the restriction in (c) above is likely to apply only in 'exceptional' circumstances, where, for example, artificial arrangements are made to convert shares that do not qualify for disposal relief into qualifying shares (VCM52020).

Identification rules

16.47   It may be necessary to identify shares disposed of with particular acquisitions of shares, in order to establish whether a disposal relates to shares acquired in excess of the permitted maximum for a particular tax year. For this purpose, the following rules replace the normal rules for identification of share and securities (see **4.2**):

•   disposals of shares acquired by the same person on the same day are identified first with any shares acquired in excess of the permitted maximum, and then with other shares;

•   a first-in, first-out basis applies to disposals of shares acquired on different days – disposals are identified first with the earliest acquisitions, and then with later acquisitions (*TCGA 1992, ss 151A(4), 151B(1)*); and

•   a person who disposed of VCT shares acquired at a time when the company was not a VCT is treated as having disposed of those shares before he disposed of any other shares acquired in the same company when it did qualify as a VCT (*TCGA 1992, s 151A(5)*).

Reorganisations and rights

16.48   On a reorganisation of share capital of a VCT within *TCGA 1992, s 126*, the rules in *TCGA 1992, s 127* (equation of original shares and new holding) are to be applied separately to each of the following kinds of shares:

(a)   VCT shares that are eligible for both CGT disposal relief and income tax relief;

(b)   VCT shares that are eligible for CGT disposal relief but not income tax relief;

(c)   VCT shares that are eligible for income tax relief but not CGT disposal relief; and

(d)   other VCT shares *(TCGA 1992, s 151B(2), (3))*.

The effect of this rule is that shares of each kind are treated as a separate holding of original shares and identified with a separate new holding following the reorganisation.

Where there is a rights issue in respect of an existing holding of ordinary shares, and either but not both of the existing shares or the new shares fall within (a)–(c) above, the provisions of *TCGA 1992, ss 127–130* (which broadly treat the old and new shares as a single holding) do not apply to the existing holding *(TCGA 1992, s 151B(4))*.

Exchange of shares

16.49   Where the rules in *TCGA 1992, ss 135* and *136* apply to exchanges of shares and securities in a company (A) for those in another company (B), their broad effect is that there is no disposal of the original holding in company A. Companies A and B are treated as if they were the same company, and the exchange is treated as a reorganisation of its share capital.

Those rules do not apply to an exchange of shares where:

•   the shares in company A are shares falling within **16.48**(a) or (b) above; and

•   the shares in company B are not ordinary shares in a VCT *(TCGA 1992, s 151B(5))*.

Withdrawal of company's approval as a VCT

16.50   A person holding shares eligible for disposal relief is deemed to dispose of and reacquire those shares at their market value if the company's approval as a VCT is withdrawn. He is deemed to dispose of the shares at the time the withdrawal takes effect (ie the date on which the notice of withdrawal is issued) and to reacquire them immediately for a consideration equal to their market value at that time. The effect of this rule is to preserve the benefit of disposal relief for the period for which approval applied.

There are detailed rules relating to identification of shares in these circumstances, the effect of any reduction in income tax relief, any chargeable event under the deferral relief rules, and the death of the shareholder (*TCGA 1992, s 151B(6), (7), (8)*).

If a provisional VCT approval is withdrawn and the company does not meet the conditions for approval subsequently, disposal relief is not available at all.

If full approval is withdrawn – so that the investor's shares are deemed to be disposed of and reacquired as mentioned above – and the company subsequently regains its VCT status, HMRC consider that the shares do not become eligible again for disposal relief, because the company will not have been a VCT at the time of the deemed reacquisition (VCM52140).

VCT deferral relief

16.51   An individual could defer a chargeable gain on the disposal of any asset by subscribing for ordinary shares in a VCT before 6 April 2004. Relief was available for subscriptions of up to £100,000 per tax year. No deferral relief was available unless the taxpayer received income tax relief on the subscription. The relief was withdrawn with effect for VCT shares issued after 5 April 2004 (*TCGA 1992, s 151A(3), Sch 5C*, repealed by *FA 2004*).

Although new investments in VCTs do not qualify for deferral relief, gains already deferred may be brought back into charge by reason of a chargeable event (see **16.53**), so a brief summary of this relief remains relevant.

The relief was available to individuals who were resident in the UK both at the time when the gain accrued and at the time the qualifying investment was made. An individual was excluded from relief if he was regarded for the purposes of double taxation relief arrangements as resident in a territory outside the UK and the effect of those arrangements was that he would not be liable to UK tax on a gain arising on a disposal (ignoring, for this purpose, the disposal relief in **16.46**).

The shares had to be subscribed for within a period beginning one year before, and ending one year after, the disposal on which the gain accrued. It was possible, therefore, to use VCT deferral relief to defer gains accruing up to 5 April 2005. HMRC have statutory powers to extend these time limits, but no extension can result in deferral relief being available for VCT shares issued after 5 April 2004 (*TCGA 1992, Sch 5C, para 1*, repealed by *FA 2004*).

Deferral relief for investment in VCT shares operated in a broadly similar manner to deferral relief for investment in EIS shares (see **16.10**).

Claims

16.52 Deferral relief using VCT shares must be claimed within five years after 31 January following the later of:

- the tax year in which the gain accrued; and

- the tax year in which the VCT shares were issued.

The last possible accrual date for a gain that could be deferred using VCT shares was 5 April 2005. A claim for deferral relief for 2004/05 had to be submitted to HMRC by 31 March 2010. This date is the deadline for the five-year claims period, which became four years on 1 April 2010 (see **1.39**).

Chargeable events

16.53 The deferred gain becomes chargeable if, broadly speaking:

- there is a disposal of the VCT shares (other than a no gain, no loss disposal to a spouse or civil partner);

- the investor's spouse or civil partner disposes (to someone other than the investor) of VCT shares originally acquired from the investor under a no gain, no loss disposal;

- VCT shares are exchanged for non-VCT shares;

- the investor, or a spouse or civil partner who has received the shares on a no gain, no loss transfer, becomes non-resident within a three-year qualifying period (five years for shares issued before 6 April 2000);

- HMRC withdraw the company's approval as a VCT; or

- income tax relief for the VCT investment is withdrawn or reduced in circumstances other than those outlined above.

The deferred gain is not clawed back on the death of the investor or on the death of a spouse or civil partner who acquired the shares on a no gain, no loss disposal (*TCGA 1992, Sch 5C, paras 3–6*, repealed by *FA 2004* with effect for shares issued after 5 April 2004).

When the deferred gain becomes chargeable, it is taxed at the rate of CGT that applies at the time of that chargeable event, which may be 18% or 28% in 2013/14. It is possible for the taxpayer retrospectively to claim entrepreneurs' relief in respect of the deferred gain (see **11.49**), in which case the deferred gain may be subject to CGT at 10% when it comes into charge.

Chapter 17

Other reliefs

SIGNPOSTS

This chapter examines the following CGT reliefs:

- **Proposed reliefs** – As suggested in recent consultation papers (see **17.1**).

- **Employee shareholder status** – Surrender of employment rights, income tax and NIC exemption, CGT treatment, corporation tax deductions and conditions (see **17.2–17.8**).

- **Loans to traders** – CGT relief for losses on irrecoverable loans or for amounts paid under guarantee (see **17.9–17.13**).

- **Share loss relief** – Income tax relief for the capital loss realised on the disposal or complete loss of value of unquoted shares held in trading companies and for EIS shares. Similar relief is available to investment companies (see **17.14–17.18**).

- **Gifts to the nation** – Nature of the scheme, alternative tax exemptions for similar gifts, which gifts qualify, how the tax relief is given (see **17.19–17.23**).

PROPOSED RELIEFS

17.1   The new reliefs listed below are proposed in consultation documents and are likely to be brought in by provisions in the Finance Bill 2014.

- *Social investment tax relief* – This relief is to be based on the Enterprise Investment Scheme (see **Chapter 16**), but the investment will be directed to social enterprise ventures instead of into private trading companies. Income tax relief will be given on the investment at a rate to be announced in the 2014 Budget, on up to £1 million invested per taxpayer per year. The cap on income tax reliefs will not apply to this type of investment. Reinvestment relief will be available to defer CGT on gains reinvested in the social enterprise. Gains on disposals of the qualifying investment may also be exempt from CGT. The investment will not necessarily be made in the form of equity, but is likely to be in the form of a debt instrument. However, the investment must not be secured on assets or subject to a guarantee. The debt instruments will not be permitted to pay more than a commercial rate of interest, and any interest paid should be linked to the performance of the organisation. Investors must not be connected to the social enterprise venture and must not obtain relief under the SEIS or EIS for their investment in the social enterprise. The investor will have to hold the investment for a minimum of five years. A 'social enterprise' will be defined by legislation and, to qualify for the relief, it must have less than 250 employees.

- *Relief on transfer to employee ownership* – Gains on the disposal of a controlling interest in a business or a company will be exempt from CGT, where the interest is transferred to an indirect employee-ownership structure, such as an employee benefit trust (EBT). The relief will be available to individuals and personal representatives of deceased individuals. Where a family controls the business, and control does not lie in the hands of one person, the relief may be available to all connected owners who transfer their interest to the EBT. 'Controlling interest' is to be defined, and may be less than 51%. There will also be income tax and NIC reliefs for employees of companies controlled by the EBT.

EMPLOYEE SHAREHOLDER STATUS

New contract

17.2   A new type of employment contract called 'employee shareholder' is introduced by *Growth and Infrastructure Act 2013, s 27*. Provisions inserted into *Employment Rights Act 1996, s 205A* broadly provide that, if the company and individual agree to the individual being an employee shareholder, the company must issue or allot shares worth at least £2,000 in exchange for the employee accepting reduced employment rights (see **17.3**).

FA 2013, Sch 23 sets out the tax reliefs for shares acquired as part of the adoption of employee shareholder status. This new employment status should be available for employers to offer to employees from 1 September 2013, but it will be brought in by Treasury order.

Surrender of rights

17.3   By signing an employee shareholder agreement (to amend, or take up, an employment contract which provides employee shareholder status), the employee surrenders all of the following employment rights:

- unfair dismissal, apart from when this is automatically unfair or relates to anti-discrimination law;

- right to request leave for studying or training;
- right to flexible working; and
- statutory redundancy pay.

In addition, the employee must give 16 weeks' notice (instead of eight weeks' notice) when returning from maternity or adoption leave.

> **Focus**
>
> All of the above employment rights must be surrendered under the employee shareholder agreement to obtain the tax-favoured shares.
>
> The employee cannot opt to keep some rights and surrender others.

Income tax exemptions

17.4   The first £2,000 of the shares awarded to an employee taking up employee shareholder status are free of income tax and NICs, and the employee is deemed to have paid £2,000 for those shares acquired (*ITEPA 2003, ss 226A–226D*). If more than £2,000 of shares are acquired, the excess value is treated as earnings and is subject to income tax and NICs, under *ITEPA 2003, Pt 7*.

> **Focus**
>
> Only up to £2,000 of shares will be free of tax and NICs on acquisition.

No income tax charge arises if the exempt shares are sold back to the company after the employee has left the company (*ITTOIA 2005, s 385A*). This provision allows the company to effectively provide a market for the shares, using a 'purchase of own shares' mechanism. The proceeds for the shares should still be exempt from CGT in the hand of the ex-employee if the £50,000 limit has not been breached (see **17.5**).

CGT treatment

17.5   Up to £50,000 of shares acquired under an employee shareholder agreement are exempt from CGT on disposal. The value of the shares that qualify for this exemption is measured as their unrestricted market value on acquisition. If the shares were acquired in several tranches from the same employing company or an associated company, all those shares are taken into account when considering the £50,000 limit (*TCGA 1992, s 236C*).

The shares cease to be exempt from CGT when the employee disposes of them (*TCGA 1992, ss 236B–236G*). This also applies where the shares are transferred to the employee's spouse or civil partner. The no gain, no loss provisions do not apply on the transfer of the exempt shares between spouses or civil partners (*TCGA 1992, s 58(2)*). This has the effect that the transferor benefits from the CGT exemption, and the transferee acquires the shares at market value at the date of the transfer.

On disposal of the shares, any amounts treated as earnings for income tax purposes on acquisition of those shares (see **17.4**) are deductible in calculating the chargeable gain, but no other consideration is treated as having been given for those shares. The employee is not treated as disposing of an asset by relinquishing employment rights under an employee shareholder agreement.

The share pooling rules in *TCGA 1992, ss 104, 105* and *106A* do not apply to the employee shares acquired under an employee shareholder agreement. Instead, the employee is given the freedom to determine which shares he has disposed of, out of the exempt shares and non-exempt shares of the same class from the same company.

The identification of shares on a reorganisation of share capital (*TCGA 1992, ss 127, 135* and *136*) do not apply to exempt shares acquired under the employee shareholder agreement.

Corporation tax deduction

17.6   A company that awards shares to employees would normally be entitled to a corporation tax deduction for the value of the shares awarded (*CTA 2009, Pt 12*). However, in the case of employee shareholder shares, the deemed payment of £2,000 for the shares on acquisition is disregarded for the corporation tax deduction under *CTA 2009, Pt 12*. If shares worth more than £2,000 are awarded, the excess in market value over £2,000 will qualify[as a deduction for corporation tax purposes.

Advice for employees

17.7   Where employees are offered employee shareholder status, they may need to take independent legal and tax advice about the terms of the employee shareholder agreement, to help them make an informed decision. Where this advice is paid for by the employer, either directly or as a reimbursement of the employee's costs, that expense does not constitute a benefit in kind for the employee, and thus is free of tax and NICs (*ITEPA 2003, s 326B*).

Conditions

17.8   An employee of the company cannot benefit from the tax exemptions for the shares acquired under an employee shareholder agreement if that employee, or any person connected with him, holds a material interest in the employing company or in its parent company, at any time in the 12 months prior to the acquisition of the shares.

For this purpose, a material interest is a holding of shares carrying 25% or more of the voting rights, or an entitlement to at least 25% of the net assets on a winding up of the company. The entitlement to, or arrangement to acquire, such rights is also considered to be a material interest. The interests of the employee and his associates are taken together to determine if the 25% threshold is breached.

LOANS TO TRADERS

17.9   Where a person (A) incurs a debt to another person (B), no chargeable gain accrues to the original creditor (B) on his disposal of the debt, except in the case of a debt on a security (*TCGA 1992, s 251*).

For individuals, trustees and personal representatives, a debt is, therefore, not normally subject to CGT unless it is a 'debt on a security', meaning, broadly, marketable loan stock (see **4.35**).

Most loan stock is a type of 'qualifying corporate bond', which is an exempt asset (*TCGA 1992, s 115*). Therefore, as a general rule, gains on simple debts are exempt from CGT and no relief is available for losses.

However, *TCGA 1992, s 253* provides for allowable capital losses incurred on loans made to UK traders. Relief is not available for amounts taken into account in computing income for tax purposes.

For companies, profits (and losses) on loans are generally treated as income (and deductions in computing income) under the 'loan relationship' rules. Such profits and losses are outside the scope of corporation tax on chargeable gains, regardless of whether the company is a borrower or a lender. Where part of a loan becomes irrecoverable, relief under *TCGA 1992, s 253* is available only to a company if the loan relationship rules do not apply to the loss. For further discussion of the loan relationship rules, see Chapter 15 of *Corporation Tax 2013/14* (Bloomsbury Professional).

Conditions

17.10   Relief is available for a 'qualifying loan', ie a loan in relation to which:

17.11   *Other reliefs*

(a)   the borrower uses the money wholly for the purposes of a trade, profession or vocation, other than a trade etc involving the lending of money, which he carries on;

(b)   the borrower is UK resident; and

(c)   the borrower's debt is not a 'debt on a security' as defined in *TCGA 1992, s 132*, (*TCGA 1992, s 253(1), (2)*).

In *Taylor Clark International Ltd v Lewis* [1998] STC 1259, the judge identified three characteristics of a 'debt on a security' in relation to a business debt: it should be assignable, interest-bearing, and have a structure of permanence. If the debt is not marketable or assignable, it is not a 'debt on a security'.

Where the money is lent to company A and that company lends it on to company B, and company B is a trading company in the same group, relief is available for the loan to company A as if company A had used the money for the purpose for which company B used it while a member of the group (*TCGA 1992, s 253(2)*).

HMRC accept that bank overdrafts and credit balances on directors' loan accounts, but not ordinary trade debts, are capable of being qualifying loans. HMRC consider that a loan used for 'mixed purposes' would not qualify. However, a proportion of a loan used partly for trade purposes and partly for non-trade purposes would qualify – for example, a loan for the construction of premises part of which are used for trade purposes (HMRC Capital Gains Tax Manual at CG65932, CG65933).

Relief for irrecoverable loans

17.11   A taxpayer who has made a qualifying loan may make a claim for an allowable capital loss in respect of that loan if, at the time he makes the claim (or at an earlier time, see below), all the following apply:

- any amount of the outstanding principal has become irrecoverable;

- the claimant has not assigned his right to recover the amount; and

- the claimant and the borrower were not each other's spouses, civil partners, or companies in the same group, either at the time the loan was made or at any later time.

The amount of the allowable loss is the amount of the outstanding principal that has become irrecoverable. It is specifically provided that no relief is due if that amount is treated as a debit on a loan relationship (as discussed in **17.9**) (*TCGA 1992, s 253(3)*).

The taxpayer may specify an earlier time than the date of the claim (and possibly obtain the benefit of the allowable loss in an earlier tax year) if the outstanding amount was irrecoverable at that earlier time. However, the earlier time must be:

- for CGT purposes, not more than two years before the beginning of the tax year in which the claim is made; or

- for corporation tax purposes, not before the first day of the earliest accounting period ending not more than two years before the time of the claim (*TCGA 1992, s 253(3A)*).

HMRC accept that a loan has become irrecoverable where they come to the view that there was in fact 'no reasonable prospect' of recovery of the loan at the date of the claim (or at the earlier time mentioned above). They take account of funds potentially available as well as those currently available, and take the view that the initial presumption should be that the loan remains recoverable if the borrower continues to trade, even at a loss (CG65950).

If there is a short period between the loan being granted and the date on which it is claimed to have become irrecoverable, HMRC may wish to establish what happened to the business in that period, and may examine in particular:

- what happened to make the loan irrecoverable so soon after it was made; and

- whether there was a reasonable prospect of recovery at the time the loan was made (CG65951).

> **Focus**
>
> A loan is not treated as becoming irrecoverable if it has become so in consequence of the terms of the loan, any arrangements surrounding the loan, or any act or omission by the lender.

These conditions are anti-avoidance measures, to exclude arrangements ranging from a gift presented as a loan to sophisticated schemes 'such as the siphoning of resources out of a company which then becomes unable to repay its loan' (*TCGA 1992, s 253(12)*; CG65958).

Relief for payments made by a guarantor

17.12 Relief may be available to a taxpayer who has guaranteed the repayment of a qualifying loan (or a loan that would be a qualifying loan, but for the condition in **17.10**(c)). An allowable loss is treated as accruing to such a taxpayer who has made a claim to relief if, at the time he made the claim:

- any amount of the outstanding principal or interest has become irrecoverable from the borrower;

- the taxpayer has made a payment under the guarantee, either to the lender or to a co-guarantor, relating to that amount;

- the taxpayer has not assigned any right, accruing to him in return for making the payment, to recover that amount;

- the lender and the borrower were not each other's spouses or civil partners, or companies in the same group, either at the time the loan was made or at any later time; and

- the taxpayer and the lender were not each other's spouses or civil partners, or companies in the same group, either at the time the guarantee was given or at any later time.

The amount of the allowable loss is:

- the amount of the payment made by the taxpayer in respect of the outstanding principal or interest that has become irrecoverable from the borrower, *less*

- any contribution payable to him by any co-guarantor (*TCGA 1992, s 253(4)*).

A loan is not treated as becoming irrecoverable if it has become so in consequence of the terms of the loan, any arrangements surrounding the loan, or any act or omission by the lender or guarantor (*TCGA 1992, s 253(12)*).

A claim in respect of a payment made under a guarantee must be made:

- for CGT purposes, by the fourth anniversary of the end of the tax year in which the payment was made; and

- for corporation tax purposes, by the fourth anniversary of the end of the accounting period in which the payment was made (*TCGA 1992, s 253(4A)*).

Recovery of loan or payment made under guarantee

17.13   If the taxpayer recovers any part of a loan or guarantee payment that has given rise to an allowable loss, the amount recovered is treated as a chargeable gain accruing at the time of recovery. The amount of the gain is so much of the loss as corresponds to the amount recovered. There are corresponding provisions for companies (*TCGA 1992, s 253(5)–(8)*).

The taxpayer is treated as recovering an amount if he receives – or directs someone else to receive – money or money's worth either in satisfaction of his right of recovery or in return for assigning that right. If he assigns the right under a bargain made otherwise than at arm's length (see **3.5**), he is treated as receiving money or money's worth equal to the market value of the right (*TCGA 1992, s 253(9)*).

Example 17.1

Patricia lent £10,000 to her sister Judy in June 2003 to help her continue in business. In May 2012, Judy's business collapsed and it was clear that she would not be able to repay the loan.

Patricia made a claim in her 2013/14 tax return that the loan had become irrecoverable at 6 April 2013. She may set off the resulting loss of £10,000 against any chargeable gains accruing in 2013/14, and carry forward indefinitely any unused allowable loss. Any part of the sum of £10,000 that is repaid at a later date will give rise to a chargeable gain equal to the amount repaid.

SHARE LOSS RELIEF

17.14   This relief turns an allowable capital loss into a loss qualifying for income tax relief under *ITA 2007, Pt 4, Ch 6* or corporation tax relief under *CTA 2010, Pt 4, Ch 4*. It may arise on the loss, disposal or negligible value of shares that qualify for EIS or SEIS (see **Chapter 16**) [or other unquoted shares. The EIS shares do not have to satisfy any further requirements for this loss relief, but the other shares do have to satisfy a number of requirements, as discussed in **17.17**.

This relief is available only to individuals and investment companies, not trustees. HMRC guidance says it is intended 'to encourage entrepreneurs to invest in unquoted trading companies' (*ITA 2007, s 131*; HMRC Venture Capital Schemes Manual at VCM70110).

Focus

FA 2013, Sch 3 limits certain income tax reliefs from 6 April 2013 to the greater of:

●   25% of the taxpayer's adjusted total income for the year; and

●   £50,000.

This cap applies to share loss relief, but it does not apply to losses arising from shares that qualified for EIS or SEIS.

Relief for individuals

17.15 An individual who has subscribed for shares in a 'qualifying trading company' (see **17.17**), and incurs an allowable loss for CGT purposes on the disposal of the shares in a tax year, may claim relief from income tax on:

(a)   an amount of his income for that tax year equal to the amount of the loss; or

(b)   the whole of his income, where his income is less than the amount of the loss.

Alternatively, he may claim relief for the amount in (a) or (b) for the preceding tax year. No part of any loss may be relieved more than once. Once a loss has been relieved against income, it is no longer an allowable loss for CGT purposes. This relief must be claimed no later than 12 months after 31 January following the end of the tax year in which the loss was incurred (*ITA 2007, s 132*).

For this purpose, an individual 'subscribes' for shares if:

•   the company issues the shares to him in return for money or money's worth; or

•   he acquires them from his spouse or civil partner by means of a lifetime transfer made while the individual was living with the spouse or civil partner, and the spouse or civil partner acquired the shares by subscription, although the subscription need not have been made during the marriage or civil partnership (*ITA 2007, s 135*).

An acquisition of shares from another family member, such as a father or brother, does not meet the conditions for subscribed shares (*Fard v HMRC* [2011] UKFTT 63 (TC)). HMRC previously regarded jointly held shares, or those acquired through a nominee (common for EIS shares), as not meeting the 'subscribed' condition for share loss relief. This position was reversed, as announced in Revenue & Customs Brief 41/10. Any claims for share loss relief denied due to jointly held shares can be resubmitted, if the claim is still in time.

Any bonus shares connected to the shares the individual subscribed for are treated as subscribed shares.

The disposal giving rise to the loss must be:

•   a disposal by way of a bargain made at arm's length for full consideration;

•   a disposal by way of a distribution in a dissolution or winding up of the company;

•   a disposal involving the entire loss, destruction, dissipation or extinction of the asset (see *TCGA 1992, s 24(1)*); or

- a deemed disposal arising on a claim that the value of the asset has become negligible under *TCGA 1992, s 24(2)* (see **2.10**) (*ITA 2007, s 131(3)*).

There are detailed rules concerning company reorganisations and exchanges of shares, identification of shares disposed of with acquisitions, and value shifting (*ITA 2007, ss 145–149*).

Order of reliefs

17.16   The share loss relief claim under *ITA 2007, s 132* for the tax year in which the loss accrued takes priority over income tax relief claimed for the preceding year, for the purpose of establishing what losses remain and what income remains chargeable.

The share loss relief claimed under *ITA 2007, s 132* for either the year of the loss or the preceding year takes priority over trading losses for which a claim has been made under either *ITA 2007, s 64* (set-off against general income) or *ITA 2007, s 72* (losses in early years of a trade available for set-off against general income of preceding years) (*ITA 2007, s 133(4)*).

Qualifying trading company

17.17   The shares must have been subscribed for in a 'qualifying trading company', but the requirements of such a company have changed over the years, so it is necessary to check that the company qualified at the time the shares were issued (see VCM72040).

The current conditions for a 'qualifying trading company' are given in (a)–(d) below:

(a)   The company either meets the following four requirements on the date of the disposal:

- the trading requirement (*ITA 2007, s 137*);
- the control and independence requirement (*ITA 2007, s 139*);
- the qualifying subsidiaries requirement (*ITA 2007, ss 140, 191*); and
- the property management requirement (*ITA 2007, ss 141, 188, 190*); or

it ceased to meet any of those requirements at a time within three years before the disposal date and, since that time, it has not been:

- an excluded company,

- an investment company, or

- a trading company.

(b) The company has either:

- met all of the requirements in (a) for a continuous period of six years ending on the date of disposal; or

- has met all of the requirements in (a) for a shorter continuous period ending on that date (or at that time) and has not, before the beginning of that period, been an excluded company, an investment company or a trading company.

(c) The company has met the following requirements:

- gross assets of no more than £7 million before the issue of the shares and no more than £8 million after the issue of the shares (*ITA 2007, s 142*); and

- it was an unquoted company when the shares were issued and there were no arrangements in existence for the company to become quoted (*ITA 2007, s 143*).

(d) The company has carried on business wholly or mainly in the UK throughout the period from incorporation or, if later, 12 months before the shares were issued, and ending on the date of disposal (*ITA 2007, s 134(5)*).

Focus

The gross asset limits in (c) above have not been amended to align with the higher gross asset limits which apply for EIS companies from 6 April 2012 (see **16.1**).

Several detailed definitions are provided, including:

- 'the trading requirement' is defined by reference to the qualifying trade rules for the purpose of the EIS (*ITA 2007, s 189*);

- 'excluded company' means, broadly, a company which falls into one or more of the following:

  – its trade consists wholly or mainly of dealing in land, commodities or futures, or in shares, securities or other financial instruments, or is not carried on a commercial basis;

  – is the holding company of a group other than a trading group; or

  – is a building society or a registered industrial and provident society.

Relief for companies

17.18   A similar relief to that described in **17.15** is available to an investment company that incurs an allowable loss for corporation tax purposes on the disposal of shares, for which it subscribed, in a qualifying trading company. The company disposing of the shares must meet both of the following conditions:

(a)   it is an investment company on the date of disposal and has been an investment company for a continuous period of six years ending on that date, or has been an investment company for a shorter continuous period ending on that date and was not a trading company or an excluded company before the beginning of that period; and

(b)   it was not, at any time when it held the shares, associated with (or a member of the same group as) the qualifying trading company (*CTA 2010, s 69*).

The company may make a claim, within two years after the end of the accounting period in which the loss was incurred, for the allowable loss to be set against income for corporation tax purposes as follows:

●   income of that accounting period; and

●   income of preceding accounting periods ending within a specified period (see below) if the company was then an investment company.

The specified period is the period of 12 months ending immediately before the accounting period in which the loss is incurred, and an apportionment may be required if that period was longer than 12 months. The loss is relieved against income of later periods before income of earlier periods (*CTA 2010, ss 70–72*).

There are detailed rules setting out the interaction between losses, charges and management expenses; specifying the order of reliefs; and providing various definitions (*CTA 2010, s 71*; VCM77050).

GIFTS TO THE NATION

Nature of the scheme

17.19   This scheme was known as 'gifts of pre-eminent objects' during the consultation stage, and is referred to as the 'cultural gifts scheme' (CGS) by the Department for Culture, Media and Sport. The aim of the scheme is to encourage the owners of pre-eminent works of art or historical objects to give such objects to the nation during their lifetime, rather than as a bequest on death.

17.20 *Other reliefs*

The legislation is found at *FA 2012, Sch 14 (Gifts to the Nation)*. At the time of writing, there was no published HMRC guidance on this scheme other than the guidance notes to the Finance Bill 2012. The Department for Culture, Media and Sport has published guidance: http://www.artscouncil.org.uk/media/uploads/pdf/DCMS_Guidance_15_March.pdf.

Alternative tax exemptions

17.20   When considering donating objects under the 'gifts to the nation' scheme, the taxpayer should also be advised about the following tax measures which exist to provide tax reliefs or exemptions for similar gifts:

- IHT exemption for transfer of qualifying heritage assets (*IHTA 1984, s 30*);

- deferment or exemption of CGT on the above gift (*TCGA 1992, s 257 or s 258*);

- IHT and CGT exemption for private treaty sales to certain bodies of heritage assets (*IHTA 1984, s 32; TGCA 1992, s 258*); and

- payment of IHT liability (acceptance in lieu scheme) by transferring heritage assets to public ownership (*IHTA 1984, ss 230, 231*).

For further information on the above exemptions and reliefs, see *Inheritance Tax 2013/14* (Bloomsbury Professional). HMRC provide guidance on the above tax reliefs in a memorandum called 'Capital Taxation and the National Heritage' (available at www.hmrc.gov.uk/inheritancetax/conditionalexemption.pdf).

Which gifts qualify

17.21   The scheme is to apply to gifts of pre-eminent objects, collections of objects, and objects associated with an historic building, by an individual or corporate owner. The object must not be jointly owned, or owned in common with other persons. The type of objects specified as being pre-eminent include: any picture, print, book, manuscript, work of art, scientific object or other thing the relevant Minister is satisfied is pre-eminent for its national scientific, historic or artistic interest. The scheme does not extend to land or buildings. A donor can claim income tax or corporation tax relief for gifts of land or buildings made to a charity under the Gift Aid scheme.

Gifts by trustees or personal representatives do not qualify, but those donors may find one of the other tax reliefs described in **17.20** more suited to their circumstances.

To be accepted as a qualifying gift, the object must be assessed by an expert panel administered by the Arts Council. This is the same panel which assesses objects offered under the 'acceptance in lieu' (AiL) scheme for inheritance tax. The panel will recommend which objects should be accepted, using defined criteria. They will agree valuations of the objects for determining the amount of the tax reduction due, and decide where the objects should be located. However, the panel will be constrained by an annual budget of £30 million for tax relief to cover both gifts under AiL and gifts to the nation, so an application made late in the tax year may be rejected because the budget for the financial year has been accounted for.

The scheme applies for complete tax years or accounting periods starting on or after 1 April 2012 (*Finance Act 2012, Schedule 14 (Appointed Day) Order 2013, SI 2013/587*).

Tax reliefs

17.22   When an object is offered under the 'gifts to the nation' scheme, the offer date (also known as the registration date) is recorded by the Arts Council panel and reported to HMRC. This registration date is important, as it signals the start of the negotiation period (see **17.23**) and the date for which the value of the object is agreed.

If the object is accepted under the scheme, the donor is granted a tax reduction of 30% of the value of the gift as assessed by the panel. Corporate donors will receive a 20% tax reduction.

Any gain arising on the making of the gift under the scheme is an exempt gain for CGT and corporation tax (*TCGA 1992, s 258*). The value of the gift is an exempt transfer for IHT (*IHTA 1984, ss 25, 26A, 32*). Where the object has been remitted into the UK by a non-domiciled person who uses the remittance basis, the value of the gift is not treated as a remittance (*ITA 2007, s 809YE*).

How the tax relief is given

17.23   These tax reductions may be applied to offset income tax and/or CGT or corporation tax arising for the tax year or accounting period in which the registration date falls. Individuals may also apply for the tax relief to be spread over tax liabilities for the four subsequent tax years. However, the pattern of the tax set-off must be agreed with HMRC at the time the gift is accepted.

Where the tax reduction is applied for a tax year, the donor is treated as paying the reduced tax on the due date, or on the registration date of the gift if the tax payment date falls before that registration date.

17.23 *Other reliefs*

The negotiation period, between the registration of the gift and the acceptance of the gift by the relevant Minister (acting on the recommendation of the panel), could take some months. To provide the donor with some protection against tax levied in that period, all interest and late payment penalties accrued in respect of the tax reduction amount are cancelled for the negotiation period (*FA 2012, Sch 14, para 6*).

Index

[All references are to paragraph number]

Index

Annuities – *contd*
retiring partners, and
generally, 6.20
introduction, 6.18
lump sum paid in addition, 6.23
partner for at least ten years, 6.21
partner for less than ten years, 6.22
Anti-avoidance provisions
capital losses, and
companies, 9.29
generally, 10.16
disclosure of tax avoidance schemes
(DOTAS)
hallmarks, 10.25
HMRC guidance, 10.27
method, 10.26
outline, 10.23
relevant tax arrangements, 10.24
disqualification arrangements, 16.28
Enterprise Investment Scheme, and
disqualification arrangements, 16.28
investment-linked loans, 16.36
pre-arranged exits, 16.28
put and call options, 16.29–16.32
reinvestment in same company or group
company, 16.27
replacement value, 16.35
value received by investor, 16.33
value received by other person, 16.34
General anti-abuse rule (GAAR)
application, 10.17
generally, 10.16
pre-arranged exits, 16.28
put and call options
generally, 16.29
granted after shares issued, 16.30
granted before shares issued, 16.31
relevant period, 16.32
principal private residence relief , and
Finance Act 2006, and, 12.42
'washing' gain, 12.38–12.41
Ramsay decision, 10.22
reinvestment in same company or group
company, 16.27
remittance basis charge
computation of gains, 5.48
definitions, 5.44
election for remittance basis, 5.42
generally, 5.38
introduction, 5.37
liability to tax, 5.50
losses, and, 5.49
order of remittances, 5.46
'relevant debt', 5.44
remittances, 5.43
'small income or gains' rule, 5.39

Anti-avoidance provisions – *contd*
remittance basis charge – *contd*
'stay away' rule, 5.41
unremitted gains of more than £2,000,
5.40
temporary non-residence, 5.47
replacement value, 16.35
targeted anti-avoidance rules (TAARs)
clearance procedure, 10.21
generally, 10.18
HMRC guidance, 10.20
scope, 10.19
tax planning, and
disclosure of schemes, 10.23–10.27
General anti-abuse rule (GAAR),
10.16–10.17
introduction, 10.2
Ramsay decision, 10.22
targeted anti-avoidance rules,
10.18–10.21
temporary non-residence, 5.33–5.34
value received by investor, 16.33
value received by other person, 16.34
'washing' gain through a trust
introduction, 12.38
operation, 12.39
statutory change, 12.40
transitional relief, 12.41
Appeals
generally, 1.56
Apportionment
non-resident company's gains
calculation of tax charge, 5.56
corporate participators, 5.59
disposal of interest in company, 5.55
exceptions, 5.53
introduction, 5.51
losses, 5.57
participators, 5.58
set-off on distribution of gain, 5.54
trustees, 5.60
UK-resident participator, to, 5.52
Appropriate proportion
disposal in series of transactions, and, 3.14
Appropriation
assets from trading stock, of
election, 4.37–4.38
generally, 4.36
Approved share schemes
share identification rules, and, 4.3
Armed forces
statutory residence test, and, 5.23
Arm's length
gifts of business assets, and, 13.2
Art works
exempt assets, and, 1.9

488

491

Index

Index

Gain and loss computation – *contd*
deductible reliefs – *contd*
no gain, no loss transfers, 3.61–3.62
rebased assets, 3.58
derivative contracts, and, 3.3
disposal of assets on no gain, no loss
transfer
civil partners, 3.62
generally, 3.61
spouses, 3.62
double tax relief
deduction, by, 3.69
double tax agreements, 3.65
introduction, 3.64
special withholding tax, 3.68
unilateral tax credit relief, 3.66–3.67
employment-related liabilities, 3.54
entrepreneurs' relief, 3.57
indexation allowance
generally, 3.60
no gain, no loss transfers, 3.61–3.62
instalment payments of CGT, and
due dates, 3.35
generally, 3.34
intangible fixed assets, and, 3.3
introduction, 3.1
loan relationships, and, 3.3
losses
capital allowances, 3.55–3.56
claims, 3.48
employment-related liabilities, 3.54
interaction with other reliefs, and,
3.49
introduction, 3.47
non-domicile UK residents, 3.51
non-residents, 3.50
trading losses, 3.52
market value rule
ascertaining market value, 3.7
introduction, 3.6
no gain, no loss transfers
civil partners, 3.62
generally, 3.61
spouses, 3.62
non-residents' losses, 3.50
post-cessation expenditure, 3.53
rebased assets, 3.58
share loss relief, 3.57
spouses, 3.62
trading losses, 3.52
VAT, and, 3.2
Gaming winnings
exempt assets, and, 1.9
General anti-abuse rule (GAAR)
application, 10.17
generally, 10.16

Gifts
business assets, of
agricultural property, 13.18
claims, 13.43
conditions, 13.3
consideration received, 13.7
definitions, 13.12–13.14
disposal of QCBs, 13.27
dissolution of civil partnership, 13.16
divorce, 13.16
dual-resident trusts, to, 13.25
emigration of transferee, 13.21–13.23
entrepreneurs' relief, and, 13.46
exceptions, 13.4
foreign-controlled companies, to, 13.24
generally, 13.2
incorporation of business, on, 13.19
inheritance tax, and, 13.15
non-residents, to, 13.20
operation, 13.6
other reliefs, and, 13.45–13.46
overview, 8.31
partial claims, 13.44
partial relief, 13.8–13.11
qualifying assets, 13.5
separation, 13.16
settlor-interested settlements, to, 13.28–
13.34
transfer of shares to company, 13.26
trust disposals, and, 13.17
disposals, and, 2.20
hold-over relief, and
business assets, of, 13.2–13.34
inheritance tax is chargeable, on which,
13.35–13.42
introduction, 13.1
overview, 8.29–8.32
partnerships, and, 6.1
valuations, 13.47
inheritance tax is chargeable, on which
claims, 13.43
conditions, 13.36
consideration received, 13.38
emigration of transferee, 13.42
inheritance tax, and, 13.40
introduction, 13.35
non-residents, to, 13.41
operation, 13.37
overview, 8.29–8.30
partial relief, 13.39
nation, to
alternative tax exemptions, 17.20
claims, 17.23
nature of scheme, 17.19
qualifying gifts, 17.21
tax reliefs, 17.22

502

Index

Index